$5.00

A GUIDE TO GREAT
ORCHESTRAL MUSIC

>>>

The publishers will be pleased to send, upon request, an illustrated folder setting forth the purpose and scope of THE MODERN LIBRARY, *and listing each volume in the series. Every reader of books will find titles he has been looking for, handsomely printed, in unabridged editions, and at an unusually low price.*

>>>

A GUIDE TO GREAT

ORCHESTRAL MUSIC

BY SIGMUND SPAETH

THE MODERN LIBRARY

NEW YORK

CONTENTS

PREFACE

THIS IS meant to be a practical book of facts, for both reading and reference. It contains no tricks, no short cuts, no sugar-coating. It is written for the layman or average listener as well as the informed music-lover. Technical knowledge or experience is not required for its understanding. It is meant to answer all the questions that are most likely to be asked by people who hear orchestral music, in concerts, on records or over the air, no matter whether they are novices or trained musicians.

These questions inevitably cover a few all-important points: the biographical background of the composer concerned, especially in its relation to a particular piece of music; the history of the composition, beyond the life of its creator; the recognizable elements within the composition, which means primarily the significant themes or melodies; and the details of workmanship which the listener can be expected to grasp, at least after an adequate number of hearings. So far as possible, this information is given in connection with every important piece of orchestral music that is likely to be heard today.

The tunes themselves are of course the best means of identification, and there is perhaps no harm in the reminder that symphonic music definitely has tunes which anyone at all can recognize and remember. These tunes, or themes, are given in notation, generally without harmonization, so that it is not difficult to play them on the piano or some other instrument. They should be heard repeatedly, in order to be stamped indelibly on the memory. (Enough of each theme is given to serve as a means of identification). Beyond this the details of structure are described in everyday language, avoiding technical terms and seeking to analyze and perhaps explain the effect on the listener himself. In no case is there any indulgence of personal evaluation, preference or prejudice.

The compositions themselves have been selected on the basis of the frequency of their performance by the leading orchestras, and the established standards of musical taste are accepted without question or argument. Time alone determines the permanent value of a piece of music, and the greater part of the orchestral repertoire has been in existence long enough to eliminate any doubts as to such values. In general the materials are presented chronologically, grouped according to their composers. While the general classifications of the classic, romantic and modern schools are observed and recognized, there is some attempt to arrive at categories of more individual significance, with the convenience and enlightenment of the reader always of prime importance. American music, for instance, is given an entire section of its own, even though it contains compositions in all the conventional categories. Again the basis of selection is frequency of performance, and in many cases the analyses are supplied by the composers themselves.

This book is in a sense a companion and sequel to *The Metropolitan Opera Guide,* by Mary Ellis Peltz and Robert Lawrence, also published by Random House in the Modern Library. But where there is only one Metropolitan Opera Company, there are in America many first-class orchestras, and the programs of all these orchestras have been studied and analyzed in determining what compositions should be included in this volume. It has been made as comprehensive as possible, within the necessary limits of its pages, and it is hoped that all those who love the music of a symphony orchestra, or would like to arrive at the enthusiasm and understanding that others have already acquired, will find in this volume some help toward the development of their own enjoyment of a most important branch of the most popular of all the arts.

Sigmund Spaeth

Westport, Conn.
September, 1942

A NOTE CONCERNING PHONOGRAPH RECORDS

Records are available of many important pieces of orchestral music, sometimes several interpretations of the same composition. The best orchestral records issued by Columbia and Victor are listed in an appendix, and thanks are due to these companies for their practical help in preparing the lists. Listening to records is recommended to all music-lovers as both a preliminary and a supplement to the enjoyment of concerts and the radio.

ACKNOWLEDGMENTS AND BIBLIOGRAPHY

Necessarily this book has leaned heavily on researches already made in the orchestral field, particularly the program notes of the leading symphony orchestras of America. These sources of information have been most helpful, although there are surprising disagreements as to facts and statistics on the part of the experts, and often a majority vote had to settle a disputed point. The program notes of the Chicago Symphony Orchestra are perhaps the clearest and most satisfying of all. But there is real meat also in those of the New York Phil-

harmonic, the Boston, Philadelphia, Los Angeles, Cleveland,
St. Louis, Detroit, Minneapolis and Pittsburgh Orchestras.

Biographical books on music have proved helpful, particularly *Men of Music,* by Brockway and Weinstock (Simon &
Schuster, New York) and Baker's *Biographical Dictionary,*
as well as Grove and other recognized sources. *The Victor
Book of the Symphony,* by Charles O'Connell, contains a
wealth of material, and *Symphony Themes,* compiled by Raymond Burrows and Bessie Carroll Redmond (Simon &
Schuster, New York) is the first really practical collection of
symphonic melodies ever published. Copyright restrictions
prevent the unlimited quotation of modern themes, and it was
finally decided to restrict such quotations largely to the classic
materials in the public domain. The co-operation of living
composers in supplying data is greatly appreciated, and in
many cases the publishers proved equally co-operative. Two
books by David Ewen have supplied treasures of information
on modern music, *Twentieth Century Composers* (T. Y.
Crowell, New York) and *Composers of Today* (The H. W.
Wilson Company, New York). On our own American composers the standard authority is of course John Tasker
Howard, who has thoroughly covered the older men in *Our
American Music* and then brought the subject up to date with
Our Contemporary Composers (both T. Y. Crowell, New
York). All these books naturally go into far more detail than
is possible within the space of this volume.

The author has occasionally permitted himself some refer-
ence to his own books, particularly *Great Symphonies* and
Great Program Music (both Garden City Publishing Co.,
New York). He has been greatly aided by the willing workers
of the Music Department of the New York Public Library.
Credit for the Index belongs chiefly to Katharine Lane
Spaeth, who also deserves the traditional dedication, if any.

I

INTRODUCTORY

A SYMPHONY ORCHESTRA is no longer a mystery. Through radio, records and the concert stage it has become almost as familiar a phenomenon as the jazz band. Therefore only a brief reminder is needed here of the make-up of such an orchestra and the kinds of music that it plays.

The symphony orchestra has been a logical development from the early groups of haphazard instruments to the perfectly balanced organization of eighty to one hundred players that we hear today. This ensemble is based upon the four-part harmony of all music. It has four sections or "choirs": the strings, the wood-wind, the brass and the percussion. Each section in turn contains enough instruments to play at least four parts simultaneously.

The strings are the biggest part of a symphony orchestra, and much music has been written for strings alone. Multiply the basic string quartet many times over, adding eight bass viols to solidify the foundation, and you have the string section of a modern symphony orchestra. There may be from sixteen to twenty first violins, fourteen to eighteen second violins, ten or a dozen violas and eight or ten cellos. (The convenient abbreviation is for violoncello.) In the old seating arrangement the violins were all at the front, with the firsts and seconds facing each other. Nowadays the second violins are quite likely to be behind the first, with the cellos at the front on the right side of the audience. Leopold Stokowski has even experimented with a seating arrangement that put the wind instruments in front, with the strings in the background, where their tone is amplified by a special sounding-board.

The wood-wind choir consists of two or three flutes, one of which can be exchanged for a piccolo (literally a small flute), two or more clarinets, one or two oboes, perhaps including an English horn (cor anglais) which is really an alto oboe, two bassoons, and contra-bassoon and bass clarinet as needed. A quartet of French horns (the real forest horns, compactly curled, with wide bells and mellow tone) are generally associated with the wood-wind rather than the brass.

The real brass choir contains two or more trumpets, at least two trombones and a tuba for the bass. The "battery" or percussion section is a variable quantity, with wide possibilities of noise-making through the striking of different surfaces. Three kettle-drums, or tympani, are essential, tuned according to the key of the composition. The big bass drum and the little side drum or snare drum have no definite pitch, but supply plenty of rhythm. Besides these fundamental percussive instruments, you may hear at various times cymbals, a tambourine, a triangle, xylophone, bells, chimes, a gong, castanets, rattles, a tinkling celesta, and even a piano. The harp is a stringed percussion instrument, as is the piano, and a symphony orchestra must have one or two harpists available as needed. Often they are the only females in the entire orchestra, although there is no law against having women play even a bass tuba or kettle-drums.

What kinds of music does this elaborate combination of strings, wind and percussion instruments play? The most important type is the symphony itself, from which the orchestra derives its name. A symphony is a large work, lasting at least a half hour or more. It is regularly in four movements or sections (again the basic division into four parts), and these movements do not necessarily have any connection of key or theme.

The opening movement of a symphony is traditionally in the so-called Sonata form, appearing also in actual sonatas, as well as in overtures, concertos, string quartets, etc. Sonata form is not at all hard to follow, so long as you know the tunes or themes of a symphony. It is similar to the structure of a play or a novel.

There are at least two important themes, corresponding to the hero and the heroine. They are generally in related keys but of contrasting character. These outstanding tunes are introduced early in the Sonata form, and this part of the movement is called the exposition, as when the chief characters of a play are introduced. Each tune may have some slight development immediately, and there is often a connecting melody or bridge to hold them together.

The exposition is followed by the development or free fantasia, corresponding to the plot of the play or novel. Here the technique of the composer is allowed complete freedom, and this is the part of a symphony that is hardest for the novice to follow. The tunes are broken up, inverted, put into different keys, turned over to various instruments, imitated, rhythmically distorted, treated in every possible way to create contrast, conflict, suspense, as in an actual plot.

Finally the leading melodies return in their original form, although often in new keys, and this section is called the recapitulation, suggesting the happy or at least logical ending of the play or novel. There may be an additional section, often quite short, called the Coda, literally a tail-piece. Sometimes there is also an Introduction, particularly in the older symphonies, and it was formerly customary to repeat the entire exposition before starting the development. Obviously Sonata form is quite definite and logical, a fine example of the basic aesthetic principle of statement, contrast, and reminder, which runs through all the related arts of music, literature, drama and the dance.

Sonata form, characteristic of the first movement of a symphony, may be conveniently outlined as follows:

Introduction (?)
Exposition: (A) First Theme
                     Bridge (?)
              (B) Second Theme
    (Repetition of Exposition?)
Development (using materials of A and B and possibly of
    Introduction)
Recapitulation: Return of A and B, generally in new keys
Coda (?)

With this outline in mind, and some familiarity with the melodies themselves, the first movement of any symphony can be analyzed without difficulty, and its Sonata form followed by the average listener, with mental as well as physical and emotional pleasure. A symphony is actually a sonata on a larger scale, written for a big orchestra. The hearing of piano or violin sonatas is a good preliminary to its enjoyment.

The first movement of a symphony is generally the most important, but the other three may be equally beautiful and even more appealing on a first hearing. The second movement is likely to be in a slow tempo, in contrast to the livelier pace of the first. Sometimes it is a single theme with variations or musical embellishments. This is a popular form in the classic school of music, and has its counterpart in the decorations given to a popular tune by the swing players of today, who often improvise their variations. The slow movement of a symphony may also be in the straightforward song form, with a first section, a contrasting second section, and a return to the first strain, once more employing the fundamental principle of statement, contrast and reminder.

The third movement of a symphony is generally lively. In the old days it was traditionally a Minuet, or *Menuetto,* the latter representing a somewhat faster tempo than the regular dance. The Minuet was always in triple time, rather slower than the modern waltz, and it had a definite form, again built on the A-B-A principle (statement, contrast, reminder). The first section contained the main theme, usually in two parts, each of which was repeated. The middle section was called the Trio, because it was originally played by only three instruments. This also consisted of two parts, with repetitions. Finally, the first section, or main theme, was played again, this time without repetition.

Beethoven upset the tradition of the Minuet, as he did so many others, by substituting a still faster movement which he called Scherzo, literally meaning "happy" or "jocular." The term was applied by Chopin to elaborate piano pieces, by no means consistently cheerful, and even Beethoven was occasionally ponderous in his musical jokes.

The Finale of a symphony is more often fast than slow, perhaps balancing the mood and the pace of the first movement. It often turns the minor key into major, and most composers have considered it almost obligatory to end their symphonies happily. A Finale may have Sonata form, possibly some form of Variations (as in the last movement of Brahms' Fourth Symphony), perhaps a dance form like the Rondo. This was originally a round dance, and it became popular with the classic composers as an instrumental form. A Rondo generally has several themes, of which the first is continually brought back after other tunes have been inserted for contrast. If each tune were lettered, the Rondo form could be summed up as A, B, A, C, A, D, etc. A concluding Coda is quite common. Occasionally an independent Rondo has been written. Richard Strauss, for instance, applied this title to his orchestral tone poem, *Till Eulenspiegel and His Merry Pranks*.

The classic ancestor of the symphony is the Suite, which was originally nothing more than a series of dance tunes strung together with some regard for contrast. Since most of the early instrumental music was intended for dancing, it was quite natural that the better composers should combine their most successful pieces in this way, and eventually Suites were written for their own sake, without regard to actual dancing.

The earliest dances to be thus contrasted were the Pavane and the Galliard, both of Italian origin. To these were added the Allemande, from Germany, and the Branle, originating in France. A later addition was the Spanish Sarabande, and this became a regular movement in the classic Suite. One of the commonest combinations was that of a Prelude, Courante (French), Sarabande and Gigue (English, i.e., Jig). But many other dance movements were included in the Suite from time to time. The Minuet appeared here before it took its place in the symphony. The Gavotte was a favorite movement, and there were also the Bourrée, Loure, Passepied and Polonaise, possibly even an Aria or Air, as a contrasting slow movement. (The Sarabande was also slow, in triple time, and the Gigue was naturally fast.)

Modern Suites are generally sets of pieces drawn from a larger work, such as an opera, a ballet or the incidental music to a play. Examples are the familiar *Nutcracker Suite* of Tschaikowsky, the two *Peer Gynt Suites* of Grieg, and the two made up of Bizet's music for *L'Arlésienne*.

Concertos are of two kinds. The classic Concerto Grosso was an orchestral piece in several movements, with a small group of instruments playing ensemble passages in contrast with the orchestra as a whole, sometimes emphasizing the difference between wind instruments and strings. This type of Concerto was perfected by Bach and Handel.

Today the title of Concerto is applied mostly to large works written for a solo instrument with orchestral accompaniment. Most of these Concertos are for the piano or the violin, but there are other possibilities, and occasionally you will hear a double concerto, like the familiar one written by Bach for two violins and the one by Brahms for violin and cello, each with orchestral background. A solo Concerto may have four movements, like a symphony, or three, like the average sonata. Its first movement is generally in Sonata form, and it is, in effect, a sonata, with the orchestra taking the place of the conventional piano accompaniment.

Among the classic forms the name of Passacaglia is occasionally found. This is strictly a member of the Variation family, closely related to the Chaconne. Both the Chaconne and the Passacaglia have their melody in the bass, with Variations written above it. The distinction is generally made that a Passacaglia must keep its theme in the lower voices, while a Chaconne may use it as a soprano melody. Both types have been arranged for symphony orchestra from the music of Bach, and Brahms uses the form in the Finale of his Fourth Symphony.

Another form of music frequently encountered in orchestral programs is the Overture or Prelude, generally connected with an opera or the incidental music to a drama. Technically an Overture is an independent piece, coming to a full stop, whereas a Prelude leads directly into the opera of which it is a part. There are also concert Overtures, written on some special subject, without any connection with a larger work. Overtures and Preludes may show Sonata form, or any of the other symphonic patterns.

Finally there is the Symphonic Poem, often called merely a Tone Poem, especially in its smaller forms. Franz Liszt is credited with the invention of the Symphonic Poem, and it has been used effectively also by Richard Strauss, Saint-Saëns and other composers. It is regularly in one movement, and therefore much shorter than a symphony, but it may contain any of the devices appearing in the symphonic structure, including even Sonata form.

The Symphonic Poem is almost necessarily program music, by which is meant a composition that tells a story or paints a picture in tones. Program music, which may be narrative, descriptive or merely suggestive, with its meaning indicated by the title, or by the composer's explanatory notes, is in contrast with pure or absolute music, whose content consists of tonal patterns, without any attempt to express an emotional or dramatic meaning that could be put into words. In general the music of the classic school is of the absolute type, while the later romantic and modern compositions are likely to show programmatic tendencies. A Ballet is definitely program music, even when it is played without dancers.

This covers the types of composition generally heard on the programs of symphony orchestras in the concert hall or over the air. In the succeeding analyses it will be assumed that the general nature and structure of the compositions discussed are familiar to the reader, who can, if necessary, refer to this introductory chapter whenever a technical term seems to require explanation.

If you know what is meant by a Symphony, a Symphonic Poem, a Concerto, an Overture, a Suite, as well as Sonata Form, Variations, a Minuet, a Rondo and possibly a Passacaglia or Chaconne, you will have no difficulty in following the details of any individual piece of music. Recognition of the outstanding themes or tunes is all-important; the rest is largely a matter of repeated hearings, leading gradually toward complete knowledge and appreciation. For such repeated hearings and detailed study the use of phonograph records is highly recommended. Opportunities to hear the great orchestral music of the world directly or through radio are not frequent enough to provide for the desirable familiarity that anyone can acquire with a picture or a book. The phonograph has solved this problem for music-lovers and brought the entire orchestral repertoire within reach of every listener. It is always more satisfactory to hear music than merely to read about it.

II

TONAL ARCHITECTS

THE SO-CALLED CLASSIC SCHOOL of musical composition was characterized by a mastery of design, not necessarily devoid of emotion, but with consistent emphasis on form rather than content. It is fair to call the "classical" composers architects of tone, and when Ruskin referred to architecture as "frozen music," he doubtless had in mind the formal music produced by such men as Bach, Handel, Haydn and, to a certain extent, Mozart and Beethoven.

These men wrote mostly absolute or pure music, giving their compositions titles which were in no sense descriptive or programmatic, merely stating the type of piece, Symphony, Concerto, Suite, Quartet, etc., with a key signature and an opus number. (The Latin word *opus,* often abbreviated to op., means "work" and is regularly used to indicate the exact point in a composer's career when a certain piece of music was written. Obviously, the higher the opus number, the later the work, at least in publication.)

JOHANN SEBASTIAN BACH

There was a large Bach family, mostly musical, but when people say "Bach," without any initials, they mean Johann Sebastian, generally considered the father of music as we know it today. He was born in Eisenach, March 21, 1685,

and died at Leipzig, July 28, 1750. The youngest son of Johann
Ambrosius Bach, he was left an orphan at ten, living with his
older brother, Johann Christoph, who treated him cruelly and
handicapped his musical development.

Nevertheless the boy soon showed extraordinary talent,
winning free tuition at the convent school of St. Michael at
Lüneburg, through his beautiful soprano voice, and learning
to play the violin, the clavier and the organ. He often walked
great distances to hear such masters as the Danish organist,
Buxtehude, and constantly studied the creations and interpretations of other musicians.

His entire life was dedicated to music, supported by a deeply
religious feeling. At eighteen Johann Sebastian Bach was organist of the "new" church at Arnstadt and four years later
he moved to St. Blasius in Mühlhausen and married his cousin,
Maria Barbara Bach, by whom he had seven children, including two of his most musical sons, Wilhelm Friedemann and
Karl Philip Emanuel.

Bach went to Weimar in 1708 as court organist. In 1717 he
was appointed director of the orchestra at Cöthen, with Prince
Leopold as a patron, and it was here that he composed much
of his instrumental music. His wife died in 1720, and a year
later he married Anna Magdalena Wülken, by whom he had
thirteen more children.

In 1723 Johann Sebastian Bach became cantor at the
school of St. Thomas in Leipzig and director of music in the
churches of St. Thomas and St. Nicholas. He spent the rest
of his life there, writing a Cantata for every Sunday, just as
the minister would write a sermon, and incidentally composing
such masterpieces as the Passions and the Mass in B minor.
His works include also a vast amount of organ music, *The
Well-Tempered Clavier,* a collection of forty-eight Preludes
and Fugues in all the keys of the tempered scale (as it is known
on the modern pianoforte), The Art of the Fugue, Inventions

in two and three voices (written for his children), the Gold-
berg Variations, etc.

The greatness of Bach is taken as a matter of course today, but after his death he was practically forgotten until
Mendelssohn drew public attention to his genius over seventy-
five years later. His orchestral works include Concertos of
both the grosso and the solo type, and four Suites which he
called Overtures. Much of his organ and clavier music has
been transcribed for the modern symphony orchestra.

THE BRANDENBURG CONCERTOS

Prince Christian Ludwig, Margraf of Brandenburg, was a
collector of Concertos, like the modern enthusiast for stamps
or coins. He met Bach, probably at Carlsbad, in 1719, and
commissioned some works of this character. They were delivered by Bach in 1721, six in all, with an outrageously
humble letter in French. A few lines are enough to make you
squirm: "Two years ago, when I had the honor of playing
before your Royal Highness, I experienced your condescending interest in the insignificant musical talents with which
Heaven has gifted me, and understood your Royal Highness's
gracious willingness to accept some pieces of my composition.
In accordance with that condescending command, I take the
liberty to present my most humble duty to your Royal Highness in these Concerti for various instruments, begging your
Highness not to judge them by the standards of your own refined and delicate taste, but to seek in them rather the expression of my profound respect and obedience."

It is not recorded whether the Margraf paid Bach anything
for his trouble. But the works were definitely not catalogued
in his library, and eventually they were sold in a job lot at an
average price of ten cents each. They became the property
of a sister of Frederick the Great, and finally landed in the

Royal Library of Berlin. Peters first printed them in 1850, over a century and a quarter after they had been created.

The Brandenburg Concertos may be considered Bach's first attempts at orchestral composition in the larger forms. He used the principle of the Concerto Grosso, with a small group of instruments known as the "concertino" in contrast with the "tutti," or full orchestra (here limited to strings), but he improved upon it and gave the form a new individuality. Evidently he tried to show the variety of instrumental combinations that could be used in the concertino or solo group, and each of the Brandenburg Concertos is different in this respect.

BRANDENBURG CONCERTO NO. 1

This is one of the least familiar of the series. It was played by the Philadelphia Orchestra in its home town and in New York in 1926, when Stokowski gave the entire set of Brandenburg Concertos in two programs, with some other Bach numbers filling in. The first Concerto is in F major, and the solo group consists of a violin, three oboes, a bassoon, and two horns, with a harpsichord to bridge the gaps and the regular strings for the orchestral body.

There are four movements, one more than customarily. The first movement (Allegro, in F major) was used by Bach as the Introduction to his Cantata, *False World* (No. 52). Its most important thematic material follows:

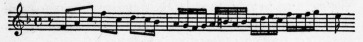

The second movement is an Adagio in D minor, "woeful" in effect. Here is its chief melody:

The third movement is again an Allegro in F, but in 6-8 time, with this main theme:

The fourth movement is a concession to the popular taste for Minuets, and goes beyond the traditional Concerto form. Bach gave this Menuetto three Trios, the second of which is a Polacca played by the strings. The first is for two oboes and bassoon, and the last for horns and oboes. The chief tunes are as follows:

BRANDENBURG CONCERTO NO. 2

This is one of the most popular of the series, with a record of nineteen performances in Philadelphia, New York and Boston. The key is again F major, and the concertino consists of a solo violin, a flute, an oboe, and a trumpet, all high-pitched instruments. The opening Allegro in F is a model of clearness and simplicity, starting thus:

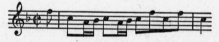

The second movement is an Andante in D minor, written for a quartet consisting of flute, oboe, violin and cello, with harpsichord accompaniment. Here is the chief melody:

The Finale, Allegro assai, in F, is a Fugue for the concertino, sparsely accompanied by the rest of the orchestra, on this subject:

The trumpet part in this Concerto lies very high, and has been revised in various ways by modern orchestrators. Richard Strauss solved the problem with a piccolo-heckelphone, invented by Heckel, producing a tone resembling that of the oboe.

BRANDENBURG CONCERTO NO. 3

This Concerto has been played more often than any of the others, and must therefore be considered the favorite with the public. It has had at least twenty-five performances by major orchestras in America. The key is G major, and the instruments are grouped in threes, three violins, three violas, and three cellos, with a double bass and cembalo (represented by the modern piano). There is no slow movement—merely two Allegros, separated by two sustained chords. The first of these was used by Bach as an Introduction to his Cantata *I Love the Highest* (No. 174). The thematic material follows:

BRANDENBURG CONCERTO NO. 4

The key is again G major, and the instrumentation is for solo violin and two flutes, against the regular strings and cembalo. This Concerto is seldom heard, with less than a half dozen performances in recent years.

It opens with an Allegro in G, in 3-8 time, emphasizing the concertino, with this melodic basis, the flutes alternating at the start:

There is an Andante in E minor, of mournful character, in 3-4 time, based on this theme:

The Finale is a Presto in G, consisting of a Fugue, which is ranked among Bach's best. The chief subject follows:

BRANDENBURG CONCERTO NO. 5

This Concerto is heard fairly often. The key is D major, and it presents a solo violin, flute and clavier in contrast to the conventional strings. (The term "clavier" is applied to practically any early keyboard instrument except an organ. It may refer to the clavichord, the harpsichord, or its equivalent, the cembalo.)

The first movement, Allegro, in D major, has a brilliant cadenza for the clavier near the close. Its chief melodic material is as follows:

The second movement, Affettuoso, in B minor, is a trio for the solo instruments, with this thematic material:

The Finale, Allegro, in D major, has been called "an Irish jig," and it creates that impression with this tune:

BRANDENBURG CONCERTO NO. 6

Seldom heard, this Concerto has an instrumentation of two violas, two viole da gamba, a cello and double bass, with cembalo or piano for a filler. The viola da gamba was literally a "leg viol," as contrasted with the viola da braccio, played in the arm position. The latter is the familiar violin of today, while the viola da gamba has been replaced by the cello.

The opening Allegro of this Concerto, in B-flat, its basic key, begins with a canon for the two violas, accompanied by the other instruments. (A canon is fundamentally the same as a round, with a melody harmonizing with itself, in the same or a related key.) Here is the opening measure:

The second movement, Adagio ma non tanto, begins in E-flat, 3-2 time (but with two flats in the signature), and has a cantabile theme of "noble gravity," fugally treated, with the two gambas silent:

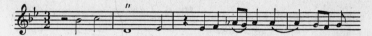

Next comes an Allegro in B-flat, 12-8 time, jig-like in its
fast tune, and described as "exhilarating" and "zestful." The
melodic material follows:

BACH'S FOUR ORCHESTRAL SUITES

Bach called these compositions "Overtures," but they actually follow the form and style of the classic Suite. The first
two were probably written at Cöthen, and the others possibly
in Leipzig, for the Telemann Musikverein, which Bach conducted from 1729 to 1736 in concerts that foretold the Gewandhaus programs of a later period.

Each of these Suites begins with an actual Overture, in the
French style established by Lully, and is followed by a series
of dance movements. The first is in C major, and contains, in
addition to the Overture, a Courante, a two-part Gavotte, a
Forlane, a Minuet, a Bourrée in two parts, and two Passe-
pieds. This Suite is scored for two oboes, bassoon and strings.
The Forlane is a stately dance of Venetian origin, and this
example has the following theme:

The second Suite, in B minor, is for flute and strings. The
Overture begins with free counterpoint for all the instrumental
voices. There follows a charmingly idyllic Rondo, after which
comes a Sarabande of "majestic sadness." There are two
Bourrées, the first showing a strumming effect in the bass, in
the manner of a hurdy-gurdy. The next movement is a Polon-

aise (quite different from the type later popularized by Chopin), followed by a Minuet, and the Finale is called Badinerie, suggesting the style of a Gavotte. All of these dances are gracefully and charmingly carried out, in the courtly atmosphere of the period.

The two Suites in D are more elaborate than the earlier works. Each of them calls for three trumpets, as well as kettle-drums (tympani), in addition to oboes and strings. The first of these, numbered 3 in the series, is by far the most popular of them all, containing the melody now known almost universally as the "Air on the G String" (having been arranged thus for the solo violin by Wilhelmj).

The Overture begins with a slow theme, marked *grave*, and really serving as an Introduction:

Then comes a fast section, Vivace, fugally treated, with the slow theme returning at the close:

After this fine example of polyphonic (many-voiced) writing, comes the famous Aria or Air, whose sustained melody is considered one of the most beautiful ever created. Notice that it was originally in D major, instead of C, as it is when played on the G string of the violin:

This slow movement is followed by two Gavottes, the first of which is a well-known Bach tune, of lively character:

The second Gavotte also has a tune that is full of vitality:

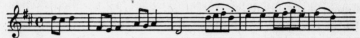

Then comes a Bourrée, with this sturdy melody:

The Finale is a rollicking Gigue, in 6-8 time, running along in this fashion:

It was this Suite that Mendelssohn used for his revival of Bach at one of the Gewandhaus concerts in Leipzig, in 1838.

In the fourth Suite, also in D, the "continuo" or keyboard accompaniment is indicated merely by a figured bass (i.e., numbers showing the harmonies to be used), and it may be assumed that this part was regularly improvised, probably by the conductor (and by Bach himself) on the harpsichord.

It begins with the conventional Overture, containing a theme that Bach also used in his Christmas Cantata, *Let Our Mouth be Full of Laughter* (No. 110), where it serves as the foundation for a vocal Fugue. Here is its original form:

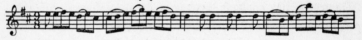

This Suite contains also a Bourrée, a Gavotte, a two-part Minuet, and a Finale with the fanciful title of Réjouissance.

THE PIANO AND VIOLIN CONCERTOS

Johann Sebastian Bach wrote seven Concertos for piano (clavier) and orchestra. These were actually transcriptions of earlier works, most of them written originally for the violin, made for the Telemann Society in Leipzig, after 1730. Six of the Concertos (in D minor, E major, D major, A major, F minor and G minor) have only strings for accompaniment. The one in F has two flutes added,* and there are two others, in A minor and D major, with flute and violin obbligato parts.

The first of these Concertos is perhaps the most important. Bach used its first two movements in his Cantata No. 146, making an Introduction of the opening, with the addition of three oboes, and turning the Adagio into a full chorus. The first movement of this Concerto has been described as a "series of repetitions on a cheerful theme, in different tonalities." There is an Interlude which gives the piano spectacular opportunities, and the solo instrument is prominent throughout.

The Adagio begins and ends with a ground bass, played by all the orchestral instruments, with the piano taking the melody above this bass, followed by the strings in canon (round) style.

The Finale has a quick ascending motive, balanced by the piano in a descending figure, with the strings developing this material.

The second Piano Concerto is in E major. Its Introduction and Siciliano turn up again in Bach's Cantata No. 169, and its Finale serves as Introduction to Cantata No. 49. This Concerto seems to have been written originally for a keyboard instrument, and may be the only one in the series that is not actually a transposition.

Piano Concerto No. 3 is merely a remake of the Violin Concerto in E major, with the key changed to D. No. 4 seems also based on a work for the violin, although its origin is uncertain and the final effect is definitely pianistic. No. 5, in F minor, is unquestionably based upon a lost Violin Concerto in G minor. The one in F, identified with the fourth Brandenburg

---

* This is identical with the fourth Brandenburg Concerto, except for the difference in key. See page 16.

Concerto (in G) is generally numbered sixth among the Piano Concertos.

The seventh Piano Concerto, in G minor, was originally the Violin Concerto in A minor. Its manuscript contained also the start of another Piano Concerto, in D minor, which later became the Introduction to Cantata No. 35.

Much of the piano music in these Concertos is carelessly written, probably because Bach himself customarily played the solo parts, requiring only a few notes for guidance and improvising the rest on the spot.

The Concerto in A minor, with flute and violin solos added to the piano, is generally considered a "triple Concerto" and makes a deep impression whenever it is heard. Its basic materials are in Bach's Prelude and Fugue in A minor for clavier, whose themes are as follows:

The slow movement of this Concerto was taken from the Organ Sonata in D minor. While the themes belong to the Cöthen period and earlier, the Concerto as a whole represents the years in Leipzig when Bach was conductor of the Telemann Society.

Bach wrote three Concertos for two pianos (claviers) and orchestra. The first, in C minor, was based upon a lost Concerto for two violins. The second, in C major, is a real double Piano Concerto, with an opening movement which may have been written originally for the keyboard instruments alone, emphasizing their independence throughout.

The third of these double Concertos, again in C minor, is a literal transcription of the well-known Concerto for two

violins in D minor (described below). It is surprising to find
the composer adapting this decidedly violinistic music to claviers, particularly the sustained melodic line of the slow movement.

There are also two Concertos for three pianos and orchestra, supposedly written by Bach for performance with his
two eldest sons, and therefore dated between 1730 and 1735.
A Concerto for four pianos is based upon a similar composition for four violins by Vivaldi, whose music Bach greatly
admired.

BACH'S VIOLIN CONCERTOS

Himself a fine violinist in his youth, Bach wrote much
music for the violin, some of which has unfortunately been
lost. At least three Concertos which he left to his son Wilhelm
Friedemann have disappeared completely. Three others are
known only through their clavier versions. (See above, p. 21.)

Three Violin Concertos, left to Karl Philip Emanuel Bach,
have survived, and of these the first, in A minor, is most
often heard. In this work, as well as the second, in E major,
there are fine Adagio movements, with the violin moving over
a sustained bass (basso ostinato), creating an effect which has
been compared with the relentless march of Fate. The third
Concerto, in G, is seldom heard. There is also a fragmentary
Allegro in D with orchestral accompaniment.

More popular than any of these works is the double Concerto in D minor, for two violins and string orchestra (often
heard with piano accompaniment). It was doubtless written at
Cöthen, and its later transcription into the third Piano Concerto in C minor has already been mentioned. (See above,
p. 22.)

The first movement is marked Vivace, opening with this
lively theme, played by the two violins in fugal counterpoint:

The second movement contains a beautiful slow melody, strongly suggesting the familiar Largo of Handel, and proving that two composers who never met could independently and accidentally arrive at a very similar idea, each one expressing it in his own way, with complete effect. Bach marked this movement Largo ma non tanto, and its theme begins thus in a slow 12-8 time:

The Finale is a fast Allegro, in triple time, with this opening:

The first piano Concerto, in D minor, is now also available in a version approximating its original form, for solo violin and strings (see p. 21). It has been recorded thus by Szigeti for Columbia (See Appendix).

OTHER ORCHESTRAL WORKS BY BACH

Many of Bach's piano and organ pieces have been transcribed for symphony orchestra by modern musicians, and these are perhaps more often heard than his actual orchestral music. Of the latter there should be mentioned the Pastoral section of the *Christmas Oratorio,* which dates from the year 1734 and is really a collection of the six Cantatas which Bach wrote for the holiday season. This Sinfonia is not at all like the corresponding part of Handel's *Messiah,* with its gentle and definitely pastoral quality. (See p. 31.) Bach's music is restless and makes little attempt to suggest a dramatic or pictorial program. He uses strings and flutes in combination, and it is generally assumed that the former represent the angels and the latter the shepherds. But beyond this rather arbitrary interpretation, the music must be considered of the absolute type.

Most famous of all the orchestral transcriptions of Bach is the great Passacaglia in C minor, originally written for a two-manual clavicembalo and then the organ, and skillfully put into symphonic form by Leopold Stokowski, who has made it one of the most exciting show-pieces of the Philadelphia Orchestra. (There is also an orchestral arrangement of the Passacaglia by Frederick Stock.) Strictly speaking, this is not a real Passacaglia, as the theme is not restricted to the bass, thus making it rather a Chaconne, according to most of the scholarly definitions. By any name and in any form, it would still be a most important work.

The basic theme of eight measures was played on the pedals of the organ, beginning thus:

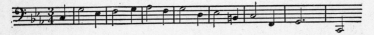

There are twenty Variations on this material, followed by a double Fugue which uses the first half of the Passacaglia theme and then adds a new one.

Stokowski has also orchestrated the Chaconne, written by Bach for the unaccompanied violin, as the Finale of his second Partita for that instrument, in D minor, during the Cöthen period. Another successful Stokowski transcription for orchestra is the organ Toccata and Fugue in D minor (best known to the public through Walt Disney's *Fantasia*). The same transcriber has orchestrated the Fantasia and Fugue in D minor, originally written for the organ, two of the Preludes from *The Well-Tempered Clavier,* and other typical compositions of Bach. A number of the Choral Preludes are also available in orchestral form, completing a fairly large and increasingly popular repertoire of Bach material for modern symphonic organizations.

CONTEMPORARIES OF BACH

While the name of Handel is the only one generally considered worthy of being bracketed with that of Johann Sebastian Bach in the early classical period, a few other composers of that time deserve mention here, since their works are still occasionally played by symphony orchestras. Of these perhaps the most interesting is Antonio Vivaldi, chiefly because Bach himself greatly admired his music and gave some of it the benefit of his own arrangements. Vivaldi, a native of Venice, was primarily a violinist, but also a skilled composer and conductor. He directed the first girls' orchestra in history, at the Foundling Hospital in Venice, from 1713 until his death, in 1743. A Concerto Grosso by Vivaldi, in D minor, is in the modern orchestral repertoire, and this was once attributed to Bach's son, Wilhelm Friedemann, who claimed its authorship on the strength of a transcription for organ in his father's handwriting. This Concerto has three movements. The concertino (solo group) consists of two violins and a cello, with the regular strings as "tutti" (full orchestra).

In Bach's own day great respect was paid to Georg Philipp Telemann, who outlived him by seventeen years, although born four years earlier. It was perhaps ironic that Bach himself should have conducted a musical society named in honor of Telemann and composed for it some of his finest instrumental works (see page 18). Telemann was a good technician and enormously prolific, composing about six hundred Overtures in the French style, besides forty operas, a number of

oratorios and much church music. Modern orchestral programs occasionally include his works.

Bach's most gifted son, Karl Philip Emanuel (also spelled
Carl and Emmanuel) has real significance as a connecting link
between the old contrapuntal style of composition and the
symphonic form developed by Haydn, Mozart and Beethoven.
He himself wrote four symphonies while living in Hamburg
in 1776, of which the second, in E-flat, is the most popular.
(The others are in D, F and G.) He laid the foundations of
Sonata form, thematic development and the modern treatment of the orchestra, besides contributing much to the ad-
vancement of the piano, as player and composer.

A Concerto in D by the younger Bach is still heard, and its
instrumentation of wood-wind and horn contrasting with
strings strongly suggests the modern orchestra. The Andante
movement opens with a solo passage for the English horn.

GEORGE FREDERICK HANDEL

B. Halle, February 23, 1685; d. London, April 14, 1759.

(The English spelling of the name is used here, although the
owner eventually signed his middle name as "Frideric.")

It is curious that Handel and Bach, born in the same year,
and the outstanding musicians of their day, never met. Handel
spent much of his life in England, where he tried unsuccessfully to compose and produce operas, but left a deep and lasting impression with his oratorios, particularly *The Messiah.*

Handel was a master of the clavier and organ and wrote
with equal skill for voices and instruments. His music is
characterized by a flowing melodic line and a thorough command of the polyphonic style. His orchestral works include
twelve Concerti Grossi for strings and harpsichord, some oboe
Concertos and the two Suites known today as the *Water Music*
and *Fire Music.*

HANDEL'S WATER MUSIC

This piece has an interesting history, on which most scholars agree, with some variation in details. Handel had enjoyed the patronage of the Elector of Hanover, but after visiting England found still greater pleasure in the royal favor of Queen Anne, the Elector's sister. When the Queen died, to be succeeded by her brother, Handel found himself in an embarrassing position and was uncertain how to win back the good-will of his former master, now King George I. A friend (Baron Kilmannsegge) suggested the successful trick of the *Water Music*, which was composed for a fete on the Thames and played from a barge which followed that of the King up the river. The date is generally given as 1715, although it may have been two years later. In any case, Handel was soon restored to royal favor.

The *Water Music* is actually a series of twenty pieces, beginning with the conventional "French" Overture and including such dance forms as the Bourrée, Minuet and Hornpipe. There are also slower movements, generally called Arias.

The music is definitely in a popular style, with no real attempt at any larger unity, and it is seldom heard today in its entirety. Hamilton Harty has arranged the most important movements in a Suite, opening with the Allegro, which has this principal theme, first announced by the trumpets:

Then comes an Air, with this main melody played by the string quartet:

The middle section brings in the full orchestra, with this theme announced by the oboe:

The next movement is the Bourrée, marked Vivace, and beginning thus:

The Hornpipe follows, in 3-2 time, but rather lively nevertheless, with the oboe taking the lead:

Next is the Andante movement, opening with this slow melody, espressivo, in the flute:

The Finale is marked Allegro deciso, again in a lively tempo that belies the 3-2 time signature:

HANDEL'S FIRE MUSIC

Handel wrote his *Fire Music* in 1749, to celebrate the Peace of Aix-la-Chappelle. He called it a Concerto, but its form is really that of a Suite. In addition to the Overture, the *Fire Music* contains a Bourrée, a Minuet, a slow Air, two movements called La Réjouissance and La Paix and a Siciliano. The orchestration is almost entirely for wind instruments, the score calling for nine horns, nine trumpets, twenty-four oboes and twelve bassoons.

History relates that Handel's music was more successful than the actual fireworks, which first fizzled outrageously and then set fire to the wooden Temple of Peace, which was promptly burned down.

The Overture to Handel's *Fire Music* has been described as a "stately march." The key is D major, and the material is drawn from the orchestral Concertos in F and D.

The Bourrée is in D minor, and La Paix is marked Largo alla Siciliana. La Réjouissance is an Allegro in D, and there are actually two Minuets. It is said that over twelve thousand people paid to hear a rehearsal of this work at Vauxhall Gardens, blocking traffic on London Bridge for three hours.

HANDEL'S CONCERTOS AND
PASTORAL SYMPHONY

Handel wrote twelve Concerti Grossi for string orchestra, using two solo violins and a solo bass viol as concertino, with cembalo for the continuo. The keys in order are G, F, E minor, A minor, D, G minor, B-flat, C minor, F, D minor, A and B minor.

The composer created this entire series in the month of October, 1739. The Concertos were published by Walsh in April, 1740, and had many public performances within a short time. Today they are seldom heard, although they represent the purest Handelian style.

Handel also wrote some Concertos for oboe and orchestra, and in two of these he made use of Fugues from his clavier pieces. One of them was turned into the second Overture to his opera, *Amadigi,* and another had its opening movement transferred to the opera *Ottone.*

More interesting to modern audiences is the *Pastoral Symphony* from Handel's *Messiah,* a charming orchestral interlude, following the chorus, *For unto Us a Child Is Born,* and preceding the soprano recitative, *There Were Shepherds Abiding in the Field.*

Handel called this Christmas music *Pifa,* probably in reference to the Calabrian Piferari or pipers, from whom he seems to have borrowed his chief melody:

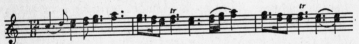

Handel is said to have heard this old chant in Rome, and to have remembered it for thirty-two years. Another story is that he was imitating Scarlatti's *Christmas Oratorio* in this orchestral portion of *The Messiah.* In any case, the music definitely represents the vigil of the shepherds on the night of the Nativity.

CHRISTOPH WILLIBALD VON GLUCK

B. Weidenwang, July 2, 1714; d. Vienna, Nov. 15, 1787.

Gluck's importance lies chiefly in the field of opera, where he instituted lasting reforms. (See *Metropolitan Opera Guide,* p. 19.) But his Overtures are significant as orchestral pieces and his music is still heard occasionally on symphonic programs.

Much of Gluck's life was spent in Paris, where he had to

overcome the rivalry of Piccinni, now a completely forgotten composer, and also the intrigues and jealousies that have always been characteristic of the operatic world. His outstanding operas are *Orpheus and Eurydice, Alceste, Iphigenia in Aulis* and *Iphigenia in Tauris,* all based upon classic subjects.

GLUCK'S OVERTURES AND BALLET MUSIC

Three of Gluck's Overtures have kept their place in the orchestral repertoire, introducing the operas *Alceste* and the two *Iphigenias.* The Overture to *Orpheus and Eurydice* is merely a lively curtain-raiser, with little significance as an independent piece of music.

The *Alceste* Overture has been called by Ernest Newman "a notable triumph of dramatic expression." Its first performance was in Vienna, Dec. 16, 1767. A French version of the opera was given (unsuccessfully) in Paris, April 23, 1776. The text is by Calzabigi. Gluck explained the failure of this opera by saying that it was "founded upon nature and has nothing to do with fashion."

The Overture to *Alceste* begins with a short, somber phrase in D minor (Lento), leading into an Andante "of a dolent expression."

There is a passage of "storm and stress," which leads back to the slow Prelude, now transposed to the key of A minor, and then to a repetition of the Andante.

Most important of the Gluck Overtures is the one to *Iphigenia in Aulis,* which was greatly admired by Wagner, who not only analyzed its contents in detail but wrote a concluding section of thirty-three measures so that it could be played as a concert piece. (Originally the music led right into the opening recitative of Agamemnon. The Wagner ending is now regularly used.)

The text of this opera was adapted by Bailly de Roullet from Racine, whose drama was based on that of Euripides. Its first performance was at the Paris Opéra, April 19, 1774.

The rehearsals of *Iphigenia in Aulis* were not promising. There was little co-operation from the singers, and the orchestra was described as "an old coach drawn by consumptive horses and led by one deaf from his birth." But the performance was a success, and the ladies of Paris adopted a hair-do called *"à l'Iphigénie."*

Wagner found four themes in the Overture, which he described thus:

1. A motive of Appeal, from the gnawing anguish of the heart:

2. A motive of Power, of an imperious, overbearing demand:

3. A motive of Grace, of maidenly tenderness:

4. A motive of Sorrowing, of agonizing pity:

For the orchestral Introduction to *Iphigenia in Tauris*, the opera which represented Gluck's final triumph over Piccinni,

the composer supplied program notes, indicating that the
music suggests "calm, a distant storm, the nearer approach
of the storm, rain and hail" and that finally "the storm ceases."
He was sixty-five years old when this work was introduced in
Paris (1779). The libretto was adapted directly from Euripides by Nicolas-François Guillard.

Here is the opening thematic material of this Introduction,
which leads directly into the action:

Some of Gluck's best orchestral music is found in the ballet
interludes of his operas. Two Suites of this Ballet Music were
arranged by Felix Mottl and published in 1900. The one most
often heard in concert contains an *Air gai* and Lento from
Iphigenia in Aulis, with an Introduction from Gluck's ballet-
opera, *Don Juan.*

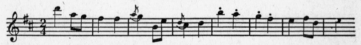

Then comes the familiar Dance of the Blessed Spirits from
Orpheus and Eurydice:

There is also a Musette from the opera *Armide,* with this
theme:

The Finale contains another *Air gai* from the first *Iphigenia* and a Sicilienne from *Armide*.

FRANZ JOSEF HAYDN

B. Rohrau, March 31, 1732; d. Vienna, May 31, 1809.

Generally known as "the father of the symphony," Haydn actually owed much to the men who immediately preceded him, particularly Karl Philip Emanuel Bach and Karl Johann Stamitz. He did, however, perfect the Sonata form, and his genius gave a new vitality and significance to outlines already established.

Haydn was fortunate in being able to test his theories with an excellent orchestra, supplied him by Prince Esterhazy, on whose estate at Eisenstadt he spent the most important years of his life.

Haydn wrote about 125 symphonies, and many of these are still active in the orchestral programs of today. In general they are characterized by a slow Introduction, followed by an Allegro (fast) movement in Sonata form. The second movement regularly has a slow theme, often with Variations, and this is followed by the conventional Minuet (Menuetto), with the symphony ending in a fast Finale, often in Rondo form.

In addition to his symphonies, Haydn wrote a wealth of chamber music (string quartets, trios, sonatas, etc.), much ecclesiastical material and two significant oratorios, *The Creation* and *The Seasons*. He experimented also with opera and song writing, but is known today chiefly by his absolute music. As an architect in tones he ranks among the highest.

THE HAYDN SYMPHONIES

The actual total of Haydn's symphonies may be as high as 154, and fourteen more have been attributed to him, but perhaps wrongly. His earlier works in this form require little attention, often representing mere elaborations of his chamber music.

Among the symphonies composed at Eisenstadt are many with programmatic titles, such as *Le Midi* (1761), *Le Soir* (1761), *Der Philosoph* (1764) and *Le Matin* (1767). The most famous of these early works is the *Farewell Symphony,* composed in 1772 as a hint to Prince Esterhazy that the orchestra deserved a vacation. The dramatic effect occurred in the Finale, when all the musicians, two at a time, blew out their candles and left the stage. The last notes were played by the two remaining violinists, whose exit left the hall in silence and total darkness. The Prince naturally took the hint.

The *Farewell Symphony* omits any Introduction, opening immediately with this Allegro theme in F-sharp minor:

The slow movement is built upon this melody:

There is a Minuet, with the following thematic material:

A fourth movement, Presto, starts with this lively tune:

The Finale is an Adagio in G, beginning thus:

Other symphonies composed at the estate of Esterhaz carry such names as *Mercury* (1772), *Trauer* (Sadness) (1772), *Lamentations* (1772), *Maria Theresa* (1773) (composed for a visit by the Empress), *La Passione* (1773), *The Schoolmaster* (1774) and *La Chasse* (1781).

Some of the so-called "Paris" symphonies also have descriptive titles. They were composed at Esterhaz for the Parisian Concerts Spirituels (or Concerts de la Loge Olympique) between 1784 and 1789 in two sets of six each. (The final symphony in this series remains unidentified, and may never have been written.)

The first Paris symphony is called *L'Ours* (The Bear), for no particular reason, and the second bears the name of *La Poule* (The Hen), with some justification in its realistic imitation of cackling sounds. The fourth of the series is known as *La Reine de France,* probably in honor of Marie Antoinette. All of the first six in this set may safely be dated 1784-6.

The first of the second Paris set, in G major, is often played today. It is numbered 13 in the Breitkopf & Haertel list, and the date of its composition is 1787.

The Adagio Introduction covers less than two measures, with staccato chords, leading immediately into an Allegro in 2-4 time, the strings softly playing the first theme:

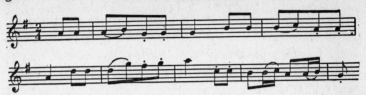

This theme is repeated forte by the full orchestra, and the second and third themes are derived from it:

The development is elaborate and full of counterpoint. After a recapitulation of the melodic material, there is a short Coda, based on the first theme.

The second movement is a Largo in D major, triple time. The oboes and cellos sing the slow tune, accompanied by violas, basses, bassoons and horn:

There is a transition to other material, with some development, all ending in a short Coda.

The Minuet is marked Allegretto, in the basic key of G and the conventional 3-4 time. Its chief theme is as follows:

The Finale is a Rondo on a peasant dance tune, Allegro con spirito, 2-4 time, key of G. Here is its opening melody:

The tenth symphony of the dozen presumably written for Parisian listeners is known as the *Oxford,* because it was played at that University when Haydn, on his first visit to England in 1791, was given a doctor's degree, along with other honors. He wrote a special symphony for the occasion, but there was not enough time for proper rehearsal, and the older work was happily substituted. It ranks among the best of Haydn's entire output. The key is G major.

The Introduction to the *Oxford Symphony* is more important than usual, announcing this charming melody at the outset:

With the start of the Allegro section, the music becomes almost boisterous:

A second theme suggests the mood of the Introduction, but in a much faster tempo:

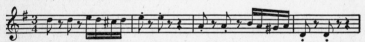

There is some development, dealing mostly with the first Allegro theme, and after its complete return (recapitulation) in the original key of G, a short Coda leads to the concluding chords.

The slow movement, Adagio, is in D major, the strings introducing this main melody:

A flute part is added on its repetition, and Haydn then treats it in various ways, including one transposition into minor key. Some contrasting material follows, and after an interlude by the wood-wind, the movement ends very softly.

The Menuetto (slightly faster than the conventional Minuet) has this lively tune for a start:

The Trio of this Minuet movement emphasizes the bassoons and trumpets, with amusing effects of syncopation, quite in the spirit of modern rag-time. The first section then returns, without repeats, according to the accepted formula.

In the Presto Finale the chief tune is again lively, with wide jumps by the cellos and other instruments and the general effect of a country dance:

This theme is repeated in minor key and, after some development, reappears in major. The solo flute then introduces a passage for the wood-wind which develops into a dialogue with the strings. In a brief Coda the flute once more suggests the main theme, but is impatiently answered by the strings, and the full orchestra brings the symphony to a fortissimo conclusion.

HAYDN'S "SALOMON" SYMPHONIES

Twelve symphonies written by Haydn in two sets of six each, for the impresario Johann Peter Salomon and the English public, represent the climax of his work in this form. They were written mostly in London, where the composer arrived on the first day of the year 1791. His patron, Prince Ester-hazy, had died in September of the previous year, leaving Haydn a substantial pension and the freedom to go where he pleased. Salomon, who had been trying by letter to bring the great musician to England, seized the opportunity for a per-sonal visit and quickly sold him the idea. They crossed the Channel together, and Haydn became an immediate sensation in London.

Unquestionably his association with the youthful Mozart had a beneficial effect on Haydn's creative work. He had begun by teaching Mozart what he could, and ended by learning much from his genial pupil, whom he admired without reservation. They spent a final day together in Vienna, and at their parting Mozart burst into tears, predicting that they would not meet again. He was right, but it was Mozart him-self, and not his aging friend, who died before the year was over.

The first two of the Salomon symphonies, in C and D, are not often heard today, but the third is the familiar *Surprise,* in G. All three were probably written in 1791. The *Surprise Symphony* had its first performance at the Hanover Square Rooms, March 23, 1792, this being the sixth concert given by Salomon with Haydn in London. It was an immediate success, and the famous Andante had to be repeated.

The Introduction to the *Surprise Symphony* is Adagio cantabile, with this dignified slow theme announced by the strings:

After seventeen measures the real opening theme enters, also in the strings, Vivace assai, in a fast 6-8 time:

There is considerable development of this lively tune, until in the eightieth measure a second theme is announced, also by the strings, its key of D contrasting with the basic G that had thus far prevailed.

The repetition of this melody adds the flute to the first violins, followed by a wood-wind interlude. The development deals mostly with the first theme, and the recapitulation uses alternating strings and wood-wind on both melodies.

The second movement contains the surprise which gives the symphony its name. This is a sudden crashing chord in the sixteenth measure, after the first half of the main theme has been repeated. It is a typical Haydn joke, of which he has been quoted as saying "This will make the ladies scream," and suggesting that it would at least wake up the audience.

The theme itself, in C major, is very simple, played by the violins in unison over a pizzicato (plucked) accompaniment of the other strings. Haydn used it again later as accompaniment to the air sung by the whistling plowboy, Simon, in *The Seasons*, to the words "With eagerness the husbandman his tilling work begins."

There are eight Variations on this theme, the last one fragmentary, in the manner of a Coda. Then comes the Menuetto, Allegro molto, back in the basic key of G. Its opening tune goes like this:

The Finale is a Rondo, Allegro di molto, again in G, and in a fast 2-4 time. The chief tune is as follows:

A secondary theme alternates with it thus:

While all twelve of the symphonies written by Haydn for Salomon are generally grouped under the name of *London,* the title has been particularly applied to the first of the second series, in D major, composed in 1795 on Haydn's return trip. (It may have been written in 1792 and saved up.) By many critics this *London Symphony* is considered the finest in the entire Haydn list. Its first performance was at Haydn's benefit concert, May 4, 1795.

It begins with a slow Introduction in D minor, played by the full orchestra, in the manner of a trumpet call:

After three repetitions of this clarion call, twice in minor and once in major, the first theme enters in a smooth melodic line:

The second theme is characterized by widely spaced intervals:

The development dwells upon short snatches of the first tune, and both themes are heard again in recapitulation. There is a Coda of eighteen measures, based upon material from the first theme.

The slow movement is in G major, opening with a plaintive melody of great charm (possibly a Croatian folk song):

This theme is repeated and then imitated, with various orchestral embellishments.

The Menuetto begins with a lively tune, again in the basic key of D, with a suggestion of artificial accents on the final beats of the measures, as in a Mazurka.

For his Finale Haydn writes a typical dance based upon the Croatian ballad, *Oj Jelena,* starting with a drone bass in imitation of the bagpipe:

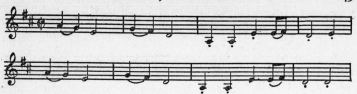

Subsidiary themes follow, and there is considerable development of the main tune. The movement is carried out in Sonata form, closing with loud chords in D major.

The eighth of the *London Symphonies* (Number Two in the second series) is in E-flat, and has the descriptive title "with the drum-roll." This mark of identification is heard at the very start in the tympani, introducing a slow, portentous melody, perhaps of Croatian origin, sung by the cellos, basses and bassoons.

The first violins play the real opening theme, Allegro con spirito, very softly, in 6-8 time.

The second theme is in B-flat, introduced by the first violins and oboe:

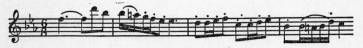

After some development, the drum-roll is heard again, with the Adagio theme of the Introduction, and the movement ends in a short Coda.

The Andante is in C minor, consisting of a theme with Variations. This melody is generally regarded as a Croatian folk-tune:

There are five Variations, the first dealing with the first half of the theme, and the second with the second half. The third introduces a violin solo.

The Menuetto is unusual in having its Trio in the same key as the main theme (E-flat), which is as follows:

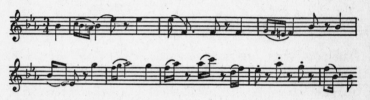

Allegro con spirito indicates the mood and tempo of the Finale, whose chief melody is built up gradually.

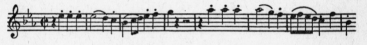

The date of this symphony is probably 1795.

The last two symphonies written for Salomon (in their published order) bear the titles *Clock* and *Military*, and are both usually dated 1794. The *Clock Symphony* is in D major, but with its Introduction beginning in D minor, in a slow, ascending scale:

A Presto theme in D major supplies the first real tune, in a lively 6-8 time:

The second theme is a definite imitation of the first, and the development concentrates upon this main melody. Both themes reach a climax in recapitulation, with the Coda going back once more to the first.

The *Clock Symphony* gets its name from the second movement, which starts with a fairly realistic imitation of the ticking of a timepiece. Over this accompaniment a charming melody is heard:

A noisy passage interrupts in minor key, but the naive tune returns in the first violins, with only a flute and a bassoon carrying the tick-tock accompaniment. A long pause leads to another repetition, this time with the clock ticking in the second violins. The full orchestra finally plays the complete theme most effectively.

The chief melody of the Menuetto is gay and lively, containing some of Haydn's favorite octave jumps:

The Trio plays scale passages over a drone bass, with one rather daring harmony that was once suspected of being a misprint.

A sturdy scale tune opens the Finale:

Its answer is also robust, with suggestions of peasant song and dance:

A noisy interlude in minor key leads to a return of the first theme, with unexpected decorations and some fugal effects. The final statement is simple and quiet, in the manner of a farewell, and this impression is heightened by the repetition of the last five notes. After this little sentimental touch, Haydn runs quickly, almost shamefacedly, into his closing chords.

The *Military Symphony,* in G major, had its first performance at the Hanover Square Rooms, London, May 12, 1794. Its name is derived from the use of the bass drum, cymbals and triangle in the second and fourth movements, presumably with martial effect. Actually the work possesses a delicate charm, far removed from what would today be considered a military atmosphere.

The Introduction offers an immediate strain of appealing tunefulness, often imitated by later composers:

The main theme is itself slightly reminiscent of the Introduction:

There is considerable experimenting with this material before the strings bring on the second theme, in D major:

The real development section deals with this second tune rather than the first. Both reappear toward the close of the movement (recapitulation), and the Coda carries a suggestion of the first theme into scales and chords for a finish.

The slow movement of the *Military Symphony* is built upon a melody of French origin, whose innocence is not disguised by the percussion effects of the orchestration:

This theme is later played in minor key and broken up for purposes of development. A trumpet fanfare introduces rolling drums to start a big crescendo which reaches its climax in the full orchestra, with the usual closing chords.

A catchy, whistling tune opens the Menuetto and is imitated in scale figures, including chromatic effects:

The Trio provides another lively melody, this time alternating skipping scale tones with smoother patterns taken from chords:

The Minuet form is strictly observed, including the repetitions.

The Finale is in 6-8 time, beginning with another attractive tune of folk-song character, which is immediately repeated:

Haydn then tries various experiments with sections of this galloping theme, in different keys. Soft, hesitating chords by the strings are interrupted by a loud drum-beat. At the end the complete melody is heard again, with a few extra touches of development in the Coda, and two loud chords bring the *Military Symphony* to a close.

HAYDN'S CONCERTOS

Of about twenty Piano Concertos written by Haydn, only one is heard often today. It is in D major, and was published along with another in G by Artaria of Vienna in 1784.

The opening theme is introduced at once, Vivace, with six measures played softly and the rest loud. The piano alternates with the orchestra for the most part and has a Cadenza (technically brilliant interlude) near the close. Here is the chief theme:

The second movement is a Larghetto (un poco Adagio) in A major. The orchestra announces the principal theme, which is then taken up by the piano:

The Finale is a Rondo all' Ongharese (Allegro assai, in D), with its chief theme based on a Croatian dance called the Kolo. It is first played by the piano and then taken up by the orchestra, with a Coda at the end.

Haydn's Cello Concerto in D was written for his friend and pupil, Anton Kraft, who played in the orchestra at Esterhaz from New Year's Day of 1778 until 1790. He was the son of a Pilsen brewer, evidently a fine artist, as both Mozart and Beethoven also wrote music for his personal use.

This Concerto is one of six (and the only survivor) written by Haydn between 1771 and 1783, catalogued as opus 101. It is still a favorite with concert cellists and was often played by Casals.

The first movement, Allegro moderato, has two themes, each introduced by the orchestra and then taken up by the soloist. This is the first:

In the Adagio, in the related key of A major, the cello sings an expressive theme which constitutes the chief melodic material:

The Concerto ends with a Rondo, containing a familiar theme, with its climax in a brilliant Coda:

WOLFGANG AMADEUS MOZART

B. Salzburg, Jan. 27, 1756; d. Vienna, Dec. 5, 1791.

Mozart remains the eternal model of the "wonder child" in music. Playing and composing at the age of four, and a public performer at six, he continued to astonish the musical world to the day of his untimely death at thirty-five. Improvident and unpractical, he lived most of his life in poverty and was buried in a pauper's grave. His wife was Constanze Weber, a cousin of the composer, Carl Maria von Weber.

Mozart stands high in the field of opera, with such works as *Don Giovanni, The Marriage of Figaro* and *The Magic Flute,* but he reached equal or even greater heights in symphonic and chamber music, besides writing great ecclesiastical works and some charming songs. He was the last of the great tonal architects, but his music contains far more than a mere technical skill and is definitely a forerunner of the romantic period that was to follow.

MOZART'S SYMPHONIES

The miraculous Mozart is credited with forty-one symphonies, besides twenty-eight Divertimenti, Serenades and "Cassations," about forty Concertos of various kinds, and a number of orchestral marches, dance pieces, etc. These works are generally numbered according to the chronological catalogue worked out by Dr. Ludwig Koechel, a botanist and mineralogist who devoted much time and money to the study of Mozart's music and made possible the complete edition of his compositions, as published by Breitkopf & Haertel. The numerals preceded by the letter K, regularly found in program notes on Mozart, indicate the listing according to Koechel.

Mozart's earliest symphonies were written in London and The Hague, and were limited to three movements. He began to include the Minuet in 1767, in Vienna, and his treatment of this conventional dance form eventually marked a great advance over the work of Haydn.

The Serenades were actually experiments in symphonic form, and the most famous of these is the so-called *Haffner Serenade* in D (K.250). It was written for the marriage of Elisabeth (or Elise) Haffner, daughter of Sigmund Haffner, burgomaster of Salzburg, to a man named Spaeth, July 22, 1776. There were originally eight movements to this *Haffner Serenade,* three of which may have been taken from a Mozart violin Concerto. Only three are now generally played. The first is marked Allegro maestoso-Allegro molto and contains this theme:

The Andante is built chiefly on this melody:

Finally there is a Rondo, with the following tune as a basis:

Mozart also supplied a march for the Haffner-Spaeth wedding, and six years later he created a symphony for the same family. This work is also in the key of D major (K.385) and was written in Vienna in less than two weeks, during the summer of 1782. Originally it was actually a Serenade, with a March and two Minuets. But two of these movements were later dropped, and the work is known today as the *Haffner*

Symphony. On March 22, 1783, it was performed in Vienna for the Emperor, with Mozart conducting. Flutes and clarinets were added to the original score for this performance.

The first movement of the *Haffner Symphony,* Allegro con spirito, in D, has only one theme, with a brief development section, and does not repeat the first part (exposition). Here is the theme:

There is an Andante in G, emphasizing this melody:

The Menuetto, again in D, has this opening theme:

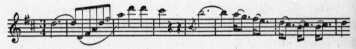

The Finale is a Rondo, marked Presto, also in D, with this main tune which has been compared with actual rounds:

Also in the category of the Serenades is the "Little Night Music" (*Eine kleine Nachtmusik*) (K.525), written for strings, but far more than a piece of chamber music. Its four movements are an Allegro in G, a Romanza in C (Andante), a Menuetto (Allegretto) in G, with Trio in D, and a final Rondo (Allegro) in G.

Mozart wrote twenty symphonies in Salzburg, and two of these stand out prominently, one in G minor (K.183), a serious, almost melancholy composition, forerunner of the later masterpiece in the same key, and the other in A (K. 201), contrastingly bright and sunny. There is also a Salzburg symphony in C (K.338). (Mozart wrote at least eight in this basic key.) The score is dated August 29, 1780. It has only three movements, Allegro vivace, Andante di molto and a final Rondo (Allegro vivace). The start of a Minuet shows in the manuscript, but was crossed out.

A symphony in D (K.297) was written in Paris in June, 1778, and is generally known by the name of that city. It also has no Minuet. The first movement, Allegro assai, begins with a loud chord, after which the first theme is introduced by the violins. The Andante, in G, has a sustained melodic line, comprising a three-part theme. The final Allegro is in Sonata form, with consistent alternation of tonic and dominant.

Far more important is the so-called *Prague Symphony*, also in D (K.504), written in December, 1786, and first performed at Prague, Jan. 19, 1787, in the first of two concerts conducted by the composer. It marks the transition from the earlier and smaller works to the gigantic trio of 1788, in E-flat, G minor and C (the *Jupiter*).

Prague at this time was "Figaro-mad," and Mozart's popular opera had been turned into waltzes and country dances to satisfy the enthusiastic public. The *Prague Symphony* made such a hit that Mozart had to improvise at the piano for half an hour. Still they would not let him go, and when cries of "Figaro, Figaro" arose, he returned and improvised Variations on the air, *Non più andrai*, from the opera.

The *Prague Symphony* has a slow Introduction, which is rare with Mozart, suggesting the opening of the *Jupiter* of later date:

The main theme of the first movement, Allegro, is as follows:

The Andante is developed from this thematic material:

Finally comes a Rondo with two themes, of which this is the first:

THE THREE MASTERPIECES

Mozart wrote his three outstanding symphonies within a period of six weeks, in the summer of 1788. The first, in E-flat, is dated June 26; the second, in G minor, July 25; the third, in C (known as the *Jupiter Symphony*) August 10. These three masterpieces are among the most popular in the entire symphonic literature, and are regularly heard on orchestral programs today. They represent the climax of Mozart's powers as a creator of absolute music.

The E-flat symphony (K.543) opens with a slow Introduction of twenty-five measures, starting thus, with impressive chords:

The first theme is in triple time, still in the basic key of E-flat:

The Andante, in A-flat, starts with this slow, lyric melody:

There is a second theme, which gives the movement Sonata form:

The third movement of this E-flat symphony is one of Mozart's most famous Minuets, with a sturdiness that is seldom found in this old-fashioned dance form. The chief melody is well known:

There is a gentle Trio in this movement, a rhythmic fore-runner of the slow *Jupiter* theme (see page 62) with possible influence also on Beethoven's Finale in his Fifth Symphony (see page 91). The tune could actually be used as a waltz.

The Finale (Allegro) starts with a rushing theme, which develops into a typical country dance, with fiddles playing furiously above a heavy bass. Snatches of counter-melody pop up here and there, but most of the movement is devoted to this one tune:

Loud chords finally silence the main theme, with a pert interruption of the basic scale passage near the close and then an almost comically sudden finish.

The symphony in G minor (K.550) is Mozart's real masterpiece, and has been called one of the few perfect things in art. It is a model of form, yet full of human interest, and open to a variety of interpretations. Dramatic values may safely be set aside in view of its purely musical significance.

The symphony starts right in with its opening theme, a marvel of construction, built largely on a two-note pattern:

After a partial repetition, this goes into a connecting theme in B-flat major, of which G is the relative minor:

The actual second theme is made of chromatic sequences, in striking contrast to the opening melody:

There is some development of the first theme, chiefly by way of experiments with the two-tone pattern, of which the composer seems entirely aware. The real development section also deals chiefly with the first theme, making use of instrumental variety for its most striking effects. All three themes return in the recapitulation, completing the Sonata form, and three loud chords finish the movement (Allegro molto).

The slow movement (Andante) is in E-flat major, with an overlapping effect in its main theme:

A second melody is derived from the first, with echo effects:

Actually this is a rare example of Sonata form in a slow movement.

The Menuetto begins robustly, in G minor, with decided syncopation (rag-time):

The Trio of this Minuet is in G major, with a quiet dance rhythm:

In the Finale (Allegro assai) Mozart lets loose with one of his daintiest and most captivating tunes, whose basic pattern

was directly imitated in the Scherzo of Beethoven's Fifth
Symphony some years later (see page 90):

Sonata form is again established by a second theme, in B-
flat, of enchanting beauty:

The development section deals almost entirely with the first
seven notes of the opening theme of the movement, with a
fascinating dialogue between strings and wind instruments.
Both tunes return for a recapitulation, with the second showing some alteration, and after orchestral arguments as to the
advisability of staying in the minor key, a compromise is ef-
fected in the final G octave.

The third of this trio of great symphonies is in C major
(K.551) and generally known as the *Jupiter*. But it is not
Olympian in mood, possessing a thoroughly human gaiety,
far from divine dignity. J. B. Cramer has been credited with
suggesting the title of "Jupiter," because of the "loftiness of

ideas and nobility of treatment." The triplets in the first
measure have been compared with the thunderbolts of Jove.
Possibly the power and brilliance of the symphony are enough
to justify the title. The first performance may have been in
Leipzig in May, 1789.

The *Jupiter Symphony* opens with a sturdy announcement
of the key of C major, pointing toward the first theme of
Beethoven's First Symphony (see page 76) which was its fitting successor.

The orchestra comments noisily on this theme, which is soon
repeated softly, with the wood-wind adding a counter-melody,
on which the orchestra also works to some extent. Blustering
chords lead to a second theme of quiet charm:

A chattering motive provides material for the development
section, which also deals with the first theme. The recapitulation brings back this melody in its original key, with the
second theme also put into C major, plus a reminder of the
chattering passage. Scales and chords provide a satisfactory
finish.

The slow movement (Andante cantabile) opens with a melody that harks back to the Minuet of the E-flat symphony
(see page 57) and points forward to the Finale of Beethoven's
Fifth (page 91). But in each case the effect is entirely different. Here it is a portentous theme, with implications of Olympian grandeur:

The second theme has a reassuring sound:

Development and recapitulation are carried out in Sonata form, with some decorations and a change of key to F major for the second melody. The movement closes very simply and softly.

The Minuet begins with a distinct reminiscence of the chromatic scale effects in the second theme of the G minor symphony (first movement). But again the effect is quite different:

The Finale is practically unique in music, being a mathematical demonstration that would have done credit to Bach, but always expressed in thoroughly human terms. The melodic materials are limited, chiefly based upon this short theme:

Still shorter patterns are added to this, and the movement does not actually reach a climax until the Coda, which is an amazing five-part Fugue, combining the chief theme and four subordinate motives. Most astonishing is the fact that all this musical arithmetic never approaches dullness but maintains a vivid and dramatic reality throughout. The symphony ends with triumphant chords in its basic key of C major.

MOZART'S CONCERTOS

Of the forty or more Concertos for solo instruments and orchestra written by Mozart, at least twenty-five are for the piano, and several of these must be considered of real importance in his orchestral catalogue. The first four were composed in Salzburg during the year 1767 (at the tender age of eleven), and six more were added there between 1773 and 1777. The last fifteen belong to Vienna, and are dated through the ten years from 1781 to 1791. There is also a Concerto for three claviers (K.242), dated 1776, and one for two claviers (K.365) of the year 1780.

The form of the modern Concerto was really established by Mozart and has undergone little change. Before his time the so-called Concertos were either of the Grosso type, with a small group of instruments alternating with the tutti (full orchestra), or at best they treated the solo instrument as merely the outstanding voice in the ensemble. Mozart gave the soloist a definite importance, but at the same time increased the significance of the orchestral accompaniment, so that he actually achieved a musical balance between the two.

The first movement of a Mozart Concerto is regularly in Sonata form (see page 3). But it always begins with an orchestral passage, in which the chief theme and generally the second as well are introduced. The solo instrument then enters, generally picking up the main melody, but often beginning with a brilliant introductory passage. Both themes are then repeated by soloist and orchestra in co-operation. A short tutti leads to the development section, generally begun as a solo. The orchestra then brings back the important melodic material in recapitulation, alternating once more with the soloist, and a final tutti brings the movement to a close.

The older Concertos always introduced a Cadenza for the

soloist near the end of the first movement, and Mozart often followed this formula, writing out as many as thirty-five Cadenzas for his Concertos. Traditionally this feature could be left to the soloist to prepare or improvise, and Mozart himself unquestionably did a lot of ad libbing when he played, even to the extent of decorating the written music according to his whim of the moment.

The second movement of a typical Mozart Concerto is always in a slow tempo, with a single predominating melody. Sometimes it includes Variations on this theme, and the solo part regularly ornaments the main subject in florid style. Sometimes there is a Cadenza near the close, but a shorter one than in the first movement.

The Finale is mostly in Rondo form, often interrupted by changes of tempo, and with opportunities for Cadenzas (sometimes more than one). The Variation form appears occasionally, and interludes of the Adagio or even the Minuet type may appear unexpectedly.

Three important piano Concertos were written by Mozart between November, 1785, and April, 1786, evidently for a series of Lenten subscription concerts in Vienna. The first of these is in E-flat (K.482) and was completed Dec. 16, 1785.

One of its modern interpreters, Wanda Landowska, describes the opening Allegro as "powerful and joyous," pointing out also its solid, symphonic character, the breadth of its themes and the brilliance of the ornamentation. The first theme is as follows:

The Andante is considered one of Mozart's finest, and had to be repeated at the first performance. Its main theme, "sorrowful and touching," interrupted only by an interlude of the wood-winds, is really a lament:

The Finale is happy and spirited, full of grace and sprightliness, a combination, according to Mme. Landowska, of "Neapolitan Sicilienne and Viennese Waltz." Its chief tune goes like this:

The second of these three piano Concertos is in A major (K.488) and was finished on March 2, 1786. It is a perfect example of the form created (or, better, perfected) by Mozart. The orchestra first has a long passage in which both themes of the first movement are introduced. Here is the opening melody:

The second theme is in the same key (the tonic, A), which is quite unusual:

The piano takes up both of these tunes, either alone or with a minimum of orchestral accompaniment, and then becomes a weaver of musical designs in the web of the ensemble. This ornamentation continues through the development section.

The thematic material is greatly reduced in the recapitulation, and a solo Cadenza ending in a long trill leads to a closing Coda by the orchestra alone.

The Andante is in F-sharp minor, and its theme has been called one of the "most touching and beautiful" in all music:

In the Finale (Presto) this leading theme is heard in the Concerto's fundamental key of A major:

The Lenten series concludes with a less-known piano Concerto in C minor (K.491), completed March 24, 1786. All three were written during the time that Mozart was working on his highly successful opera, *The Marriage of Figaro,* and producing some of his happiest music. Yet the C minor Concerto is full of melancholy and poignant emotion. Sir Donald Tovey calls its Finale "sublime" and Beethoven is said to have been deeply affected by it. This is the outstanding theme:

Among the earlier Mozart piano Concertos there is another in A major (K.414) which has been called "perfect in design and full of youthful charm." The one in B-flat (K.450) suggests Haydn in its first movement and foretells Schumann in its Finale, but with a set of Variations in the middle that are typically Mozart.

The same key of B-flat was used by Mozart for the last of his piano Concertos (K.595), finished in Vienna Jan. 5, 1791, the year of his death and also of his great opera, *The Magic Flute.* At this time the composer was already a sick man, but wrote much carnival music for Vienna of the pot-boiling type.

This last B-flat Concerto contains echoes of Mozart's earlier

works. The first theme has been compared with the opening of
the Romanze in his D minor Concerto (see below, p. 68):

The Larghetto, in E-flat, starts with a melody similar to
that of the Andante in Haydn's *Military Symphony* (p. 49):

In the final Rondo, started by the piano solo, there is actually a brief reminiscence of the Larghetto movement in the
middle, but this is the chief tune:

The next to the last of Mozart's piano Concertos is known
as the *Coronation* and bears the Viennese date of Feb. 24,
1788, the year that was to produce the three great symphonies.
The key is D major (K.537) and the Concerto owes its title
to the fact that it was played by Mozart for the coronation of
Leopold II, on the 14th of October, 1790. It had first been
played for a court audience in Dresden, April 14, 1789, and
for this performance Mozart received 100 ducats. But he had
to pawn his silver plate to get to Frankfort for Coronation
Week and to start a concert tour.

The themes of the *Coronation Concerto* are not particularly
noteworthy. It has a modern Cadenza by Wanda Landowska,
who has also recorded the work.

The D minor Concerto already mentioned above is dated
Feb. 11, 1785 (K.466). It was probably first performed by
Mozart himself at the opening concert of a series in the Mehl-
grube, Vienna. The parts were copied barely in time for the

concert and the final Rondo was played at sight. The Romanze begins as follows:

The Concerto for two pianos and orchestra in E-flat (K.365), written by Mozart in 1780, in Salzburg, is still heard occasionally. It has been recorded by Artur Schnabel and his son Karl with the London Symphony Orchestra, Adrian Boult conducting (V.Album M-484). There is also a Concerto for three pianos, in F (K.242) written in February, 1776, for three Countesses, Antonie, Luise and Josepha Lodron.

Mozart was an excellent violinist, although in later years he preferred to play viola in a string quartet. His father constantly urged him to keep up his virtuosity on the violin, and it was perhaps to please the elder Mozart that the composer, at the age of nineteen, wrote his five violin Concertos in Salzburg (1775). A sixth was added the following year, and a seventh was discovered as recently as 1907, but without satisfactory proof of its authenticity.

The keys of the six recognized violin Concertos are B-flat (K.207), D (K.212), G (K.216), D (K.218), A (K.219) and E-flat (K.268). They all have much the same form, and the orchestration is invariably two oboes, two horns and strings, with flute and bassoons added for the sixth Concerto.

All of these Concertos are in three movements, an Allegro at the start, then a slow movement (Andante or Adagio) and finally a Rondo of the cheerful type. There is a suggestion of the Aria rather than Sonata form in the characteristic first movement, with alternating solo and tutti passages.

Mozart was employed as court musician at Salzburg when these Concertos were written, and since one of his duties was to play the violin, he doubtless composed them for his own performance. Even in so short a time they show a steady advance in technique and musical content.

The first three Concertos are not often heard today, although the third, in G, has been recorded by Yehudi Menuhin with the Paris Symphony Orchestra, conducted by his teacher, Georges Enesco (V.Album M-485), and by Huberman with the Vienna Philharmonic, Dobrowen conducting (C.M-258).

The fourth, in D, is deservedly popular. There is a record by Fritz Kreisler with the London Philharmonic Orchestra (V.Album M-623) and one by Szigeti with the same orchestra, conducted by Sir Thomas Beecham (C.M-224).

Perhaps the best known of them all is No. 5 in A. Its most familiar subject is in Tempo di Menuetto, interrupted by a long Allegro in A minor.

The sixth violin Concerto, in E-flat, dating from 1776 (K. 268), begins with an Allegro moderato of gay charm. The soloist often plays as one of the first violins (as at the outset) and the part is actually marked "violino principale." Here is the first theme:

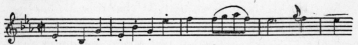

The second is in the same key (an eccentricity frequently indulged by Mozart):

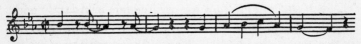

For the middle movement the composer uses only stringed instruments, with one outstanding melody, Un poco Adagio:

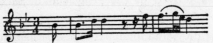

There is an after-theme, given to the solo violin, which is not a real second subject. The final Rondo (Allegretto) is full of merry abandon, with the soloist leading the way throughout. This is the chief tune:

There is a contrasting melody of more dignity and finally a third theme in minor key, following the conventional Rondo alternation.

A Concerto for flute, harp and orchestra is sometimes heard (K.299). It was composed in Paris in 1778, when Mozart was giving lessons in composition to the daughter of the Duc de Guisnes. She was a good harpist and her father played the flute, so he tossed off this Concerto as a tribute to their abilities. There are also two Concertos for the flute, one for clarinet and one for the bassoon.

THE MOZART OVERTURES

Mozart's greatness as an operatic composer gives importance to his Overtures, several of which are frequently heard as concert numbers. The most popular are those which preceded the operas of *Figaro, Don Giovanni* and *The Magic Flute*.

The Marriage of Figaro was written in Vienna and had its first production there on the first of May, 1786. Lorenzo da Ponte supplied the libretto, adapting it from the Beaumarchais play after securing the consent of the Emperor Joseph II, who had disapproved of the story on moral and political grounds.

There were plots and intrigues against the opera, which included even the majority of the singers, but in spite of all these handicaps it was an enormous success, most of the numbers being encored on the opening night.

The music of the *Figaro* Overture suggests the pomp and gaiety of an actual wedding, although this event does not take place until the end of the opera, whose plot is mostly concerned with Count Almaviva's attempts to prevent the marriage of the maid, Susanna, to his barber-valet, Figaro. There are no actual quotations from the opera.

The Overture opens in the key of D major (Presto) with a fast passage for strings and bassoons in octaves, leading into four measures of melody by the wind instruments:

To this material the full orchestra adds seven measures of joyous music, and after the repetition and a short subsidiary theme the real second subject appears in A major, a merry tune played by the violins, with bassoon and later flute for added color.

There is no real development section, but the Coda is unusually long. Mozart resisted the temptation to interpolate a slow section. He wrote a few such measures, but rubbed them out.

Don Giovanni is generally considered Mozart's greatest opera, and one of the greatest of all time. The Overture, however, is by no means as popular as some of the vocal music and is not often heard independently. The opera was written in Prague and had its first performance there Oct. 29, 1787. Da Ponte was again the librettist, and once more Mozart scored an unqualified success. (Vienna, however, received

Don Giovanni rather coldly when it was presented there on May 7, 1788.)*

The Overture to *Don Giovanni* was a last-minute job, with the composer working at it most of the night preceding the initial performance. His wife reported later that she had kept him awake by telling him stories and feeding him glasses of punch. It was completed at 7 A.M. and played at sight that evening.

The music plunges at once into the climax of the opera, the heavy chords that announce the coming of the statue to keep its gruesome appointment with Don Juan. The scale passages are taken from the ghastly denunciation. The outstanding melody of the Overture is as follows:

There is a fast theme, perhaps representing the life of the hero, and an orchestral cry of warning leads to a sardonically frivolous reply, again in character.

The Magic Flute was composed during the final year of Mozart's short life, 1791. It was suggested by a Masonic friend, Emanuel Schikaneder, who was trying desperately to make a success of his little theatre "Auf der Wieden." With the help of an actor named Gieseke, Schikaneder made a libretto from a fairy story by Liebeskind, *Lulu, or the Enchanted Flute*.

Mozart wrote his music mostly in a little pavilion provided by the impresario in a garden near his theatre. The composer's wife, Constanze, had gone to Baden for her health, and when Mozart became bored and despondent, Schikaneder sent members of his company to amuse him, evidently with good effect.

---

* For the plot of *Don Giovanni* see *The Metropolitan Opera Guide*, pp. 27-35.

The plot of the opera is an absurd mixture of Masonic ritual and artificial farce, saved only by the great music with which Mozart adorned it. Schikaneder himself played the comedy part of Papageno, the bird-man, and later, after he had been enabled to build a new theatre, "An der Wien," with the money he made from *The Magic Flute*, he adorned the roof with a statue of himself in his feathered costume.

The first performance was on the evening of Sept. 30, 1791, with Schikaneder's name in large letters at the top of the program, and Mozart's in very small print below the list of the cast. It was by no means a success at first, but gradually found increasing favor and eventually made a fortune for its producer.

The Overture to *The Magic Flute* is as fine as anything in the opera itself and successfully sums up its entire mood. (It was written only two days before the production.) Solemn calls of the trombones suggest the rites of the High Priest, Sarastro, while the lighter atmosphere is supplied by the lively fugal tune introduced by the violins in the sixteenth measure and carried through a brilliant succession of musical patterns. (It was originally in a Sonata by Clementi.)

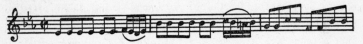

Occasionally one still hears the Overtures to *The Abduction from the Seraglio, Idomeneo, Cosi fan Tutte* and *La Clemenza di Tito*. The last of these represents Mozart's final opera, written on order and produced in eighteen days for the coronation of Emperor Leopold II in Prague, September, 1791. The opera was a failure, but all these Overtures have their moments of Mozartian greatness.

III

ROMANTIC REBELS

IT IS IMPOSSIBLE TO SAY just where and when musical classicism gave way to romanticism. Actually a number of composers have shown a combination of the two, and even today some music is still being written in the classic style, alongside the ultra-modern versions of the romantic.

It is difficult also to draw hard and fast distinctions between the classic and the romantic in music. In general the former type concentrates on technique, form, design for its own sake, while the latter emphasizes the content rather than the form. Pure or "absolute" music is generally associated with the classic style ("tonal architecture"), while "program" music, which tries to tell a story or paint a picture, or at least to suggest a program of some sort, with the help of a title or an explanatory note, belongs definitely to the romantic school.

Mozart is remembered as an outstanding technician, perhaps the greatest of the tonal architects, yet his music clearly showed romantic tendencies, and a longer life would probably have established him as the creator of a new style. As it is, however, the romantic movement may fairly be said to begin with Beethoven, the next great composer after Mozart, who had all the classic formulas at his command but rebelled against mere tonal abstractions and insisted on the consistently human and dramatic significance of music. Thus he became the first great heretic in the history of the art and the pioneer in a rebellion against musical convention that continues to this day and has produced its full share of masterpieces.

LUDWIG VAN BEETHOVEN

B. Bonn, Dec. 16, 1770; d. Vienna, March 26, 1827.

The life of this genius is a cross-section of the whole history of music. His early works sound like those of Haydn and Mozart. Later he developed a style of his own, full of drama and emotional vitality. Finally he arrived instinctively at a musical idiom close to actual modernism.

Beethoven wrote all kinds of music, including one opera, *Fidelio*. His nine symphonies are a monumental contribution to the orchestral repertoire. His Overtures, Concertos and chamber music are of equal importance. His Sonatas created a new kind of piano-playing. He wrote beautiful songs, and his *Missa Solemnis* is one of the masterpieces of sacred music.

All this was accomplished in the face of cruel handicaps, the greatest of which was the deafness that afflicted him throughout most of his creative career. He rebelled against social as well as musical conventions and tortured himself with frustrations of all kinds. He loved feminine society but never married, despised aristocracy yet depended constantly on patronage, gloried in personal liberty but succumbed to the inevitability of circumstances over which he had no control. He was misunderstood during his lifetime, but fully appreciated after his death. In any list of the world's great musicians his name must stand at or close to the top.

BEETHOVEN'S SYMPHONIES

The First Symphony of Beethoven, in C major, op. 21, is definitely reminiscent of Mozart. Its first theme has been compared with the opening of Mozart's *Jupiter Symphony* (see p. 61).

But Beethoven follows Haydn's custom of preceding this Allegro tune with a slow Introduction, in the manner of a proclamation.

The second theme enters in the key of G major, and this tune may have influenced Wagner's *Walküre* many years later:

A slight development of this theme leads to a repetition of the first, now in G, and the entire exposition is then repeated, this time going right into the real development or free fantasia that regularly serves as the middle section in Sonata form. Here the material is taken mostly from the first theme. In the recapitulation both melodies return in the basic key of C, and the movement closes with a Coda that is more elaborate and brilliant than had been customary with Haydn and Mozart.

The second movement, Andante cantabile con moto ("moving along with a singing quality") again reminds one of Mozart in its opening theme, which starts like the corresponding melody of the great G minor symphony, also using the Mozartian trick of counterpoint by letting the tune harmonize with itself:

The second theme contributes substantially to the development, which pays particular attention to its first four notes:

The recapitulation adds a running accompaniment of staccato notes to the first theme and introduces some interesting drum rhythms (severely criticized at the time) before going into another fairly elaborate Coda which ends in a violin-horn dialogue, once more emphasizing the pairs of tones at the start of the second theme.

The third movement is given the title of Menuetto (Allegro molto e vivace) but is really the first of Beethoven's symphonic Scherzos, a faster and more jocular piece than the conventional Minuet of Haydn and Mozart. The Scherzo (literally a joke) is one of Beethoven's individual contributions to symphonic literature. The chief tune in this part of the first symphony is little more than an ascending scale but used with great rhythmic effect:

The Trio starts with a succession of chords, interrupted by more scale passages in the violins.

The Finale begins with a musical joke worthy of Papa Haydn himself. Beethoven strikes a loud G octave and then starts to play the scale upward, softly, a few notes at a time, first three, then four, then five, then six, then seven. When he is ready to complete the octave, he turns it into his first theme:

The second theme has a definite dancing quality:

A syncopated passage leads to another series of false starts, finally arriving at a complete repetition of the exposition.

The development section combines the scale tones of the first theme with the opening notes of the second, with the scale effects becoming more and more prominent. Both tunes are then heard in recapitulation, with the second in the key of F, and another long Coda follows, introducing some new material in the manner of a march, with scales and chords creating a conventional finish.

Beethoven's First Symphony was completed in 1800 and had its first performance at his own benefit in the National Court Theatre, Vienna, on April 2d of that year. The conductor was Paul Wranitzky, and contemporary accounts indicate that the work was not well played.

The Second Symphony of Beethoven is in D major, op. 36, written in 1802, but not performed until April 5, 1803, at the theatre "An der Wien" in Vienna. The composer was in a wretched state of health and spirits at the time, already suffering from deafness and intestinal troubles, to which was added his greatest disappointment in love, the failure to win the hand of the Countess Giulietta Guicciardi. There were quite naturally parental objections, and the "immortal beloved" eventually became the Countess Gallenberg, with sincere regrets.

Yet this Second Symphony (called by Camille Bellaigue

"a heroic lie") is full of serenity, courage, even gaiety. Again there is a slow Introduction, in the manner of Haydn, but of considerable length, starting with what is really a complete theme:

The actual first theme is fast and spirited, introduced by the violas and cellos in unison:

The clarinet sings the second theme softly, a tuneful strain which has often been imitated in popular music:

The development deals largely with a few notes of the first theme, and the recapitulation puts the second theme into the symphony's basic key of D. A long and elaborate Coda ends in a rhythmic suggestion of the introductory theme, creating a strong sense of unity at the close.

The slow movement, Larghetto, starts with a melody that has become quite familiar as a hymn tune, known as *Alsace*, with words by Isaac Watts beginning "Kingdoms and thrones to God belong." It is first announced by the strings:

This part of the theme is repeated before the answer is heard:

Then comes another melody, later imitated by Schumann, and somewhat livelier in character:

The middle section puts the opening strain into minor key and then develops it with fascinating harmonies and decorations. All the melodic material is recapitulated, and the Coda is quite short, merely suggesting a change in the opening melody.

For the third movement Beethoven uses the title Scherzo for the first time in a symphony. It is in triple time, but much faster than a conventional Minuet. The opening tune has a tricky character, with the phrases cleverly imitating each other:

The Minuet form is preserved, in spite of the fast tempo, and the following scale melody corresponds to the Trio:

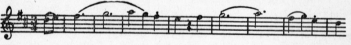

The Allegro vivace returns at the close, in regular Minuet style, giving the movement a lively finish.

The Finale (Allegro molto) was called by Berlioz "a second Scherzo," and he added that "its playfulness has perhaps something still more delicate, more piquant." It begins with a suggestion of recitative, but going right into a fast tune that lives up to the Berlioz description:

There is an interlude consisting of a solemn melody in the bass, like a fugal chant of sacred character:

The actual second theme is also largely in the bass, shared by several instruments, and built on the tones of the common chord:

The regular processes of development and recapitulation follow, and the long Coda gives importance to the solemn bass melody, with echoes of the first theme right up to the finish.

Beethoven's Third Symphony, in E-flat, the famous *Eroica*, marks an enormous step forward in his development as a composer. For the first time it reveals his own style, free from any traditions or influences. The composer himself called it his favorite symphony, in spite of the fact that it represented one of the great disappointments of his life.

He had originally dedicated it to Napoleon Bonaparte, who was unquestionably the hero indicated by his title. But when Napoleon accepted the crown as Emperor, Beethoven tore the name from the title-page and stamped upon the music in a rage. When the symphony was published, in October, 1806, there was a mere statement in Italian that it celebrated "the memory of a great man."

The actual composition took place from 1803 to 1804, and the first performance was at a private concert in the home of Prince Lobkowitz (to whom the symphony was dedicated) in December of the latter year. Beethoven conducted, and the orchestra broke down during the first movement and had to begin again. The first public performance was in the theatre "An der Wien," April 7, 1805, Beethoven again conducting, this time without mishap. But someone is said to have shouted from the gallery, "I'd give another kreutzer if they would stop!"

The *Eroica Symphony* opens with two E-flat chords by the full orchestra, followed immediately by the first theme, introduced by the cellos. This melody is note for note the same as a tune written by Mozart at the age of twelve for his one-act opera, *Bastien et Bastienne,* but this identity is possibly accidental.

This theme is developed at some length and there is a subsidiary theme before the second subject, of plaintive character, announced by alternating wood-wind and strings:

There is an elaborate development section, full of new ideas and materials, and after the recapitulation of both themes, a long Coda assumes new importance, becoming for the first time an intrinsic part of the movement instead of a mere "tail-piece."

The second movement again shows complete originality by taking the form of a funeral march, one of the most famous in all music. Beethoven later called it a foreboding of the death of his hero. The chief theme is in C minor, Adagio assai, first played softly by the strings, and then repeated by the oboe with wood-wind and string accompaniment:

The second portion of this theme goes into the major key (E-flat):

After some development by the full orchestra, the second subject (in C major) is given out by various wood-wind instruments, accompanied by triplets in the strings, an early suggestion of the C major melody that became the triumphal march of the Fifth Symphony (see p. 90).

There is a section of development, with snatches of the main melody, and then a lengthy reminder of the whole march, with new touches of rhythmic decoration. At the very end Beethoven breaks up the minor melody, as though it were heard through stammering sobs, a poignantly dramatic effect.

The Scherzo (Allegro vivace) is a cheerful contrast, starting softly, with the oboe leading a merry little tune (possibly originating in Austria's folk-music):

In the Trio one hears a distinct hunting call, played by the horns, with soft answers from the strings:

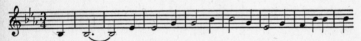

The Finale starts with a headlong rush and then announces a skeleton-like theme which turns out later to be merely the bass to the main melody:

After several treatments of this pattern, the actual theme suddenly enters, a lilting, joyous tune, introduced by the oboe:

This melody must have been a favorite with Beethoven, for he had already used it three times, first in his *Prometheus* music, then as the basis for a set of Variations and a Fugue for piano, and finally as a Country Dance (Contredanse). It alternates with the bass theme, each showing a variety of treatment, until a climax is reached in a slow version, played first by the wood-wind and then by the strings an octave lower:

One more variation is presented by the combination of brass and percussion (drums) and finally there is a profoundly thoughtful Coda. The full orchestra rushes into a Presto con-clusion, shaking out scraps of melody with violent rhythmic attacks and landing at last on the same E-flat chords that were heard at the start of the symphony, a heroic finish that lives up to the title of this masterpiece.

In his Fourth Symphony, in B-flat, Beethoven returned temporarily to the style of Haydn and Mozart, perhaps to quiet the fears of those who considered him already quite mad. It is the least played and perhaps the least interesting of the nine. Yet it is a fine example of the more obvious type of sym-phonic music and cannot fairly be called a step backward.

It has been suggested that the general spirit of contentment in this symphony is due to the fact that it was written when he was in love, possibly even engaged to the Countess Therese Brunswick, but this is mere conjecture.

Musically Beethoven had little reason to feel happy in 1806, when this symphony was written, for his opera, *Fidelio,* had been twice produced in Vienna by that time, without success. Moreover the city had been in the hands of the French, and the operatic audiences were largely composed of French officers under Napoleon.

The Fourth Symphony had its first performance at the home of Prince Lobkowitz in March, 1807, at a benefit concert for Beethoven himself. It was dedicated to Count Franz Oppersdorff, whom Beethoven had met while visiting Prince Lichnowsky. Actually the Count had commissioned a symphony and paid 350 florins in advance. Beethoven had already begun the symphony in C minor, known as the Fifth, and intended this for his patron, but changed his mind and eventually gave Oppersdorff the Fourth. It was not particularly successful, and the Count was not particularly pleased.

The symphony opens with a slow Introduction, but definitely superior to the old-fashioned form. There is a suggestion of the start of the third *Leonore Overture* (see p. 105) as the strings pick their way slowly down a series of octave steps, until the violins softly ask this musical question:

The answer comes in a light-hearted tune which serves as the first theme (Allegro vivace):

The wood-wind (bassoons, oboe and flute) co-operate in presenting the second theme:

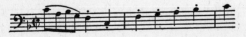

Development occupies itself largely with the skipping notes of the first Allegro tune and then a remarkable crescendo starts with a very soft drum roll, over which the strings play snatches of scales, gradually increasing in volume until the full orchestra is playing the first theme once more. The second theme also returns, in a new key, and the Coda is unusually short for Beethoven, using the skipping notes once more, to build the chords for a lively finish.

The slow movement (Adagio), in E-flat, concentrates on a simple but beautiful melody, coming right down the scale, somewhat in the manner of Handel's *Joy to the World*:

Various decorations and independent materials are added to this theme, which is heard completely four times, with a final echo in the brief Coda, ending on an E-flat chord topped by the flute.

Beethoven called the third movement of this Fourth Symphony a Menuetto, again showing a partiality to the earlier style, although it is in effect a Scherzo, full of original ideas. The first tune displays unexpectedly shifting accents, the notes running in pairs, yet in triple time:

The Trio has the effect of a country round dance, with woodwind and horns prominent and echoes from the first violins:

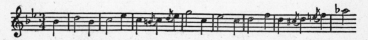

These melodies are treated far more freely than in a conventional Minuet, and the atmosphere is rural rather than of the drawing room. A tiny Coda is content with a single saucy phrase by the horns and one loud final chord.

The Finale maintains the mood of a country fiddler, and its fast opening strain is naturally played by the strings:

A second theme is of definitely lyric character, presented by the oboe and flute in turn:

Following the Sonata form, Beethoven develops both these tunes interestingly and eventually arrives at their complete restatement. The Coda is fairly long and quite brilliant. At the end the violins experiment with the notes of the first theme and are finally drowned out by the chords of the full orchestra.

Beethoven's Fifth Symphony, in C minor, op. 69, is one of the most popular ever written, and unquestionably one of the greatest. It was taking shape in his mind as early as 1800, as is proved by notes in his sketch-books. (He had the habit of jotting down themes and other snatches of music as they occurred to him, and it is interesting and enlightening to see how some of his most familiar melodies were gradually evolved from quite different origins.)

This symphony was interrupted by the composition of the Fourth, and it was not finished until 1807, probably at Heiligenstadt. The dedication is to Prince Lobkowitz and Count Rasoumowsky and the publication date April, 1809. The first public performance was at the theatre "An der Wien," Vienna, Dec. 22, 1808.

It is generally believed that this great symphony represents man's struggle with Fate, and it has often been called "program music." Beethoven himself is quoted as saying of the opening four notes (the "motto" of the first movement) "Thus Fate knocks on the door." It is not difficult to read such a significance into these portentous notes and their immediate repetition a tone lower:

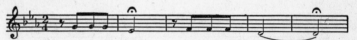

These notes have recently assumed a new meaning, for it has been pointed out that the rhythmic pattern of three short and one long dash represents the letter V in the telegraphic code. The motto thus became a popular expression of the faith in victory felt by all adherents of democracy in the Second World War.

Out of this simple but prolific pattern the entire first theme is built, repeating the four notes at various levels of pitch no fewer than forty-five times within the boundaries of its first statement and extension:

The horns finally interrupt with a raucous imitation which introduces the second theme, lyric in character, first played by the violins:

Even during this complacent melody, the mutterings of the Fate motif are heard in the bass. A connecting passage of scale formation leads to the loud proclamation of the motto at different intervals of the major chord, and the horns once more announce a change of mood. This time it sounds like a challenge to battle, immediately accepted by the strings.

The development section then begins quietly, as though the opposing forces were trying each other out, but soon the orchestra is in an uproar, with the Fate motif predominating. A return of the horn call inspires a series of chords, musically beautiful yet still in conflict.

Between the two returning themes there is a mild little interlude by the solo oboe. The Coda is a long one, with Fate still holding the upper hand.

The second movement, Andante con moto, starts with a sustained melody of quiet confidence, announced by violas and cellos in unison over a plucked bass (pizzicato).

The second half of the theme maintains the mood of serenity:

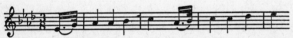

This two-part melody now goes through a series of Variations, with the embellishments becoming each time more elaborate. At one point the clarinet imitates the opening tune, with answers from bassoon and flute, resulting in fascinating interweaving of the wood-wind. Again, at the start of the Coda, the bassoon gives the melody a "blue" twist, over a flippantly rhythmic bass. The last reminder of the first half of the theme brings in a melodic change in the leap from the third to the major seventh that produces a heartrending effect of unique inspiration:

The third movement of this Fate symphony is neither a Minuet nor a Scherzo. It is marked Allegro but opens in a mysterious, unearthly fashion, with a melody that comes from the very depths of the orchestra. The sequence of notes is melodically identical with that of the opening of Mozart's Finale in his G minor symphony (see p. 60) but the rhythm, tempo and key are so different that one is hardly aware of the relationship.

After a repetition of these eight measures, the horns once more take up the Fate motif, this time with a regular triple beat:

There is considerable conflict between these two themes, and the atmosphere of strife continues in the Trio, which finds the strings playing against each other in a blustering style, led by the double basses in C major:

There is a satirical treatment of the second theme on its return, and the first melody gradually emerges triumphantly, soaring higher and higher in obvious preparation for the climax. On the final chords the approaching key of C major is already indicated by a discordant C in the bass and the transition to the great march of triumph is made without a break. The first theme is made up of the simplest of chord and scale tones but the effect is inevitably thrilling:

The second theme, also built on tones of the major chord, is strongly reminiscent of the slow movement of Mozart's *Jupiter Symphony* and the Trio of the Minuet in the E-flat symphony by the same composer (see pp. 61 and 57).

A third melody has a skipping motion, created by triplets, increasing the effect of light-heartedness:

A fourth melody creates the suggestion of gloating, and adds still more to the atmosphere of triumphant victory:

There is some development, concentrating chiefly on the skipping tune, and suddenly Beethoven brings back the Fate motif as it appeared in the third movement, but quite softly, keeping the rhythmic pattern going for some time. This leads to a recapitulation of all the themes, and finally a long Coda introduces still more original ideas, including an entirely new treatment of the second melody. The gloating theme returns at top speed, following the deliberately clumsy chords of a triumphal dance, and after an equally speedy snatch of the first tune the final page of the symphony is entirely filled with chords, first alternating between tonic and dominant (C and G) and then merely repeating the C major harmonies at various levels and with different rhythmic effects. When it seems to be all over, Beethoven still adds six more tonic chords, as if to make sure that there is no mistaking the key or the major mood, and ends with a solid C over several octaves, a satisfying finish to a great symphony.

After the monumental Fifth Symphony, Beethoven again relaxed. The Sixth is known by the title of *Pastoral*, simple and melodious, and definitely a piece of program music, with the composer himself supplying explicit directions for its interpretation. It was written in the Heiligenstadt country in the summer of 1808 and first performed along with the premiere of the Fifth in the concert of Dec. 22, 1808, at the theatre "An der Wien," Vienna. The dedication also parallels that of the Fifth, to Prince Lobkowitz and Count Rasoumowsky.

Beethoven was a real lover of Nature, and he expresses this love throughout the Sixth Symphony, even to the extent of imitating bird-calls, a brook and a storm. He asked that this music be considered "more as an expression of feeling than painting," but its programmatic character is obvious. (Walt Disney, in his *Fantasia,* turned Beethoven's shepherds into stylized nymphs, fauns, centaurs and satyrs.)

The key of the *Pastoral Symphony* is F major and the opus number 68. The first movement, Allegro ma non troppo, carries the composer's explanatory note: "Awakening of pleasant feelings on arriving in the country." Over a droning bass the strings immediately sing a bit of folk-music that is completely in the pastoral spirit:

There are other thematic materials in this movement, but they are of minor importance. The development deals mostly with the opening tune, and there is a complete recapitulation and a long Coda.

The second movement, Andante molto moto, starts with a slow theme in 12-8 time which definitely carries out the title "Scene by the Brook." The triplets of the accompaniment might easily represent the murmuring of the brook itself.

There is a second theme of melodious and lilting character imitated by Schumann many years later (see p. 141):

Near the end of this movement Beethoven introduces his imitations of bird-song, the flute trilling in the manner of the nightingale, the clarinet representing the cuckoo with the traditional two notes, a third apart, and the oboe adding the high monotone of the quail (the German variety, not our whistling Bob White).

The third movement, Allegro, is marked by the composer "Merry gathering of country people," followed by a musical thunderstorm. The main tune is again of a distinctly rural type and might be an actual country dance:

The storm itself is not particularly convincing. There is mild thunder by the kettle-drums and the whistling of the wind is conventionally suggested. There is no pause as the symphony goes into its Finale, Allegretto, which Beethoven calls "Shepherd's song" and also describes as "Happy and thankful feelings after the storm." The clarinet gives an introductory impression of the shepherd's pipe, and then comes the clear song of thanksgiving:

There are two subordinate snatches of melody, but the shepherd tune stands out, dominating even the long Coda, where its relationship to the opening theme of the symphony is emphasized. This melody is actually brought back for a moment in a soft echo of the horns, to be cut off by two crashing chords in F which bring the *Pastoral Symphony* to a close.

Beethoven's Seventh Symphony, in A major, op. 92, was called by both Wagner and Liszt "the apotheosis of the dance." The first sketches were made as early as 1810 or 1811, and the score was completed in the spring of 1813, dedicated to Count Moritz von Fries. It was probably played privately at the home of the Archduke Rudolph in Vienna, April 20, 1813. The first public performance was at the University of Vienna on Dec. 8th of the same year.

This concert also introduced the notorious *Battle Symphony* of Beethoven, whose real title is *Wellington's Victory or the Battle of Vittoria*. The composer wrote this distinctly bad piece at the suggestion of Johann Nepomuk Maelzel, inventor of the metronome and also of an early juke-box which he called Panharmonicon. It was for this mechanical player that Beethoven created his jumble of patriotic airs, using the tune of *God Save the King* for a fugue, with the old *Malbrough* (*We won't go home until morning*) representing the French army, and simply turned into minor key to indicate their defeat. *Rule, Britannia* also appears as a march.

The concert, however, was a great success, chiefly because of the Seventh Symphony, and it had to be repeated four days later. Spohr tells of "the uncertain and often ridiculous conducting by Beethoven," and it is also reported that the violinists declared some of the music unplayable, whereupon the composer told them to take it home and practice it.

It is entirely proper to consider the Seventh a dance symphony, and its prevailing mood is definitely joyous. There is a long, slow Introduction, as though the dancers were being given plenty of time to choose their partners. Then, after a suggestion of tuning fiddles, with repeated sounding of the top string (E), this note serves as the start of a lively first theme (Vivace):

A second theme emphasizes the skipping rhythm created by the 6-8 time:

There is repetition, development and recapitulation, as regularly in Sonata form. The Coda contains a highly original touch in the repetition over twenty-two successive measures of a syncopated bass pattern derived from the opening theme:

Of this passage the younger Weber declared that "Beethoven is now ripe for the madhouse."

The second movement is in A minor, Allegretto. Its opening theme concentrates on the monotonous repetition of the same note, as though emphasizing the inevitability of time itself. It is introduced by the violas, after a single loud chord of introduction:

In repeating this melody, whose effect depends so much on the harmony, Beethoven brings in a counter-tune in the violas and cellos, which fits in perfectly:

This material is developed in the manner of a theme with Variations, but also with suggestions of Rondo form. Beethoven introduces a second melody in A major, with an accompaniment in triplets:

The Coda repeats this major tune, besides using bits of the first theme, which is finally brought back almost in its entirety. At the end the violins deliberately accent the wrong notes of this pattern, and a soothing chord by the wind instruments brings the movement to a close.

The third movement (Presto) is much faster than an ordinary Minuet or even a Beethoven Scherzo. The opening tune is very lively:

There is a more restful mood in the Trio:

The Finale, after two rhythmic exclamations, goes into a fast Irish reel (Allegro con brio) in A major. The chief tune is actually of Irish origin, appearing in Beethoven's accompaniment to the folk-song, *Nora Creina,* and at the end of an authentic Irish melody, *Kitty Coleramie*. (Beethoven was working on the arrangement of Irish tunes at the time this symphony was written.)

There are snatches of subordinate melody, but this one whirlwind dance tune suffices for most of the movement. It is an exuberant finish to a definitely joyous symphony.

Beethoven's Eighth Symphony was probably played on the same evening as the Seventh, at the Archduke Rudolph's in Vienna, April 20, 1813. Its first public performance was in the Redoutensaal, Vienna, Feb. 27, 1814. Beethoven considered this symphony superior to the Seventh and was annoyed when it failed to make an equal impression. He blamed it on the fact that the two were played in direct competition.

The key of the Eighth Symphony is F major and the opus number 93. It was written at Linz in the summer of 1812, while Beethoven was visiting his brother Johann, who incurred his displeasure by falling in love with his housekeeper, Therese Obermeyer, and eventually marrying her. The composer got even by referring to her thereafter as the "Queen of the Night."

The Eighth Symphony opens with a Mozartian melody of simple beauty:

The second tune is also disarmingly simple in its scale progressions:

Both the exposition and the development of these themes are comparatively short. The recapitulation presents the first theme in the bass, and puts the second into a new key. The Coda is fairly long but not intricate, concentrating chiefly on establishing the key of F major.

The main melody of the second movement is said to have originated at a dinner in honor of Maelzel, when Beethoven improvised it in the form of a canon, with the words "Ta-ta-ta, ta-ta-ta, lieber Maelzel." They were good friends at the time, although they ended by suing each other. The accompaniment to this little tune suggests the rhythm of the metronome:

The second theme imitates this material, with some syncopation:

The third movement is a real Minuet (Tempo di Menuetto), with this opening theme:

The melody of the Trio is as follows, with staccato triplets in the accompaniment:

A fast Finale (Allegro vivace) opens with this quivering theme in the violins:

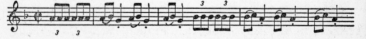

A broader melody enters later, again in the violins:

The development works mostly on the latter part of the first tune, with the triplets appearing prominently in the Coda.

It was a long time before Beethoven completed his final symphony, the choral Ninth. He had made sketches for it as early as 1815, but the score was not finished until February, 1824. The idea of using a chorus in the Finale did not occur to him until quite late, although he had long planned to set Schiller's *Ode to Joy* to music.

This symphony is unquestionably the climax of Beethoven's work and has become exceedingly popular, in spite of necessarily limited performances. The choral Finale was unique at the time, but has since been imitated, with varying success. The instrumental movements are considered by many superior to the Finale, which makes cruel demands upon the human voice.

The basic key is D minor, op. 125, and the dedication to Friedrich Wilhelm III, King of Prussia, who sent Beethoven a ring which he sold for 300 florins. The first performance was at the Kärntnerthor Theatre, Vienna, May 7, 1824, along with the *Missa Solemnis*. The choral singers were supplied by the Society of the Friends of Music. Michael Umlauf conducted, and the soloists were Henrietta Sontag, Karolina Unger, Anton Haitzinger and J. Seipelt. Beethoven sat in the orchestra following the score. At the end he was unaware that it was over until Mme. Unger led him to the front of the stage, so that he could see the audience applauding. In spite of this success, the net return to the composer was only about sixty dollars.

Beethoven's Ninth Symphony goes far beyond the ordinary restrictions of form, particularly in the first movement. It is possible to pick out as many as eight separate themes in this movement (Allegro, ma non troppo, un poco maestoso). The most important is in D minor, after a groping Introduction and a tearing at the tones of the chord.

The Scherzo which follows is far easier to grasp at a first hearing. It begins Molto vivace with several announcements of the rhythmic pattern, employing even the kettle-drums alone. When the tune gets under way, it proves to be gay and full of humor, starting in the second violins and bringing in various instruments in the manner of a round.

A counter-melody is heard in the wood-wind, with the triple rhythm continuing in the background:

Then comes the real second theme, heavier and more solid than the first, and suggesting a country dance:

This scale tune is disguised so as to form a new theme in 4-4 time in what amounts to a Trio (Presto):

There is a mocking accompaniment by the bassoon, and fugal passages lead to a Coda, completing a most unusual Scherzo.

The slow movement (Adagio molto e cantabile) is also highly original, starting with a serene melody in which the inner voices of the harmony play an increasingly important part:

The second theme has a plodding character, as though expressing the stubborn striving of the eternal idealist:

There are variations on the first melody, and finally, in the Coda, a new note is sounded, like a trumpet call, indicating that something startling is about to happen.

The unique Finale starts in utter confusion, with all the wind-instruments arguing at the top of their voices. The bass viols stop the noise with an unaccompanied recitative, clearly suggesting a symposium to discover a fitting melody for the choral climax. A bit of the first movement is heard but immediately rejected. The chief tune of the Scherzo dances in timidly, but meets with no more success, the kettle-drums casting the negative ballot. Two measures of the slow movement are more favorably received, but after some modulation the bass viols again break in with their protesting recitative.

Finally a snatch of scale melody is suggested by the woodwind and this brings the orchestra to attention while the low strings announce the complete theme in unison:

This simple melody, mostly contained within five notes of the scale, is gradually developed instrumentally. First a mere note of harmony is added here and there. Then the upper strings weave in a counter-melody. Next the full choir of the wood-wind chants the theme with complete harmony, while the strings mark the time in chords. An attempt at further development is cut short by the vociferous reminder of the full orchestra that human voices were to be used.

A solo baritone voice enters immediately, using the same recitative that had previously served for the protest of the bass instruments. The soloist then sings the complete melody to the words of Schiller's *Ode to Joy* (the half notes turning into quarters where necessary, to fit the text):

Joy, by fairest gods inspired, daughter of Elysium,
We, with new ambition fired, to thy sacred shrine have come.
Through thy spell in bonds supernal, free and joyful once again,
All mankind unites, fraternal, where thy gentle wings remain.

The lower voices of the chorus pick up the theme, after which the solo quartet and full chorus alternate in a completely harmonized version. The quartet repeats it with decorations, and after orchestral interludes the chorus reaches a climax of religious chords.

Now comes a strange, syncopated treatment of the choral melody by the orchestra, actually jazzy in its effect, distorting the rhythm, the melody and even the tone color, with the unsymphonic combination of brass, wood-wind, triangle, cymbals and drums:

The orchestra repeats this Variation, with the solo tenor adding an explosive counter-melody, later joined by the male voices of the chorus. After further orchestral development the full chorus once more delivers the opening stanza of the *Ode to Joy*.

There is a pause, and suddenly the male voices utter a new and majestic theme:

This is imitated by the full chorus in a remarkable harmonization, leading to a contrapuntal treatment in which the sopranos sing the main tune in a skipping rhythm, while the contraltos imitate the majestic theme in even time. When the male voices join in, the skipping effect appears in the basses. At the climax the sopranos are forced to hold an A above the staff for thirteen measures.

A solemn hush precedes the Coda, which is introduced by strings and wood-wind. The solo voices gradually work up to a round, in which the chorus also joins, in complicated counterpoint. Suddenly the quartet changes the key with a surprising chord and goes into a slow Cadenza, or decorative interlude, sung very softly in a high register, one of the most difficult passages in the entire symphony.

Another surprising modulation leads to a Prestissimo finish, both voices and instruments moving at top speed in a compressed version of what was once the majestic masculine theme. One more brief interlude momentarily stops the mad rush of the music, and then the orchestra runs away with the closing measures, apparently placing its seal of approval upon the entire performance.

BEETHOVEN'S OVERTURES

Next to his nine symphonies, the Overtures of Beethoven are his most important orchestral works, and several of them are frequently heard in concerts and over the air. There are no fewer than four Overtures to the opera *Fidelio*, and two others, to the dramas of *Coriolanus* and *Egmont*, serve as independent compositions of equal popularity.

The *Coriolanus Overture* has the opus number 62. It was written in 1807 and published a year later. Beethoven composed this Overture to a tragedy by Heinrich von Collin, produced in Vienna in 1802, but he doubtless had Shakespeare's play also in mind. Beethoven wanted to write an opera with Collin, but they never arrived at a satisfactory libretto.

The key of the *Coriolanus Overture* is C minor. It begins with three loud, sustained unison C's in the strings, each answered by an abrupt chord from the full orchestra, perhaps depicting the proud character of Coriolanus himself. The agitated first theme may refer to the banishment of the hero by the Roman plebeians.

The second theme is lyric, in major key, and seems to portray the pleading of the Roman women, including the wife and the mother of Coriolanus, that he withdraw the Volscian army which he has led to the very gates of the city.

In the Collin drama Coriolanus kills himself after giving in to the entreaties of the women. (Some versions of the story have him killed by the Volscians.) His death is indicated at the close of the Overture by soft pizzicato octaves in the strings, after the blasting motif of the start has been heard once more, following a conventional development and recapitulation of the two outstanding themes.

Of the four Overtures written by Beethoven for his opera *Fidelio*, three bear the name of *Leonore*, the heroine, who saves the life of her husband, Florestan. (For the complete plot of the opera see *The Metropolitan Opera Guide*, pp. 84-90.)

There is some uncertainty as to the exact order of the three *Leonore Overtures*, but it is generally assumed that the first was discarded during rehearsals as unsatisfactory, although it may have been written later. At the first performance of the opera, at the theatre "An der Wien," Vienna, Nov. 20, 1805, the *Leonore Overture* No. 2 seems to have been played. *Fidelio* was revived on March 29, 1806, and on this occasion the Overture was *Leonore* No. 3.

Only one theme is common to all three of the *Leonore Overtures*. It is the melody sung by Florestan in the first scene of the second act, when he recalls in prison the happy days of his youth. Here is the form in which it appears in the third Overture:

Both the second and the third *Leonore Overtures* show a descending scale at the start, probably representing the halting steps of the heroine as she goes down to the dungeon in which her husband is imprisoned by order of the cruel Don Pizarro. (She is disguised as a man, and calls herself "Fidelio.")

The courage of Leonore is suggested by a syncopated theme which plays an important part in both the second and the third Overtures.

There is a broader melody, derived from the Florestan theme, expressing hope and confidence, and also occurring in both Overtures:

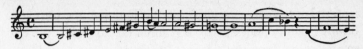

The climax of both these Overtures comes in an off-stage trumpet call announcing the arrival of help, almost as it occurs in the opera itself.

This call is heard twice (in the third Overture), each time followed by a calmly optimistic melody whose accompaniment keeps up the rhythm of the trumpet signal. (This is from Leonore's song of thanksgiving.)

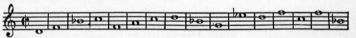

The final section of each of these Overtures (No. 2 and No. 3) is introduced by a brilliant display of passage-work in the strings, which leads naturally to an unmistakably happy ending.

The *Leonore Overture* No. 3 was called by Wagner a complete drama in itself, and it has become one of Beethoven's most popular compositions as an independent concert piece. When the opera is produced, it is generally played between scenes during the second act.

The actual Overture to Beethoven's only opera, as played today, has the title *Fidelio* and was written for the second revival, which took place in May, 1814. It is far more conventional than the *Leonore Overtures,* and quotes none of the material of the opera itself. The key is E major, and the music begins brightly and attractively, but with immediate Adagio reminders of the tragic phases of the plot.

The opening phrases are developed into a complete theme which supplies the Overture with most of its melodic material:

Echoes of the mournful contrast are heard, but with the cheerful three-tone pattern predominating and turning the whole *Fidelio Overture* into a charming and thoroughly musical curtain-raiser.

Beethoven's Overture to *Egmont,* op. 84, is one of nine numbers written as incidental music to Goethe's play of the same name. It was composed in 1810 and published in 1811. The first performance was at the Hofburg Theatre, Vienna, May 24, 1810. All the music was used on this occasion, with Antonie Adamberger playing the part of the heroine, Clärchen, in the drama. In addition to the Overture there are four Entr'actes, two songs sung by Clärchen, "Clärchen's Death," "Melodrama" and a "Triumph Symphony" (identical with the Coda of the Overture) to close the play.

This Overture is in effect a Symphonic Poem, far ahead of its time. It concentrates upon the historical significance of the Goethe tragedy rather than its human relationships. There are actually three sections, representing in turn oppression, conflict and victory. The first part has been described as "the stern command of iron-willed tyranny and the wails and plaints of the down-trodden." This mood is definitely suggested by the opening measures (Sostenuto ma non troppo) in F minor:

There is a second introductory strain, which might represent the heroine and her love for Count Egmont. When the main theme arrives it is a clear expression of the gathering discontent of the Netherlanders, finally breaking out in open revolt against Spanish tyranny, under Egmont's leadership:

In the final section the opening measures become a complete melody, representing the ultimate triumph of liberty:

At the close there is a terrific fanfare of brass, perhaps indicating the actual trumpets which the Duke of Alva ordered to drown out the farewell speech of Egmont himself. The shrill voice of the piccolo, between crashes of the full orchestra, adds to a climax such as no composer had written up to that time.

Beethoven wrote some other Overtures, but none to compare with those already mentioned. One of the earliest was for the *Prometheus Ballet*, numbered as opus 43 and dated 1801. In 1811 he contributed incidental music to two of Kotzebue's dramas, *King Stephen* and *The Ruins of Athens*. The Overture to the former is given a Hungarian flavor by the brilliant Czardas at the close. (King Stephen was Hungary's first benefactor.) The latter presents the shortest and least pretentious of the Beethoven Overtures. But the music also includes the *Dance of the Dervishes*, frequently heard in a transcription for violin, and the ever popular *Turkish March*, which has undergone every variety of instrumentation, with its familiar two-tone theme:

In 1814 Beethoven wrote an Overture in celebration of the Emperor's "Name Day" (*Zur Namensfeier*), thus creating the type of concert Overture later used by Mendelssohn and other composers. He called it "an Overture for any occasion or for use in the concert hall."

Finally, in 1822, Beethoven composed one more Overture, *Die Weihe des Hauses* (The Consecration of the House), for the inauguration of the new Josephstädter Theatre in Vienna. It is numbered as opus 124, and therefore belongs among the most mature of Beethoven's works, although its style strongly suggests that of Gluck or Handel.

BEETHOVEN'S CONCERTOS

Among the Concertos written by Beethoven for a solo instrument and orchestra, the one in D major for the violin demands first attention. It has been called the greatest music ever written for the violin, and it has only one real rival, the violin Concerto in the same key by Johannes Brahms (see p. 201).

Beethoven composed this masterpiece in 1806 for Franz Clement, who introduced it at the theatre "An der Wien" on Dec. 23 of that year. The violinist played it at sight, as a result of the composer's typical procrastination. On the same program Clement offered a Sonata of his own, played on one string, with the violin held upside down.

Under the circumstances the Concerto could hardly have been a real success. It was only when Joachim revived it many years later, adding his own Cadenzas, that the public discovered the musical value of this unique contribution to the literature of the violin.

The first movement of this Concerto uses the orchestra for a long time before the solo instrument enters. The first theme is introduced by the oboes, clarinets and bassoons, preceded by four taps of the kettle-drums.

A brief second theme is announced by wood-wind and horns, repeated in minor key and then considerably developed.

The solo violin plays both of the important melodies, besides adding ornamentation. Near the end comes the conventional opportunity for a Cadenza and the movement closes with a short Coda.

The second movement, Larghetto, is in G major, and might be called a Romance, freely constructed. There is only one real melody, carried chiefly by the orchestra, with the solo violin supplying embellishments.

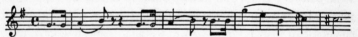

Another Cadenza leads to the Finale, which is a Rondo in G, based on a theme believed to be a Russian folk-song:

There is a second theme, introduced by the solo violin, with accompaniment of the horns in the manner of a hunting call.

Again there is a chance for a Cadenza, and the Concerto ends brilliantly, with satisfaction for the players and hearers alike.

In addition to this masterpiece, Beethoven wrote two Romances for violin and orchestra, op. 40 in G, and op. 50 in F. Both are heard frequently in concert, supplying soloists with much-needed material in the shorter forms.

Beethoven wrote at least five Concertos for piano and orchestra, two of which have become permanently popular, the one in G, op. 58, and the so-called *Emperor,* in E-flat, op. 73. The first was in B-flat, numbered op. 19, and the second, in C, had the opus number 15, although definitely written later than the first. A third Concerto in C minor, op. 37, belongs to the year 1800 and was published four years later, with a dedication to Prince Louis Ferdinand. Its first performance was on April 5, 1803, on the same program with the Second Symphony. This Concerto has been described as the first real indication of the greater Beethoven.

The fourth piano Concerto of Beethoven probably dates from the year 1805, and was certainly performed by the composer at a private subscription concert of his works given at the home of Prince Lobkowitz in Vienna, some time in March, 1807. The first public performance was at the theatre "An der Wien," Dec. 22, 1808, when the Fifth and Sixth Symphonies were also introduced. This Concerto is dedicated to the Archduke Rudolph of Austria.

It opens, Allegro moderato, with the solo piano immediately announcing the first theme, a definite departure from tradition.

The orchestra enters in B major, using the opening note of the Concerto as its tonic, a highly individual touch. Returning to the basic key of G, it develops the theme and soon there is a second melody, sung by the first violins:

A third theme is announced fortissimo, supplemented by the wood-wind:

Finally there is a fourth melody in B-flat played by the solo piano, with string accompaniment:

The slow movement, Andante con moto, is in E minor and very free in form. Beethoven directed that it be played throughout with the soft pedal down. The chief melodic material, starting as "a stern and powerful recitative for strings," alternates with gentler passages for the piano. (Liszt compared this with Orpheus taming the wild beasts by his music.)

The Finale is a Rondo (Vivace). The strings announce the opening theme "of a sunny and gay character":

The piano plays a variation on this material, and then there is a short melodic phrase in the strings, again taken up by the piano.

A final theme originates with the solo instrument (borrowed a century later by Richard Strauss for his *Don Juan*) and all these melodies are carried out in the traditional Rondo form, with reckless gaiety, ending at top speed (Presto).

The *Emperor Concerto* was not so called by Beethoven himself. The name was added some years after its composition, which dates from 1809, the year that Vienna was occupied by the French. Possibly it refers to the grandiloquence of the first and third movements.

This Concerto was not performed publicly until Nov. 28, 1811, in Leipzig, when Friedrich Schneider was the pianist. Beethoven was present at the first Viennese performance, by Karl Czerny, Feb. 12, 1812.

The first movement, Allegro, in E-flat, opens with a loud chord by the full orchestra, followed by an immediate Cadenza for the piano. The first theme is announced by the strings and then taken up by the clarinets:

A second theme, also introduced by the strings, is first heard in E-flat minor and then in E-flat major, legato, by the horns:

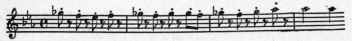

Beethoven wrote his own Cadenza, bringing in the orchestra before its close.

The second movement, Adagio un poco mosso, in B major, starts with a beautiful slow melody played by the muted strings:

(It is interesting to note the evolution of this theme in the Beethoven sketch-books.) After some development of the variation type, the piano hints at the first theme of the Finale and then, from a sustained B-flat, goes right into this Rondo (Allegro).

The piano announces the second theme as well as the first and both are elaborately developed.

In the Coda the piano is heard in a long series of descending chords, gradually growing softer, with the kettle-drums marking the rhythm of the first theme.

Beethoven's piano Concerto in C major is generally called his first, although it may actually have been the fourth in the series. It was published in 1801 as Number 1, and its first performance was probably in the Vienna concert of April 2, 1800. Its date of composition may have been as early as 1797.

There is also a Beethoven Concerto for violin, cello, piano and orchestra, in C, generally known as the "triple concerto," op. 56. It was probably written in 1804. The dedication is to Prince Lobkowitz and the date of publication 1807.

CARL MARIA VON WEBER

B. Eutin, Dec. 18, 1786; d. London, June 5, 1826.

Weber is a popular composer today chiefly through the Overtures to his operas, *Der Freischütz, Euryanthe* and *Oberon.* One of the first romantic composers, he definitely pointed the way toward the music dramas of Wagner. His operas were a complete departure from Italian and French models, strongly nationalistic in character, with considerable dramatic realism.

Oberon was written on order for England, to an English libretto, and this work really brought on Weber's untimely death at the age of only 39.

WEBER'S OVERTURES

The three Overtures of Weber have become staples of the orchestral repertoire, and two of them are among the most familiar of all concert works. They provide ideal material for opening or closing a program.

The earliest of the three operas that supplied these familiar concert pieces was *Der Freischütz* (The Freeshooter), originally called *Die Jägersbraut* (The Huntsman's Bride). Its first performance was in Berlin, June 18, 1821, and it proved an immediate success. The Overture, which was encored at the premiere, was begun February 22, 1820, and finished on May 13th of the same year. (Compare this deliberate schedule with the methods of Mozart.)

The plot of *Der Freischütz* concerns a Faustian character, Max, who, at the suggestion of his fellow-huntsman, Caspar, sells himself to the devil, represented by the evil Samiel, for some magic bullets with which he wins a shooting competition. The final bullet is intended for Agatha, the inamorata of both rangers, but luckily hits Caspar, who is carried off to his well-earned fate in place of Max. (The libretto is by Friedrich Kind.)

In the Overture nine measures of Introduction, Adagio, in C major, lead to a beautiful slow theme played by the horn quartet, often used as a hymn tune:

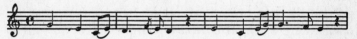

The Samiel motif is then suggested, with a direct quotation from Max's aria, "What evil power is closing round me?" In the main section of the Overture, Molto vivace, in C minor, some of the sinister music of the Wolf's Glen (scene of the casting of the magic bullets) is heard, with its thunderstorm and flames starting from the earth.

The key changes to E-flat major, with the clarinet voicing another theme associated with the hero ("No ray will shine upon my darkness"), followed by Agatha's chief melody, expressing the triumph of virtue over evil:

There is a repetition of some of the earlier material, dominated by the Samiel motif, leading to a Coda, in the opening key of C, representing the apotheosis of Agatha.

Euryanthe, an old-fashioned, chivalric opera, with an inadequate book by the amateurish Helmine von Chezy, based on an old French story, also used by Boccaccio in his *Decameron* and by Shakespeare in *Cymbeline*, was first performed at the Kärntnerthor Theatre, Vienna, October 25, 1823, with Weber himself conducting.

The plot concerns the noble Adolar, who wagers all his possessions with the villainous Lysiart that his intended bride, Euryanthe, is faithful to him. Euryanthe is a victim of the duplicity of Eglantine, herself in love with Adolar. A ring is stolen from the tomb of Emma, a sister of Euryanthe, who had committed suicide, and Lysiart produces this as evidence of Euryanthe's guilt. When Emma's ghost appears, Eglantine confesses the plot and is stabbed by Lysiart, who is led away to execution, as Adolar and Euryanthe are reunited.

The opera itself was completed on August 29, 1823. Weber began the Overture September 1st and finished it in Vienna, October 19.

The Overture opens in the key of E-flat, Allegro marcato, con molto fuoco, and after eight measures of brilliant Introduction, the first theme is announced by wind instruments. It is taken from Adolar's phrase "I trust in God and my Euryanthe," in the first act:

After some effective development and a crashing B-flat chord, the cellos lead into a second theme, sung by the first violins, based on a part of Adolar's air in the second act, "O bliss, I scarce can fathom!"

Before the development of this material there is a short Largo, representing the appearance of the ghost and the fatal ring. The recapitulation indicates the triumph of virtue, as always in opera.

Weber's final opera, *Oberon,* was commissioned by the English actor-impresario, Charles Kemble, for Covent Garden, London, where it was introduced on April 12, 1826, with the composer conducting. (He died less than two months later, of tuberculosis.) The book was by James Robinson Planche, in English.

Its plot tells of the quarrel between Oberon and Titania, the fairy king and queen, who will not speak to each other until a pair of faithful lovers has been found. Oberon's sprightly little errand-boy, Puck, finds the necessary couple in Huon of Bordeaux, a knight of the court of Charlemagne, and Rezia, daughter of the Caliph of Bagdad, Haroun al Raschid. On their way home from Bagdad, the lovers are shipwrecked and captured by pirates, who sell Rezia to the Emir of Tunis and Huon to his wife, Roxana. Each resists the temptation to infidelity, and when they are condemned to death by fire, Huon blows upon the horn of Oberon, which magically transports them to the court of Charlemagne, where all ends happily, with a reconciliation between Titania and her husband.

Weber began work on *Oberon* January 23, 1825, and finished the opera on the morning of April 9, 1826, in London, where it had been rehearsed in sections, as fast as they were ready. The composer received $2500, which he felt he needed for the future support of his family. He carried out the contract against his doctor's orders.

The Overture opens in D major (Adagio sostenuto) with the sound of Oberon's horn, played by the actual French horn, echoed by muted strings:

Soft passages in the flutes and clarinets, taken from the opening scene of the opera, lead to a pianissimo fanfare of fairy trumpets, which in turn introduces the real opening theme in the strings:

A crashing chord leads to the main body of the Overture (Allegro con fuoco), starting with a brilliant string passage taken from the accompaniment of the quartet, "Over the dark blue waters," in Act II.

The next melody is a familiar one, from Huon's air in the first act, originally written for Oberon himself and sung here by the clarinet, followed by the first violins:

The final theme, Presto con fuoco, is from the peroration of Rezia's "Ocean, thou mighty monster" in Act II, when she believes that help is at hand:

After a free fantasia, all three themes are brought back, with some additional material, the Overture ending brilliantly with the triumphant song of Rezia.

Less well known than the Overtures, but still occasionally played, is Weber's *Concertstück* (Concert Piece), op. 79, for piano and orchestra, originally planned as a Concerto in F minor. This work, completed in 1821, has a definite program, which the composer revealed to his wife when he first played it for her and his pupil, Julius Benedict.

It represents an elaborate story of knighthood and faithful love, with the lady sitting in her tower, gazing sadly into the distance, waiting for the return of her lord from the Holy

Land. Her mind calls up a vision of her lover dying on the battlefield. But just as she falls, exhausted, the sound of trumpets proclaims the return of the knight, and all ends happily.

The mournful sighs of the lady are represented by this opening theme in the wood-wind:

The hero's return is indicated by a stirring march, announced by clarinets and trumpets:

The rest of this Concert Piece maintains a mood of pure joy, with the piano running wild in rapid scale passages (Presto giojoso) and the full orchestra finally describing what Weber called "a commotion of love," "an infinite, indescribable happiness."

Perhaps the most popular music written by Weber is his *Invitation to the Dance,* a set of waltzes, also used for the ballet, *Spectre de la Rose,* for which Fokine supplied the choreography. The composer gave this piece also a detailed program, although it really applies only to the introductory section.

The composer calls the opening measures "first approach of the dancer":

"The lady's evasive reply" is represented by this passage:

A slight alteration of the same material serves for "his pressing invitation" and "her consent." Then "they enter into conversation" thus:

These measures are elaborated as "he speaks with greater warmth" and "she sympathetically agrees." In the final section of the Introduction, he asks the lady to dance, she accepts, "they draw together," take their places and wait for the music to begin.

The first waltz opens with a robust strain, repeated, followed by quieter music.

After some lively interludes comes the waltz which may be considered the chief melody of the series:

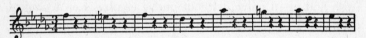

One more waltz theme is worth quoting, again in a lively mood:

This is followed by fast scale passages, repetitions and recapitulations, with various changes of key. At the end the music of the Introduction returns, as the dancers utter "his thanks" and "her reply," the composition closing with three soft chords.

Weber wrote the *Invitation to the Dance* for piano, in 1814. It was orchestrated by Hector Berlioz in 1819, and again, even more brilliantly, by Felix Weingartner, in 1896. Both versions are frequently heard in concert and on the air. Among other orchestral works by Weber are two symphonies in C major and the *Jubilee* and *Preciosa Overtures,* none of which can be considered really active in the modern concert repertoire.

FRANZ SCHUBERT

B. Vienna, Jan. 31, 1797; d. Vienna, Nov. 19, 1828.

Another natural prodigy of music, astonishingly prolific in his short life of thirty-one years, Schubert is perhaps best known through his songs, of which he wrote more than 600, including the popular *Serenade, The Erlking, Ave Maria,* etc. But he is credited with ten symphonies, of which at least two are exceedingly popular, and his chamber music and piano compositions are of real importance.

Schubert spent most of his life in and near Vienna, typically poverty-stricken, but with an apparently inexhaustible supply of melodic inspiration. His music is of the spontaneous type, fresh and often naive, without undue emphasis on technical detail.

THE SCHUBERT SYMPHONIES

Unquestionably the most popular of all symphonies is the *Unfinished* by Schubert. It is variously numbered as his eighth or seventh, depending on the assumed total, and its key is B minor. There are only two movements, although the composer wrote nine measures of a Scherzo, from which it may be gathered that he found it impossible to live up to the standards established by the opening Allegro and the Andante.

The *Unfinished Symphony* was written in 1822, when Schubert was only 25 years old. It was intended for a musical society in Graz, of which the young composer had been elected an honorary member. But it was never played until December 17, 1865, more than thirty-seven years after Schubert's death.

The manuscript fell into the hands of Anselm Hüttenbrenner, a mutual friend of both Beethoven and Schubert, who had actually brought these two together. (Beethoven is quoted as saying on his deathbed, "You, Anselm, have my mind; but Franz has my soul.")

Hüttenbrenner and his brother Joseph worked hard to gain recognition for Schubert, Anselm even going so far as to write a set of *Erlking Waltzes*! In 1860, Joseph Hüttenbrenner applied for membership in the Vienna Friends of Music and wrote to the conductor, Johann Herbeck, of a symphony in B minor by Schubert in his brother's possession. Five years later Herbeck visited the dying Anselm and secured from him the precious manuscript, whose music is now familiar to millions all over the world.

The *Unfinished Symphony* begins with an Introduction of eight measures, whose theme later proves of real importance:

After four measures of rhythmic preparation, the first theme is announced by oboe and clarinet over quivering strings:

This melody is interrupted by heavy chords, and the horns and bassoons sustain a unison D which leads directly into the second theme, introduced by the cellos. (This is the tune used by Sigmund Romberg for his *Song of Love* in *Blossom Time,*

an operetta based on the life of Schubert and employing several of his melodies.)

Agitated chords, on the opening notes of the first theme, interrupt this theme, which is then developed to some extent, including a series of overlapping imitations in the wood-wind, suggesting a fragmentary round.

The real development section, or free fantasia, starts by working on the introductory theme, now in E minor instead of B minor. The second theme is merely suggested by an echo of its syncopated accompaniment, and the first appears only in the crashing chords of its first two notes until it arrives at a complete recapitulation in the original key. The reminder of the second tune, again introduced by unison horns and bassoons, and played by the cellos, is in D major instead of the former key of G. The substantial Coda uses the introductory theme to get back to the basic key of B minor.

The slow movement starts with plucked strings moving down the scale and has its main theme (in E major) announced by the wood-wind:

This material is immediately developed, with emphasis on the pizzicato strings and wood-wind chords, and then the clarinet introduces a second melody, in E minor, again with strongly syncopated accompaniment:

There is development of this theme also, with one change to major key. Recapitulation of both melodies follows, the second now in A minor. The Coda makes a new tune out of the chords and plucked strings of the introductory measures, and makes use of two violin interludes for surprising modulations. The close is in a spirit of calm resignation.

Schubert's symphony in C major, generally numbered seven but also known as his tenth, was, like the *Unfinished Symphony,* never heard by its composer. He wrote it for Vienna's Society of the Friends of Music, at whose concert of Dec. 14, 1828, it had its first performance (less than a month after Schubert's death). It was repeated March 12, 1829, and then completely forgotten until Schumann, on a visit to Vienna in 1838, found it in the possession of Schubert's brother Ferdinand. Schumann immediately had it copied and sent to Mendelssohn, who produced it at a Gewandhaus concert in Leipzig, March 21, 1839. The symphony was finally published in January, 1850.

The influence of Beethoven may be seen in this final symphony by Schubert. Its Introduction is a broad, unaccompanied melody, sung by the horns, in the manner of the choral theme of Beethoven's Ninth Symphony:

Harmonies are gradually added (as also in Beethoven's Finale), until the full orchestra gives the theme a majestic interpretation. The actual first theme is little more than a reminder of the basic key of C and its dominant, G.

The second theme is the one that remains inevitably in the memory, suggesting a Hungarian character, and introduced with charming gaiety by the wood-wind:

The materials are developed to what Schumann called a "heavenly length," with emphasis on the second theme, which eventually returns in the key of C minor. After the recapitulation, a long Coda brings back the broad melody of the Introduction, with which the movement ends.

The second movement, Andante, opens with a mysterious Introduction, after which the oboe plays a melody of definitely pastoral mood:

There are melodic interludes, related to this theme, partly in major and partly in minor key, after which the real second theme appears:

The rhythm of the Scherzo had been used by Schubert in his string quartet in B-flat, and the movement once more suggests comparisons with Beethoven's Ninth Symphony. The first theme is introduced by the strings.

This Scherzo follows the Sonata form rather than that of the Minuet. The second theme has the spirit of a country dance:

Following the development of these themes, the horns, clarinets and trombones play a one-note interlude which leads to a Trio, whose tune was later echoed by Franz Liszt in *Les Preludes* (see page 167):

The Finale opens with portentous trumpet calls, which supply much of the material of the movement, merely adding rhythmic decorations:

The second theme is again a memorable melody, creating a fascinating effect by its repetition of a single note:

During the development section a new tune is evolved which presents a curious mixture of Schubert's own *Marche Militaire* and the choral theme of Beethoven's Ninth Symphony, whose influence is given this final tribute of recognition:

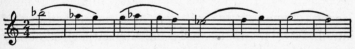

This melody appears again near the close of the symphony, after the elaborate Coda has brought back reminders of the first and second themes.

SCHUBERT'S EARLY SYMPHONIES

Of the six symphonies written by Schubert while still in his 'teens, only two, the Fourth and Fifth, are frequently heard today. But they are all interesting as early evidences of genius, frankly derivative, with a clear background of Haydn and Mozart, yet with individual touches that already indicated the far greater orchestral music to come.

Schubert wrote his First Symphony, in D, when he was only sixteen years old (1813). The Second, in B-flat, dates from December, 1814, to March, 1815. A Third Symphony, again in D, was begun on May 24, 1815, just two months after the completion of the Second. It was interrupted during the writing of the first movement, but eventually finished July 19, the last three movements being written in four days.

When Vienna's Society of the Friends of Music gave a concert of Schubert's "Symphonic Fragments" on December 2, 1860, Johann Herbeck conducted the Finale of the Third Symphony, as well as the first two movements of the Fourth and the Scherzo of the Sixth (known as the "little" symphony in C, dating from the year 1818). The first complete performance of the Third Symphony seems to have been at the Crystal Palace, London, February 19, 1881, from manuscript, under the direction of August Manns. It was published in 1884 by Breitkopf & Haertel.

Schubert's Fourth Symphony, in C minor, was called "Tragic" by its composer, although the title now seems unnecessarily weighty. It opens with a slow Introduction, starting with a unison C by the full orchestra. The first theme, introduced by the violins, has a rather melancholy character even though the tempo is fast:

A second melody, also in the strings, maintains the plaintive mood:

A typical slow theme dominates the second movement, revealing at once the distinctive melodist that Schubert was by nature:

The chief tune of the Menuetto is chromatic in character, introduced by the wood-wind:

The Trio of this movement has a sturdy character, in the manner of a Mazurka:

The Finale is in fast time, starting softly with this theme:

A second subject is full of echo effects, alternating violin and clarinet tones:

Schubert's Fifth Symphony, in B-flat (1816), which is now the most popular of his early orchestral works, remained undiscovered until 1867, when Sir George Grove and Sir Arthur Sullivan found the parts in Herbeck's possession in Vienna. The score turned up in the Berlin Royal Library in 1882 and was published the same year.

There are definite echoes of Mozart in this charming symphony. The first theme, entering after four measures of Introduction, uses the old reliable major triad for a start:

The sprightly second subject is really in the dominant key of F:

A beautiful melody, worthy of Mozart himself (and actually reminiscent of the Rondo of his violin sonata in F) opens the slow movement, Andante con moto:

The Menuetto also suggests Mozart, with the full orchestra starting a theme in G minor possibly related to the Minuet of the earlier symphony in the same key (see page 59):

The Trio also follows Mozart's model in going into G major in the strings:

The Finale begins with a lively scale tune in the violins:

The second theme of the Sonata form maintains the lilting quality and leads to a cheerful and straightforward finish:

SCHUBERT'S ROSAMUNDE MUSIC

Schubert tried for ten years to write a successful opera, but without effect. From the librettist of Weber's *Euryanthe*, the pretentious Helmine von Chezy, he accepted a thoroughly artificial play, *Rosamunde*, for which he wrote some charming incidental music, of which an Entr'acte and Ballet are often heard. The lovely melody of the Entr'acte shows a relationship with Schubert's *Impromptu* for piano:

The ballet music also has a relative in the familiar *Moment Musical* in F minor, so often used by classic dancers. The *Rosamunde* tune is in G major, with identical rhythmic effect:

Rosamunde was produced at the theatre "An der Wien," Dec. 20, 1823, and ran for two nights only. Its music was rediscovered in Vienna in 1867 by Sir Arthur Sullivan and Sir George Grove. It has recently been adapted for school use and now appears in many transcriptions, in addition to its original orchestral form.

ROBERT SCHUMANN

B. Zwickau, June 8, 1810; d. Endenich, July 29, 1856.

Here is the arch-romanticist of them all, and a leader in the movement to free music from the restrictions of classic form. Schumann was a critic as well as a pianist and composer, expressing his views in a musical journal which he edited for years, and keeping up an imaginary organization of "Davidsbündler," whose mission it was to defeat the Philistines of art. He was exceedingly helpful to such newcomers as Chopin and Brahms.

Schumann's own romance was with the daughter of his piano teacher, Clara Wieck, whom he eventually married after a long struggle against paternal objections. He turned to composition largely because of the crippling of a finger as the result of overzealous attempts to improve his piano technique. Clara Schumann is recognized as one of the greatest women pianists of all time.

Schumann's piano pieces are outstanding, and he is also one of the leading songwriters of the world. But his orchestral music is also important, including four symphonies, a popular piano Concerto and several Overtures, and he wrote much significant chamber music. Schumann died in an insane asylum at the age of 46, after an unsuccessful attempt at suicide.

The orchestral compositions of Schumann have a romantic appeal that has kept them actively in the repertoire.

SCHUMANN'S SYMPHONIES

Schumann wrote four symphonies. They have been criticized as pianistic rather than orchestral, yet they have a definite individuality and their influence on the later symphonies of Brahms would alone justify them.

The First Symphony is in B-flat major, op. 38. It was written in the winter of 1840-41, just after Schumann's marriage to Clara. The composer himself called it a "Spring" symphony, and its music is full of the happiness of that season, added to the bliss of romantic fulfillment. The instrumentation was completed February 20, 1841. It was performed less than two months later by Mendelssohn at a Gewandhaus concert in Leipzig.

Schumann's First Symphony opens with a fanfare of trumpets and horns, majestically announcing the advent of Spring:

The first real theme imitates this Introduction, in lighter fashion:

The second theme suggests whispering winds and running brooks, with an ecstatic quality that preserves the vernal mood:

There is an orthodox development, but the recapitulation emphasizes the melody of the Introduction, although the first theme also returns, considerably disguised. The second theme

also reappears in a new key, and a long Coda makes use of
snatches of the main melody.

The slow movement, Larghetto, introduces a melody of
great beauty, over a syncopated accompaniment, full of pomp
and circumstance, yet suggestive of suppressed gaiety:

This movement develops into a Rondo, with two more
themes alternating with the principal tune. At the close the
main melody assumes a new form, directly foretelling the
theme of the Scherzo, into which it leads with only a momentary pause.

This Scherzo, Molto vivace, begins in G minor but later goes
into D minor, D major and B-flat major. The first theme is
syncopated and full of animation:

The answer is in major key, still full of the spirit of spring:

The first Trio, in D major, changes the time from 3-4 to
2-4, with this theme:

A second Trio goes back to the triple beat, with its melody
in B-flat, somewhat reminiscent of a passage in Schumann's
Papillons:

The Finale opens with a broad, syncopated scale, suggestive of stormy weather, and assuming real importance later in the movement:

The first theme is a dainty, elfin dance tune, developed by strings and wood-wind:

A second melody is also full of elfin characteristics, interrupted by a minor version of the Introduction, threatening in its effect:

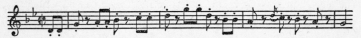

This introductory melody finally co-operates with the other themes, and becomes a leading feature of the development. A slow interlude emphasizes a chord pattern in the horns, which Beethoven had used in his Fifth Symphony, and Wagner was to employ dramatically in years to come. The flute plays a long trill and a flowery Cadenza, against all the rules, and back comes the elfin dance, plus the second theme and interruptions of the Introduction as before. The Coda is moderate, with occasional high winds, and builds up conventional B-flat chords for a finish.

Schumann's Second Symphony is in C major, op. 61. Actually it is his third, but its predecessor, in D minor, was revised and published much later. The C major symphony was composed in 1845 and '46, and published in November, 1847. It was first conducted by Mendelssohn at a Leipzig Gewandhaus concert, November 5, 1846. Schumann was a sick man when he composed this work, and it is the least successful of his four symphonies.

It opens with a curiously subdued fanfare of trumpets, horns and alto trombone, against a flowing counterpoint in the strings:

The first theme has a light-hearted, skipping rhythm:

There is a fragmentary second theme, built on chromatic scales, and the exposition is unusually short. The development is more elaborate, using both the first theme and the Introduction, and in the recapitulation the chief melody becomes loud and impressive, played in full chords by the orchestra. The chromatic scales also return, in a different key, and the Coda experiments with snatches of the skipping rhythm.

Schumann defies convention by using his Scherzo as a second movement. It begins with lively figures in the violins, exuberant in character:

There are two Trios, the first of which has a theme in triplets:

The second Trio shows a broad melody, sung by the strings, and developed against a running contrapuntal figure:

Toward the close of the Scherzo the horns and trumpets are heard again in the introductory motto.

The slow movement, Adagio espressivo, has a melody with leisurely syncopation, first sung by the violins and then by the oboe:

The material of the second theme is of slight melodic importance. In place of a development or free fantasia, Schumann uses a short polyphonic episode which is generally considered incongruous. A conventional recapitulation leads to a brief Coda, with final reminders of the first melody.

The Finale has a short, rapid Introduction which leads immediately into the lively opening theme, somewhat suggestive of the start of Mendelssohn's *Italian Symphony* (see page 145).

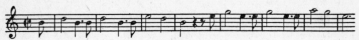

This movement develops in Rondo form, bringing back some of the materials of the slow movement, and finally creating a second melody from the progression first heard in the Introduction to the Finale:

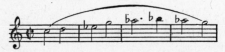

An echo of the opening motto is heard again near the close, and the symphony ends triumphantly, after an unusually long Coda.

The Schumann symphony generally numbered as his third, op. 97 (actually his fourth and last), has the title *Rhenish* because it was composed at Düsseldorf on the Rhine and contains much of the legendary spirit of that beautiful river. The composer had succeeded Ferdinand Hiller as conductor at Düsseldorf in 1850, and the symphony was written between November 2 and December 9 of that year. Its first performance was at the Geisler Hall, Düsseldorf, February 6, 1851, under Schumann's direction. It created little enthusiasm.

The *Rhenish Symphony* opens with a strongly dramatic theme, full of syncopation, in E-flat, the basic key, announced by the full orchestra:

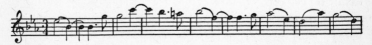

After a repetition of this melody, an elegiac theme in G minor enters in the oboe and clarinet, answered by the violins and wood-wind:

There are original touches throughout the movement, with emphasis on the heroic opening melody. The Coda is quite short.

Again Schumann makes the second movement a Scherzo, instead of the conventional slow time. He starts with the tune of the *Rheinweinlied,* "of a rather ponderous joviality," traditionally sung by the makers and drinkers of the famous Rhine wines. It is introduced by the cellos in the key of C major:

A livelier contrapuntal theme is contrasted with this folk-material, and in the Trio the wind instruments are heard in A minor over an insistent C in the bass. The movement ends quietly.

The slow movement is in A-flat, with its main theme announced by clarinets and bassoons over a viola accompaniment, in the manner of a Romance:

An extra movement is added (Maestoso), representing a scene in the famous Cologne Cathedral, where Schumann attended the ceremony of installing the Archbishop of Geissel as Cardinal, Nov. 12, 1850. He originally marked this movement "In the character of the accompaniment to a solemn ceremony," but later crossed it out. Three trombones are added in this movement, and they play an important part in the chief theme:

The Finale has been interpreted as portraying a Rhenish festival. It opens with a gay, folk-like melody in the basic key of E-flat:

The second theme has a typically Schumannesque quality:

Near the close one hears again the music of the Cathedral scene, and the symphony ends brilliantly.

Schumann's so-called Fourth Symphony is actually his

second, written in the same year as the first, 1841. It was originally called a *Symphonic Fantasia*. Schumann revised it in 1851, and it was published in November, 1853, as opus 120. The key is D minor. The first performance was in the Geisler Hall, Düsseldorf, March 3, 1853, from manuscript, with the composer conducting. Schumann expressed the wish that the symphony be played without any pauses between movements.

An introductory "dreamy motive," in triple time, leads to the opening theme, a lively figure in the violins:

The second theme is far more melodious, first sung by the violins in the related key of F major:

There is a free development of this material, but no recapitulation or Coda. The movement leads directly into a Romanze in D minor, whose chief melody was later echoed by both Cesar Franck and Brahms (see p. 193). It is introduced by the oboe and cellos.

There is a return of the "dreamy motive" of the Introduction to the symphony, and the key changes to D major, with whispering strings, the movement finally ending on an A major chord.

The Scherzo is robust and boisterous, opening with a spirited melody in the basic key of D minor:

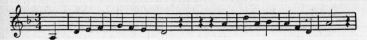

The answering theme is in a gentler mood:

The Trio goes into the key of B-flat, suggesting the whispering theme of the Romanze, and a slow version of the opening Allegro leads right into the Finale, whose chief theme is in D major:

There is a second theme of more lyric character, but the most important melody is held in reserve until the Coda, acting as a nostalgic farewell:

SCHUMANN'S CONCERTOS

Among the most popular of all Concertos for the piano is Schumann's in A minor, op. 54. He called it "a compromise between a symphony, a concerto and a huge sonata," and wrote to his beloved Clara, "I see I cannot write a Concerto for the virtuoso."

The first movement was written as a *Fantasie* in 1841, at Leipzig, and Clara Schumann played it during a rehearsal at the Gewandhaus on August 13th of that year. Two more movements were added in 1845, and the entire work was introduced by the composer's wife in Dresden, Dec. 4. A second performance was given in Leipzig, Jan. 1, 1846, under Mendelssohn's direction. The dedication is to Ferdinand Hiller.

The Concerto opens with a short prelude by the piano, after which the opening theme is announced by the wood-wind, with the piano immediately answering.

The second theme is derived from the first, and there are several subordinate melodic strains.

The development section begins in A-flat major, Andante espressivo. There is a recapitulation, practically identical with the first part, and an elaborate Cadenza for the piano precedes the Coda.

Schumann called the second movement an Intermezzo (Andantino grazioso) and it is really a Romanze of his characteristic type. The chief melody is treated as a dialogue between the solo instrument and the orchestra.

This movement leads directly into the Finale, which is in Sonata form, A major. The piano plays the first theme:

The strongly syncopated second theme is introduced pianissimo by the strings and then repeated broadly in a new key by the soloist:

The development section begins with a short orchestral fugato on the first theme. The recapitulation goes into the key of D major, with the full orchestra playing the first theme, and there is a long Coda.

Schumann also wrote a Concerto for cello and orchestra in A minor, op. 129, which is still in the repertoire of concert cellists. The date of composition is 1850. There is also a Schumann Concerto for four horns, besides several smaller pieces for piano and orchestra.

A violin Concerto in D minor was resurrected by Yehudi Menuhin a few years ago and recorded by him with the New York Philharmonic Symphony Orchestra under Barbirolli (V. Album M-451).

SCHUMANN'S OVERTURES

In 1848-9 Schumann composed incidental music to Byron's *Manfred*, which is numbered as opus 115. The Overture is frequently played and regarded by many as his finest orchestral work.

In addition to the Overture and incidental music, there were Entr'actes and several solos and choruses. The first performance of the Overture was at the Gewandhaus in Leipzig, with Schumann conducting, March 14, 1852. A complete performance was given by Franz Liszt at Weimar on June 2nd of the same year.

The mood of the *Manfred Overture* is somber, with the "surging agitation of despair." The opening theme is played by the solo oboe with the second violins, perhaps representing Manfred's own dying words to the Abbot, "Old man, 'tis not so difficult to die."

Another Schumann Overture still heard occasionally in concert is that which introduced his opera *Genoveva*. The work as a whole was not a success, and it seems agreed that Schumann was unfitted for the creation of stage music. He wrote this opera during 1847 and 1848, and it was produced in Leipzig, June 25, 1850, but had only a few performances.

The libretto was by Robert Reinick, after the tragedies of Hebbel and Tieck, telling the story of St. Genevieve of Braham, which first appears in the *Golden Legend* of the Chronicles of Matthias Emmich in 1472. It is the old story of a chaste wife falsely accused of infidelity by a rejected suitor whom the husband naively and incredibly trusts. In this case the husband is Siegfried of Treves, who goes to the Crusades, and the false friend is named Golo. Schumann revised the libretto considerably, to no avail.

The Overture is really a concert piece, with this important theme:

FELIX MENDELSSOHN-BARTHOLDY

B. Hamburg, Feb. 3, 1809; d. Leipzig, Nov. 4, 1847.

In spite of his short life, Mendelssohn must be considered one of the few happy composers, and almost the only one to escape financial problems. He came of a distinguished Jewish family, his father a leading banker of Berlin and his grandfather the famous philosopher, Moses Mendelssohn. (The name of Bartholdy was added when the family adopted the Lutheran faith.)

Like so many other composers, Mendelssohn was a youthful prodigy, producing his popular Overture to *A Midsummer Night's Dream* at the age of seventeen. Later he wrote several important symphonies, the oratorio *Elijah,* various Overtures and other orchestral works, the most popular of all violin Concertos, and a vast amount of chamber music, songs and piano pieces. His music is refined, melodious, and easy on the ear. By his revival of Bach, Mendelssohn performed an unforgettable service to music, and the significance of his own creations cannot be ignored.

MENDELSSOHN'S SYMPHONIES

Mendelssohn wrote four symphonies, of which two, to which he gave the identifying titles of *Italian* and *Scotch*, are frequently played today. A so-called "Reformation" symphony makes use of Luther's hymn, *A Mighty Fortress Is Our God*, in the Finale. The earliest symphony, in C minor, op. 11, dates from 1824, when the composer was only fifteen years old.

The *Italian Symphony*, in A major, op. 90, was begun during an actual trip to Italy in 1831. It was finished in Berlin March 13, 1833, after Mendelssohn had received and accepted an invitation to conduct the London Philharmonic Society and been paid $500 to provide a symphony and other music for the occasion. This concert took place on May 13, 1833, and the first performance of the *Italian Symphony*, played from manuscript under the composer's baton, was a definite success.

Mendelssohn, however, began to revise the score in June, 1834, and worked over it for three more years. It may have been played in its revised form at another concert of the London Philharmonic, under Moscheles, in June, 1838. But it was not heard on the continent until November 1, 1849, two years after the composer's death, when Julius Rietz conducted it at a Gewandhaus concert in Leipzig. The symphony was not published until March, 1851.

The first movement immediately introduces a lively theme in A major, played by the violins, whose opening notes suggest the actual word "Italian":

A second theme, in E major, is introduced by the clarinets:

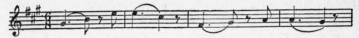

These two melodies are developed in a polyphonic (many-voiced) style, suggesting at times Bach rather than a romanticist of the nineteenth century. The recapitulation is brief, but there is a good-sized Coda, with new and original touches.

The second movement has the effect of a religious procession, starting with a dignified march, Andante con moto, in D minor:

This melody is first played by oboe, clarinet and violas, and later taken up by the violins, with the flutes in counterpoint. A second theme shows alternating clarinet and flute quality, with string tone, in major key:

There is a minimum of development, both melodies soon returning, each surprisingly in a new key. The third movement, Con moto moderato, has the effect of a Scherzo, but follows the old Minuet style in rhythm and form. The first violins introduce the lively opening theme:

Horns and bassoons are prominent in the chords opening the Trio. The Finale is the first and only movement which really justifies the name of "Italian" for this symphony. Its principal tune is a Saltarello, a dance similar to the Tarantella, played by the flutes after six introductory measures:

There are two more themes of similar character, with first and second violins alternating in a lively dialogue. This definitely Italian Finale seems to have been inspired by Mendelssohn's experience at a Carnival in Rome in 1831.

The *Scotch Symphony* is in A minor, published as opus 56. It was undoubtedly begun in 1829 during Mendelssohn's trip to Scotland, and ten measures are said to have been written in Edinburgh, under the influence of the landmarks associated with Mary, Queen of Scots. The symphony was finished in Berlin in 1842, and its first performance was at the Leipzig Gewandhaus on March 3rd of that year, with the composer conducting.

There is an introductory theme that immediately strikes a serious note, in the basic key of A minor:

The actual first theme is adapted from this material, largely through a quickening of the pace:

A second theme provides a certain amount of contrast:

Sonata form is followed out painstakingly, with elaborate development, recapitulation and Coda, all ending in a repetition of the slow Introduction and going right into a fast Scherzo. It is this movement that gives the symphony whatever Scotch character it possesses, building its first theme definitely on the five-tone scale, regularly associated with Scottish folk-music (as well as that of most other countries).

The second theme goes into conventional diatonic scale progressions, with Sonata form again controlling the development, recapitulation and Coda.

The slow third movement begins with a rather mournful theme, possibly inspired by the tragedies of Scotch history:

The second melody is robust and courageous, suggesting a battle hymn for the heroes of Scotland's wars:

The Finale starts with a skipping tune which restores the symphony to complete cheerfulness of mood:

In the second theme there is an echo of the slow Introduction once more, but now in a fast time:

Sonata form is again in command of the melodic materials, with the Coda introducing a practically new theme toward the close.

MENDELSSOHN'S CONCERTOS

The violin Concerto in E minor, op. 64, by Mendelssohn, is still the favorite of them all with the average listener, and it is easy to understand the eternal appeal of its melodious measures. The composer began it in 1838, with some hesitation, and did not finish the work until September, 1844. The first performance was at the Gewandhaus, Leipzig, March 13, 1845, with Ferdinand David as soloist. This fine violinist is believed to have been very helpful to Mendelssohn in making the Concerto delightful to the performer. Even the Cadenzas sound musical and melodically significant.

After two measures of orchestral Introduction, the solo violin immediately plays the opening theme, high on the E string:

The second theme, of definitely sentimental character, is introduced by the wood-wind and then taken up by the soloist:

The development of these materials is handled with great skill, giving the impression of a constant flow of varied melody. Near the close of the movement a well-wrought Cadenza leads right into the final reminder of the first theme by the orchestra, with the solo violin playing decorative arpeggios (broken chords).

The slow movement, starting without a pause, has a short orchestral Introduction, after which the solo violin plays a sweetly sentimental melody in the uncompromising key of C major:

A middle section brings in a new theme, with the violin making considerable use of double stops and octaves:

The return of the first melody brings the movement to a quiet close.

There is a short, melodic Interlude, after which the orchestra utters peremptory chords, answered by arpeggios in the violin, from which the first theme of the Finale is derived:

A robust second theme enters in the full orchestra after rapid scale passages in the violin:

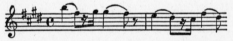

The Rondo form is followed in this brilliant Finale, with the solo violin providing a variety of embellishments for the principal themes.

Mendelssohn wrote two piano Concertos, which are now seldom heard. The first, in G minor, op. 25, dated from 1831, and was played for the first time by Mendelssohn himself in Munich, October 7th of that year. It was dedicated to Delphine Schauroth, a young pianist of Munich. The composer requested that the Finale be played "as fast as possible," and created a sensation by the speed of his own performance in this movement.

A second Concerto for piano and orchestra, in D minor, op. 40, bears the date of August 5, 1837, when it was completed at Horchheim.

MENDELSSOHN'S OVERTURES

The composition by which Mendelssohn is best known is of course the popular Overture to *A Midsummer Night's Dream,* which remains one of the miracles of youthful precocity in musical history. The boy of seventeen had spent part of the summer of 1826 reading Shakespeare with his beloved sister Fanny in the translation of Schlegel and Tieck. He composed the Overture in July and August of that year, writing it first as a piano duet and playing it with his sister at a musicale in their Berlin home, November 19, 1826. Later it was performed by an orchestra in the garden house, which had room for a fairly large audience. Karl Löwe conducted the first public performance at Stettin in February, 1827. The orchestral parts were published in 1832 and the score in 1835, with a dedication to the Crown Prince of Prussia.

The Overture begins in E major, with four sustained chords in the wood-wind. A very soft E minor chord in the violins and violas then introduces the "fairy music," played softly by divided violins:

A subsidiary theme by the full orchestra suggests the splendor of Duke Theseus and his court:

The real second theme is a romantic melody, representing
the two pairs of lovers, Hermia and Lysander and Helena and
Demetrius:

A clownish passage interrupts, clearly depicting the little
theatre of Nick Bottom and his companions. The bass strings
provide a droning accompaniment, while the melody definitely
imitates the braying of the ass's head worn by Nick after the
spell has been cast upon him:

All of these materials are excitingly developed, after which
there is a recapitulation of themes in regular Sonata form. The
Theseus theme returns quietly at the close, indicating the
blessing of the elves on his home, and after an echo of the fairy
music the Overture ends on the same chords that first created
the illusion of the dream.

Seventeen years later, in 1843, King Frederick William IV
of Prussia asked Mendelssohn to compose incidental music for
the entire play of *A Midsummer Night's Dream,* as well as for
Athalia and *Antigone.* (The *Priests' March* from the *Athalia*
music has become a popular tune.) The composer wrote a
total of twelve additional numbers, and the score was performed with the play at Potsdam, October 14, 1843, on the eve
of the King's birthday, with Mendelssohn conducting.

The most important of these additional numbers are the
Scherzo, occurring between Acts I and II, the *Nocturne,* after

Act III, and the familiar *Wedding March*, at the close of Act IV. Themes from the Overture were used in much of this incidental music, and the *Scherzo* suggests the mood of the fairy measures once more. The chief theme is this:

The *Nocturne* is played while the lovers are asleep in the forest, with Puck straightening out the mischief that his magic has caused. The chief melody is of quiet beauty, effectively using the tone color of the French horn:

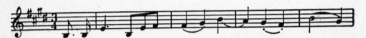

The *Wedding March* introduces the two marriages, presided over by Theseus and Hippolyta and blessed by the reconciled royal couple of Fairyland, Oberon and Titania. Its opening scarcely needs quotation:

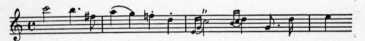

This has become the traditional exit march for all weddings.

Sharing the popularity of the unique *Midsummer Night's Dream Overture* is the one variously known as *Fingal's Cave* and *The Hebrides,* op. 26. It was inspired by the great cave in Staffa, off the coast of Scotland, which Mendelssohn saw in 1829. The opening theme came into his head immediately, and he wrote down twenty-one measures of music in a letter to his sister Fanny. The Overture was first played at a concert of the London Philharmonic Society at Covent Garden, May 14, 1832, from manuscript, with Thomas Attwood conducting.

The main theme, imitating the surging of the sea in and out of Fingal's Cave in the Hebrides, shows this constantly repeated figure:

Another popular Mendelssohn Overture is the *Ruy Blas,* op. 95, written for Victor Hugo's historical drama in 1838, and performed at a benefit for the Theatrical Pension Fund in Leipzig that year. The composer also wrote a *Romance* for the occasion. Mendelssohn disliked the play, perhaps because he knew it only in a very bad German translation, but he wrote the Overture in three days and it turned out to be one of his most successful orchestral pieces. The most important theme is the following:

Calm Sea and a Prosperous Voyage is the title of still another Mendelssohn Overture, written in 1828 and completely revised in 1834, based on a poem by Goethe and perhaps influenced by the composer's visit to the shores of the Baltic Sea in 1824. Mendelssohn himself considered *The Lovely Melusina* his best Overture, but this composition is practically never heard today. It dates from the year 1834 and was based on the story of the beautiful mermaid who became involved in a human marriage.

SPOHR AND CHOPIN

A minor romanticist whose works are still heard occasionally was Louis (or Ludwig) Spohr (b. Brunswick, April 5, 1784; d. Cassel, Oct. 22, 1859). He was not only one of the greatest violinists of his day, but an astonishingly prolific composer, having to his credit no fewer than seventeen violin Concertos, nine symphonies, ten operas, four oratorios and thirty-three string quartets.

Of the violin Concertos of Spohr only two have been pro-
grammed in recent years, the eighth, in A minor, and the
ninth, in D minor. The latter was written in 1822, and first
played by the composer at Cassel, July 28, 1823, to celebrate
the birthday of the Elector.

Spohr's Overture to his opera, *Jessonda,* op. 63, is also
heard occasionally. The entire work was exceedingly popular
in its day, but is now completely forgotten except for the
Overture.

Far more important in the romantic movement is the work
of Frederic Chopin (b. near Warsaw, March 17, 1810; d.
Paris, Oct. 17, 1849), but since he wrote almost exclusively
for the piano, he requires only passing mention in a guide to
orchestral music.

Chopin wrote two Concertos for piano and orchestra, the
first in E minor, op. 11 (actually the second in composition, but
published ahead of its companion) and the second in F
minor, op. 21. The date of the E minor concerto is 1830, and it
was first performed by the composer at Warsaw on October
11th of that year. It was published in September, 1833. There
are three movements, Allegro, maestoso, a Romance: Larghetto, in E major, and a Rondo: Vivace, returning to the basic
key of E minor. Its opening melody was later echoed by Victor
Herbert's *Gypsy Love Song* and the popular *Play, Fiddle,
Play*:

The second piano Concerto of Chopin was dedicated to the
Countess Delphine Potocka, an early love, who sang to him
at his deathbed. The publication date of the F minor Concerto
was April, 1836, and the first performance was by the composer at Warsaw, March 17, 1830. The orchestration has been

revised by Richard Burmeister and others. The three movements are marked Maestoso (F minor); Larghetto (F major); and Allegro vivace (F minor). The opening theme is as follows:

HECTOR BERLIOZ

B. Grenoble, Dec. 11, 1803; d. Paris, March 9, 1869.

Hector Berlioz was one of the strangest figures in the history of music, a frustrated soul, generally attempting more than he could accomplish, yet a pioneer in modern orchestration, to whom Wagner, Liszt, Richard Strauss and many other composers were unquestionably indebted.

The music of Berlioz is largely programmatic, including even his symphonies, which bear such titles as *Fantastique* (*Episode in the Life of an Artist*), *Lelio, Harold in Italy,* and *Romeo and Juliet.* His best known work is the oratorio, *The Damnation of Faust.* An opera, *Benvenuto Cellini,* is remembered chiefly because of two Overtures, one of which, known as *Carnaval Romain,* has become permanently popular. An elaborate *Requiem,* requiring "four orchestras of brass instruments ... placed around the grand orchestra and the mass of the voices" is occasionally heard when the necessary staging can be accomplished.

THE SYMPHONIES OF BERLIOZ

Berlioz' *Fantastic Symphony* was written in 1828, a year after the Irish actress, Henrietta Smithson, had appeared in Paris for a series of Shakespearian performances. Berlioz fell violently in love with her, and they were eventually (and unhappily) married. The *Fantastic Symphony,* with its sub-title, *Episode in the Life of an Artist,* was primarily an expression of the apparently futile passion of its composer.

Berlioz gave out three different versions of the program of this symphony, agreeing in the following essential details: "A young musician of a morbid sensibility and an ardent imagination poisons himself with opium. The dose of the narcotic, too weak to kill him, plunges him into a heavy sleep, accompanied by strange visions, during which his sensations, sentiments and recollections are translated in his sick mind into musical thoughts and pictures. The beloved woman, she herself, has become for him a melody and, as it were, an *idée fixe,* which he finds and hears everywhere."

This "fixed idea" is represented thus, as the principal melody of the opening Allegro, reappearing from time to time throughout the symphony:

In the next movement the artist attends a ball, where he hears the theme of the beloved even through the music of a brilliant waltz:

In the third movement, Adagio, the hero, according to Berlioz, "hears from afar two shepherds dialoguing a *ranz des vaches;* this pastoral plunges him into a delicious reverie." Here is the pastoral melody, played by English horn and oboe in turn:

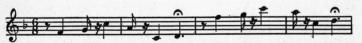

After the attempted suicide, the artist believes that he has killed his beloved. He sees himself at his own execution, and the music gives a gruesome suggestion of the march to the scaffold:

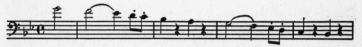

The Finale represents the Witches' Sabbath, in which the theme of the beloved is distorted, with a parody also of the *Dies Irae*. Here is the chief dance theme of the orgy:

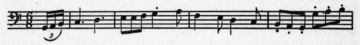

The first performance of the *Fantastic Symphony* was at the Paris Conservatoire, December 5, 1830, under the composer's direction. He married Miss Smithson three years later.

The violinist Paganini was so impressed with the music of Berlioz that he asked him to write a Concerto for the viola, as he owned a fine Stradivarius instrument which he wished to play in public. Berlioz did not succeed in creating anything of sufficient virtuosity to suit Paganini, who said "I must be playing all the time." But the sketches for this Concerto developed into the symphony, *Harold in Italy,* which so pleased Paganini that he gave the composer 20,000 francs. (Some say that he merely acted for an anonymous benefactor.)

The music was unquestionably influenced by an actual visit to Italy, as winner of the Prix de Rome, and also by the poem of Byron, *Childe Harold*, although the symphonic program has nothing to do with this story. The four movements of the symphony have the titles (1) *Harold in the Mountains: Scenes of Melancholy, Happiness and Joy;* (2) *March of Pilgrims Singing the Evening Prayer;* (3) *Serenade of a Mountaineer of the Abruzzi to His Mistress;* (4) *Orgy of Brigands: Recollection of the Preceding Scenes.*

Harold in Italy was written in 1834, and the first perform-ance was at the Paris Conservatoire on November 23rd of that year, the composer conducting. The theme representing the hero runs through all four movements and is first announced by the solo viola:

The *Romeo and Juliet Symphony* was written in 1839, and dedicated to Paganini, out of gratitude for the violinist's help. (Paganini, however, died in 1840 without having heard the work.) It is a mixture of choral and instrumental music, and only three movements are commonly heard in the concert hall.

To the first of these Berlioz gave the descriptive heading: "Romeo alone. Sadness. Concert and ball. Grand Fete at Capulet's house." Another movement has this program: "Love Scene. Adagio. Capulet's Garden at Night. Juliet on the Balcony. Romeo in the Garden below."

The most popular movement is the Scherzo, "Queen Mab, or the Dream Fairy," based upon the familiar speech of Mer-cutio in Shakespeare's play. The chief theme of this fairy music is as follows:

There is an Introduction, describing the "Combats, Tumults and Intervention of the Prince," with the royal voice heard in a recitative of trombones and other brass instruments. The Finale attempts to portray "Romeo in the Tomb of the Capulets; Invocation; Awakening of Juliet; Delirious Joy, Despair, Last Anguish and Death of the Two Lovers."

FAUST AND OTHER MUSIC OF BERLIOZ

The Damnation of Faust is also a mixture of the vocal and the instrumental, strongly programmatic throughout. Berlioz had been persuaded by Franz Liszt to read Goethe's *Faust* and therefore dedicated this score to the Weimar impresario-conductor. He first wrote some songs to Goethe's words, which he then produced under the title *Eight Scenes from Faust*. By 1846 he had completed the instrumental music. Only three excerpts from *The Damnation of Faust* are regularly heard in concert, but these three are deservedly popular. The general order of performance is (1) *Dance of the Will-o'-the-Wisps*, (2) *Ballet of the Sylphs*, (3) *Hungarian March (Rakoczy)*, although these numbers appear in reverse order in the actual score.

The famous *Rakoczy March* was originally created by a gypsy violinist, Michael Barna, court musician to the Transylvanian Prince Franz Rakoczy, who won fame by his resistance against Austria. The march was later revised by another gypsy named Ruzsitka and eventually became a recognized piece of Hungarian folk-music. Berlioz orchestrated it, and its first performance in Budapest produced such a frenzy of patriotic enthusiasm that he decided to include it in *The Damnation of Faust*. He brought it in by the simple device of having Faust watch the Hungarian army departing for the battlefield. The opening theme hardly requires quotation:

The *Ballet of the Sylphs* occurs near the end of the second part of *The Damnation of Faust*, when Mephistopheles, after showing Faust a vision of Marguerite, lulls him to sleep on the bank of the Elbe. The music combines the rhythm of a charming waltz with the mood of a lullaby:

The *Dance of the Will-o'-the-Wisps* is in the third part, when Mephisto tries to bewilder Marguerite and make her an easy prey to the advances of Faust. Its music has been described as a "grotesque Minuet."

Berlioz wrote the opera *Benvenuto Cellini* (op. 23) in Paris in 1838, and it had its premiere at the Opera on September 10 of that year, with Habeneck conducting. It was dedicated to Ernest Legouvé, who lent the composer 2000 francs to make its creation possible.

The Overture is based on themes from the opera, using first the carnival music, then the Cardinal's speech, pizzicato by cellos and basses, then the Ariette of Harlequin, the love music, the carnival again, and finally the Cardinal's music once more, fortissimo in the brass.

More popular and significant is the *Roman Carnival Overture*, op. 9, which also employs themes from the opera, *Benvenuto Cellini*, and has generally been used as an entr'acte. The first and most important tune is from the Saltarello in the second act:

Berlioz dedicated this Overture, now heard mostly as a concert piece, to the Prince of Hohenzollern-Hechingen. Its first performance was in Paris, February 3, 1844, with the composer conducting.

There are several other Overtures by Berlioz appearing occasionally in the orchestral repertoire, but of no great importance. *The Corsair,* op. 21, was composed in Rome in 1831, but was not performed until April 1, 1855, by the St. Cecilia Society. It was dedicated to the English critic Davison, and may have been influenced by the poem of Byron.

A *King Lear Overture* also belongs to the year 1831, written between Nice and Rome, with a first performance in Paris in 1834. Its music is intended as a portrait of the King. The unison theme played by violas, cellos and basses at the start is generally interpreted as representing the selfishness of the two daughters.

An Overture to *Waverley,* op. 2, is headed by a quotation from the poem, *Mirkwood Mere,* in the fifth chapter of Sir Walter Scott's book. The *Overture des Francs-Juges,* op. 3, 1828, is a crude but powerful work, portraying in music the sensations of a prisoner brought before the Vehmic Tribunal, with his appeals for mercy vehemently denied.

GIOACCHINO ANTONIO ROSSINI

Of all the Italian composers of opera, only one is heard with any frequency on the orchestral platform. That one is Gioacchino Antonio Rossini (b. Pesaro, Feb. 29, 1792; d. Paris, Nov. 13, 1868). At least three of Rossini's Overtures remain hugely popular with concertgoers and radio listeners, and several others are still played occasionally.

The best-known Rossini Overture is of course the *William Tell,* which is available in practically every possible combination of instruments. The *Semiramide Overture* is an important number in brass band literature, and also a radio staple in its original form. One also hears the sparkling Overture to *The Barber of Seville* with some frequency.

William Tell was Rossini's most serious opera, strongly influenced by Beethoven (and not always to its advantage). It was first performed in Paris, August 3, 1829, and it remains today a mere background to the popular Overture.

The Introduction to this Overture represents dawn in the Alps, opening with the solo voice of the cello, which soon grows into a quartet of these instruments. They announce this broad melody:

An Alpine storm occupies the second section of the *William Tell Overture*, with realistic lightning flashes in the cymbals, and the drums imitating the roll of thunder. The ensuing calm (all of this reminiscent of Beethoven's *Pastoral Symphony*), with the thanksgiving of the shepherds, is suggested by a slow melody played by the English horn, to which the flute is soon added with brilliant embellishments:

The final section of the Overture contains the familiar quick-step, representing the march of the Swiss troops, long a stand-by of the movies and vaudeville:

The Barber of Seville was first produced at the Teatro di Torre Argentina, Rome, February 20, 1816, and scored a complete failure. But this initial set-back was soon forgotten in a series of triumphs all over Europe and also in America, where it was presented as early as 1825 by Manuel Garcia. (See *The Metropolitan Opera Guide*, pp. 38-44).

The Overture to *The Barber of Seville* is merely a lively prelude to the comic action of the opera, without any dependence on its themes. In fact, it had been used by Rossini for two earlier operas, *Elisabetta* and *Aureliano*. Here is the chief theme:

Semiramide was introduced at the Teatro Fenice in Venice, February 3, 1823, running for a solid month and continuing to win favor for many years. It was revived at the Metropolitan Opera House in 1895, with Melba, Scalchi and Edouard de Reszke, but without success, and is now a mere memory except for the Overture, which has this opening theme:

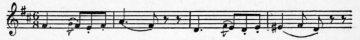

Another Rossini Overture occasionally heard is that of the comedy, *L'Italiana in Algeri,* full of youthful melody and wit, and also first performed in Venice. The Overture to *La Cenerentola* is largely borrowed from earlier Rossini works. It was first produced at Rome, Jan. 25, 1817. Far more important musically is the Overture to *La Gazza Ladra,* introduced at La Scala, Milan, in May, 1817, and this orchestral prelude stands comparison even with the *William Tell Overture.*

FRANZ LISZT

B. Raiding, Oct. 22, 1811; d. Bayreuth, July 31, 1886.

Generally considered the greatest pianist in history, Liszt is important also as the inventor of the Symphonic Poem and as a composer in various forms, with considerable influence on Richard Wagner, who became his son-in-law and heavy financial and artistic debtor.

Primarily a technician, Liszt was helpful to his fellow-composers through brilliant piano arrangements of their works. His own success was phenomenal, and he dominated the musical world to the day of his death at the ripe age of nearly seventy-five. In addition to his twelve Symphonic Poems, Liszt contributed a *Faust Symphony* to the orchestral literature, and many of his piano pieces have been orchestrated. An oratorio, *The Legend of St. Elizabeth,* has been performed both in its original form and as an opera. He wrote church music and songs, in addition to a wealth of material for the piano.

LISZT'S SYMPHONIC POEMS

While some of the earlier concert Overtures (particularly those of Beethoven) had had the effect of miniature symphonies, it was Franz Liszt who clearly established a form that is still popular, which he called the Symphonic Poem. Such a composition is in one continuous movement, although including a variety of themes, symphonic in effect, and almost necessarily programmatic, as it concentrates on the musical portrayal of a single dramatic subject, indicated by its title.

The first of Liszt's Symphonic Poems has the title *What One Hears on the Mountain,* based on the fifth of Victor Hugo's *Autumn Leaves,* with the poem prefixed to the score. It represents "a mystic dialogue of two voices," Nature and Humanity, arguing on Destiny, the soul, God and the universe. The music is not particularly important.

Far more significant is the second of the series, *Tasso: Lamento e Trionfo.* This fine composition was written and produced in Weimar in 1849, in connection with the celebration of the centenary of Goethe's birth, although the subject matter derives from Byron's poem, *The Lament of Tasso,* rather than Goethe's drama.

Liszt wrote in his preface to *Tasso* that the poet "loved and suffered in Ferrara; he was revenged in Rome, and he lives still today in the folk-songs of Venice. These three moments are inseparable from his imperishable fame. To render them musically we called up first his great shade as it still haunts the Venetian lagoons; we then saw his proud, sad face pass through the festivities of Ferrara, where he gave birth to his masterpieces; finally we followed him to Rome, the Eternal City, which, in bestowing on him her crown, glorified in him the martyr and poet."

Liszt himself declared that the principal theme of his *Tasso* was a melody which he had heard the Venetian gondoliers sing to the opening stanzas of the Italian poet's *Jerusalem Delivered*:

The best known and most popular of the Liszt Symphonic Poems is unquestionably the third, *Les Preludes*. It was written in Weimar in 1850 and first performed there February 23, 1854, with publication two years later. This music was inspired by one of Lamartine's *Poetic Meditations* (the 15th), which Liszt translated thus: "What is our life but a series of preludes to that unknown song, the first solemn note of which is sounded by death? Love forms the enchanted daybreak of every life; but what is the destiny where the first delights of happiness are not interrupted by some storm, whose fatal breath dissipates its fair illusions, whose fell lightning consumes its altar? And what wounded spirit, when one of its tempests is over, does not seek to rest its memories in the sweet calm of country life? Yet man does not resign himself long to enjoy the beneficent tepidity which first charmed him on nature's bosom; and when the 'trumpet's loud clangor has called him to arms' he rushes to the post of danger, whatever may be the war that calls him to the ranks, to find in battle the full consciousness of himself and the complete possession of his strength."

The first of these rather grandiloquent questions seems to

be asked by this theme, which appears at the start of *Les Preludes*:

The "sweet calm of country life" may be represented by this melody, reminiscent of Schubert (see page 127):

Finally there is a martial theme, with plenty of trombone volume, uttering this call to battle (also appearing earlier in *Les Preludes*):

Liszt's fourth Symphonic Poem is called *Orpheus*, suggested by Gluck's opera and the decoration on an Etruscan vase in the Louvre. The fifth is *Prometheus*, another popular subject with composers, written to introduce some dramatic scenes by Herder performed at Weimar in 1850 to dedicate a statue of the poet. Neither of these works is heard nowadays.

A piano Etude supplied the material for the sixth Symphonic Poem, *Mazeppa*, which becomes orchestrally a dramatic and highly imitative piece of music. Its story is from one of the poems in Victor Hugo's *Les Orientales*. The music moves in galloping rhythms, with realistic touches when the wild horse tries to scrape off the unfortunate Mazeppa, tied to its back.

Festal Sounds (*Festklänge*) is the name of the seventh in the series, evidently written in 1851 when Liszt's marriage to the Princess Wittgenstein seemed a possibility. This piece shares the oblivion of number eight, *Heroïde Funébre*, nine, *Hungaria*, and ten, *Hamlet*. Number eleven is *The Battle of the Huns*, first performed at Weimar, December 29, 1857. It had its inspiration in a fresco by Kaulbach in the Berlin Museum, portraying the fighters of Attila and the Roman army continuing their battle in the skies after being killed on the Catalaunian Plain.

The twelfth and last Symphonic Poem of Liszt is called *Die Ideale* (Ideals) after Schiller's poem, which supplies nine quotations, prefixed to various parts of the music.

THE LISZT SYMPHONIES

Liszt wrote two symphonies, each of which is really a combination of Symphonic Poems. The first is called *Faust,* and consists of three "Character Pictures," bearing the names of the hero, Gretchen (Marguerite) and Mephistopheles. This symphony was first performed at the Grand Ducal Theatre in Weimar, September 5, 1857. The dedication is to Hector Berlioz.

Faust himself is introduced by a brooding theme which later goes through various transformations:

The Gretchen theme of the second movement is as follows, introduced (dolce semplice) by the oboe, accompanied only by a solo viola:

In the Finale the Faust theme is parodied, with sardonic, Mephistophelian implications, while Gretchen's theme remains in its pure simplicity. At the close a men's chorus, with tenor solo, sings Goethe's famous words concerning things transitory and indescribable, ending with his tribute to "the eternal feminine." The music is a rhythmic alteration of the

Gretchen motive, with harp eventually added to the accompaniment.

Liszt's second symphony is called *Dante,* and its two movements have the titles *Inferno* and *Purgatorio.* (Wagner is said to have persuaded his benefactor not to attempt a musical portrayal of Paradise.) This symphony was composed during the years 1847 to 1855 and published in 1858. Its first performance was in Dresden, November 7, 1857. The dedication is to Richard Wagner.

Trombones and tuba introduce a musical picture of the gates of Hell, illustrating the words written in the score: "Through me you pass into the city of woe. Through me you pass into eternal pain." Trumpets and horns, mostly on one note, add the familiar line, "Abandon hope, all ye who enter here."

The episode of Paolo and Francesca is represented by a love duet, interrupted by the mocking laughter of demons. The *Purgatorio* begins with twenty-seven measures on one chord, expressing Dante's "infinite longing for godliness." There is a fugue on a lamentoso theme. At the close comes a Magnificat, sung by women's voices, in place of the conventional Coda.

LISZT'S CONCERTOS AND RHAPSODIES

There are two piano Concertos by Franz Liszt, both maintaining their place in the virtuoso repertoire. The first, in E flat, was completed in June, 1849, revised in 1853 and published in 1855. The first performance was at the palace of the Grand Duke in Weimar, February 17, 1855, with the composer

at the piano and Bülow conducting. (Some give the honor to
Berlioz, who was present.) The dedication is to Henri Litolff.
The Concerto is in one movement, divided naturally into several sections. It was severely criticized by Hanslick for its use
of the triangle, and was long known as "the Triangle Concerto."

The opening theme, sounded by the strings, with interruptions of wood-wind and brass in chords, has become very familiar. Liszt himself used to sing to it the words "Das ver-
steht ihr alle nicht" ("This is a mystery to all of you"), and it
has been suggested that the chords mean "Nur ich," in the
sense that he alone understood it.

There are three more themes, but the opening notes may be
considered the motto of the entire Concerto, which ends in a
brilliant Presto.

The second piano Concerto is in A major. Its composition
runs through the decade of 1839-49. The dedication is to Hans
von Bronsart, who played it for the first time at the Grand
Ducal Theatre in Weimar, January 7, 1857, with Liszt conducting. Like its predecessor it has only one movement, and
was originally called *Concert Symphonique*. It has also been
called a Symphonic Poem for piano and orchestra and "The
Life and Adventures of a Melody." Here is its opening and
outstanding theme:

Several of Liszt's popular *Hungarian Rhapsodies* have
been orchestrated, notably the second, which is often heard as
a brilliant climax to a symphonic program. The fourteenth
Rhapsody is also known orchestrally as the *Hungarian Fan-*

tasy for piano and orchestra. Its chief theme is taken from the Hungarian folk-song, *The Heron*:

RICHARD WAGNER

B. Leipzig, May 22, 1813; d. Venice, Feb. 13, 1883.

Wagner is recognized as the greatest of all dramatic composers, and his Overtures, Preludes and orchestral excerpts from the music dramas have won permanent popularity in the concert hall as well as the opera house.

Wagner was raised in the theatre, with an actor as a step-father, and his early leanings were dramatic rather than musical. But he became a conductor at 21, and with the help of Meyerbeer his opera, *Rienzi*, was produced at Dresden in 1842.

Wagner was a revolutionary, politically as well as musically, spending part of his life as an exile from Germany. After much financial and domestic trouble his problems were finally solved by the "mad King," Ludwig of Bavaria, who subsidized him and made possible the creation and completion of his greatest works.

The despicable character of Wagner does not affect the genius of his music. He turned conventional grand opera into a new form, in which the orchestra is actually more important than the singing or acting. After *Rienzi* he wrote *The Flying Dutchman, Tannhäuser, Lohengrin, The Mastersingers of Nuremberg*, the cycle of the *Nibelungen Ring*, consisting of *Das Rheingold, Die Walküre, Siegfried* and *Götterdämmerung, Tristan und Isolde* and *Parsifal*. Wagner is also known orchestrally by his *Faust Overture* and *Siegfried Idyl* and as the composer of several songs.

WAGNER'S OVERTURES AND PRELUDES

Of Wagner's first important opera, *Rienzi,* only the Overture is heard today, but this attractive orchestral piece remains a popular feature of the concert repertoire. The opera, with a sub-title, *The Last of the Tribunes,* was based on Bulwer-Lytton's *Rienzi,* which Wagner read in the summer of 1837 in Dresden, in a German translation. The Overture was completed October 23, 1840, and the opera was produced nearly two years later, October 20, 1842, at Dresden's Royal Saxon Court Theatre. The original instrumentation of the Overture included a serpent and an ophicleide, now replaced by double bassoon and tuba.

All the themes in the Overture are from the opera itself. There is a slow Introduction in D major, opening with a long sustained A on the trumpet, representing the signal for the uprising of the people against the nobles. The first outstanding melody, played by violins and cellos, is the theme of Rienzi's prayer in the fifth act:

Several other melodies from the opera are introduced, one of which is the battle hymn of the revolutionaries, announced and later repeated by the brass instruments. Rienzi's prayer returns in a fast tempo, played by the violins over a dance-like accompaniment. At the close (Coda) the battle hymn is robustly developed.

The Flying Dutchman is the first of Wagner's operas that might be considered a music drama. It was produced in Dresden, January 2, 1843, but departed too much from traditional forms to make a success and ran for only four performances.

The story of the accursed Vanderdecken, condemned to sail the seas in his ghostly ship until redeemed by the love of a woman, was suggested by Heine's treatment of the legend, and its background of storm and ocean waves unquestionably took shape in Wagner's mind when crossing the North Sea from Riga, with his actress wife, Minna Planer. (He originally called his heroine of *The Flying Dutchman* Minna, but later changed the name to Senta.) The Overture was completed November 5, 1841, in Paris. In 1852 Wagner changed the ending, and in 1860 he changed it again, for a Parisian concert.

The Overture to *The Flying Dutchman* immediately introduces the motive of the ghostly sailor himself, given out by horns and bassoons:

The music develops stormily. A gentler, more melodious theme soon enters, taken from Senta's Ballad, and representing the love and self-sacrifice of the heroine:

These two themes provide most of the melodic material of the Overture.

The Overture to *Tannhäuser* is perhaps the most popular in the entire Wagner list. It was written in Dresden in the spring of 1845, and the opera had its premiere under the composer's direction at the Royal Opera House in Dresden, October 19th of that year. The Overture was first performed as a concert piece at the Leipzig Gewandhaus, February 12, 1846, with Mendelssohn conducting from manuscript.

Wagner himself wrote a detailed programmatic analysis of the Overture, which was published in the *Neue Zeitschrift*, Jan. 14, 1853. He emphasizes the familiar *Pilgrims' Chorus*, played by the wood and brass at the start:

There follows a musical description of the Venusberg and its revelries, with Venus herself playing the temptress to the Minnesinger Tannhäuser. These bacchanalian strains are introduced by the violas:

The triumphant song of Tannhäuser forms a climax to the Overture:

At the close the *Pilgrims' Chorus* is heard again, this time with elaborate decorations by the strings. There is no musical indication of the heroine, Elisabeth, nor does the Overture actually suggest the plot of the opera. It is really an independent piece of program music, heard far oftener in the concert hall than in the opera house.

The Prelude to *Lohengrin* is also a popular concert number, besides serving as an admirable introduction to the opera. (Technically a Prelude leads directly into the action of the opera itself, whereas an Overture comes to a complete stop before the curtain rises.)

The opera had its first performance at the Court Theatre in Weimar, August 28, 1850, with Liszt conducting, after many hardships and disappointments. Nor was it an immediate success. Wagner himself was in exile at the time, and could hear about it only at a distance.

Liszt described the Prelude to *Lohengrin* as "a sort of magic formula which, like a mysterious initiation, prepares our soul for the sight of unaccustomed things, and of a higher signification than that of our terrestrial life." (For the plots of the operas and music dramas of Wagner see pages 91-192 in *The Metropolitan Opera Guide*.)

The *Lohengrin* Prelude opens with mystic chords high up on the strings, representing the Holy Grail, to which service the knight is dedicated.

This theme creates the mood of the entire composition, which again makes no attempt to sum up the plot or the melodies of the opera itself, but contents itself with establishing the right atmosphere for the action which is to follow. The Prelude ends as it began, with the mysterious Grail music.

There is an orchestral Prelude to the third act of *Lohengrin* which is also popular as a concert piece. It represents a torchlight procession, preceding the marriage of Elsa and Lohengrin (and actually leading into the familiar *Wedding March*). Its music is robust and hearty, in strong contrast to the ethereal strains that precede the opera as a whole. The main theme, played by the brass over agitated strings, is as follows:

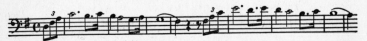

The Mastersingers of Nuremberg has been called the greatest musical comedy of all time, and it is the only opera of this type written by Wagner. He was working on it as early as 1845, but the score was not completed until 1867. The first performance was in Munich, June 21, 1868, under the direction of Hans von Bülow.

The *Meistersinger Prelude* is a sustained song of joy, summing up the whole spirit of the opera itself and introducing its leading themes. It bursts forth immediately with the pompous march of the Mastersingers, representing the ancient Guilds of Nuremberg:

There is a suggestion of the love music of Eva and Walter, followed by the second strain of the march, which is based on an actual melody of the Mastersingers of history, known as the "long tone":

A bit of the Prize Song is next heard, as sung by Walter in the opera, but in 4-4 time:

A caricature of the march, with staccato bassoons, suggests the absurdities of Beckmesser, who represents music critics in general and particularly the Viennese Hanslick, who was hostile to Wagner. The climax of the Prelude exhibits all the themes in an astonishing five-part counterpoint, and after this impressive feat of musicianship Wagner lets the brass blare out the march tune once more in a brilliantly exciting finish.

Tristan und Isolde, considered by many to be Wagner's greatest opera, was also a long time in the process of creation, with frequent interruptions to the work. Wagner had it in mind as early as 1854, and wrote the words in the summer of 1857 while in exile at Zurich. The first act was completed by the end of that year, and the second act is dated March, 1859, at Venice. The score was finished near Lucerne in August of that year. After an unsuccessful attempt to produce the music drama in Vienna, it finally arrived at a first performance in Munich, June 10, 1865, under von Bülow's baton.

The *Prelude* (which leads directly into the action) begins with a theme of yearning, sometimes identified with the love potion, introduced by the cellos and answered by an upward chromatic scale in the wood-wind:

The *Prelude* consists chiefly of a free development of this material, with a variety of imitations, gradually reaching a climax after a slow crescendo. When played in the concert hall it is generally followed by an orchestral version of the "Love death" (*Liebestod*) which Wagner himself arranged. This also works up to a climax from this basic melody:

The *Prelude* and *Liebestod* combine in a practically perfect expression of human love, presenting in miniature the entire music drama of *Tristan und Isolde*.

The four music dramas comprising the cycle of *The Nibelungen Ring* (referring to the actual ring which brought disaster to all its owners) have no extended Overtures or Preludes, but there are orchestral passages which provide splendid concert material, and several of these have become popular as independent numbers.

Best known perhaps is the *Ride of the Valkyries*, from *Die Walküre*. It is an enormously exciting portrayal of a storm, with lightning flashes revealing the war-like daughters of Wotan, calling to each other and uttering their battle cries as they prepare to carry off the dead heroes to Valhalla, the abode of the gods. The music moves with a consistently galloping rhythm, the violins tossing off broken chords, against sustained trills from various instruments, all presenting a remarkable piece of orchestration. The main theme is actually a bugle call, given in both major and minor keys:

This music occurs at the start of Act III in *Die Walküre*.

The *Magic Fire Music,* which comes near the close of the same work, is often played in concert along with the wild *Ride of the Valkyries*. The flames around the couch of the sleeping Brünnhilde are suggested musically by a series of staccato figures, interrupted at times by the motives representing sleep and the hero Siegfried, who will eventually fight his way through the magic fire and awaken Brünnhilde from her sleep.

This music is generally preceded in concert by the strains of Wotan's Farewell.

Wagner spent many years in the work of writing *The Ring of the Nibelung,* with its Prelude, *Das Rheingold,* and the three great music dramas, *Die Walküre, Siegfried* and *Götterdämmerung*. It was interrupted for a period of twelve years, while he worked over *Die Meistersinger* and *Tristan und Isolde*. The text alone occupied the composer for four years, from 1848 to 1852, and the music was not completed until 1874. Separate performances of the *Rheingold* and *Walküre* were given in Munich in 1869 and 1870, by command of King Ludwig, Wagner's patron, and the entire cycle was finally performed at the festival theatre in Bayreuth during the summer of 1876.

A popular concert number is the *Entrance of the Gods into*

Valhalla, which comes at the end of the introductory music drama, *Das Rheingold.* Wotan, through stealing the golden treasure from the dwarf Alberich, who in turn had stolen it from the Rhine Maidens, has employed the Giants to build the great castle of Valhalla, as a permanent abode of the gods. The work is now completed, although the troubles of all concerned have scarcely begun.

Thor, god of thunder, hammers upon the rocks; lightning flashes and a storm breaks. As the clouds lift, the distant pile of Valhalla is revealed, with a rainbow bridge leading up to it. The gods and goddesses prepare to ascend to their home, as the wailing song of the Rhine Maidens is heard from the depths below. Here are the chief melodic materials:

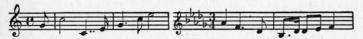

With *Die Walküre* supplying its *Ride of the Valkyries* and *Magic Fire Music* to the concert stage, the remaining dramas of the cycle add some imposing numbers to the orchestral repertoire. *Siegfried* contributes the *Waldweben* (*Forest Murmurs*), arranged by Wagner himself for concert performance from various portions of the second act. The sounds of the forest mingle with the definite bird-calls, which on the stage are eventually translated into words, as Siegfried learns the language of animals by having tasted the dragon's blood. Here the voice of the forest bird is represented by oboes, flutes and clarinets, and the operatic orchestration is considerably reduced for practical purposes. The melodic line of the bird song runs as follows:

Götterdämmerung contains a wealth of orchestral music that is well adapted to the concert hall. One frequently hears the combination of the *Dawn* music (which comes at the start of the music drama, right after the departure of the Norns) with *Siegfried's Rhine Journey*. This is the instrumental interlude which follows the scene between Siegfried and Brünnhilde in the first act of *Götterdämmerung*, during which a change of scene takes place. Siegfried has left his bride on the rock where he had found her, and now goes down the Rhine in search of adventure. The music of the interlude is built upon the hero's familiar horn call, with suggestions of the "Fire Music" and "Rhine Music" as well.

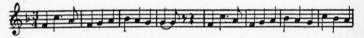

The climax of the entire cycle of the *Nibelungen Ring* comes in *Siegfried's Funeral March*, in which all the important motifs appear, some of them in entirely new forms. Most impressive is the metamorphosis of Siegfried's horn call, which is now heard as a broad, dramatic theme:

The *Funeral March* occurs on the stage after Siegfried had been killed by Hagen, when his dead body is born aloft on his shield. In concerts the *Immolation Scene* is often added, but this really needs a singer to make it effective.

One of the most popular of Wagner's orchestral works is the *Siegfried Idyl,* written as a Christmas and birthday gift for his wife Cosima in 1870. It is known as the *Treppenmusik* (Staircase Music) because its first performance was on the stairs of the villa Triebschen, near Lucerne, on Christmas morning. Siegfried Wagner, the son of Richard and Cosima (daughter of Franz Liszt and formerly the wife of Hans von Bülow) was then a little over a year and a half old.

Wagner had planned the *Siegfried Idyl* as a surprise for his wife, and everything was carried out with the greatest care and secrecy. Hans Richter rehearsed the orchestra, himself playing the short trumpet part as well as one of the violas. The entire instrumentation included two each of the upper strings, one cello, one bass viol, two clarinets, two horns and a flute, an oboe and a bassoon. The result is a significant answer to those who think that Wagner could write only for a huge orchestra.

The score of the *Siegfried Idyl* (often spelled *Idyll*) was not published until February, 1878, and the work had few if any public performances before that time. (Wagner conducted it privately at Mannheim December 20, 1871, and at the Ducal Palace in Meiningen, March 10, 1877.)

This is a tender and charming piece, quite different from the typical Wagnerian music drama. Its themes are mostly taken from the *Siegfried* of the stage, including the sleep motif, and it is not generally realized that the chief melody is an ingenious alteration of Siegfried's horn call:

(Compare this with the horn call itself, as given on page 180.)

There is also a lullaby, taken from an actual folk-song, *Schlaf', mein Kind* (Sleep, my child):

Wagner's final music drama was *Parsifal,* a "stage-consecration-festival play," composed at Bayreuth and for a long time heard only in that sacred place. The *Prelude* is often heard today as a concert number, and this had its first performance privately in the Villa Wahnfried, at Bayreuth, on Christmas day, 1878, as a birthday gift for Cosima. The first public performances were in July, 1882, and the score and parts were published in October of that year. (See *The Metropolitan Opera Guide* for the story of *Parsifal* and other Wagnerian music dramas.)

The *Prelude* to *Parsifal* begins with a broad melodic phrase, played in unison, without accompaniment, by the violins, cellos, English horn, clarinet and bassoon. It is generally known as the motif of the *Lord's Supper,* and is sung by mystic voices in the religious scene of the first act:

Trombones and trumpets announce the second theme, which represents the *Holy Grail* and is based upon the *Dresden Amen* of the church service:

This theme was also used by Mendelssohn in his *Reformation Symphony*.

With a mere change of tempo and rhythm, the third theme is introduced, again by the brass. This is known as the "Faith" motif, and it is played four times in succession, with changes of key:

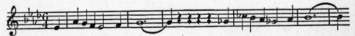

The remainder of the *Prelude* to *Parsifal* is built largely upon the opening theme of the "Lord's Supper," from which a new theme of suffering is also derived. On the concert stage the *Prelude* is generally paired with the *Good Friday Spell,* which carries on the atmosphere of mysticism and tender com-

passion. This music occurs in the last act of *Parsifal,* when
Gurnemanz and Kundry set out with Parsifal for Monsalvat.
It expresses the beauty of the awakening meadows and the
peacefulness of a spring day, but includes also reminders of
the Parsifal and Grail themes and the motif of Faith. The
chief melody, which has been described as a "hymn of thanksgiving," is played by the flute and the oboe, over muted strings:

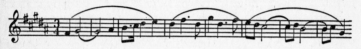

Wagner is said to have created some of these themes as early
as 1857.

A *Faust Overture* by Wagner is frequently heard in concert. It was intended as the first movement of a symphony
and was sketched in Paris in the darkest days of the composer's
poverty. The first performance was at Dresden, July 22, 1844.
A revised version was played in Zurich, Jan. 23, 1855.

The score contains a quotation from Goethe's *Faust* (lines
1566-71 of the First Part) and was originally called "Faust in
Solitude." The music presumably portrays the aged scholar
of the start of the drama, with a second theme which may refer
to Marguerite.

These are the most important orchestral works of Richard
Wagner in the concert repertoire, but many other excerpts
from his music dramas are heard from time to time, with the
inclusion of the vocal parts. There is an elaborate *Bacchanale*

which was inserted into the score of *Tannhäuser* long after its composition and is now often played with the Overture, which eventually led directly into it, this additional music representing a far more advanced style.

The *March of the Knights* from *Parsifal* is sometimes heard as a concert piece, with a melodic foundation of only four notes, C, G, A and E. Wagner also wrote three instrumental marches, which are now almost forgotten. They are known as the *Huldigungsmarsch*, the *Kaisermarsch* (celebrating the German victories of 1870 and first performed in Berlin, May 5, 1871, with a musical quotation from Luther's chorale, *A Mighty Fortress Is Our God*) and the *Centennial March*, written for Philadelphia's celebration in 1876 for a fee of $5000 (a definite case of inflation). The Overture to Wagner's early opera, *Die Feen* (The Fairies) still has an occasional performance. It dates from 1833-4, but Wagner never heard the work, as its first production (for reasons of purely historical interest) was in Munich in 1888, five years after the composer's death.

IV

MODERN CLASSICISTS

AFTER THE REBELLION against formalism which started with Beethoven and progressed through Schubert, Schumann, Mendelssohn, Berlioz, Liszt and Wagner, it was only natural that there should be a revival of the classic spirit, with the advantage that the new classicists could make use of all the devices and techniques which had been developed by their romantic predecessors. The symphonies and other absolute music written by the classic masters of the second half of the nineteenth century were something quite different from the formal works of Haydn, Mozart or even Beethoven. They had the freedom of the romantic school, yet they went far beyond its representatives in the skill and musicianship which they applied to the classic traditions. It is generally agreed that the ideal combination of the romantic and the classic in music was found in Johannes Brahms, who has rightly become one of the most popular of all symphonic composers.

JOHANNES BRAHMS
B. Hamburg, May 7, 1833; d. Vienna, April 3, 1897.

Here is a musician who lived a singularly uneventful life, but turned out consistently great music. As a boy Johannes Brahms improvised waltzes for the dancing sailors in Hamburg dives, meanwhile reading a book propped up in front of

185

him. He accompanied the violinist Remenyi as a young man and thus picked up much Hungarian gypsy music. Schumann early recognized him as a genius, but later Brahms was stupidly and unnecessarily set up as a rival to Wagner, even though their work was along entirely different lines, and for a long time this controversy was harmful to both.

Brahms was an excellent pianist and conductor as well as a composer of the first rank. He never married and he never wrote an opera. But he has to his credit four of the outstanding symphonies of orchestral literature, one of the greatest of all violin Concertos and two of similar importance for the piano, a wealth of chamber music, sonatas and piano pieces, two Overtures and other orchestral works, a *Requiem* and other choral music, and several volumes of remarkable songs.

Brahms has been called a cerebral composer, and for many years it was the fashion to consider his music abstruse and difficult, even dull. Today it is acclaimed as full of sensuous beauty in addition to its impressive musical scholarship. The traditional sign "Exit in case of Brahms" has been replaced with one that reads "By Special Request" and the poor joke of the turn of the century, "What *are* Brahms anyway?" long ago gave way to sincere interest, enthusiasm and understanding on the part of an ever-growing audience. Brahms belongs with Bach and Beethoven in the mighty triumvirate of the "Three B's."

THE BRAHMS SYMPHONIES

It was characteristic of Brahms' careful and studious workmanship, as well as his modesty, that he refused to attempt a symphony until he was well over forty years old. His first work in this form is listed as opus 68 and the key is C minor, the same as that of Beethoven's Fifth. The first performance was by the Grand Duke's orchestra at Carlsruhe, November 4,

1876, with Dessoff conducting from manuscript. Brahms himself conducted the symphony a few days later at Mannheim. It had its first American performance in Boston, January 3, 1878, by the Harvard Musical Association, when it was severely criticized.

As early as 1854 Schumann was urging Brahms to write a symphony, with Beethoven as a model. After hearing Beethoven's choral Ninth, the young composer did attempt something in the symphonic form, but he eventually used this material for his piano concerto in D minor (see page 202) and for a chorus in the *German Requiem*. Brahms is quoted as saying "I shall never compose a symphony! You have no conception of how the likes of us feel when we hear the tramp of a giant like him (Beethoven) behind us." But when the First Symphony of Brahms was completed, Hans von Bülow called it "the tenth," as the logical successor to the nine masterpieces of Beethoven.

The first movement of this symphony starts with an Introduction in fairly slow 6-8 time, un poco sostenuto, the kettledrum beating portentously in groups of three, suggesting the knocking on the door by Fate, which Beethoven had put into a rhythmic pattern of three short tones and a long one (see page 88).

This soon turns into a belligerent Allegro, with this outstanding theme:

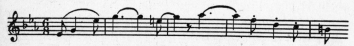

This material develops into a quietly melodious version in major key, which is eventually interrupted by a vicious tearing at the strings, resulting in this defiant theme:

A broader melody also appears, both in major and in minor key:

The second movement is slow and full of melancholy. The key is E major, and this is the opening theme:

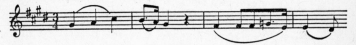

Over a syncopated accompaniment in the strings, the oboe soon sings a tranquil melody that clearly foretells the first strain of the third movement to come:

This parallel is even more clearly indicated in major key, and its purpose becomes evident when the third section, un poco allegretto e grazioso, begins thus:

The quiet calm of this music, introduced by the clarinets, gives way to a distinct reminiscence of Beethoven's Fate motif which develops into the second theme of the movement:

The Finale begins with a wailing cry from the orchestra, followed by mysterious progressions of pizzicato effects, reaching several climaxes. Suddenly a solo horn is heard, giving out a melody which Brahms heard in the Alps, and also suggesting the tones of the Westminster Chime:

A choral motif follows, intoned by trombones and bassoons, and later to be heard in a great climax of the brass:

All this is merely an Introduction to the main theme of the *Finale*, a broad, sustained melody, which in its second part suggests the corresponding measures of Beethoven's choral setting of Schiller's *Ode to Joy* in the Finale of his Ninth Symphony (see page 102):

The similarity of these melodies must be considered purely accidental, although Brahms may have been paying a deliberate tribute to the "giant" in whose footsteps he was following and whom he so greatly revered.

Toward the close of the movement the Alpine song of the horn is heard again, with a variety of treatment, and finally the brass choir bursts forth with a climactic utterance of the Chorale quoted above, whose effect has been compared with "the opening of the Heavens." From there on to the end the symphony is completely triumphant, as was its precursor in the same key by Beethoven, ending in the solid, uncompromising tonality of C major.

The Second Brahms Symphony, in D major, op. 73, was composed in the summer of 1877, about the time that the first was published. Hans Richter conducted the first public performance on Dec. 30 of that year, and Brahms himself conducted it at the Leipzig Gewandhaus January 10, 1878.

This Second Symphony is distinctly pastoral in spirit and may be considered the clearest and easiest of the four at a first hearing.

It begins with a motto of four notes, D, C-sharp, D and A (below) which may be heard all through the opening movement, leading immediately into the first theme, built on the tones of the D major chord:

This leads to a bridge which is really an elaboration of the basic idea and serves chiefly to decorate and develop the four-note motto:

The actual second theme then enters in minor key, introduced by the violas and cellos, a broad, singing melody, possibly influenced by the gypsy music with which Brahms had become so familiar:

These materials are developed in Sonata form, with a recapitulation of the chief melodies and a Coda of great originality, the movement ending softly on a D major chord.

The slow movement has another broad melody, of rather uncertain outline, but great emotional power:

A syncopated contrast creates the equivalent of a second theme:

The music flows steadily onward to a Coda, again ending in a soft chord.

The third movement, Allegretto grazioso, quasi andantino, is really a Scherzo, although the tempo is not particularly fast. The wood-wind announces the first tune, with the cellos plucking out a rhythmic accompaniment:

The triple time suddenly changes to a very rapid 2-4 Presto, producing an entirely new effect with the same melodic basis:

Still another change brings fast scale passages and syncopations in 3-8 time, in the manner of a Trio:

Toward the close the main tune wavers between major and minor, bringing in new and appealing harmonies, with a final leap of an octave to indicate the finish, which is once more on soft chords.

The Finale, Allegro con spirito, starts with an exuberant theme that promises a happy ending to the symphony:

A second theme produces an even greater feeling of satisfaction, with a broadly sweeping march time:

The development deals mostly with the first theme, experimenting with both rhythms and harmonies before going into a straightforward recapitulation, to arrive eventually at a brilliant close in D major.

The Third Symphony of Brahms, in F major, op. 90, is now considered by many the best of the four. Certainly it is the most consistently appealing, and its popularity has grown steadily, with the continued proof of its wearing qualities. This great work was begun in 1882 and finished in the summer of 1883. Its first performance was at a Vienna Philharmonic concert, December 2, 1883, with Richter conducting. Both Richter and Hanslick gave this symphony the title of Eroica. But Max Kalbeck says it was inspired by the statue of Germania near Rüdesheim; Joachim found the story of Hero and Leander in it, and Clara Schumann called it "a forest idyl." Actually it is a fine piece of absolute music, without any waste notes.

Again there is a motto at the start, consisting of the three notes F, A-flat and the F an octave above. Brahms indicated that these letters represented the words "Frei aber froh" ("Free but joyous"), a variation of Joachim's "Frei aber einsam" ("Free but lonesome"). Chords built on these notes lead right into the opening theme, of exultant character:

A second theme, sung as a duet by clarinet and bassoon, over a gently syncopated accompaniment, has the effect of a lullaby:

The development shows interesting treatment of this material, with the second theme appearing in minor key, emotionalized by cellos and bassoons. The Coda ends tranquilly with descending notes on the chord of F major, a reminder of both the opening theme and the key of the symphony.

The second movement starts with an Andante pastoral theme, played by the wood-wind in the manner of actual shepherds' pipes, and this really sums up the melodic material:

The third movement is definitely romantic, almost sentimental, with an opening melody of Schumannesque character sung by the cellos, with decorations by the other strings. (It actually suggests the Romanze of Schumann's Fourth Symphony. See page 140.)

A second theme is slightly reminiscent of the Allegretto of the Second Brahms Symphony, including the treatment of the accompaniment:

This is twice interrupted by a passage that deserves to be quoted independently as an example of sheer and characteristic beauty:

When the first melody returns it is given to the solo French horn, with decorations by the oboe.

The Finale is definitely heroic. It opens in a mood of suppressed excitement, rather mysteriously and portentously:

The mystery is heightened by a distinct reminiscence of the Fate motif used by Beethoven in his Fifth Symphony (see page 88):

There are clear indications of a terrific struggle, perhaps once more between man and Fate, and another theme expresses the unquestionable spirit of triumph:

This is played by the cellos in a cross rhythm of three against two. It leads to an even more exultant series of phrases in the strings:

One climax follows another, with Brahms apparently inexhaustible in his musical resources. A treatment of the opening theme of the Finale by muted strings in triple time creates new interest near the close. Then suddenly the opening motto of the first movement returns, much as it did when finishing

that movement, and the symphony ends with another glorification of the F major chord, in a calm serenity that represents the composer at his best, a characteristic Amen to a
typical work, entirely free from the conventional noise that
closes so many symphonies.

The Fourth (and last) Symphony of Brahms was written
in the summers of 1884 and 1885, and the manuscript was
nearly destroyed by fire just before its completion. The key is
E minor and the opus number 98. The first performance was at
Meiningen, October 25, 1885, with the composer conducting.
It was also played on the occasion of his last appearance in
public, March 7, 1897, less than a month before his death, by
the Philharmonic Orchestra in Vienna.

The symphony as a whole is more austere and forbidding
than the other three, harder to grasp at a first hearing, yet full
of beauty and impressively solid in its workmanship. The start
is almost naively simple, immediately announcing a theme
which is built upon combinations of two notes at various levels
of pitch:

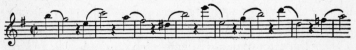

The second theme has two parts, the first leaping boldly to
unexpected intervals, the second broadly displaying the solid
tone of the strings:

All these materials are used with great variety of effect in development and recapitulation, a mere slowing of time values

often serving as a complete contrast. In the Coda the two-tone pattern of the opening alternates in an almost startling progression between treble chords and bass octaves, in melodic imitation.

The slow movement which follows, Andante moderato, is a fine example of Brahms in a tenderly romantic mood of untroubled serenity. The melody is suggested immediately, in the key of C major, but actually enters in E major, after a surprising change in which the third interval suddenly becomes the key-note:

The second theme is a broad chorale, sung by the cellos through a soft tracery of orchestral patterns:

Toward the close of the movement there is a momentary return to the opening key of C major, but immediately modulating into E major again, to create an astonishingly effective ending.

The third movement, Allegro giocoso, is a real Scherzo, starting off with a cheerful scale tune, comically interrupted by dismal chords and rolling drums, but coming right back to continue its undaunted course:

A subordinate melody gracefully carries out the implications of folk-music already suggested:

An individual treatment of the first theme by the wood-wind stands out in the development, and there is much arguing between chords representing the cheerful and the gloomier aspects of the music. At the finish there is a return to the key of C major, with a concluding gesture of complete nonchalance.

The Finale is strictly a Passacaglia, consisting of Variations on a theme generally appearing in the bass. This theme is little more than an ascending scale of E minor, the basic key of the symphony:

There are actually thirty-four Variations on this theme, two of which, however, amount to little more than restatements of the theme itself. In most cases the treatment of the basic melody is amazingly ingenious. Sometimes it appears only by implication, but its course can always be followed through the eight measures which it regularly covers. One of the most effective Variations is the Twelfth, in which the flute plays a fascinating countermelody:

Another beautiful moment comes in a solemn trombone passage (Variation 14), which creates an entirely new melodic effect in major key, while still implying the minor scale as a foundation:

The technical complexities of this unique Finale are easily overlooked in the face of such obvious and impressive beauties.

OTHER ORCHESTRAL WORKS OF BRAHMS

Two Overtures by Brahms are frequently heard in concert, of completely contrasting character, the *Academic Festival*, op. 80, and the *Tragic*, op. 81. Both were written at Ischl in the summer of 1880. Actually the *Tragic Overture* was composed and performed before the lighter *Academic Festival*, being heard for the first time at Vienna's fourth Philharmonic concert in the fall of 1880. It was published in 1881.

The *Tragic Overture* does not deal with any particular tragedy or tragic hero, but rather with the spirit of Tragedy itself. It is impersonal in character, yet full of deep emotion. The chief theme is this:

The *Academic Festival Overture* was written in acknowledgement of the degree of Doctor of Philosophy, bestowed upon Brahms by the University of Breslau, March 11, 1879. Its first performance, however, was nearly two years later, with Brahms himself conducting in the presence of the Rector, the Senate and members of the Philosophical Faculty of the University. The composer called it "a very jolly potpourri of students' songs," and brought in several of the best-known melodies from the college song-books of Germany.

Beginning with a soft and mysterious Introduction, slightly reminiscent of the *Rakoczy March* (see page 160), the Overture takes its first real theme from the Binzer song, *Wir hatten gebauet ein stattliches Haus* (We had built a stately house), announced by the trumpets in a truly dignified fashion:

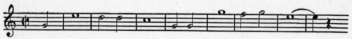

The beautiful melody of *Der Landesvater* (The Country Father) is introduced by the second violins:

Then comes the familiar *Fuchslied* (Freshman Song), basically the same tune as *The Farmer in the Dell,* presented with comic effect by the two bassoons:

The Overture reaches its climax in the universally known *Gaudeamus Igitur* (Let us then rejoice), a very old Latin song of Europe's wandering scholars, here played majestically by the full orchestra, with considerable ornamentation:

Another popular orchestral piece by Brahms is the set of *Variations on a Theme by Haydn,* op. 56a, also known as a composition for two pianos. It is not certain which version came first, but it may well have been the orchestral. Brahms played the piano work with Clara Schumann at Bonn in August, 1873, for an audience of friends, and it was published in November of that year.

The theme was originally called *Chorale St. Antoni,* occurring in a Haydn Divertimento for wind instruments in B-flat (two oboes, two horns, three bassoons and a serpent). Brahms announces the theme in a similar instrumentation, substituting a double bassoon for the third bassoon and serpent, and adding cellos and bass viols to the accompaniment.

There are eight Variations and a Finale, the latter using a phrase adapted from the theme in Passacaglia style, as a ground bass. At the climax of the Finale the complete theme returns in the strings, with the wood-wind playing scale passages and the brass supplying the harmony. It is then repeated by the wind instruments with a running accompaniment by the strings. These *Variations* have been given programmatic significance in connection with the temptation of St. Anthony, but it is best to think of them merely as excellent examples of scholarship in absolute music.

For early practice in orchestration Brahms wrote two *Serenades*, op. 11 and 16, dated 1858 and 1859, strongly influenced by Mozart and perhaps inspired by the performances of the wind players in the Detmold Orchestra. The first of these *Serenades* was introduced at Hamburg, March 28, 1859, under the direction of Joachim. Later it was rescored for full orchestra and had its first performance in this form at Hanover, March 3, 1860, with Brahms himself conducting. It was published in the same year.

The basic key of this first *Serenade* is D major, in which it begins, Allegro molto. The second movement is a *Scherzo* in D minor, and the following slow movement is marked Adagio non troppo, in B-flat. There are two Minuets (G major and D minor), a second Scherzo, and a final Rondo (Allegro) in the opening key of D major.

The second *Serenade* is in A major, also published in 1860, and first performed by the Hamburg Philharmonic Orchestra February 10th of that year. (This was the first composition by Brahms to be played in America. The date of this performance was February 1, 1862, by the New York Philharmonic, under Carl Bergmann.)

There are no violins in the instrumentation of this *Serenade*, violas, cellos and bass viols supplying the string tone for two flutes, piccolo, two oboes, two clarinets, two bassoons and two horns. There are five movements, Allegro moderato, in A, Scherzo, Vivace, in C, Adagio non troppo, A minor, Quasimenuetto, in D (6-4 time), and a final Rondo (Allegro) in A.

THE BRAHMS CONCERTOS

Brahms wrote a violin Concerto in D major, op. 77, the same key as Beethoven's, and there is an eternal argument as to which is the greater of the two. Admittedly they stand at the top in the literature of the violin.

Brahms composed his Concerto during the summer and fall of 1878. It was dedicated to Joachim and first played by him, with the composer conducting, at a Gewandhaus concert in Leipzig, on New Year's Day of the year 1879. Two of the original movements were later rejected, the Adagio being completely rewritten and the Scherzo abandoned entirely. Brahms may have intended to use these materials in a second violin Concerto, which was never written.

The opening theme of the Brahms violin concerto is built on the tones of the D major chord, somewhat in the manner of the start of his Second Symphony and the song, *Sapphic Ode*, both of which are in the same key:

This is given out by the orchestra, which also introduces a contrastingly violent second theme:

The solo violin enters with a cadenza-like passage in octaves and then takes up the first theme in the upper reaches of the

E string. Another melody of great beauty stands out both in the violin and in the orchestra:

Near the close of the first movement the soloist has an elaborate Cadenza, originally supplied by Joachim, with later soloists, such as Kreisler and Heifetz, writing their own.

The chief melody of the slow second movement is introduced by the oboe and then repeated with decorations by the solo violin high in the upper register:

The Finale is the most conventional of the three movements, with the soloist immediately playing a fast theme in double stops, suggesting a gypsy background, with trills in the woodwind and generally heavy orchestration:

The two piano Concertos of Brahms are also among the outstanding masterpieces written for that instrument. The first, in D minor, op. 15, dating from as early as 1854, when the composer was only twenty-one years old, was projected as a symphony (see page 187). Brahms, however, wisely decided that he was not yet ready for this supreme form of absolute music, and turned the three completed movements into a sonata for two pianos, which he often played privately with Clara Schumann and with Julius Otto Grimm, who had helped him with his orchestral problems. It was Grimm who suggested the further change into a piano Concerto, and this was the final form of the first two movements, Maestoso and Adagio. The opening thematic material is as follows, mostly in the strings:

The Finale is a Rondo: Allegro non troppo, with this opening theme boldly announced by the solo piano:

The piano Concerto in D minor was first played at Hanover, January 22, 1859, with Brahms as soloist and Joachim conducting. Brahms played it again at the Leipzig Gewandhaus, five days later. On both occasions the critics and public failed to respond, and Brahms himself called the Concerto "a brilliant and decided failure." It was published in 1861.

Actually the second piano Concerto of Brahms, in B-flat, op. 83, is a far greater work, representing the maturity of his style and the summit of his creative powers. Vladimir Horowitz, who has both played and recorded it with his father-in-law, Toscanini, calls it the greatest music ever written for the piano.

This Concerto was definitely influenced by two visits to Italy and is full of melody and the joyous spirit of springtime. It may contain the Scherzo movement originally intended for the violin Concerto. Brahms completed this masterpiece for the piano at a villa near Vienna in the summer of 1881. It was played for the first time, from manuscript, at Budapest, November 9, 1881, with the composer at the piano.

The first movement, in a complex Sonata form, opens with the immediate statement of the first theme by the solo horn, followed by the flute and other wood-winds in the answering strain:

The piano, which merely added rolling arpeggios to the opening melody, breaks in with a stormy interlude, tempting the orchestra to an equally vehement restatement of the horn theme, greatly transformed, in heroic mood. A second theme of lyric quality soon enters and supplies much of the body of the movement:

The second movement, Allegro appassionato, is in the nature of an Intermezzo, starting vigorously in the solo piano, with a suggestion of free improvisation:

A tranquil theme of very simple construction presents an effective contrast:

Later a third theme adds still further contrast, in a vigorous triple time:

The third movement is a slow Andante, with the main melody sung at the start by a solo cello over subdued orchestral accompaniment. A definite reminiscence of the Brahms song, *Immer leiser wird mein Schlummer* (Ever softer grows my slumber), may be noticed in this broad melody:

The Finale is a buoyant, highly original Rondo, Allegretto grazioso, with five distinct melodic ideas. Its opening theme has a bubbling, effervescent quality which is irresistible:

A more plaintive note creeps into this bit of melody:

Then comes a highly emotional and expressive theme of yearning, again reminiscent of Brahms as a songwriter, with a suggestion of Hungarian gypsy background:

A contemplative calm serves as a contrast in the next motive:

Finally the buoyant spirit returns in another gay melody which keeps the Concerto sparkling with a wealth of brilliant decoration by the piano to the close:

A double Concerto for violin, cello and orchestra by Brahms is less frequently heard than the solo works. Its key is A major and the opus number 102. The first public performance was by Joachim and Hausmann, for whom it was written, October 18, 1887, at Cologne, with Brahms conducting. It was published in 1888. Max Bendix and Victor Herbert (an excellent cellist) introduced this double Concerto to America, January 5, 1889, in a New York concert conducted by Theodore Thomas.

The work has the quality of the classic Concerto Grosso, with the two soloists representing the concertino or small group, contrasting with the orchestra as a whole. This effect is enhanced through the frequent double-stops played by both violin and cello, often creating the impression that a string quartet is playing.

PETER ILITCH TSCHAIKOWSKY

B. Votkinsk, May 7, 1840; d. St. Petersburg, Nov. 6, 1893.

There are many different opinions on the music of Tschaikowsky. Even his name is found in several different spellings, some insisting on a v instead of the w (which is pronounced like an f), and some starting the final name Tchai or even Chai. The first and second names are sometimes found as Piotr and Ilyitch.

There are those who consider Tschaikowsky an obvious, even vulgar, sentimentalist. To others he represents a genius in symphonic music to be ranked close to Beethoven and ahead of Brahms. Recently Tin Pan Alley has discovered him, and Tschaikowsky has supplied the "Schmalz" for a number of deservedly popular tunes.

Tschaikowsky was late in getting started as a composer, trying his hand unsuccessfully at civil service before entering the St. Petersburg Conservatory of Music at twenty-two and graduating there four years later, with considerable help from Anton Rubinstein.

The pianist's brother Nicholas gave Tschaikowsky a badly paid job at the new Conservatory in Moscow and eventually gained for him the interest of a wealthy widow, Nadejda von Meck, with whom the composer carried on a long and famous correspondence. They never met in person, but she practically supported him for the greater part of his creative life.

Tschaikowsky's music has been called consistently melancholy, but this is not a fair description, as he expressed a great variety of emotion, and was not only an outstanding melodist but one of the greatest of all masters of orchestration. His output includes six symphonies, eleven operas, Concertos for the piano and the violin (among the most popular of their kind), songs, chamber music, ballets, piano pieces, and such effective orchestral works as the *Nutcracker Suite,* the *Romeo and Juliet Fantasie Overture, Francesca da Rimini,* the *1812 Overture, Marche Slave,* etc.

Tschaikowsky toured the United States in 1891, at the height of his fame, conducting his own works in New York, Philadelphia and Baltimore. His death from cholera, two years later, at the age of 53, has often been considered suicide, since he deliberately drank unboiled water during an epidemic in St. Petersburg (now Leningrad).

THE TSCHAIKOWSKY SYMPHONIES

The first three symphonies of Tschaikowsky are seldom heard, although the second contains some attractive music and is well worthy of performance. The First Symphony, written while the composer was teaching at the Moscow Conservatory, in 1866, had the title *Winter Day-dreams*. It was criticized by Anton Rubinstein and coldly received in St. Petersburg, but met with some success in Moscow at its first performance there (February, 1868).

The Second Symphony, bearing the name of *Little Russia*, and containing folk melodies of the Ukraine, appeared in 1872. The third is known as *Polish*, for no particular reason, and dates from 1875. It is mostly light and graceful music, with a noisy *Finale*, meeting with more success than its predecessors, but still far below the standards that were set by Tschaikowsky in his last three symphonies.

The Fourth Symphony, in F minor, op. 36, marks the beginning of the composer's friendship with Mme. von Meck and his consequent release from financial difficulties. It is dedicated to his benefactress, described as "my best friend," and it was composed mostly in 1877, running into January of 1878. The first performance was in Moscow, February 22nd of that year, with Nicholas Rubinstein conducting.

In his letters to Mme. von Meck the composer gave a complete program to this Fourth Symphony, comparing it with the "Fate" program of Beethoven's Fifth. (For a complete account of this program, see the author's *Stories Behind the World's Great Music*, page 234 ff.)

There is a definite motto at the start, clearly a challenge to Fate, uttered by horns and bassoons and later heard in various forms, giving the entire symphony a cyclic form.

This portentous Introduction leads naturally into a theme composed mostly of syncopated scale passages:

After much expansion of this material, a second theme enters, rather mocking in character, with gently satirical chromatic runs by various members of the wood-wind:

There are two subordinate themes, acting as interludes, and the development section begins with a loud reminder of the opening motto, played by the trumpets over a long drum roll. All the melodic material is treated in considerable detail, and after a recapitulation the Coda enters with another tremendous blast on the notes of the motto, rushing on to the close with a new version of the second theme and ending with octaves on F.

The second movement, Andantino in modo di canzona, begins with an ingratiating melody sung by the oboe in plaintive style, but going immediately into a more robust strain, emphasized by the strings:

The second theme is approached through distinct echoes of the chief tune of the first movement, but assumes an individual character, emerging as a straightforward march melody:

The return of the first theme introduces a novel touch in using the chromatic scale passages of the first movement as decorations, with the flute and clarinet alternating. The Coda interestingly combines the two parts of the main melody, with the courageous chords interrupting the plaintive notes in a musical picture of indecision.

The third movement is a highly original Scherzo, starting with all the strings plucked in a rapid pizzicato. Tschaikowsky himself described this movement as representing "vague thoughts, dreams and visions" of those who are trying to forget the cares of life and enjoy themselves. Here is the main pizzicato theme:

The wood-winds enter in the Trio, with a gay tune suggestive of folk-music:

This is interrupted by the brass with a slower version of the pizzicato theme, played staccato, with very short notes:

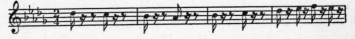

With the wood-wind and brass competing for attention, the strings make several false starts and finally run through the entire pizzicato section once more. A whimsical Coda finds all three choirs in competition, each insisting on its individual tone-color, with the strings finally winning out by a shade.

The Finale opens with a noisy announcement of the descending scale, reminiscent of Handel's hymn-tune, *Joy to the World*:

Sustained tones by the horns then introduce the main theme of the movement, a literal quotation of the Russian folk-song known as *The Birch Tree*:

This tune is decorated in various ways, finally appearing brazenly in the bass, while the strings play it four times as fast up above. The motto suddenly rings out again, loudly and confidently, in the brass choir, and another echo of the first movement leads to an essentially new melody, which increases in volume and importance toward the close:

The symphony ends triumphantly in the solid key of F major.

Tschaikowsky's Fifth Symphony was written in 1888 and had its first performance in St. Petersburg on November 17th of that year, with the composer conducting. The immediate reception was unfavorable, and Tschaikowsky was depressed by its apparent lack of success, asking his patroness if he were "played out" and comparing the new work despondently with the Fourth Symphony, which he considered much better (and perhaps with justice). The Fifth Symphony, in E minor, op. 64, has, however, become one of the most popular in the entire orchestral literature and is heard today more often than the Sixth.

It is again a Fate symphony, and the program is fairly obvious, representing once more the struggle of man against unseen forces. Tschaikowsky begins his Fifth Symphony, as he did his Fourth, with a motto, which is actually an extended melody in minor key, introduced by the clarinets, and later to be turned into a major climax:

The main theme of this movement is said to be based on a Polish folk-tune, and is introduced by clarinet and bassoon, again in minor key:

There is a plaintive second theme, given to the strings:

After considerable development, with the occasional introduction of new materials, a long Coda ends pianissimo, with a dying tremolo.

The slow movement begins with an introductory minor scale, played in chords, after which the solo horn sings a melody that has become familiar through its use in the popular song, *Moon Love*. (It was also used some years ago as a musical theme for the play *The Song of Songs*.)

A second theme contains a distinct note of optimism:

These two melodies supply most of the material of the movement, with a tentative reminder of the motto just before the
Coda, which ends in a long, soft chord.

The third movement is a waltz, unique in symphonic literature. It takes the place of the old-fashioned Minuet, or the
later Scherzo. This is the melody, which is variously treated:

At the very end of this movement the foreboding tones of
the motto are heard again, still in minor key. But at the start
of the Finale this introductory theme suddenly appears in
major, and the listener realizes for the first time that its apparent pessimism can easily be given a completely triumphant
character.

A subordinate theme carries out the triumphant mood, over
a strongly marked, rhythmic accompaniment:

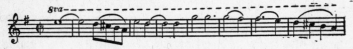

After some elaborate development, the motto is once more
heard in its ominous minor key, but this is its last gasp. The
full orchestra starts an overwhelming march, with two introductory measures of accompaniment, and this final version
exhibits the full possibilities of the motto as a major melody,
sweeping on to a majestic finish. Near the close a surprising
reminder of the first theme of the first movement is trumpeted
by the brass, also in major key, and with this final bond to
emphasize the cyclic form, the symphony ends gloriously on E
major chords.

For a long time the most popular of Tschaikowsky's works was the Sixth Symphony, in B minor, op. 74, known as the *Pathétique*. It was his swan song, and he himself liked it better than anything he had previously written. Today this symphony no longer creates hysteria, but it has taken its place among the great and lasting inspirations of orchestral music.

The Sixth Symphony was composed during the final year of Tschaikowsky's life, 1893. It had its first performance at St. Petersburg on October 28th of that year, the composer conducting (evidently not to the best advantage). It was coolly received, but made an overwhelming impression when conducted by Napravnik nearly a month later (November 18th). But by that time Tschaikowsky was dead. While he felt instinctively that it was his best work, he never knew of the adulation it was ultimately to receive.

When the music was ready for the publisher, Tschaikowsky wanted a title beyond the mere number, stating definitely that it was "a program symphony." His brother Modeste first suggested the name "Tragic," and finally hit upon "Pathetic," which the composer gratefully accepted. Whatever program he may have had in mind, it was decidedly melancholy and pessimistic.

The first movement opens with a mournful strain, in the manner of a motto, played by the deep notes of the double bassoon:

The opening notes of this doleful motive soon supply the start of the actual first theme, which is lively and courageous in character:

After considerable expansion, with consistent emphasis on the basic four notes of the start, the strings introduce a second theme, of lyric quality, combining pathos with optimism:

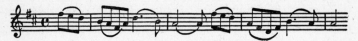

This leads directly into still more thematic material, with wood-winds alternating in the melody, imitated in the bass, over a sprightly accompaniment:

The exposition ends quite softly, and is interrupted by a sudden and startling crash, which sends the development off at top speed, mostly on snatches of the first theme. When the Coda is reached, a repeated scale of B major serves as the basis of a new and solemn theme, played by the brass:

The second movement, Allegro con grazia, is practically unique in its sustained use of a 5-4 beat, actually representing alternating twos and threes. The effect is one of great charm and originality.

After several variations of this tune, with some counter-melody, a subordinate theme brings back the mood of melancholy which had prevailed in so much of the first movement:

The more cheerful melody is repeated, but the movement ends on the note of sorrow.

There is decided contrast in the third movement, which is in effect a triumphal march, Allegro molto vivace, comparable to the Finale of Beethoven's Fifth Symphony. But Tschaikowsky employs the individual device of building his main theme gradually from mere snatches of the melody. At the start one hears nothing but galloping triplets in the strings, softly at first, and gradually becoming louder. Then from various instruments short phrases are heard, easily distinguished by their common rhythmic pattern, ending always in a decided syncopation, and these phrases become steadily more prominent. Finally after a variety of experiments the complete theme emerges:

This is really all the melodic material that the movement requires, but its treatment is full of invention and high spirits.

After this gay and confident Scherzo, the Finale plunges into the depths of despair, an unhappy ending without parallel in symphonic literature. The start, Adagio lamentoso, is a terrific wail of human disappointment and self-pity:

Each time that this strain appears it is given a more despairing effect. The more melodious second theme, in major key, does little to relieve the prevailing gloom:

Throughout the rest of the symphony this second theme of the Finale is the more prominent, but it also descends eventually to the depths, in minor key, with muttered syncopations in the bass. At the close the effect is completely tragic, rather than merely pathetic, completing the most thorough expression of introspective misery in the entire literature of music.

TSCHAIKOWSKY'S SMALLER ORCHESTRAL WORKS

One of the best and most popular of all the works of Tschaikowsky is also one of his earliest, the *Romeo and Juliet Fantasie Overture*. It was written at the suggestion of Balakireff, a ringleader in the group of five Russians at that time striving for a nationalistic expression and a revival of their native folk-music. (See pages 258-282.)

This composition belongs to the year 1869, but was later twice revised, unquestionably to its advantage. Nicholas Rubinstein introduced it in Moscow, March 16, 1870, and it was published in its revised form in 1871. A second edition, published in 1881, contained still further revisions.

Tschaikowsky had evidently intended to write an opera on the subject of Romeo and Juliet, and there exists a duet for soprano and tenor, representing the famous second balcony scene, and containing the most important themes of the *Fantasie Overture*.

At the start of this orchestral piece, clarinets and bassoons are heard in solemn harmonies, suggesting the character of Friar Laurence. Soon the music grows exciting, with clashing cymbals and much syncopation. This clearly describes the fighting of the Montagues and the Capulets, and it gives way in turn to the two love themes which provide the most memorable melodies of the Overture. One of these themes has become almost too familiar through the popular song, *Our Love:*

The other depends for its effect on harmonies rather than the melodic line, using mostly muted strings for its expression:

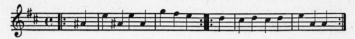

There is a return to the music of strife and brawling, with the soft love theme once more asserting itself and leading to a climactic repetition of the sentimental melody of Romeo. At the close the muffled beat of drums, with bass viols pizzicato, would seem to indicate the death of the lovers. Romeo's theme is heard in a final wailing imitation, and soft chords of the wood-wind bring the *Fantasie Overture* to an end.

Less popular than the *Romeo and Juliet*, but sometimes credited with greater musical value, is Tschaikowsky's *Francesca da Rimini*, a tone poem perhaps influenced by Liszt's *Dante Symphony*, but based directly on the famous episode of Paolo and Francesca in Dante's *Divine Comedy* itself. Its first performance was conducted by Nicholas Rubinstein in Moscow, March 9, 1877. Here is its most important theme (recently turned into a popular song by Alec Templeton):

Tschaikowsky wrote a number of minor works for orchestra that are practically never heard today. These include an early Overture to Ostrowsky's drama, *The Thunderstorm*, a Fantasia on Shakespeare's *Tempest*, a *Hamlet Overture*, a symphonic ballad, *Le Voyevode*, and a *Manfred* which the composer called "a symphony in four pictures after the dramatic poem of Byron." These are all examples of program music, of varying degrees of interest, with *Manfred* perhaps the most significant, dramatically and musically.

The *Overture Solenelle, 1812*, however, is still a popular number in the orchestral repertoire, even though the composer said of it "I wrote it without much love, on which account it is probably without much artistic value." This well-known *Overture* is a musical description of Napoleon's attack on Moscow, using the tunes of the *Marseillaise* and the Czarist national anthem (also known as *Hail, Pennsylvania*) to stage an exciting tonal battle, with the Russian air finally triumphing. There is much noise of drums and bells, sometimes supplemented by actual cannon shots, especially in outdoor performances. The Overture contains one broad melody, of religious significance, similar in effect to the main theme of Sibelius' later *Finlandia*. (See page 344.)

Equally popular, or even more so, is the *Marche Slave*, written at the request of Nicholas Rubinstein, and first played at a benefit concert for the Serbian victims of Turkish aggression, with an obvious appeal for all those who wished to involve Russia in a war with Turkey. The main theme of this march is a folk-tune of Serbian origin, used also by Cesar Cui as the basis of his popular *Orientale:*

There is a *Suite* called *Mozartiana* by Tschaikowsky, of potential popularity, but almost never played in public. Far better known is his *Italian Caprice,* op. 45, which contains some excellent folk-tunes, of which this is a sample:

This lively piece was written at Rome in the winter of 1880. The trumpet fanfare at the start is a cavalry signal, heard by the composer at the barracks, and the Finale is a brilliant Tarantella.

The music of Tschaikowsky's ballets, particularly *The Lake of Swans* and *The Sleeping Beauty,* is occasionally heard in orchestral concerts. It is not always realized also that the ever-popular *Nutcracker Suite* was originally a ballet. It was produced thus for the first time on December 17, 1892, along with Tschaikowsky's one-act opera, *Iolanthe.* Both were complete failures.

But when the composer strung together the best numbers from this ballet in the form of a Suite, it was immediately successful, and every number had to be repeated. The themes are among Tschaikowsky's best known today, and the story behind the *Nutcracker Suite* scarcely needs retelling. It is all about little Marie and her Christmas-Eve party, after which she dreams of the battle between the toys, led by the nutcracker, and the mice, whose King is finally killed when Marie throws her slipper at him. The nutcracker then turns into a Prince, who takes Marie to the land of the Sugar-Plum Fairy, where various dances are staged in her honor. These dances form the greater part of the *Nutcracker Suite.*

It opens with an Overture Mimature, establishing the Christmas spirit, violins and flutes carrying the silvery theme:

One of the best of the succeeding sections is the dainty Dance of the Sugar-Plum Fairy. Here for the first time the celesta was used in orchestral music, with a bass clarinet for contrast. The tune is charmingly graceful:

There is also a gay and fantastic March of the Toys, built upon this theme:

An Arabian Dance, of Oriental flavor, makes clever use of the bassoon and English horn. The Russian Dance is a Trepak.

A Chinese Dance uses a novel combination of flute, piccolo and bassoon, and this is followed by one of the most popular of all the numbers in the *Nutcracker Suite*, the Dance of the Mirlitons or toy pipes. A realistic effect is secured by using three flutes against pizzicato strings, with decorations by the piccolo. Here is the theme:

The Finale of the *Nutcracker Suite* is the familiar Waltz of the Flowers (appearing with an entirely different program in Walt Disney's *Fantasia*). This waltz has a flowing theme played by the full orchestra:

The Tschaikowsky orchestral repertoire is occasionally expanded with such pieces as his *Serenade for Strings*, op. 48, particularly the Elegy, the Letter Scene from *Eugen Onegin*, as well as the Waltz and Polonaise, and an amplification of the *Andante Cantabile* from the String Quartet.

TSCHAIKOWSKY'S CONCERTOS

The Concertos written by Tschaikowsky for the violin and the piano, with orchestra, are among the best known in all music. His first piano Concerto, in B-flat minor, op. 23, after years of popularity with musicians of all grades, suddenly became the darling of Tin Pan Alley, and its opening theme appeared with several different sets of words (most of them unspeakably bad) and in various "simplified" versions. It is still a good Concerto, and sure fire in its effect on the concert platform.

This work was written in 1874, and actually had its world premiere before an American audience, in Boston, where it was played by Hans von Bülow in October, 1875. Tschaikowsky had showed it to Nicholas Rubinstein on the previous Christmas Eve, and was greatly upset by the harsh criticism of his friend and teacher.

Rubinstein found no merit whatever in the work, but was later honest enough to confess his error and actually played the Concerto many times. Tschaikowsky, however, changed the dedication, giving the honor to Bülow.

This enormously popular Concerto allows its first movement only a brief Introduction, in minor key, and then goes right into the familiar, broad melody, played by the orchestra, with the piano hammering out the triple beat in crashing chords. (This melody never appears again.)

The real first theme, supposedly derived from a blind beggar's song, creates a more lyric mood:

The piano alternates between supplying decorations for these materials and carrying the melodies itself. There is considerable development, in a decidedly free style, and the movement proceeds to a brilliant finish, Allegro non troppo e molto maestoso; allegro con spirito, with a Cadenza near the close.

The slow movement begins with a charming melody, first announced by the flute and then by the piano, Andante semplice:

The tempo quickens, Prestissimo, with this lively theme in the manner of a French waltz song:

In the Rondo Finale, Allegro con fuoco, the brilliancy of the first movement returns and maintains its pace to the end. Here is the opening tune, a wild Slavic dance:

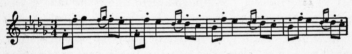

There are other important melodies in this last movement, particularly this one, first sung broadly by the violins in octaves, and eventually taken by the piano in sweeping triumph:

Tschaikowsky's violin Concerto, op. 35, like the classics of Brahms and Beethoven in this form, is in the key of D major. It shares with these two and Mendelssohn's in E minor the greatest popularity accorded to violin music throughout the world.

But as with his even more popular piano Concerto, Tschaikowsky had to overcome much criticism and disapproval before his masterpiece for the violin was generally accepted. The Viennese Hanslick earned a permanent place in the Exhibition of Bad Taste when he wrote that this music "stinks in the ear." Leopold Auer, to whom it was originally dedicated, called it too difficult to play, although, like Nicholas Rubinstein, he

later changed his mind and gave it many brilliant performances, besides teaching it to all his famous pupils. The dedication was made over to Adolf Brodsky, who had the courage
to introduce the Concerto in Vienna, at a Philharmonic concert, December 4, 1881, with Hans Richter conducting.

The music had actually been written three years earlier,
during the fruitful period that produced also the Fourth
Symphony, the opera, *Eugen Onegin,* and various minor
works. The Concerto was finished in April, 1878, on the estate
of Mme. Davidowa at Kamenka, just before Tschaikowsky
made a summer visit to the home of Nadejda von Meck (in the
absence of its owner).

The Tschaikowsky violin Concerto begins with an orchestral Introduction of pompous character, after which the solo
violin enters with a brief recitative, unaccompanied, leading
into a sweeping, romantic theme, which provides the chief
melodic material of the movement:

The slow movement is a Canzonetta in G minor, with its
outstanding melody played by the muted violin, in plaintive
mood, with many sustained trills.

The Finale is high-spirited and jolly, in strong contrast to
the melancholy of the preceding movement, suggesting a possible background of folk-dances, with this principal tune:

Tschaikowsky also wrote a set of *Variations on a Rococo Theme,* for cello and orchestra, op. 33. The date of composition was December, 1876, and it was dedicated to Wilhelm Karl Friedrich Fitzenhagen. The piece is not often heard nowadays, although it was formerly a favorite with concert cellists. There are seven Variations, Mozartian rather than Tschaikowskian in character, on this theme in A major:

CESAR FRANCK

B. Liège, Dec. 10, 1822; d. Paris, Nov. 8, 1890.

Of all the composers of the nineteenth century, Cesar Franck best deserves the title of a "modern classicist." In his life and character he was similar to the great Johann Sebastian Bach, and like him he was one of the finest organists of his day, with the Parisian church of Ste. Clotilde as his headquarters. He was an excellent choirmaster and private teacher, and he composed music because he loved it, without any thought of public acclaim or remuneration. Among his pupils were Claude Debussy and Vincent d'Indy.

Franck's music is built on classic lines, yet full of modernism in its harmonies and freedom of structure. Like most innovators, he was little appreciated in his lifetime, but has since attained an enormous popularity, chiefly through his one symphony, in D minor. In addition to this familiar symphony, Cesar Franck wrote five oratorios and other choral works (including *The Beatitudes* and *The Redemption*), three operas, four Symphonic Poems and some smaller orchestral pieces, outstanding chamber music, including the well-known violin sonata and quintet, about twenty songs and much music for the organ and the piano.

THE CESAR FRANCK SYMPHONY

Cesar Franck's *Symphony in D minor,* one of the greatest favorites in the entire literature, was completed on August 22, 1888. Its first performance was at the Paris Conservatoire, February 17, 1889, with Jules Garcin conducting. The dedication is to Henri Duparc.

This symphony, like so many other great works, was received with decided hostility, one of its severest critics and worst friends being the rival composer, Charles Gounod, who, while a professor at the Conservatoire, dismissed it contemptuously because it made use of the English horn as a solo instrument! The composer's own comment was merely, "It sounded just as I thought it would."

The symphony has only three movements, instead of the conventional four. The opening theme is built on a motto of three notes, reminiscent of Beethoven's "Must it be?" in the String Quartet, op. 135, a Wagnerian motif, and, most closely, the start of Liszt's *Les Preludes.*

This pattern develops into a vigorous melody, in faster time:

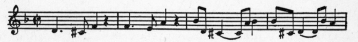

Chromatic scale progressions lead to a contrasting theme of a gentler character:

A third theme leans heavily on syncopation, and this is perhaps the most memorable melodic material in the entire movement:

In time this melody is sung softly and plaintively by horns and wood-wind, leading to highly original development and recapitulation. The Coda is introduced by a remarkable series of harmonies, and the three-note motto returns at the close with tremendous force, the movement ending quite unexpectedly on an agitated D major chord.

The second movement, Allegretto, begins with an Introduction by the harp and pizzicato strings, over which the English horn soon plays its famous solo:

This is followed by a broad, singing melody, in which the strings contribute their sustained tones for an effect of great solidity:

After some extension and amplification of this material, the English horn is heard again in its plaintive melody, and then a soft whispering of the strings leads to an entirely new treatment of the theme.

One more melody is heard in this movement, and it might be considered the basis of a fragmentary Scherzo, leading to the Finale:

This material alternates with the second melody in the Coda.

After a brief Introduction, the Finale gets under way with a cheerful syncopated tune, first heard in the lower strings:

The second theme also has its suggestions of rag-time, and was actually borrowed for the modern popular song, *Masquerade*, where it appeared in waltz time:

Instead of the conventional development, Cesar Franck completes his Finale with a striking example of the cyclic form, bringing in material from both of the previous movements. He first introduces the main melody of the slow movement, again with whispered comments by the violins, and later he gives this theme a new treatment, with surprising interruptions and rhythmic changes, finally using it with full orchestra to start the Coda. There is a complete reminder of the syncopated theme of the first movement, in two different keys, and the opening motto is also heard again, completing a unity which stands out as a rare example of symphonic workmanship.

FRANCK'S SYMPHONIC POEMS

The first of Cesar Franck's four Symphonic Poems for orchestra has the title *Les Eolides*, meaning the daughters of Aeolus, god of the winds. (He was credited with six sons and six daughters.) This was actually the composer's first orchestral work, written in 1876, with its introductory performance May 13, 1877, in Paris. The music was presumably inspired by one of Leconte de Lisle's poems, of the same name. It has a delicate, airy quality, in keeping with the subject.

In 1883 Franck composed his second Symphonic Poem, *Le Chasseur Maudit* (The Wild Huntsman), inspired by Bürger's ballad, *Der Wilde Jäger,* which was also imitated by Sir Walter Scott. The composer summed up the program thus: "It was Sunday morning; from afar sounded the joyous ringing of bells and the glad songs of the people . . . Sacrilege! The wild Count of the Rhine has wound his horn.

"The chase dashes through cornfields, brakes and meadows. Stop, Count, I pray! Hear the pious songs! No! And the horsemen rush onward like the whirlwind.

"Suddenly the Count is alone; his horse will go no farther; he blows his horn, but his horn no longer sounds . . . A lugubrious, implacable voice curses him. 'Sacrilege!' it says. 'Thou shalt be forever hunted through Hell.'

"Then flames dart from everywhere. The Count, maddened by terror, flees, faster and faster, pursued by a pack of devils."

The musical portrayal of this program is divided into four sections. The first describes the serene Sabbath landscape, with chanting chorus and pealing of bells. Then comes the Count's chase, with galloping rhythm. The curse is pronounced in the third section, after a pause indicates the failure of the horn to blow. Finally comes the infernal chase, with the pace growing fast and furious toward the close.

Cesar Franck's third Symphonic Poem, *Les Djinns,* uses a piano with the orchestra. It was composed in 1884 and introduced at a Colonne concert in Paris, March 15, 1885, with Louis Diémer at the piano, which is treated as part of the orchestra rather than as a soloist.

The program for this piece may be found in Victor Hugo's

poem of the same name, one of the series called *Les Orientales*. The Djinns are depicted as a hideous army of vampires and dragons, driven by the north wind, filling the air with infernal howls and groans, and Cesar Franck's music represents this scene quite convincingly.

A fourth Symphonic Poem (sometimes called a symphony) has the title *Psyche,* and adds a chorus to the orchestra. Its background is the story of Cupid and Psyche, with the chorus acting as commentator, in the ancient Greek style, while the orchestra suggests the dramatic emotions of the characters. A Suite of four instrumental fragments from *Psyche* was published in 1900 and is occasionally heard in concert. The program of these sections represents "The Sleep of Psyche" (Prélude), "Psyche Borne Away by the Zephyrs" and "Psyche and Eros."

FRANCK'S OTHER ORCHESTRAL WORKS

A famous set of *Symphonic Variations,* for piano and orchestra, belongs to the third and most significant period of Cesar Franck's life. This work was composed in 1885, and first performed at the Salle Pleyel, Paris, May 1st, 1886, with Louis Diémer as the soloist. The full score was not published until 1894, although a two-piano arrangement appeared earlier.

There is a fine balance between the solo instrument and the orchestra in these Variations. Alfred Cortot emphasizes the contrast between the "aggressive rhythms of the strings and the melodic supplication of the piano." The theme itself is as follows:

One hears occasional performances also of a *Chorale in B minor,* written by Franck for the organ, and arranged by Wallace Goodrich for organ and orchestra, as well as the *Prelude, Chorale and Fugue,* orchestrated by Gabriel Pierné, and the Symphonic Prelude to *The Redemption* (1873). But to the concert public the name of Cesar Franck still means the *Symphony in D minor,* and this work alone is sufficient for his established reputation in the orchestral field.

CAMILLE SAINT-SAËNS

B. Paris, Oct. 9, 1835; d. Algiers, Dec. 16, 1921.

The importance of this composer as a modern classicist is not to be ignored. He was a thorough master of composition in many styles, and an excellent performer as well on the piano and organ. His versatility permitted him to experiment also in mathematics, astronomy, archaelogy, drawing, writing, acting and other pursuits. He was famous as a sharp-tongued wit, and greatly respected by his contemporaries, including such men as Liszt and von Bülow.

Saint-Saëns is best known by his opera-oratorio, *Samson and Delilah,* a melody called *The Swan,* from his *Carnival of the Animals,* and the orchestral tone poem, *Danse Macabre.* But he also wrote five symphonies (one for organ and orchestra), five piano Concertos, four violin Concertos and one for the cello, several Symphonic Poems, a dozen more operas and an oratorio, orchestral Suites, chamber music, songs, piano and violin pieces and sacred works. He was a master of form, with a prodigious and dependable technique, which often compensated for some irregularity of inspiration. The music of Saint-Saëns maintains an honored place in the orchestral repertoire.

THE SAINT-SAËNS TONE POEMS

This French composer is credited with four orchestral pieces that perhaps deserve the title of Symphonic Poems, standing chronologically, as well as musically, between those of Liszt and Richard Strauss. The earliest (dated 1871) is called *Le Rouet d'Omphale* (*The Spinning-Wheel of Omphale*), op. 31, originally written as a Rondo for piano. It was first performed orchestrally at a Paris Concert Populaire, April 14, 1872.

Saint-Saëns wrote this description of the piece: "The subject of this Symphonic Poem is feminine seductiveness, the triumphant contest of feebleness against strength. The spinning-wheel is merely a pretext, chosen only for the sake of the rhythm and the general turn of the piece. Those interested in the examination of details will see Hercules groaning in the bonds which he cannot break and Omphale mocking at the vain efforts of the hero."

For the second in the series, *Phaeton,* op. 39, first performed at the Chatelet, December 7, 1873, the composer wrote this brief summary of the classic story: "Phaeton got permission to drive in Heaven the chariot of the Sun, his father. But his unskilled hands made the horses go astray. The flaming chariot, thrown out of its course, approached the terrestrial regions. The whole universe is about to be set on fire when Jupiter strikes the imprudent Phaeton with his thunderbolt."

Danse Macabre (generally translated "The Dance of Death"), number three among the Saint-Saëns tone poems, is decidedly the most popular, a strange combination of grotesque humor and morbid horror. Its inspiration came from a poem of the same title by Henri Cazalis, whose story is faithfully followed by the music. Here is a free translation: "Zig, zig, zig, Death in grim rhythm beats with a bony hand upon the graves. Death at the hour of midnight plays a waltz, zig, zig, zig, upon his weirdly tuned fiddle. The night is dark and the wintry winds are sighing; moans of the dead are heard through the linden trees. Through the darkness the white skeletons dart, leaping and dancing in their spectral shrouds. Zig, zig, zig, each ghost is gaily dancing; the bones are cracking rhythmically on the tombstones. Then suddenly the dance is at an end. The cock has crowed! Dawn interrupts the Dance of Death!"

Danse Macabre was written in 1874 and first performed at a Chatelet Concert, January 24, 1875. At the start the twelve strokes of the clock are heard upon the harp, with a background of soft chords. The opening of the graves is suggested by mysterious octaves in the bass. Death tunes his fiddle, with the E string half a tone flat ("zig, zig"). The first waltz is a lively tune in minor key, introduced by the flute and then taken up by the violins:

A solo violin then announces the chief melody, again in minor key and waltz time:

These two themes alternate, with various dramatic touches and technical devices, and after chromatic runs have suggested the sighing of the wind and of the spirits, they are developed in counterpoint. There is a recapitulation of both melodies, and a long Coda starts with a surprising variation of the main theme. The "Dance of Death" reaches a climax, with the xylophone suggesting the rhythm of bones on tombstones. The interruption of the rooster's crow is achieved by the solo oboe, in a high, squeaky voice. Soft, agitated chords indicate that the ghosts are scurrying back to their graves, and the solo violin is heard once more, in sad, almost regretful tones. A long trill, punctuated with brief echoes of the opening strain, leads to an abrupt close on two soft chords.

The fourth and last Symphonic Poem by Saint-Saëns is called *The Youth of Hercules*. The composer supplied this "legend": "Mythology states that on entering life Hercules saw opening before him two paths—the path of pleasure and the path of virtue. Unmoved by the seductions of the Nymphs and Bacchantes, the hero enters the road of struggles and combats, at the end of which he sees through the flames of the pyre immortality as a reward."

ORCHESTRAL SUITES OF SAINT-SAËNS

The *Carnival of the Animals* (*Le Carnaval des Animaux*) was privately performed in Paris in February, 1887, and Saint-Saëns forbade its public hearing or printing, as he considered it a musical joke. Only the familiar melody of *The Swan* was permitted to be played, and this has been heard in every variety of instrumental arrangement.

In 1922, after the composer's death, his will was found to have removed the restrictions on the *Carnival,* and since then it has had a number of performances as a Suite. There are fourteen sections, mostly touched with humor, and all full of charm.

First comes an Introduction and "Royal March of the Lions." This is followed by "Hens and Roosters," and then a series of rapid piano passages represents "Wild Asses," with a possible dig at the virtuoso style of pianism. The fourth section is called "Tortoises," burlesquing a tune from Offenbach's *Orpheus in the Nether World* by playing it very slowly:

Number five is "The Elephant," with the bass viols playing a heavy, lumbering theme, to which are added satirical suggestions of the Berlioz *Dance of the Sylphs* (see p. 160). Kangaroos follow, in a light, bouncing musical outline. The seventh episode describes an Aquarium, with the music imitating the glimmer of darting fish.

Number eight is called "Personages with Long Ears," a definite slap at the music critics. "Cuckoo in the Woods" uses the clarinet for the familiar pattern of the bird-call. Then comes a section devoted to Birds in general, with flute and piano giving realistic imitations. The name "Fossils" is given to a medley of familiar tunes, including the composer's own waltz from *Danse Macabre* (see p. 23).

The round dozen is completed by *The Swan,* whose cello melody scarcely needs quotation:

Finger exercises at the keyboard are burlesqued in "The Pianists," with the unlucky number thirteen, and a Finale recapitulates the outstanding music that has gone before, bringing the Suite to a brilliant close.

The *Suite Algérienne* of Saint-Saëns is also heard occasionally. It was composed in 1880 and published a year later as op. 60. There are four sections: a Prelude, Moorish Rhapsody, Evening Reverie and French Military March. The final part is the most popular, said to have been inspired by seeing French soldiers on Algerian soil.

There is an early Suite by Saint-Saëns, in the classic style, consisting of the conventional Prelude, Sarabande, Gavotte, Romance and Finale, dated 1863. A *Scotch Idyl,* from the ballet music of the Saint-Saëns opera, *Henry VIII,* composed in 1882 and produced in 1883, is sometimes played in concert.

Also worth mentioning is a *Marche Héroique*, op. 34, dedicated to the painter, Henri Regnault.

THE SAINT-SAËNS SYMPHONIES

Of the five symphonies by Saint-Saëns, only one is heard to-day with any regularity. Two remained unpublished, written in 1856 and 1859 respectively. The earliest symphony, in E-flat, produced in 1853 and published two years later, is dedicated to M. Seghers, who conducted the first performance. A fourth (generally numbered second), dated 1859, remained unpublished until 1878, as op. 55. It is in the classic form, written for a rather small orchestra, with reminiscences of Mozart and Mendelssohn.

All these fade into comparative insignificance beside the masterpiece in C minor, op. 78, known as Number Three, but actually the last of five such works. It was dedicated to the memory of Franz Liszt, who had heard the composer play some of it on the piano while visiting Paris for the last time. Liszt died at Bayreuth, July 31, 1886, and the symphony was performed in London by the Philharmonic Orchestra on May 19th of that year, with the composer conducting. The dedication was added later.

There are many original touches in this final symphony by Saint-Saëns, including the extensive use of the organ as well as the piano (both two and four-handed.) It has only two movements, but these divide logically into the traditional four sections. The first movement is marked Adagio; allegro moderato; poco adagio, and the second Allegro moderato; presto; maestoso; allegro.

A short, slow Introduction, described by the composer as "a few plaintive measures," leads to the first theme, in the strings, and this is later carried through various developments and transformations:

Another important theme, thoroughly French in its "sustained suavity," represents the Adagio section, in D-flat, again introduced by strings, over chords played by the organ:

The second movement, combining the materials of a Scherzo and Finale, shows further use of the initial theme, which is finally transformed into an entirely new effect, with divided strings and four hands at the piano, repeated by the full orchestra and organ in a thrilling climax. The symphony ends in a brilliant Coda, with the initial theme finally turned into a figure for the violins and a broadening of the rhythm into long, sustained beats, grouped in threes. The whole work is an impressive piece of absolute music.

THE SAINT-SAËNS CONCERTOS

Saint-Saëns wrote five piano Concertos, two of which have become popular with audiences. The first of the series, dated 1859, is merely a promising, youthful work, in the classic style. The second, in G minor, op. 22, dates from 1868 and is frequently heard. It contains a light, melodious Allegro scherzando, with this popular theme:

The final Presto is in the form of a Tarantella.

The third piano Concerto, in E-flat, op. 29, is less known. But the fourth, in C minor, op. 44, generally considered the best of the series, more than holds its own with pianists and listeners alike. It was composed in 1875 and first performed on October 31st of that year, at a Colonne concert in the Chatelet Theatre, Paris, with the composer as soloist. The dedication is to Anton Door, a professor at the Vienna Conservatory.

A final piano Concerto in F, op. 104, composed in 1896, shows Egyptian influence, with a Finale representing a sea voyage, including a short storm.

Of the violin Concertos of Saint-Saëns the favorite is the third, in B minor, op. 61. A forgotten Concerto in A (probably his first) became the *Concert Piece,* op. 62, for violin and piano. Another early violin Concerto dates from the year 1859, numbered op. 17. The one usually called the second, op. 58, was not published until 1878.

More popular than any of the Concertos are two shorter pieces for violin and orchestra, the *Introduction and Rondo Capriccioso,* op. 28, and the *Havanaise,* op. 83. The latter contains this familiar theme:

Saint-Saëns wrote two Concertos for cello and orchestra, the first of which is well established in the concert repertoire. It is in A minor, op. 33, written in 1872 and introduced by Auguste Tolbecque (to whom it was dedicated), January 19, 1873, at a Paris Conservatory concert. This Concerto is in one movement but three distinct sections, closing brilliantly in A major. A second cello Concerto was composed by Saint-Saëns in 1902.

This composer's output also includes a *Tarantella* for flute, clarinet and orchestra, op. 6, a *Romance* for the French horn, op. 36, and one for the flute, op. 37, both with orchestral accompaniment.

VINCENT D'INDY

B. Paris, March 27, 1851; d. Paris, Dec. 2, 1931.

This French composer of symphonic music belongs definitely among the modern classicists. He studied the organ with Cesar Franck and in 1885 won the Paris Grand Prize of the City with his orchestral piece, *Le Chant de la Cloche.* With several other musicians he founded the famous Schola Cantorum in 1894 and became its President in 1900.

His first symphony, *Jean Hunyadi,* dates from 1874-5, op. 5, after which he wrote an Overture, *Anthony and Cleopatra,* op. 6 (1876) and a "symphonic legend," *The Enchanted Forest,* op. 8 (1878). A *Wallenstein Trilogy,* op. 12, was started in 1874 with the middle section, "The Piccolomini" (Max and Thecla). The first part, "Wallenstein's Camp," was added in 1880, and the Finale, "The Death of Wallenstein," in 1884.

One of the important works of d'Indy is his symphony *On a French Mountain Song,* op. 25, for orchestra and piano. The latter is in the nature of an obbligato, and not to be regarded as a solo instrument.

The theme of this piece is a folk-song of the mountains of the Cevennes, where the composer spent many summers. It is heard almost at the start of the Introduction, sung by the English horn over muted strings:

All three movements are built on this tune. It first becomes a lively theme, played by bassoon and strings. A variant opens the second movement, played by the piano, and it later becomes a horn fanfare above a drum-roll, finally appearing also on a stopped horn, with a suggestion of funereal accompaniment. The third movement opens with another transformation of the mountain tune, introduced by piano and harp. This Finale is lively, and the symphony ends with the return of the original theme, loudly proclaimed by trumpets and piano.

Even more popular is the set of symphonic variations called *Istar*, op. 42, dating from 1896. This work is based on the French version of a Babylonian poem, *Ishtar's Descent into Hades*, originally in the Library of Sardanapalus.

Istar (corresponding to Astarte or Astaroth) is the goddess of fertility. She goes to the Land of No-Return, passing through seven gates on the way. At each gate she is stripped of an ornament, finally arriving naked before Queen Allatu, of Hades, who has her smitten with plagues in all parts of her body. As a result all procreation ceases on earth, and no new life is born.

Queen Allatu relents and Istar is sprinkled with the waters of life. She returns through the seven gates, each time getting back some of her apparel.

These seven gates are represented musically by seven variations on a theme. But d'Indy uses the original device of approaching this theme gradually, so that it does not appear in full until the seventh episode, the variations thus preceding the statement. In its complete form it is sung by various groups of instruments in unison and octaves, finally appearing in full orchestral harmony:

The first performances of the *Istar Variations* were given simultaneously, Jan. 10, 1897, by Willem Mengelberg in Amsterdam and Eugene Ysaye in Brussels.

D'Indy wrote his Second Symphony, in B-flat, op. 57, during 1903, and it was first performed at a Lamoureux concert in Paris, February 28, 1904. Many consider it the composer's masterpiece.

This symphony shows the cyclic style used by Cesar Franck and others, with common thematic materials appearing in all four movements. The opening is austere, developing in the classic Sonata form. The second movement is in Rondo form, thematically related to the first, with a dance theme that suggests a Greek or possibly Egyptian background.

The third movement might be called an Intermezzo and Scherzo, again echoing earlier themes and ending with un-expected brilliance. The Finale continues this cyclic form, reaching a climax in the glorification of the second theme of the first movement, in chorale style.

The last of this important series of symphonic works is called *Summer Day on the Mountain*, op. 61, designated by the composer as a series of "symphonic pictures." It was composed in 1905 and first performed by Colonne at the Chatelet Theatre, February 18, 1906.

This composition was suggested by Roger de Pampellone's *Les Heures de la Montagne: Poèmes en Prose*. Each move-ment has a title, with excerpts from the prose work prefaced.

The first is called "Dawn," and the quotation starts with the command "Awake!" ending with "Laugh or weep, you who people this world. Awake, harmonies! God harkens!"

This movement begins with muted strings, gradually creat-ing the mood of a Wagnerian *Waldweben*. Bird-songs are heard in the wood-wind. A trombone proclaims the theme which is to be heard in all three movements:

The second section has the title "Day: Afternoon under the Pines," with a preparatory note: "How sweet it is to cling to the mountain sides, broad staircase to Heaven!" There is a peasant dance tune, with the brief suggestion of a summer storm, as in Beethoven's *Pastoral Symphony* (see p. 93).

The last part of this work is called "Evening," with a Preface that says in part "O Night! Eternal Harmony dwells beneath your veil; joy and grief are but sleeping." This movement begins exultantly with a theme derived from the first part. It ends with a definite echo of the atmospheric opening, but this time reversing the modulation and working from B major to the closing key of C minor.

Other orchestral works by Vincent d'Indy include *Tableaux de Voyage*, op. 36 (1891); *Souvenirs*, op. 62, dedicated to his wife (1906); a third symphony, *De Bello Gallico*, op. 70 (1916-18); *Le Poème des Rivages*, op. 77 (1920-21); and a Concerto for piano, flute, cello and strings, op. 89 (1927).

D'Indy was by instinct a classicist, a worshipper of Nature, deeply religious in a Pantheistic fashion, spiritually steadfast, a believer in God, counterpoint and artistic integrity.

ANTON BRUCKNER

B. Ausfelden, Austria, Sept. 4, 1824; d. Vienna, Oct. 11, 1896.

Here is a symphonist of unquestioned genius, bitterly attacked and strangely misunderstood during his lifetime, and only now beginning to arrive at the appreciation that is his due. Unfortunately much of Bruckner's music sounds dull to modern ears, yet there are pages of such inspiration that his significance cannot be ignored.

He was largely self-taught, but became one of the outstanding organists of his time, concertizing, teaching and composing throughout his long life, with little encouragement from the critics or the public. Hanslick was consistently and venomously hostile, partly because the Wagnerites, whom he hated, chose to pick Bruckner as their symphonic representative, in opposition to Brahms, whom Hanslick adored.

Outside of an early Overture in G minor (1863), Bruckner's orchestral writing is summed up in his nine symphonies, several of which have established their permanent place in the repertoire. This does not include a symphony in F minor, published posthumously, and also dating back to the year 1863. The Andante is often played alone.

The first Bruckner symphony in the recognized list is in C minor, written at Linz in 1865 and revised in 1891. It was first performed at Linz May 9, 1868, and proved too difficult for the players. Hans Richter introduced the revised version in Vienna at a Philharmonic concert, December 13, 1891. This symphony was dedicated to the University of Vienna, in appreciation of a doctor's degree. It is seldom heard today.

There are four movements, of the conventional type, the first in Sonata form. The Adagio has two themes and is followed by a Scherzo. The Finale shows a fiery opening by the full orchestra, followed by a tranquil second theme.

Bruckner's Second Symphony is also in C minor, written in 1871-2, and first performed in Vienna, Oct. 26, 1873, with the composer conducting. The dedication is to Franz Liszt. There are three themes in the first movement. The second is a Rondo, with one outstanding theme to which the others are subordinate. The Scherzo has a peasant humor, and the Finale, with three themes, achieves considerable complexity, ending in a C major climax.

The Third Symphony was dedicated to Bruckner's idol, Richard Wagner, whose orchestral technique he attempted to adapt to symphonic writing, not without success. The key is D minor. It was composed in 1873 and first performed in Vienna, December 16, 1877.

The opening movement is in Sonata form. The Adagio has three themes, freely developed. The Scherzo shows a whirling violin figure, with a Trio on a waltz theme. The Finale is free in form, suggesting a Rondo, although there are only two themes.

The Fourth Symphony of Bruckner is in E-flat, with the title "Romantic." (It is also known as the "Wald" or "Forest" Symphony.) It was first played in Vienna in 1881.

This symphony is full of the love of Nature. It begins contemplatively, and the slow movement (Andante) is full of melancholy. The Scherzo seems to represent a hunting scene. The Finale starts impressively with a long and gradual crescendo, going into a musical description of a folk festival and closing in a triumphant mood. This work has by this time attained considerable popularity. Here is the final theme:

Number Five is not so well known. It is in B-flat, with a first performance at Graz, April 8, 1894, conducted by Franz Schalk. Although Bruckner composed this symphony in Vienna between 1875 and '77, and revised it in 1878, he never heard it performed. It has been given the title "Tragic," and is contrapuntally brilliant, with a cyclic use of thematic material.

The first movement contains a so-called "Hymn to Holy Love," written when the composer was in a desperately unhappy state of mind. The second movement starts with a pizzicato which becomes the foundation of the Scherzo. The Finale is fugal and makes use of earlier themes.

The Sixth Symphony of Bruckner is seldom heard. The key is A major, and it was written between 1879 and 1881. Two movements were performed in Vienna in 1883, with Jahn conducting, and the first complete performance was given by Gustav Mahler with the Vienna Philharmonic in 1899.

The Seventh is unquestionably the most popular of the Bruckner symphonies today. Its key is E major, and it was completed September 5, 1883, with a dedication to the mad King Ludwig II of Bavaria, who had been Wagner's generous patron. The Adagio of this symphony was called by its composer a "Dirge to Wagner's memory," although it must have been written before his idol's death, February 13, 1883. The first performance was under the baton of Arthur Nikisch in Leipzig, December 30, 1884, and the symphony was published the following year.

The Dirge has been called Bruckner's "most celebrated page." It is the second movement, and its principal theme is played by five tubas, doubled by the low strings:

This slow movement is followed by a Scherzo, and the Finale ends with a triple fortissimo on the chief theme of the first movement.

Bruckner's Eighth Symphony is again in his favorite key of C minor, with the title "Apocalyptic." The composer worked at it from 1884 to 1890 and it was first played in Vienna by Hans Richter, December 18, 1892. Even Hanslick admitted its triumphant success. There are four movements, with the Scherzo preceding the Adagio.

This symphony is generally considered programmatic. Commentators have found Prometheus in the first movement, the German Michel in the Scherzo, the All-loving Father of Mankind in the Adagio and a Finale devoted to "heroism in the service of the Divine." The ending recalls themes from the earlier movements, again suggesting the cyclic form of which Bruckner was so fond.

Bruckner's Ninth Symphony remained unfinished. It is in D minor, and was begun in 1887 and continued in 1891. The Adagio was completed in 1894, and Bruckner sketched a Finale, but imperfectly, working on it to the very day of his death. He knew of his approaching end, and suggested that if the symphony were not completed, his own Te Deum be used for a Finale.

It is customary, however, to play only the three complete movements, ending with the Adagio, containing an "elegiacal chant of tubas," decorated by the violins. Löwe conducted this final Bruckner symphony in Vienna in 1903 and published it the same year in his own garbled version. Like most of the others, it reveals its composer as a strange combination of naïveté, mysticism and the grand style.

GUSTAV MAHLER

B. Kalischt, Bohemia, July 7, 1860; d. Vienna, May 18, 1911.

Bruckner and Mahler had much in common, so much so that there is now a Society devoted to making propaganda for both composers. Mahler is recognized as the greater of the two, but even he did not always succeed in carrying out his grandiose conceptions. Both were greatly misunderstood within their lifetimes, both led unhappy lives, and both are today worthily honored by sincere music lovers.

Mahler was a disciple of Bruckner in counterpoint. Coming of peasant stock, and showing an early aptitude for music, he developed an enormous technique, both as a composer and as a conductor. He directed the opera at Budapest and later in Vienna, bringing the latter to its greatest heights. In 1907 he came to New York and made his debut at the Metropolitan Opera House, Jan. 1, 1908, with an impressive performance of Wagner's *Tristan und Isolde*. In 1909 he became conductor of the Philharmonic Society of New York, but he was never happy in this position and finally returned to Vienna a sick man, disappointed and frustrated, to die there in the spring of 1911.

Mahler, like Bruckner, lives primarily through his nine symphonies, and like him he sketched a tenth which was never completed. But Mahler also wrote songs and a great vocal work, *Das Lied von der Erde* (The Song of the Earth), which is in effect a symphony with tenor and contralto solos. It was based on seven old Chinese poems, paraphrased by Hans Bethge. Mahler finished it in 1908, but it was not performed until November 10, 1911, more than six months after the composer's death, when Bruno Walter conducted it in Munich.

Of the nine Mahler symphonies recognized as such, several present almost insurmountable difficulties of production, which partly accounts for the infrequency of their perform- ance. (It remained for Erno Rapee to give the first complete cycle, over the air, from New York's Radio City.) They vary in musical value, but each one presents distinct and individual points of interest. Mahler himself admitted that sooner or later he always felt the need of words to express himself musically, and this explains his frequent dependence on human voices, added to the symphony orchestra. He vigorously denied writ- ing program music, however, and insisted that his works should stand on their absolute significance as music, with every listener free to draw his own conclusions. He even fought against program notes, although he privately gave out much in the way of analysis and comment.

The very first of the Mahler symphonies, in D major, would seem to be definitely programmatic, and it was thus interpreted at its opening performance in Budapest (1891). Its composition dates back to 1883-8, and its inspiration came from a pastoral romance by Jean Paul Richter called *Titan*. This title has since been associated with it, evidently with Mahler's consent. Apparently he also approved of the sub-titles popularly attached to the five movements.

This rather obscure work was divided into two main parts. The first, called *The Days of Youth*, contained three movements: "Spring without End," "A Chapter of Flowers" (Mosaic) and "Under Full Sail." The second part, under the general title of *Commedia Umana*, covered the fourth and fifth movements: "The Hunter's Funeral March" and "Dall' Inferno al Paradiso."

The whole symphony breathes the love of Nature and the spirit of Youth, with bird songs, including even the familiar cuckoo-call. The Scherzo contains a German folk-tune, *Bruder Martin*.

The Second Symphony of Mahler, in C minor, has become fairly well known in recent years, in spite of the fact that it requires a mixed chorus, soprano and contralto soloists and an enormous orchestra, with emphasis on percussion as well as extra wind instruments. It was completed in June, 1894, and Richard Strauss conducted the three instrumental movements at a Berlin Philharmonic concert, March 4, 1895. Berlin heard the entire work for the first time on December 13th of the same year, with the composer conducting.

The opening movement, marked by Mahler "with serious and solemn expression throughout," makes it clear that this is intended as a "symphony of destiny." The death of a hero is indicated by a definite funeral march.

The second movement is marked by a charmingly naïve dance tune, played by the strings on three different occasions, once pizzicato.

A Scherzo which follows has been interpreted as the musical suggestion of St. Anthony's Sermon to the Fishes. When the entire symphony is performed, this movement goes directly into the vocal sections, numbered four and five.

The movement dominated by the contralto solo has the title "Urlicht" (Primal Light), with words taken from Mahler's favorite collection of poems, *Des Knaben Wunderhorn* (The Boy's Magic Horn). This in turn goes right into the choral Finale, with soprano solo.

This magnificent Finale has given to the whole symphony the name of *Resurrection*, with words taken from Klopstock's Ode of the same title. It has been described as "a colossal musical fresco of the Day of Judgment." "The dead arise and march forward in endless procession." At the close the organ and pealing bells join the orchestra in a jubilant climax.

Mahler's Third (variously keyed as D minor and F major) has been called the "Program Symphony," and it actually had an elaborate set of sub-titles when first produced. Its composition dates from 1895-6, but it was not performed until June 9, 1902, when the composer conducted it at Krefeld. It was published in the same year.

In spite of Mahler's later protestations, the original program may be considered fairly authentic, under the general title of "Summer Morning's Dream." This symphony is so long as to fill an entire program by itself, the first part alone equaling the length of an average symphony, and in actual performance running up to the time of the traditional concert intermission.

There is an Introduction called "Awakening of Pan," and the first section then carries the explanatory notes: "Summer

Enters. Procession of Bacchus." The music definitely supports the aptness of these titles.

The second movement, starting with an oboe solo, is a Minuet, with the sub-title "What the Flowers of the Meadow Tell Me." Then comes a Scherzo, explained as "What the Animals in the Forest Tell Me."

With the fourth movement the contralto solo enters, singing the Night-Wanderer's Song from *Thus Spake Zarathustra*. This section is explained as "What Man Tells Me."

In the fifth movement a contralto solo, women's chorus and boys' choir are added to the orchestra. The words are from *Des Knaben Wunderhorn,* and the boys' voices imitate the sound of bells by singing a continuous accompaniment of "bimm, bamm." The sub-title is "What the Angels Tell Me."

The Finale is an Adagio of profound tenderness and devotional fervor, in which Mahler attempts to express the ideal of universal brotherhood, as Beethoven did in his Ninth Symphony, but this time without the aid of words. The explanatory line for this last movement is "What Love Tells Me."

Mahler's Fourth Symphony, in G, is far more modest in its demands, and its prevailing mood is of contrasting gaiety. It was written between 1899 and 1900 and first performed by the Kaim Orchestra in Munich, November 28, 1901, with the composer conducting. The date of publication is 1900.

There are four movements, with the Scherzo standing second. This part contains a device similar to that used by Saint-Saëns in his *Danse Macabre* (see p. 233), but Mahler has the fiddle of Death tuned a whole tone higher than usual, with piercing effect.

The third movement is peaceful. A soprano solo sings words from *Des Knaben Wunderhorn* of a delightfully naïve character, suggesting the pictures of William Blake. The basic thought is "We really are in Heaven," and this idea is carried out in a detailed account of the activities of St. Peter, St. John, Herod, St. Luke, St. Martha, St. Ursula and St. Cecilia, outstripping even Gertrude Stein's *Four Saints in Three Acts*.

The Fifth Symphony of Mahler again requires a large orchestra, although it is entirely instrumental. Its key is C-sharp minor, and it is often considered program music, with the title of "The Giant." It was composed in 1901-2, and first performed at Cologne, October 18, 1904, with Mahler himself conducting. Publication was a year later.

There are five movements, but they are grouped in two parts, the first of which covers a funeral march and a section marked "stormily agitated." The third movement, which opens the second part of the symphony, has the composer's instruction "vigorously, but not too fast." The fourth movement is an Adagietto, marked "very slow," and this is the most popular section of the whole work, sometimes played alone.

The Finale is a Rondo.

The Sixth is the least known of the Mahler symphonies. Its key is A minor, and it was written in 1903-4, with a first performance at Essen, May 27, 1906, conducted by the composer. The publication date is 1905.

Mahler's Seventh Symphony has no program, and not even a key signature, although it may be considered as in E minor or possibly B minor. It was first heard in Prague, September 19, 1908, under the direction of the composer. Mahler's biographer, Paul Stefan, suggests the mood of the symphony as "on top of a mountain."

There is a slow Introduction, with three trombones in unison announcing the main theme. After complex development, this theme reappears in E major, "grandioso," with the effect of a recapitulation.

The second movement is a Serenade, or Intermezzo, which the composer himself called "Nachtmusik" (Night Music). The Scherzo is marked "shadow-like," and its Trio presents a naïve theme for three oboes.

The fourth movement is another Serenade, realistically introducing both guitar and mandolin. A solo on the kettle-drums opens the Finale. There are fanfares by the horns, and the main theme of the first movement finally returns, played by four horns fortissimo, bringing the symphony to an exultant finish.

Number Eight is generally known as "The Symphony of a Thousand," because it supposedly requires that number of choral voices to do it justice. These voices are divided among two mixed choruses and a children's choir. There are also eight solo voices: three sopranos, two contraltos, a tenor, a baritone and a bass. (Leopold Stokowski gave memorable performances of this monumental work both in Philadelphia and in New York, with a full complement of singers and instrumentalists.)

This Eighth Symphony is divided into two parts, both predominantly vocal. The first is a setting of the old Latin hymn, *Veni Creator Spiritus,* and the second takes its words from the closing scenes of Goethe's *Faust.* It was composed in 1906 and had its first performance at Munich, September 12, 1908, with publication the same year. To many this "Symphony of a Thousand" remains Mahler's masterpiece, although the second is likely to exceed it in popularity, assuming the possibility of adequate performance. The *Faust* theme is as follows:

Mahler began his Ninth Symphony (D major) in 1906, and it was first played under the baton of Bruno Walter in Vienna in June, 1912. There are four movements, the Finale being unconventionally an Adagio. It requires a large orchestra, but is consistently instrumental and by no means difficult for the listener. It was posthumously published in 1912.

Mahler's sketches for a Tenth Symphony were completed by Franz Mikorey and performed in Berlin in 1913 under the title of *Symphonia Engadiana*. It cannot be considered representative of the composer.

MAX REGER

B. Brand, Bavaria, March 19, 1873; d. Jena, May 11, 1916.

While not to be classed with either Bruckner or Mahler, Max Reger deserves an honored place among the modern classicists of orchestral music. He was strongly influenced by Wagner. A pianist of exceptional ability, he spent much of his life in Munich. His songs are outstanding and he wrote well for the organ and for the orchestra, even though his work shows an overemphasis on scholarly technique, sometimes at too great length.

Among Reger's orchestral compositions are a *Sinfonietta*, op. 90, and a *Serenade*, op. 95. His most popular work is probably the set of *Variations and Fugue on a Merry Theme*, op. 100. The theme is from Ferdinand Hiller's operetta, *The Harvest Wreath*, dating back to 1772. It covers eighteen measures, "of a simple character," Andante grazioso, in E major:

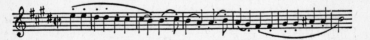

There are eleven Variations on this theme and a final
Fugue. The first statement is by the wood-wind, with the
strings supplying the conclusion. The premiere was conducted
by Reger himself at a Gürzenich concert in Cologne, October
15, 1907.

The Reger list continues with a *Symphonic Prologue to a
Tragedy,* op. 108, a *Comedy Overture,* op. 120, and a *Concerto in the Old Style,* op. 123, using Bach as a model, with
some modern touches. Then comes a *Romantic Suite,* op. 125,
in D minor, founded on poems by Eichendorff, containing
three movements: Notturno, Scherzo and Finale.

Four *Tone Poems after Böcklin,* op. 128, led to a *Ballet
Suite,* op. 130, dedicated to Josef Stransky, formerly conductor
of the New York Philharmonic Orchestra. This piece employs the instrumentation of Haydn's day, with six movements: Entrée, Columbine, Harlequin, Pierrot and Pierrette,
Valse d'Amour (in ballet style) and Finale (a Tarantella).
The Suite was introduced to America by Mr. Stransky, November 20, 1913.

Then came *Variations and a Fugue on a Theme by Mozart,*
op. 132 and a *Patriotic Overture,* op. 140, indicating an unusual volume of creative work. Reger also orchestrated his
Variations and Fugue on a Beethoven Theme, op. 86, originally written for two pianos (1904), using only eight of the
twelve Variations, and getting his tune from a piano Bagatelle,
the eleventh in a set of twelve. The orchestral compositions of
Max Reger include two *Romances* for violin and orchestra,
op. 50, a violin Concerto in A, op. 101, and a piano Concerto
in F minor, op. 114.

RALPH VAUGHAN WILLIAMS

The English composer, Ralph Vaughan Williams (generally
called Vaughan Williams) is a contemporary upholder of

classic traditions in orchestral music. He was born at Down Ampney, Gloucestershire, October 12, 1872, and became world famous as an organist and composer, making special studies in English folk-music.

Vaughan Williams is best known by his *London Symphony*, written in 1912-13, and first performed at the Queen's Hall, London, March 27, 1914, with Geoffrey Toye conducting. It was introduced to the United States by Albert Coates with the New York Symphony Orchestra, December 30, 1920.

The *London Symphony* is frankly programmatic, and the composer himself has supplied a detailed outline of its meaning. The Introduction represents daybreak on the Thames River. Big Ben is heard striking the half hour. The scene shifts to the Strand, with the bustle of morning traffic. After a glimpse of the Adelphi, the hearer is brought back to the Strand once more.

The slow movement begins with dusk in Bloomsbury. The sound of a street musician is imitated by the solo viola. In the distance the familiar cry of "Sweet Lavender" is heard.

The third movement is a combination of Scherzo and Nocturne. It is late Saturday night on the Temple Embankment, between the Houses of Parliament and Waterloo Bridge. Strange noises rise from the slums across the river. Once more the Thames is heard flowing mysteriously.

In the Finale one hears the Hunger March of the down-and-outers. The music is grim and tragic. Big Ben sounds the Westminster Chime once more. A quiet Epilogue ends with the river-music with which the symphony began.

Less known, but perhaps equally significant, is the *Pastoral Symphony* of Vaughan Williams, completed in London November 25, 1921, and first performed by the Royal Philharmonic Society under Sir Adrian Boult, January 26, 1922. The composer conducted this symphony at the Litchfield Festival, Norfolk, Connecticut, on June 7th of the same year.

The *Pastoral Symphony* has no program, not even an opus number. It is really absolute music, in spite of its title, achieving a pastoral mood by its atmosphere and spirit, rather than by direct musical description or imitation. The music is modal in character, suggesting a background of English folk-tunes, like the *Bushes and Briars,* which Vaughan Williams himself arranged. The symphony is "quiet and contemplative," in the words of the composer. The second movement ends ultra-pianissimo on high, sustained chords played by divided violins. The third is marked "of the nature of a slow dance." Six themes can be identified, of which three are important. In the Finale a wordless human voice is heard in the distance, over the soft roll of the kettle-drums, and the same effect is repeated near the close.

There is also a *Symphony in F minor* by Vaughan Williams, dedicated to Arnold Bax, and composed between 1931 and '34. It was introduced by the British Broadcasting Company Orchestra at the Queen's Hall under Sir Adrian Boult, April 10, 1935, and published the same year. Two themes run through the work, the first built on the notes F, E, G-flat, F (similar to Bach's fugal theme on his own name), and the second ascending through F, B-flat, E-flat, G-flat.

A popular piece by Vaughan Williams is his *Fantasia on a Theme by Thomas Tallis,* for double string orchestra with a solo string quartet. The modal theme dates back to the year 1567 and is treated by Williams in a free variation style, with some suggestion of the period in which it originated.

Vaughan Williams also has to his credit an Overture to *The Wasps* of Aristophanes, first performed in Cambridge, England, in 1909, and introduced at the Stadium Concerts in

New York by Albert Coates. It is playful, attractive music, without any serious attempt to suggest Greek origins.

Other orchestral works by Williams are a *Serenade,* a *Bucolic Suite,* a *Norfolk Rhapsody* in E minor (based on folk-tunes), a violin Concerto, two *Impressions,* a *Fantasy on Sussex Folk-Tunes* for cello, a piano Concerto and a Suite for viola.

ANTON RUBINSTEIN

The Russian Anton Rubinstein (b. Podolia, Nov. 28, 1829; d. St. Petersburg, Nov. 20, 1894) should be considered a classicist rather than a nationalist, for he wrote in the Teutonic style. Best known as a brilliant pianist, he nevertheless composed six symphonies, op. 40 in F; op. 42, the "Ocean," in C, with seven movements; op. 56 in A; op. 95 in D minor, the "Dramatic"; op. 107 in G minor; op. 111 in A minor, besides "character pictures" of *Don Juan, Faust* and *Ivan IV,* a *Romance and Caprice* for violin, op. 86, and five piano Concertos: op. 25 in E; op. 35 in F; op. 45 in G; op. 70 in D minor (the most popular) and op. 94 in E-flat.

V

THE RUSSIAN NATIONALISTS

WITH PERHAPS the richest treasure of folk-music in the entire world, Russia long remained unaware of these resources, imitating German, French and Italian models, much as America has done during the past century and a half. The pioneer work of Glinka, however, carried on by Balakireff and four companions, created a spirit of nationalism which has produced some of Russia's greatest music. Tschaikowsky and Anton Rubinstein cannot strictly be included among the nationalists, even though the former made frequent use of Russian folk-tunes. The work of that famous group known as "the Five," Balakireff, Borodin, Cesar Cui, Moussorgsky and Rimsky-Korsakoff, was made possible by the example of Michail Ivanovitch Glinka (b. Smolensk, June 1, 1804; d. Berlin, Feb. 15, 1857).

Glinka was of noble birth and was educated for a political life. But he studied music briefly with John Field and later with Böhm and Fuchs, learning orchestration by rehearsing scores with his uncle's orchestra.

He entered the Ministry of Communications, but spent most of his time writing songs. Finally he resigned his position and went to Italy, where he met Donizetti and Bellini and became fascinated by the technique of Italian opera. His father's death brought him back to Russia, and he began work on his

258

own first opera, *A Life for the Czar,* originally called *Ivan Soussanine.*

His second opera, *Russlan and Ludmilla,* was completed in April, 1842, and this work has been called "the foundation of real Russian music." Later Glinka visited Paris, Spain and Warsaw. His orchestral works include two unfinished symphonies, the Overtures *Night in Madrid* and *Kamarinskaya,* a *Valse-Fantaisie, Jota Aragonesa* ("capriccio brillante") and incidental music to Kukolnik's *Prince Kholmsky.*

THE GLINKA OVERTURES

Glinka lives in the modern orchestral repertoire chiefly through the Overtures to his two operas, *A Life for the Czar* and *Russlan and Ludmilla.* The first of these operas was started in 1832 and produced December 9, 1836, at the Imperial Opera, St. Petersburg (now Leningrad). The libretto was by Baron Rosen, a member of the court circle.

The musical effects of the Overture to *A Life for the Czar* grow out of Russian folk-songs. There is a characteristic melody by the oboe in the Introduction. The main part of the Overture is in Sonata form, with the chief theme in the violins. There is a transition to a second theme, announced by clarinets. The development is based on the first theme, and the Overture closes with a recapitulation and a long, elaborate Coda.

Russlan and Ludmilla has a libretto by Pushkin, and was first produced at the Imperial Opera, December 9, 1842. It was an immediate success. The Overture begins with fortissimo chords by the full orchestra, ushering in the Introduction. The first theme is also announced loudly by strings and flute, followed by a charming episode in the wood-wind, with pizzicato string accompaniment. The second theme is a graceful melody for violas, cellos and bassoons, and there is also a concluding theme. The development leads to a brilliant Coda, based on the first theme, enriched at the close by bell-like effects in the bass.

MILY BALAKIREFF

The leader of the five Russian nationalists who took their cue from Glinka was Mily Balakireff. (The last name is often spelled with a w or v instead of the ff, but pronounced as f, with the chief accent on the second syllable.) (B. Nishni-Novgorod, Jan. 2, 1837; d. Petrograd, May, 29, 1910.)

Balakireff was musically self-taught, but became an excellent pianist and composer, founding the Free School of Music and directing its concerts for years. He conducted opera at Prague and eventually became conductor of the court chapel, holding this position from 1883 to 1895. He is considered the real founder of the Russian national school of composition, and has to his credit two symphonies, two Symphonic Poems, *Russia* and *Tamar,* several Overtures, music to *King Lear,* an *Oriental Fantasia, Islamey* and other works. He was strongly influenced by Glinka, and in turn influenced not only the composers of his own nationalistic group, but even the youthful Tschaikowsky (see p. 217).

An early work by Balakireff is the *Overture on the Theme of a Spanish March,* which was completed in 1857, but revised and rescored in 1886. The composer secured the theme from Glinka himself, who encouraged the young man to go on with his music. A program for this Overture is given on a fly-leaf of the score. It was inspired by the fate of the Moors, driven from Spain by the Inquisition. The music suggests the tones of the organ, the chant of monks, pyres of the auto-da-fé, ringing of bells and rejoicing of the populace.

The first theme is of Oriental character, invented by Balakireff, and introduced by the piccolo over open fifths in the violins. The second theme is the March itself, preceded by four measures of drumming. It is first played by horns and trumpets, and later, pianissimo, by muted strings. The Overture follows the Sonata form, with both themes recapitulated by the full orchestra at the end.

An *Overture on Three Russian Themes* followed in 1858 and gave the first significant indications of Balakireff's trend toward nationalism. The three themes are actual Russian folksongs, and the dedication is to Vladimir Stassoff, a music critic who approved of the work of "the Five" and the Glinka influence already apparent.

The Introduction to the Overture is based on the second of the three songs, *In the Field Stood the Little Birch Tree,* later used by Tschaikowsky for the Finale of his Fourth Symphony (see p. 211). The first theme is then introduced by divided first violins, flute and clarinet, and this is the folk-song beginning *Lo, the white birch tree stood near the field* (not to be confused with the more familiar *Birch Tree* already mentioned). The clarinet then sings the second *Birch Tree* song as a second theme, and the oboe introduces the third, originally called *She Went to a Feast.* These second and third themes are later cleverly combined over an organ point on F-sharp. There is a double fortissimo development of the second theme by the full orchestra, and the first returns at the close.

Balakireff's *Symphony in C* was composed in 1897, dedicated to Tertius Phillippoff, and was first performed April 23, 1898. Its opening phrase of five notes pervades the entire work. There are three movements, Largo, Scherzo and Andante, but to the last is added a Finale which begins with a Russian theme of truly national ring, introduced by the cellos and bass viols. It is balanced by a section in 6-8 time, and the symphony ends with a polacca version of the main pattern, forming a distinctive Russian theme:

A Second Symphony, in D minor, by Balakireff, is dated as late as 1909. His *Islamey*, sometimes called the most difficult music ever written for the piano, and hence a favorite with Liszt, has been orchestrated by Casella (1908) and others. It appeared as a piano piece in 1869, inspired by the composer's travels in the Caucasus. Casella's instrumentation requires a large orchestra. There are three themes, freely developed. The first is Oriental in character. The second is introduced by the English horn and four solo cellos, and there is a Trio theme also played by the English horn. The Fantasia ends in a brilliant Coda.

Balakireff's masterpiece, however, is unquestionably the symphonic poem *Tamar* (also spelled Thamar and Tamara). He composed this after a poem by Michael Lermontoff, written in 1841, the year in which its author was killed in a duel in the Caucasus. The words are printed on the score in Russian and French. The music was sketched in 1866-7, completed in 1882, and published in 1884, with a dedication to Franz Liszt.

Tamar, according to the story, was a vampire queen, who lived in an ancient tower by the rushing river Terek, in a narrow defile of Darial. She had "the beauty of an angel but the soul of a demon." Tamar had the habit of luring solitary travelers to her tower, to join in her revels. Sounds of merriment are heard through the night. "At day's dawn, silence reigns once more, but the river bears along on its foaming waters a lifeless body. At a window appears Tamar's shadowy form, bidding farewell from her tower to the dead lover, in a voice laden with such tenderness that its every accent, breathing sweet promises, seems to presage for them both a happy morrow."

Balakireff's music suggests Terek's torrent at the start by a running figure in the cellos and basses, over which soon appears Tamar's theme, first in minor key, with English horn, oboe and violins, then in major, by clarinet and harp. The complex character of Tamar is indicated by a descending theme for wood-wind, representing her loveliness, a wild tarantella (her demoniac passion) and an Oriental figure (her irresistible fascination). There is increasing excitement in the music, culminating in a staccato crash by the full orchestra. Then the monotonous accents of the river are heard once more, with Tamar's theme floating languidly above, seeming to sigh a fond farewell.

ALEXANDER BORODIN

B. St. Petersburg, Nov. 11, 1833; d. there Feb. 27, 1887.

This important member of Russia's group of five nationalists showed an early talent for music, composing between the ages of nine and fourteen. He took up the study of medicine, however, eventually becoming assistant Professor of Chemistry at the St. Petersburg Academy of Medicine. He wrote valuable treatises on chemistry, and never really gave up his scientific work, considering music a side line to the end of his life.

It was Balakireff who revived Borodin's interest in the art and encouraged him to take it seriously as a composer. He visited the musical centers of Europe, meeting Liszt among others and receiving flattering comments from the master. Two trips to Belgium were particularly successful, and Borodin's compositions began to be widely played, even though he continued to consider himself an amateur.

Borodin's works included three symphonies, *Prince Igor* and other operas, the symphonic sketch, *On the Steppes of Central Asia*, a *Scherzo* in A-flat (1885), chamber music, piano pieces and songs.

The First Symphony is in E-flat, dating from 1862-7, and first performed at the Salle de la Noblesse in St. Petersburg, January 4, 1869, with Balakireff conducting. There are four movements: Introduction and Allegro, Scherzo, Andante and Allegro molto vivo. Liszt called the first movement "perfect," the Andante a "chef-d'oeuvre" and the Scherzo "enchanting." According to Moussorgsky, this symphony is "the Russian *Eroica*."

But the Second Symphony of Borodin is definitely more important. Its key is B minor, and it was begun in 1869 and finished in 1876, with a premiere at St. Petersburg, February 14, 1877, in the Salle de la Noblesse (possibly February 2nd or even March 10th. Authorities disagree on these dates). Napravnik was the conductor. The national character of this symphony is unmistakable. Stassoff says that Borodin was "haunted by the picture of feudal Russia and tried to paint it in his music." There seems to be a definite program. The first movement represents the assembling of the old Russian Princes. The Scherzo starts in the brass, as urged by Balakireff, who helped the less experienced composer greatly with his orchestration. In the Andante one hears the songs of the old Slavonic troubadours, while the Finale gives musical expression to the banquets of heroes, the tones of the guzla and bamboo flute, and the enthusiasm of the people.

A Third Symphony, in A minor, was begun by Borodin in 1885-6 and two movements were completed from his sketches by Glazounoff. A solo oboe sings the chief theme of the first movement, and the Scherzo shows considerable technical skill.

When the players found difficulty in its 5-8 time, they were told to think of each measure as fitting the name of Rimsky-Korsakoff.

Borodin's orchestral sketch, *On the Steppes of Central Asia,* was completed in 1880 and intended originally for *tableaux vivants* celebrating the twenty-fifth anniversary of the reign of Emperor Alexander III. It was dedicated to Franz Liszt, who insisted on an immediate piano arrangement for four hands. The music describes a caravan crossing the desert under escort of Russian soldiers. There are two themes, one Russian, the other Oriental, and a long, persistent note in the violins suggests the immensity of the desert. According to the program supplied by the composer, the songs of the Russians and the Asiatics mingle in harmony, gradually dying away in the distance.

Borodin's most popular orchestral piece is unquestionably the set of dances from *Prince Igor,* turned into a ballet by Diaghileff in his Paris season of 1909, with choreography by Fokine. These dances, called Polovtsian, Polovetzian and even Polovetzkian, were orchestrated in pencil by the combined efforts of Borodin, Rimsky-Korsakoff and Liadoff, and first conducted by Rimsky at the Free Music School in February, 1879. The melodies were supplied by Hunfalvi, a traveler familiar with the tribes of Central Asia.

As played orchestrally, the most popular theme (a melody sung in the opera by a women's chorus) is played by the oboe over a pizzicato accompaniment:

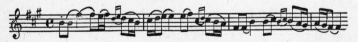

There are dances of "savage men," prisoners, buffoons, little boys, young girls, and, according to the ballet version, a wild bowmen's dance.

The complete opera of *Prince Igor* was published in 1889

and had its premiere in St. Petersburg, November 4, 1890. Its Overture is sometimes heard as a concert piece. Borodin never finished the opera, although he worked at it for nearly seventeen years, starting in 1870. Rimsky-Korsakoff and Glazounoff completed the work, the latter writing out the Overture from memory, as he had often heard Borodin play it on the piano. There are two themes in the Overture, Andante and Allegro.

Borodin wrote his own libretto for *Prince Igor*, whose plot concerns a twelfth-century expedition of Russian princes against a nomadic people, the Polovetzki (see p. 265), who had invaded Russia. The story is based on an old national poem, *The Epic of Igor's Army.*

A prolific but less important member of the Russian Five was Cesar Cui, unfortunately best known today by his popular *Orientale,* based on a folk-tune corresponding in triple time to that of Tschaikowsky's *Marche Slave* (see p. 219). Cui (b. Vilna, Jan. 18, 1835; d. Petrograd, March 24, 1918) was a pupil of Balakireff but destined for the career of a military engineer, thus carrying out the tradition of the entire group. He also reviewed music for the *Journal of St. Petersburg.*

Cesar Cui has to his credit ten operas (completely unknown today), and his orchestral works include a *Tarantella,* op. 12 (1859); a *Marche Solenelle,* op. 18 (1881); a *Suite Miniature,* op. 20; two *Miniatures* for violin and orchestra, op. 24; a *Suite Concertante* for the same combination, op. 25 (1883); two pieces for cello and orchestra, op. 36; two more Suites, op. 40 and 43; and three *Scherzos,* op. 82, of which the second, in F, is sometimes played. He also completed Moussorgsky's opera, *The Fair at Sorotschinsk.* But the public still knows only the *Orientale.*

MODEST PETROVITCH MOUSSORGSKY

B. Karevo, Pskov, March 21, 1839; d. St. Petersburg, March 28, 1881.

Here is the outstanding genius of the Russian group of nationalists. Unfortunately, only a small portion of his work can be heard in orchestral concerts.

Moussorgsky was taught the piano at an early age by his mother, but went through a military education and eventually entered the army. Dargomijsky introduced him to Cui and Balakireff, with whom he studied composition for a time. He was compelled to remain in a distasteful government position in order to make a living, and he gradually sank into habits of intemperance which finally cost him his life.

The musical inspirations of Moussorgsky are found largely in his songs and his operas. *Boris Godounoff,* his most famous dramatic work, was produced in 1874, but revised and re-orchestrated by Rimsky-Korsakoff in 1896. Another opera, *Khovanstchina,* was also revised by Rimsky. Moussorgsky's *The Fair at Sorotschinsk* and two other operas remained uncompleted.

The Prelude to *Khovanstchina* is sometimes heard as a concert piece. It was described by the composer as "Dawn on the Moskva River," but he was careful to say that this did not imply the glory of the sunrise. The Prelude consists of five variations on a theme of national character.

The opera itself was begun in 1872 and finished in 1880. Its first performance was by an amateur company at the Kononoff Hall, St. Petersburg, in November, 1886. The subject of the opera was the plotting against Czar Peter (later known as Peter the Great) by the Princes Khovansky, father and son. Peter is said to have called these plots a mere "Khovanstchina," from which Moussorgsky got the title for the opera. But the fact remains that the Khovanskys were publicly hanged.

Far better known is the orchestral tone poem generally called *A Night on Bald Mountain* (literally Bare Mountain), which figures in the Walt Disney *Fantasia* and other pictorial interpretations. This piece was begun in 1867 with the intention of using piano and orchestra. Moussorgsky twice revised it, once planning to use the music in his opera, *The Fair at Sorotschinsk,* as the dream of a peasant lad. Rimsky-Korsakoff, who heartily disapproved of this idea, finally revised and orchestrated the whole work, leaving it in the form in which it is heard today. Its first performance was at one of Belaieff's concerts in the Kononoff Hall, St. Petersburg, October 15, 1886, with Rimsky conducting.

The music has a definite program, describing "subterranean sounds of supernatural voices," followed by the spirits of darkness and Satan (Chernobog) himself. There is a celebration of the Black Mass and the Witches' Sabbath revels. At the height of the orgies, the bell of a village church is heard in the distance, dispersing the spirits of darkness and permitting the dawn to appear.

Another Moussorgsky composition heard both orchestrally and in its original form on the piano is the series of sketches called *Pictures at an Exhibition.* It was completed as a piano piece in July, 1874, and later orchestrated by Cailliet, Touschmaloff, Leonardi, Sir Henry Wood and Maurice Ravel.

The last-named composer undertook the instrumentation at the request of Serge Koussevitzky, who introduced the Ravel version at one of his Paris concerts, May 3, 1923.

The music was suggested by pictures and designs in an exhibit of the work of the architect Victor Hartmann, who died in the summer of 1873. There are eleven pictures altogether, preceded and interrupted by Promenades, representing the composer at the exhibition, loitering, walking to and fro, occasionally hurrying to look at some congenial work, and then slackening his gait in sadness at the memory of his dead friend.

The eleven subjects and the pictorial details which they represent are as follows: 1. The Gnome (Gnomus). "Waddling, awkward steps." 2. Il Vecchio Castello. A medieval castle, with troubadours singing. 3. Children at the Tuileries Gardens in Paris. Quarrels and romping, with nurses included. 4. Bydlo. A Polish wagon, drawn by oxen. (The music is a folk-song in the Aeolian mode.) 5. Ballet of the Chickens in Thin Egg-shells. A sketch for the ballet *Trilby* by Hartmann. 6. Samuel Goldenberg and Schmuyle. Two Polish Jews, one rich and laconic, the other poor and restless. 7. Market Place at Limoges. Women wrangling in the market place. 8. Catacombs. Hartmann himself exploring the Catacombs of Paris with a lantern. (Moussorgsky marked this episode "Cum mortuis in lingua mortua," "with the dead in a dead language," and added "His creative spirit leads me to the place of skulls and calls to them; the skulls begin to glow faintly from within.") 9. The Hut of Baba-Yaga. Design for a clock, with the Russian witch, Baba-Yaga, "on fowls' legs," or rather held in birds' claws. 10. The Golden Gate of Kieff. Bogatyr's Gate, a proposed design in the old Russian massive style, with a cupola in the form of a Slavonic helmet.

The original piano composition, *Pictures at an Exhibition*, was dedicated to Vladimir Stassoff, who had suggested and carried out the memorial to Hartmann.

One sometimes hears also a concert version of the *Introduction and Polonaise* from *Boris Godounoff* and a *Gopak* or *Hopak* (Russian folk-dance), one with words and the other instrumental. Moussorgsky's less familiar orchestral works include an *Intermezzo in Modo Classico*, a *Scherzo*, a *Turkish March* and such tone poems as *On the Southern Shore of the Crimea*, *Meditation* and *Une Larme* (A Tear).

NIKOLAI RIMSKY-KORSAKOFF

B. Tichvin, Novgorod, March 18, 1844; d. Liubensk (St. Petersburg), June 21, 1908.

This brilliantly gifted composer may be said to have completed the work that Glinka and Balakireff began. He was a youthful prodigy, playing the piano at six and composing at nine. He was sent to the Naval Academy in St. Petersburg, but met Balakireff in 1861 and began under his influence to compose a *Symphony in E-flat minor*.

Rimsky graduated from the Naval Academy and took a cruise around the world, visiting the United States, among other countries. On his return to Russia he completed his symphony, which was introduced by Balakireff December 19, 1865. Later the composer resigned from the Navy, but continued to serve as Inspector of Marine Bands. He taught composition at the St. Petersburg Conservatory and succeeded Balakireff as director of the Free Music School. He also conducted symphony concerts at home and abroad.

Rimsky-Korsakoff wrote a half dozen operas, of which the best known, *Le Coq d'Or,* was banned by political censorship until 1910. His services to his fellow composers, and particularly to Moussorgsky, have already been mentioned. It was Rimsky's reorchestration of *Boris Godounoff* that put it into the regular operatic repertoire in 1896. He was a master of instrumentation and a fine judge of folk materials, besides writing excellent songs and other music.

The most popular orchestral work of Rimsky-Korsakoff is unquestionably the Symphonic Suite *Scheherazade,* which is included on many modern programs in place of an actual symphony. It is based on material from *The Arabian Nights,* its title representing the favorite wife of the Sultan Schariar, who tells him a series of stories in order to keep him from killing her and his other wives. He becomes so interested that eventually he spares them all.

The story-telling Sultana is represented musically by a florid theme high up on the solo violin, and this is repeated at various times throughout the Suite, as though she were saying "Once upon a time":

The music actually begins with a contrastingly brutal theme, representing the Sultan himself, and later treated in various ways, without any particular regard for a set program:

The first episode is the story of Sinbad the Sailor, with the motion of the sea suggested by rocking tones in the cellos. The Sultan's theme is only slightly changed to fit the ship plunging through the waves:

A second theme, calmer and smoother than the first, enters by way of contrast, and this completes the melodic material of the first section:

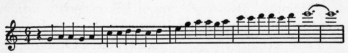

The second movement of the *Scheherazade Suite* is called "The Tale of the Prince Kalendar," and the music is again introduced by the story-telling theme in the solo violin, accompanied by the harp, this time sounding more confident, and ending with a brilliant Cadenza. The story is then unfolded by the bassoon, evidently with some comic connotation. The Kalendars were wandering fakirs, and it is possible that the mere thought of a Prince among them would be considered something of a joke.

The suggestion of exotic dances is interrupted by a loud fanfare of brass:

There is ample excitement after this, with trumpets answering each other in definite tones and a spirit of conflict in the music.

The third movement is quieter, with the title "The Young Prince and the Young Princess." In the *Arabian Nights* these were brother and sister, known as Children of the Moon. The charming melody at the start obviously fits the young Prince:

The theme of the Princess is livelier, with a suggestion of actual Oriental dancing:

The Finale has the composite title: "Festival at Bagdad. The Sea. The Vessel is Wrecked upon a Rock Surmounted by a Bronze Warrior." The music follows this program with some accuracy, although the details are not always clear. The Sultan's theme is heard at the start, answered by the soft voice of Scheherazade. The Bagdad Festival is described in a lively Oriental dance tune:

A second theme is derived from earlier materials, but with an appropriately festive ring, and still in the Oriental manner:

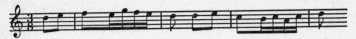

The Princess theme of the preceding movement is echoed again, and eventually the music of the sea reappears. There is a crash as the ship is wrecked upon the rock of the Bronze Warrior. Calm after the storm is suggested by the woodwind. Scheherazade begins her round of stories once more, but this time the solo violin leads to a happy ending, soaring to high harmonics as quiet chords in the orchestra bring the music to a peaceful close.

Scheherazade is numbered op. 35 among the works of Rimsky-Korsakoff. It was composed in the summer of 1881, at Neyzhgovitsy on the shores of Lake Cheryemenyetskoye, and produced at St. Petersburg the following year. The dedication is to Vladimir Stassoff.

Next to the *Scheherazade Suite*, the most popular concert work of Rimsky is doubtless the *Capriccio Espagnol*, or *Spanish Caprice*, op. 34, begun in 1886 and first performed at a Russian Symphony concert in St. Petersburg, October 31, 1887. It was intended originally as a *Fantasia* on Spanish themes for violin and orchestra, and the solo violin still has some striking passages, although the piece became a tour-de-force of orchestral virtuosity in general. Tschaikowsky called it a "colossal masterpiece of instrumentation" by "the greatest master of the present day." But Rimsky took pains to explain that the instrumentation was not mere embellishment, but a necessary part of the basic musical ideas.

There are five parts in this *Spanish Caprice*. It begins with an Alborada, corresponding to the French Aubade, or serenade at dawn. Next come five variations on a theme introduced by the horns.

The Alborada is then repeated, and a fourth section represents a "Scene and Gypsy Song," with Cadenzas by the trumpets, solo violin, flute and harp. The song itself is an impetuous strain played with rough bowing by the violins. Finally comes a Fandango of the Asturias, with suggestions of the typical guitar and castanets:

A repetition of the opening Alborada brings the piece to an end.

Several other works of Rimsky-Korsakoff are heard with some regularity on the concert stage. His tone poem, *La Grande Paque Russe,* generally known as *Russian Easter,* op. 36, has become well established as an orchestral piece. It was written and first performed in 1888, and published in 1890. There are notations on the score to indicate its basic program. First comes a quotation from Psalm 58: "Let God arise, let His enemies be scattered. Let them also that hate Him flee before Him. As smoke is driven away, so drive them away. As wax melteth before the fire, so let the wicked perish at the presence of God."

There is also a quotation from the sixteenth chapter of St. Mark, telling the familiar Easter story, followed by "Resurrexit" and other comments. The music starts with a church melody of Russian ecclesiastical origin, and this eventually proves the main theme. The effect of bells adds to the impressive instrumentation.

Rimsky-Korsakoff was a successful composer of opera, and some of this music has found its way into the concert hall. The Overture to *The Maid of Pskov,* his first opera, dates back to 1868-71, with a premiere January 1, 1873 at the Maryinsky Theatre, St. Petersburg. The libretto was from a drama of the same name by Mey, but the opera was later called *Ivan the Terrible.* The Overture is richly scored, as usual with Rimsky.

Another opera, *A Night in May,* based on a Gogol story, was first produced in St. Petersburg in 1880. The Overture is built on folk-songs and dances in the opera, and is full of boisterous comedy.

Rimsky's last opera was the popular *Coq d'Or,* from which a Suite was arranged by Glazounoff and Maximilian Steinberg. It consists of three movements: (a) King Dodon in his Palace; his dream; his departure; (b) King Dodon and the Queen of Shemakha; the dance, nuptial cortège, etc.; (c) Wedding and Lamentable End of Dodon. Wedding March. Attack of the Cockerel. Postlude.

The symphonic Suite, *Antar,* op. 9, is often heard in concert. It was first called Rimsky's Second Symphony, but the composer himself wrote: "I was wrong in calling *Antar* a symphony. My *Antar* was a poem, Suite, fairy-tale, story, or anything you like, but not a symphony. Its structure in four separate movements was all that made it approach a symphony. It has no thematic development whatever, only variations and paraphrases." The work was composed in 1868 and first performed by the Russian Music Society in St. Petersburg, March 22, 1869.

Antar was a famous Arabian warrior-poet of the sixth century, and this Suite is based on a tale concerning this hero by Semmkowsky. Antar saves the life of a gazelle, pursued by a flying monster. He dreams of a beautiful queen in a palace, and she turns out to have been the gazelle. She promises

Antar the three great joys of life, and these are described in the second, third and fourth parts of the Suite. The first joy is the delight of vengeance, the second the delight of power, and the third the delight of love.

Rimsky's First Symphony, begun in E-flat minor, at the suggestion of Balakireff, was later changed to E minor and appeared as opus 1. The subject of *Sadko* served both for a symphonic poem, op. 5, (1867) and for an opera, in which occurs the popular *Song of India,* often heard orchestrally in a variety of arrangements, but originally a tenor solo.

The opera *Tsar Saltan* (founded on a Pushkin story about a beautiful swan) supplied the material for a set of *Musical Pictures,* op. 57, and there is also a Suite from the opera, *Pan Voevoda,* op. 59. Among the earlier works of Rimsky-Korsakoff are a *Fantasy on Serbian Themes,* an *Overture on Russian Themes,* a piece called *Conte Féerique,* op. 29, a piano Concerto in C-sharp minor, op. 30, a *Symphoniette in A minor, on Russian Themes,* op. 31, a Third Symphony, op. 32, and a *Fantaisie de Concert* in B minor for violin and orchestra, op. 33 (1886).

The popular *Flight of the Bumble Bee* is often played orchestrally, as well as in various arrangements for solo instruments. It was originally a Scherzo in the first scene of the second Act of *Tsar Saltan,* with the stage direction: "Out of the sea comes a bumble bee and flies about the swan." The music is a brilliant imitation of actual buzzing, achieved through rapid scale passages.

Other titles in the orchestral list of Rimsky-Korsakoff are *Doubinouschka, Christmas Eve, Kitesch,* etc.

OTHER RUSSIAN NATIONALISTS

Alexander Dargomijsky (b. Toula, Feb. 14, 1813; d. St. Petersburg, Jan. 17, 1869) contributed somewhat to the pioneer work in Russia's musical nationalism. His opera *Russalka* is still remembered, and his orchestral works included a popular *Baba-Yaga*, a *Finnish Fantasia* and a *Cossack Dance*.

Closely associated with "the Five" was Anatol Liadoff (b. St. Petersburg, May 10, 1855; d. there Aug. 28, 1914), a pupil of Rimsky-Korsakoff, perhaps best known by his charming little *Music Box*, written for piano, but often heard orchestrally. Liadoff wrote two orchestral *Scherzos*, op. 10 and op. 16, a *Symphony in B minor*, op. 12, and six Symphonic Poems, *Baba-Yaga*, op. 56; *The Enchanted Lake*, op. 62; *Kikimora*, op. 63; *Amazon's Dance*, op. 65; *Fragment of the Apocalypse*, op. 66, and *Nänie*, op. 67. Of these *The Enchanted Lake* is most played, and it also makes effective ballet music. The *Amazon's Dance*, published in 1910, was dedicated to Ida Rubinstein. There is also an orchestral version of *Eight Russian Folk-Songs* by Liadoff, which represents one of his direct contributions to nationalism.

The contemporary Reinhold Glière (b. Kiev, Jan. 11, 1875) may likewise be considered primarily a nationalistic composer, who became in 1938 President of the Composers' Association of the U.S.S.R. His writings include three symphonies, six Symphonic Poems, three ballets, two operas, and some chamber music, songs and motion-picture scores.

Glière's *Marche Heroique* is in the modern orchestral repertoire, as is his tone poem, *The Sirens*, op. 33, composed and first produced in Moscow in 1908. The latter has a definite program, referring to the actual Sirens of Greek mythology, who lured sailors to destruction by their song. The music describes, in turn, The Sea, Isle of the Sirens, Approach of the Vessel, Song of the Sirens and Shipwreck.

Glière collected folk melodies of the Caucasus, and thereby qualifies as a nationalist, even though much of his work is absolute music. His First Symphony, op. 8, in E-flat, was composed in 1899-1900 and introduced in Moscow in 1902. His Second, in C minor, op. 25, is dated 1907, and was given in Berlin that year by Koussevitzky. A Third Symphony is in B minor, op. 42, written between 1909 and 1911, and first played in Moscow, 1912. There is also a harp Concerto, dated 1938. Glière's best-known music is probably the *Sailor's Dance* from his opera, *The Red Poppy*, often used as a ballet number (especially by Paul Haakon) and sometimes played orchestrally.

Michael Ippolitoff-Ivanoff (b. Gatschina, Nov. 19, 1859; d. Moscow, Jan. 28, 1935) deserves inclusion among the Russian nationalists, if only because of his popular *Caucasian Sketches,* considered sure-fire material by practically all symphony orchestras. The composer was a pupil of Rimsky-Korsakoff, 1872-82, at the St. Petersburg Conservatory. The *Caucasian Sketches,* op. 10, were written in 1894, and first performed in Moscow a year later, with the composer conducting. The individual numbers bear the titles: In the Mountain Pass, In the Village, In the Mosque and Procession of the Sirdar (March of the Caucasian Chief). It is the Finale that contains the best-known melody, reminiscent of *Old Black Joe* at the start:

ALEXANDER GLAZOUNOFF

B. St. Petersburg, Aug. 10, 1865; d. Paris, March 21, 1936.

· This composer may be considered the last of the Russian nationalists, bringing to a close a significant movement, whose effects are unquestionably permanent. (Stravinsky, Prokofieff and Shostakovitch are treated as all-round contemporary composers, Scriabin as an impressionist, and Rubinstein and Tschaikowsky as definite classicists.)

Glazounoff met Balakireff and Rimsky-Korsakoff in 1880, the latter as a teacher, and immediately succumbed to the spell of nationalism. His First Symphony was composed in 1882 and conducted by Balakireff in St. Petersburg the same year. (Liszt introduced it in Weimar in 1884.) The composer himself conducted his Second Symphony, with others of his works, at the Paris Trocadéro in 1889, and his Fourth in London, 1896. He visited the United States in 1929, conducting his Sixth Symphony in Detroit on November 21st of that year, eventually settling in Paris.

Glazounoff has been called "the Russian Mendelssohn," chiefly because he was financially independent and therefore free to develop his natural gifts as a musician. His most popular piece is probably the Autumn section of the Ballet *The Seasons,* to which Pavlowa used to dance.

But his symphonies are often heard, and his first violin Concerto remains in the repertoire of the virtuosi.

Glazounoff wrote two *Overtures on Greek Themes.* His First Symphony, in E, dates from 1881. These works were followed by a *Serenade,* op. 7, and an *Elegy,* op. 8. Then came the symphonic poem, *Stenka Razin,* op. 13, which is still heard quite often on orchestral programs. The title refers to a Cossack outlaw of the seventeenth century, who was executed at Moscow in 1671. He was a rebellious leader of Cossack insurgents, and many ballads were written about him.

Glazounoff's music first depicts the peaceful Volga river, using the melody of the famous *Song of the Volga Boatmen,* sung by the oboe over tremolo strings. The sudden pillaging of the peaceful countryside by Stenka Razin is indicated by a brutal theme, representing the outlaw himself. He has in his possession a beautiful Persian Princess, musically represented by a soft, sweet theme on the clarinet. The story goes that she dreamed of his capture and her death in the river. When surrounded by soldiers of the Czar, the Ataman Stenka Razin threw her overboard, thus giving up what was dearest to him and inspiring his own men to a new attack. Glazounoff uses his three themes effectively to tell the essentials of this legend.

This composer's Second Symphony was in F-sharp minor, op. 16 (1886), followed by a symphonic poem, *The Forest*, op. 19 (1889), a Fantasy, *The Sea*, op. 28, (1890) and a *Rhapsodie Orientale*, op. 29 (1891). Then came the Third Symphony, in D, op. 33 (1892), a *Carnaval Overture*, op. 45, and a Fourth Symphony, in E-flat, op. 48 (1893). This symphony was dedicated to Anton Rubinstein and published in 1894. It wavers between folk-music and the classic tradition, showing its composer definitely on the way toward absolute music. It is cyclic in character, the opening subject being later transformed into the brief theme of the Finale, with other reminiscences of earlier material. There is no independent slow movement, the Andante section leading directly into the close.

Glazounoff's popular Suite, *Scènes de Ballet*, op. 52, was written in 1895, and the same year produced a Fifth Symphony, in B-flat, op. 55, which was first played at a Belaieff concert in St. Petersburg in 1896. The first movement is marked Moderato maestoso, and the second is a Scherzo, with elements of folk-song. In the third movement (Andante), tune detectives may find an echo of Verdi's *Celeste Aida*. The Finale, Allegro maestoso, again shows touches of folk-music, using the bass drum, cymbals and triangle in the old-fashioned military style.

Glazounoff's Sixth Symphony, in C minor, op. 58, was written in 1896, dedicated to Felix Blumenfeld, and published in 1897. The opening movement is in Sonata form, with an Adagio Introduction and the main part Allegro. The second section presents seven Variations on this theme:

The third movement is an Intermezzo, and the Finale, Andante maestoso, contains a big theme by the full orchestra and a brilliant Coda.

The Seventh Symphony of Glazounoff is in F, op. 77, dating from 1902, with touches of modern harmony. It opens with a Pastoral movement, in jolly mood. Then comes a slow movement, full of pathos and charm, with a solemn air in the brass. The Scherzo is whimsical and lively, and the Finale again presents a solemn chant, with echoes of the earlier movements, in cyclic style.

Glazounoff's popular violin Concerto, in A minor, op. 82, was composed in 1904. The three movements are played without pause, with luscious, romantic themes, of which the most memorable is perhaps the second subject of the first section:

The Eighth, and last, Symphony of Glazounoff is in E-flat, op. 83, composed in 1906, and first performed in St. Petersburg, December 21st, in the same year. It was published in 1907. The composer gave titles to all four movements, according to Modest Altschuler, who introduced the symphony to America with the Russian Symphony Orchestra. The first was called by Glazounoff "Heroic," the second "Fantastic," the third "Pagan" and the fourth "Christian."

A piano Concerto in F minor, op. 92, was written by Glazounoff in 1911, and a second, in B, op. 100, in 1922. Among other orchestral works by this well-equipped Russian one sometimes hears *The Kremlin,* op. 30, dedicated to the memory of Moussorgsky, introduced in St. Petersburg in 1890 and published in Leipzig in 1892. It has three parts, representing (1) A Popular Feast, (2) In the Monastery and (3) Entrance and Greeting of the Prince. There are also two *Valses de Concert,* of which the second, in F, op. 51, is the better known.

A "tableau musical," *Le Printemps,* op. 34, (1891, St. Petersburg) was published in 1892, with a dedication to Nicholas A. Sokoloff, a colleague of Glazounoff at the Imperial Conservatory. Based on a poem by Tutcheff, it has this program: "Spring advances, and, following it joyously, in purple and luminous chorus, come the sweet, warm days of May." The music lives up to this outline, with occasional hints of bird-song.

An *Overture Solenelle,* op. 73, was introduced in St. Petersburg in 1900 as a *Festival Overture,* with publication under the new title in 1901. The dedication is "to the artists of the orchestras at the court of His Majesty, the Emperor of all the Russias." There is also a *Raymonde Suite,* a violin Concerto in E minor, and the *Ballet of the Seasons* already mentioned. Occasionally one hears Glazounoff's *Introduction and Salomé Dance,* based on Oscar Wilde's *Dance of the Seven Veils,* somewhat lighter than the Richard Strauss treatment of the same material (see p. 365).

VI

TONAL IMPRESSIONISTS

THE TERM "MODERNISM" is often applied to what should really be called "impressionism." In this respect music runs parallel to painting. A picture by Monet, for instance, shows a vagueness of outline, a misty atmosphere, strongly suggesting the effect of impressionistic music.

Scientifically these musical effects are produced by the constant employment of the higher primary overtones, the whole-tone scale and the ancient church modes. The clarity of melodic outline characteristic of the classic school is generally avoided, as are the conventional harmonies of tonic, dominant and subdominant. Traditional modulation is superseded by unprepared chords, unrelated sequences, even dissonances. Yet impressionism is still a long way from the cacophonies permitted in the really modern and ultra-modern styles. It is musical painting in subdued colors and dim outlines, but with the charm and individuality of appeal that such painting has always possessed.

CLAUDE DEBUSSY

B. St. Germain-en-Laye, Aug. 22, 1862; d. Paris, May 25, 1918.

Chopin paved the way to musical impressionism, but it was Debussy who really founded the style and thus became the virtual father of modernism in general. A prodigy, like most musicians, he entered the Paris Conservatoire at the age of eleven, studying with various masters, particularly harmony under Durand. From 1880 to 1882 he enjoyed the patronage of Mme. von Meck, the "beloved friend" of Tschaikowsky, and she encouraged his musical ambitions, besides giving him opportunities for travel in several countries.

After several attempts, Debussy won the Grand Prix de Rome in 1884 with his cantata, *L'Enfant Prodigue* (The Prodigal Son), later produced as an opera. But he was already experimenting with new harmonies and rebelling against the formulas of musical convention. His symphonic Suite, *Printemps* (1887) and *Fantaisie* for piano and orchestra (1888) showed something of his revolutionary ideas, and in 1892 he startled the musical world with the *Prelude to the Afternoon of a Faun*, which remains one of his most popular compositions. His opera, *Pelleas and Melisande*, went far beyond this in originality and may be considered unique in its field. His *Nocturnes, La Mer, Images* and other orchestral works carried on the same distinctive style, each in its own way, with impressionism entering also into his chamber music, songs and piano pieces. Debussy died dramatically at a time when the Germans were bombing Paris in 1918.

DEBUSSY'S TONE POEMS

The *Prelude to the Afternoon of a Faun*, composed in 1892, had its first performance at a concert of the National Society of Music, Paris, December 23, 1894, under the baton of Gustave Doret. A second and far more successful presentation was given by the Colonne Orchestra, October 20, 1895.

The program for this famous composition comes from a poem by Stéphane Mallarmé, of which Debussy calls his music "a very free illustration." He summed up the Prelude as evoking "the successive scenes in which the longings and the desire of the Faun pass in the heat of the afternoon."

Edmund Gosse interpreted the Mallarmé text in this poetic fashion: "A faun—a simple, sensuous, passionate being—wakens in the forest at daybreak and tries to recall his experience of the previous afternoon. Was he the fortunate recipient of an actual visit from nymphs, white and golden goddesses, divinely tender and indulgent? Or is the memory he seems to retain nothing but the shadow of a vision, no more substantial than the 'arid rain' of notes from his own flute? He cannot tell. Yet surely there was, surely there is, an animal whiteness among the brown reeds of the lake that shines out yonder. Were they, are they, swans? No! But Naiads plunging? Perhaps! Vaguer and vaguer grows that impression of this delicious experience. He would resign his woodland godship to retain it. A garden of lilies, golden-headed, white-stalked, behind the trellis of red roses? Ah, the effort is too great for his poor brain. Perhaps if he selects one lily from the garth of lilies, one benign and beneficent yielder of her cup to thirsty lips, the memory, the ever-receding memory, may be forced back. So when he has glutted upon a bunch of grapes, he is wont to toss the empty skins in the air and blow them out in a visionary greediness. But no, the delicious hour grows vaguer; experience or dream, he will never know which it was. The sun is warm, the grasses yielding; and he curls himself up again, after worshipping the efficacious star of wine, that he may pursue the dubious ecstasy into the more hopeful boskages of sleep."

The languid, chromatic tones of the flute immediately announce the main theme of Debussy's music:

This direct imitation of the pipe of the faun is developed in various ways, with oboe, clarinet and harp joining in to create a gathering excitement. Muted horns and a solo cello play their parts. The final statement of the theme, with new, soft harmonies under its chromatic scale, creates an unforgettable effect as the music dies away. The *Prelude to the Afternoon of a Faun* is dedicated to Raymond Bonheur. It was published in 1902.

The great dancer, Nijinsky, gave a ballet version of Debussy's *Prelude,* of which the composer disapproved, calling it "ugly—Dalcrozian, in fact." There was considerable criticism of this ballet and much controversy when Diaghileff brought it to America.

Debussy's three *Nocturnes* (*Clouds, Festivals* and *Sirens*) have won a similar popularity, although the third is not heard as often as the first two, since it needs a women's chorus, singing wordless tones. *Nuages* (Clouds) and *Fêtes* (Festivals) were introduced at a Lamoureux concert, with Camille Chevillard conducting, December 9, 1900, and the third part was added on a parallel occasion, October 27, 1901. The *Nocturnes* were composed in 1898 and published the following year.

Debussy himself wrote of this series of impressionistic pieces: "The title *Nocturnes* is intended to have here a more general and, above all, a more decorative meaning. We, then, are not concerned with the form of the Nocturne, but with everything that this word includes in the way of diversified impression and special lights.

"Clouds: the unchangeable appearance of the sky, with the slow and solemn march of clouds dissolving in a gray agony tinted with white.

"Festivals: movement, rhythm dancing in the atmosphere, with bursts of brusque light. There is also the episode of a procession (a dazzling and wholly idealistic vision) passing through the festival and blended with it; but the main idea and substance obstinately remain—always the festival and its blended music—luminous dust participating in the universal rhythm of all things.

"Sirens: the sea and its innumerable rhythm; then amid the billows silvered by the moon the mysterious song of the Sirens is heard; it laughs and passes."

Debussy's *La Mer* (The Sea), often considered his most important orchestral work, was written at Bichain, Dieppe and Eastbourne, from 1903 to 1904. The dedication was to Jacques Durand, who published *La Mer* in 1905. It was first performed at a Lamoureux concert, Paris, on October 15th of that year, with Chevillard conducting.

La Mer is actually a set of three Symphonic Sketches, with the individual titles: From Dawn till Noon on the Ocean, Play of the Waves, and Dialogue of Wind and Sea. The music is more masculine and emotional than one usually expects of Debussy, reaching a succession of impressive climaxes. This is a wilder ocean, more sinister and terrible, than that which Mendelssohn described in his music (see p. 154).

Iberia, the second of a set of *Images* for orchestra, has also found a place among the popular works of Debussy. (The first is called *Gigues* and the third *Rondes de Printemps*.) The time of composition runs from 1906 to 1912. *Iberia* had its first performance at a Colonne concert in Paris, February 20, 1910. (*Gigues* had to wait until January 26, 1913.)

Iberia is again impressionistic music, with more than a hint of Spain in its rhythms and tonal coloring, yet never descending to mere effects of realistic imitation. The title is justified in the mood rather than in dramatic details. There are three sections: In the Streets and By-ways, The Fragrance of the Night, and The Morning of a Festival Day.

Debussy's list of orchestral works also includes a ballet, *Jeux* (1912), incidental music to *King Lear* (1904) and a

Sacred and Profane Dance for harp and strings (1904). Many of his piano pieces have been orchestrated, with particular rewards of popularity for his *Reverie* (translated into a hit fox-trot by Tin Pan Alley), *Clair de Lune* and the familiar *Golliwog's Cake-Walk*.

MAURICE RAVEL

B. Ciboure, Pyrenees, March 7, 1875; d. Paris, Dec. 26, 1937.

This composer is often compared with Debussy, yet his style is quite different. He is less impressionistic, dealing far more with clarity and precision, and using chords of the seventh in preference to the ninths of which Debussy was so fond.

Ravel studied composition with Fauré in 1897. He had already written a *Habanera* for two pianos in 1895, which was later orchestrated as part of a *Rhapsodie Espagnole*. The charming *Pavane for a Dead Infanta*, written as a piano solo (and utilized for the popular song, *The Lamp Is Low*), also became an orchestral piece in 1912.

The composer made his debut as an orchestral conductor with the Societé National, May 27, 1899, performing his own Overture, *Scheherazade*, from manuscript. (It remained unpublished.)

Ravel's orchestral works include also *La Valse* (1920), the ballet *Daphnis and Chloe* (1909-11), an orchestral version of his *Tombeau de Couperin* (1919), the five children's pieces grouped under the title *Ma Mère l'Oye* (Mother Goose) (1912), a *Tzigane* for violin and orchestra (1924) and the immensely popular *Bolero* (1928). He also wrote a successful opera, *L'Heure Espagnole,* some chamber music, songs and piano pieces.

Daphnis and Chloe may be considered Ravel's earliest and

perhaps most important music written directly for the orchestra. Actually it was a ballet, commissioned by Diaghileff, but it is generally heard today in the form of two orchestral Suites.

The first performance of the ballet was at the Chatelet Theatre, Paris, June 5, 1912, although Ravel had been working at the composition for a year or more before that time. Fokine was responsible for the choreography, and his disagreements with Diaghileff resulted in a final break between the two. Nijinsky and Karsavina created the title parts, with Pierre Monteux conducting. The score had been published in 1911.

One of the Suites, containing three parts, Nocturne, Interlude and Danse Guerrière, had already been performed on April 2d, 1911, at a Chatelet concert, conducted by Gabriel Pierné. But it is the second Suite that is most often heard in concert today. This also consists of three parts: Daybreak, Pantomime and General Dance.

A program is printed in the score of this Suite, based upon the story of Longus, also used by Fokine. In the first part, Daphnis is discovered by shepherds, asleep before the grotto of the nymphs. Awakened, he searches in anguish for Chloe. When she appears, surrounded by shepherdesses, it becomes evident that the god Pan has honored her in memory of the nymph, Syrinx, who became the reed from which he fashioned his pipes.

The second part of the Suite is a musical pantomime, in which Daphnis and Chloe act out the story of Pan and Syrinx. Her dance follows the sounds of Pan's pipe. The lovers pledge their devotion, attended by young girls dressed as Bacchantes.

The general dance of the Finale is a "joyous tumult," with Daphnis and Chloe leading the rest.

Of perhaps equal importance as an outright orchestral piece is *La Valse*, called by Ravel a "choreographic poem," sketched during the First World War and completed in 1920. Its first

performance was at a Lamoureux concert, December 12, 1920.
It seems to have been intended also as a ballet, or possibly an
"apotheosis of the dance." The themes are of Viennese character, and the music is in three parts, for which the composer
supplied a definite program.

First comes "The Birth of the Waltz," starting with a suggestion of dull chaos, and gradually reaching the familiar form
of the waltz. The second section is devoted to the Waltz itself,
while the third represents its Apotheosis.

Ravel's own description of the music is as follows: "Whirling clouds give glimpses, through rifts, of couples waltzing.
The clouds scatter, little by little. One sees an immense hall,
peopled with a whirling crowd. The scene is gradually illumi-
nated. The light of the chandeliers bursts forth, fortissimo.
An Imperial Court about 1855."

Here is the chief waltz theme:

Ravel's most popular composition is of course the famous
Bolero, dedicated to Ida Rubinstein, and first produced by
her as a ballet in Paris, in November, 1928. The action (as
later presented also on the stage of the Radio City Music Hall
in New York) suggests a picture by Goya, a Spanish Inn, with
a dancer on one of the tables, gradually bringing in all the
spectators and rousing them to a frenzy.

Musically the *Bolero* is a trick piece, employing a persistent
rhythm and a monotonous strain of melody, working slowly
toward a tremendous climax, in which percussion plays an
important part. The basic rhythm has the triple beat of the
Bolero, but with each beat decorated by its own pattern. On

the third beat of each measure this inner pattern alternates
between two and six rapid strokes upon the drum:

The melodic theme is first announced by the flute, and later
taken up by various instruments, singly and in groups, eventually reaching a "tornado of sound":

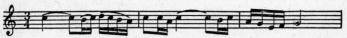

An early work by Ravel, originally written as a piano duet
and later orchestrated by the composer, is the picturesque
Mother Goose (*Ma Mère l'Oye*). The year of its actual composition was 1908, with publication in 1910, dedicated to the
children, Mimi and Jean Godebski. It was first performed
as a four-handed piano piece at the Salle Gaveau, Paris, April
20, 1910, with Christine Verger and Germaine Duramy as the
pianists, aged six and ten respectively. The orchestral version
is dated 1911, first played at the Théâtre des Arts, January
21, 1912.

There are five sections in this highly individual *Mother
Goose*. First comes a very brief "Pavane of the Sleeping
Beauty," built on the opening phrase, played by the flute,
horns and violas. The second part has the title "Hop o' my
Thumb" (Petit Poucet), which Ravel explains by this quotation from the story of Perrault: "He believed that he would
easily find his path by means of the bread-crumbs which he
had scattered wherever he had passed; but he was very much
surprised when he could not find a single crumb: the birds
had come and eaten everything up."

The third section is called "Laideronette, Empress of the
Pagodas." A *laideron* is an ugly young woman, and the French
word *pagode* is applied to grotesque little figures with movable
heads. Ravel quotes from *Serpentin Vert,* by the Countess

Marie Catherine d'Aulnoy, describing Laideronette as she takes a bath: "The pagodes and pagodines began to sing and play on instruments; some had theorbos made of walnut shells; some had viols made of almond shells; for they were obliged to proportion the instruments to their figure." The music definitely suggests this miniature orchestra in a dainty march movement.

The title of the fourth part is "Conversations of Beauty and the Beast," the latter represented by a double bassoon. Quotations from Mme. Leprince de Beaumont have Beauty starting a dialogue along these lines: "When I think how good-hearted you are, you do not seem to me so ugly." "Yes, I have, indeed, a kind heart; but I am a monster." "There are many men more monstrous than you." "If I had wit, I would invent a fine compliment to thank you, but I am only a beast." Beauty finally agrees to marry the Beast, who then turns into a handsome Prince, properly grateful for his delivery from a magic spell. The music is a slow waltz, based chiefly on a melody for the clarinet.

The Finale is "The Fairy Garden," Lent et grave, also in triple time, with its opening theme announced by the strings and interestingly developed.

Also originally written for piano are the *Valses Nobles et Sentimentales* of Ravel, composed in 1910, published in 1911, and first performed at the Salle Gaveau May 9, 1911. The orchestration dates from 1912 and was introduced as accompaniment to a ballet, *Adelaide, or The Language of the Flowers,* at the Chatelet Theatre, April 20, 1912. The dedication is to Louis Aubert. The score carries this quotation from Henri de Régnier: "The delicious pleasure, always new, of a useless occupation." There are eight sections, actually seven waltzes and a slow Epilogue, played without pause, starting and finishing in the key of G major.

One of Ravel's earliest transcriptions from piano to orchestra is the *Alborada del Gracioso* (from *Miroirs*), written in 1905 and first played in Paris January 6, 1906. The title implies an Aubade or morning serenade of a graceful buffoon, of the Figaro type. The piece has grown in popularity and is a good example of Ravel's gift of reproducing a Spanish atmosphere.

In the same spirit is the *Spanish Rhapsody,* a Suite in four movements, dated 1907. The composer's own titles and comments are as follows: (1) Prelude à la Nuit; "voluptuously drowsy and ecstatic." (2) Malaguena, "slow and sensuous," with a persistent figure in the bass viols and a theme carried by muted trumpets with tambourine accompaniment. (3) Habanera. (This was first written for two pianos in 1895, representing the Cuban form of the familiar tango rhythm.) (4) Feria, describing a Fair, in which the music rises to a tumult of excitement.

A *Tzigane* for violin and orchestra was written by Ravel in 1924 and first performed in Paris on October 15th of that year, with Samuel Dushkin as soloist. In its original form the accompaniment was intended for the "lutheal," an ancestor of the modern Solovox, attached to the piano and imitating the tone color of various other instruments.

A piano Concerto in G, on which the composer worked for two years, was completed in time for the Festival Ravel at the Salle Pleyel, Paris, and first played there January 14, 1932, with publication the same year. The composer conducted the premiere, with Marguerite Long as soloist, to whom the Concerto is dedicated. There are three movements: Allegramente, Adagio assai and Presto. The first is light and gay; the second begins with a long piano solo, and the third has an agile grace, in which the orchestral syncopation approaches American jazz. Ravel himself called this Concerto the complete expression of his own development as a composer, and stated that he had put the best of himself into the music.

Another piano Concerto, for the left hand alone, was written for the one-armed pianist, Paul Wittgenstein, by whom it is frequently and effectively played. Other orchestral pieces by Ravel, not previously mentioned, are his two *Hebraic Melodies*, a *Menuet Antique* and the *Introduction and Allegro* for harp, strings, flute and clarinet, all occasionally heard in public.

ALEXANDER SCRIABIN

B. Moscow, Dec. 25, 1871; d. there, April 14, 1915.

In any discussion of musical impressionism the name of Scriabin must be included. His *Divine Poem, Poem of Ecstasy* and "color symphony," *Prometheus,* are sufficient to give him an important place in the field of modern orchestral music in general, with a significant influence on contemporary composers.

Although born to the military tradition, and trained as a cadet, Scriabin entered the Moscow Conservatory, studying piano with Safonoff and composition with Taneieff, and winning the first prize in 1891. A year later the wealthy publisher Belaieff became interested in him, and by 1897 he had become piano instructor at the Conservatory. In 1906-7 Scriabin visited Paris, Brussels and Switzerland, later coming to the United States, and finally retiring to Moscow in 1910, where he spent the rest of his life.

Scriabin wrote five symphonies, of which three are of real significance in the literature of orchestral music. The First, a choral work in E major, op. 26, is dated 1895, and the Second, in C, op. 29, was written between 1897 and 1903. The Third is the famous *Divine Poem*, in C minor, op. 43, composed in 1903. It was first performed by Artur Nikisch in Paris, May 29, 1905, and published the same year.

The fundamental idea of Scriabin's music has been described as "art as religion and religion as something involving the conception of art." The *Divine Poem* expresses "the spirit's liberation from its earthly trammels," arriving at a "free expression of purified personality." Its performance requires a large orchestra. The Introduction presents three motives, which have been interpreted as (a) Divine Grandeur, (b) The Summons to Man, and (c) Fear to Approach, Suggestive of Flight. These motives occur throughout the symphony.

The Fourth Symphony of Scriabin is the *Poem of Ecstasy,* op. 54, composed in 1907-8. It was introduced by the Russian Symphony Orchestra, under Modest Altschuler, in New York, Dec. 10, 1908. It has been interpreted as expressing the "ecstasy of untrammeled action, the joy in creative activity."

The Prologue has two motives, the first, introduced by the flute, expressing "human striving after the ideal." The second, played by the clarinet, is "the ego theme, gradually realizing itself." The symphony then continues in Sonata form, with a subject symbolic of the "soaring flight of the spirit." The second theme is two-fold, having an upper and a lower part, in harmony. The third is "imperious," announced by the trumpet. The harmony wavers between the fairly conventional style of Scriabin's first period and the advanced ideas which he finally reached. The symphony is actually absolute music, regardless of programmatic implications.

Scriabin's Fifth Symphony has the title *Prometheus, the Poem of Fire,* op. 60. The key is F-sharp. It was begun in Brussels in 1909, and finished at Moscow in April, 1910. The first performance was conducted by Koussevitzky in Moscow, March 15, 1911, with Scriabin playing the piano part. This symphony is an expression of the composer's theosophy, a belief in reincarnation and the essential divinity of man, approaching the state known in India as Nirvana. (There was to have been a sixth work called *Mystery,* in whose appreciation all the senses played a part, even that of smell.)

The Prometheus of Scriabin's title is not the classic figure of Greek mythology, chained to a rock and fed upon by vultures. Rather is it a later Son of the Flame and of Wisdom, representing an ideal instead of an individual. An important feature of this symphony is the "color organ," whereby colors are thrown upon a screen, controlled by a keyboard. Thus the key of C produces red, G orange, D yellow, A green, F dark red, etc. It has never been proved that there is any fundamental relationship between these tones and the colors assigned to them. In actual performance, listeners found it hard to follow the colors and grasp the music at the same time, just as the music of Disney's *Fantasia* became comparatively insignificant when used as a background to his color cartoons.

Scriabin invented a "mystic chord," built upon fourths, and also a special scale: CDEF-sharp,AB-flat. The *Prometheus Symphony* requires a big orchestra, including both piano and organ. There are three important themes, the first stated by horns, the second by flutes and the third by the piano.

OTHER MUSICAL IMPRESSIONISTS

Many other composers have written music in the modern, impressionistic style. Some of them will be found among the

Contemporary Giants (see pp. 334-403) and America's Own (pp. 404-465). A few more may be included here.

Charles Martin Loeffler (b. Mühlhausen, Jan. 30, 1861; d. Medfield, Mass., May 19, 1935) was an Alsatian by birth, but an American by adoption. He studied the violin with Joachim, lived for a time in Russia, learned composition in Paris, and finally came to the United States, where for twenty years he sat next to Concertmaster Franz Kneisel at the first desk of the Boston Symphony Orchestra. He resigned this position in 1903 to devote himself entirely to composition.

Among Loeffler's orchestral works are a Suite for violin and orchestra, *Les Veillées de l'Ukraine,* after a story by Gogol (1891), a *Fantastic Concerto* for cello (1894), a *Divertimento* for violin (1895) and a *Divertissement Espagnol* for saxophone (1901). In 1897 he wrote the *Death of Tintagiles,* op. 6, which remains one of his most important compositions. It was based upon a drama for marionettes by Maeterlinck, and in its original form contained two solo parts for violas d'amour (played by the composer and Mr. Kneisel). It was thus first performed in Boston, January 8, 1898. Later one viola d'amour was omitted and the other greatly reduced in importance, and this predominantly orchestral piece was introduced by the Boston Symphony Orchestra, February 16, 1901.

Another significant work by Loeffler is *A Pagan Poem,* op. 14, first written for piano, two flutes, oboe, clarinet, English horn, two French horns, three trumpets, viola and bass viol (1901). A second version, for two pianos and three trumpets, was performed in 1903. The symphonic version dates from 1905-6, and was first played by the Boston Symphony Orchestra, November 23, 1907.

This tone poem was suggested to Loeffler by the eighth Eclogue of Virgil, sometimes called *The Sorceress.* These verses, probably written in 39 B.C., comprise two love songs, one by Damon and one by Alphesiboeus. They tell of a Thessalonian girl who by magic spells tries to win back her truant lover, Daphnis. (Virgil's poem is largely borrowed from Theocritus, whose second Idyll, *The Sorceress,* treats of a maiden of Syracuse who similarly weaves a magic spell to regain the love of Delphis.)

Loeffler's music is by no means a literal translation of Virgil's verses, but rather a free fantasy, inspired by their content. The dedication is to Gustave Schirmer.

A Pagan Poem begins, Adagio, with a short motive which appears frequently throughout the work. There is a "theme of invocation," announced by the viola and three flutes. The piano enters fortissimo with a harmonized inversion of the introductory motive, and eventually a second theme appears in the harp, first violins and piano. The theme of the sorceress is played by off-stage trumpets. At the finish there is a fanfare of "frantic exultation."

La Vilanelle du Diable (The Devil's Vilanelle), op. 9, also keeps the name of Loeffler alive in the orchestral repertoire. It was inspired by a poem of Rollinat and written at Dover, Mass., in 1901. The first performance was from manuscript, April 12, 1902, by the Boston Symphony Orchestra under Wilhelm Gericke.

The Rollinat poem has two refrains, each represented by a theme in Loeffler's music. There are echoes of such old tunes as *A la Vilette, Ça ira* and the *Carmagnole.* The alternating refrains are finally united, in the music as well as in the poem. The original words reiterate the fact that "Hell's a-burning," with a tentative question "If I should go to see Lucifer?"

Loeffler also wrote a symphony in one movement with male chorus, *Hora Mystica* (1916), and a tone poem, *Memories of My Childhood* (1925).

The German-English-American Frederick Delius (b. Brad-
ford, England, Jan. 29, 1863; d. Grez-sur-Loing, June 10,
1934) belongs among the tonal impressionists whose music
has steadily grown in popularity. Intended by his German
parents for a mercantile career, he was sent at the age of nineteen to Florida to grow oranges. Instead he developed his
musical ability, inspired by a love of Nature and the singing
of Southern Negroes. He taught music at Danville, Va., and
then went to Leipzig, where he met Reinecke, Jadassohn and
Grieg. In 1888 he settled in France, where he spent much of
the rest of his life, eventually suffering from paralysis and
blindness.

The most popular work of Delius has the title *On Hearing
the First Cuckoo in Spring,* one of two tone poems for small
orchestra. (The other is called *Summer Night on the River.*)
It was composed in 1912-3 and first performed at a London
Philharmonic concert, January 20, 1914, with Mengelberg
conducting. There are two themes, the first original with
Delius, the second taken from a Norwegian folk-song, *In Ola
Valley* (also set by Grieg, op. 66, no. 14). Delius knew Norway well, and fully appreciated its folk-music. Here is his own
opening theme:

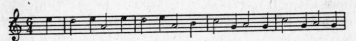

Almost as popular is Delius' *Brigg Fair,* an English Rhapsody, first performed by the Liverpool Orchestral Society,
January 18, 1908, with Granville Bantock conducting. The
music consists of variations and "commentary" on a Lincoln-
shire folk-song discovered at Brigg by Percy Grainger. It is
introduced by the oboe:

The piano Concerto of Delius, in C minor, was composed in 1897, and first played by Julius Buths at Elberfeld in 1904. Grainger brought it to America and played it at a concert of the New York Philharmonic Orchestra, November 26, 1915. This music was conceived in Florida and influenced by the singing of Negroes, particularly the slow movement, which Grainger considers the best. The Concerto is played without a pause, but has three definite parts, Moderato, Largo and Vivace.

In a Summer Garden was composed in 1908 and first played by the London Philharmonic, December 11th of that year, with Delius conducting. It was later revised. The score bears a motto from the 59th Sonnet of Dante Gabriel Rossetti: "All are my blooms; and all sweet blooms of love To thee I gave while Spring and Summer sang."

The Walk to the Paradise Garden is an interlude from the Delius opera, *A Village Romeo and Juliet* (his fourth). The opera is based on a tale in Gottfried Keller's *The Folk of Seldwyla* (1900-01). This interlude comes between the fifth and sixth "pictures," and has been called "an epitome of the whole drama."

The Prelude to *Irmelin,* the first opera of Delius, is sometimes heard. It was composed in 1890-92, to his own libretto, and published in 1938. The music begins slowly, with the flute playing an ascending phrase. The second theme is given to the strings, and the piece ends with the first theme, played pianissimo by the bass clarinet.

Delius also wrote *Life's Dance,* a revised version of *The Dance Goes On,* a Symphonic Poem (1898). Its original performance was at St. James's Hall, London, May 30, 1899, and it was given in its revised form at Düsseldorf, in February, 1904, by Julius Buths. The inspiration came from Nietzsche's *Thus Spake Zarathustra.*

Paris, a Night Piece (The Song of a Great City) was composed in 1899-00, and first played at Elberfeld in 1900, with Hans Haym conducting, to whom it was dedicated when published in 1909. It has been described as the "personal record of feelings engendered by the city." The form is free, and the melodic material comes from the actual street cries of Paris. The opening theme, Adagio, is announced by the oboe. There follows a Vivace, an Adagio con espressione (strings), an Allegretto grazioso, a Tempo di Marcia (harp and Glockenspiel), and at the end the opening theme is heard again in the oboe.

Delius also has to his credit a choral work with orchestra, *Appalachia,* introduced at the Delius Festival in London, 1929; *Sur les Cimes* (Monte Carlo, 1893) and *Over the Hills and Far Away* (Elberfeld, 1897), a *Florida Suite* (1886-7), *Hiawatha, Marche Caprice* and *Sleighride* (1888); a *Petite Suite* (1889), *Legend,* for violin and orchestra (1893), *North Country Sketches* (1913-4), *A Dance Rhapsody* 1916), a violin Concerto (1916); a cello Concerto (1921) and *Fantastic Dance* 1934).

A Polish composer who may be listed among the tonal impressionists is Karol (or Karel) Szymanowski (b. Tymoszowska, Ukraine, Sept. 21, 1883; d. Lausanne, Switzerland, March 28, 1937). He was largely self-taught, and had composed nine Preludes for piano and six songs before taking up the serious study of composition with Noskowski at Warsaw in 1903. In 1905 he produced his first orchestral work, a *Symphonic Overture in E,* op. 12. His First Symphony followed in 1906 and a Second Symphony, op. 19, appeared in 1910.

Szymanowski was at first influenced by German music, particularly that of Richard Strauss. He then turned to French impressionism, and eventually became a modernist in the best sense of the word. This final stage was marked by his Third

Symphony, *The Song of the Night*. In Berlin he formed the society known as Young Poland in Music, with Gregor Fitelberg and others. He became director of the Warsaw Conservatory in 1920. Besides his three symphonies and two violin Concertos (1917 and 1930), Szymanowski wrote two operas, *Hagith* and *King Roger*, two cantatas, *Demeter* and *Agave*, and a ballet, *Mandragora*.

The Third Symphony (*The Song of the Night*) dates from 1915-6, and was first performed at Warsaw in 1921, with Mlynarski conducting. Szymanowski originally called it a Symphonic Poem, and it remained in one movement, with tenor solo and an optional chorus, besides piano and organ. The text was taken from the second divan of Maulana Jallaluddin Rumi, a Persian mystic of the thirteenth century.

Szymanowski's first violin Concerto, op. 35, is played more often than his symphonies. It is atonal and polytonal, with no signature. The date of composition is 1917-8, and it was first performed at Warsaw in November, 1922, with publication the following year, dedicated to Paul Kochanski. There are three sections, in cyclic style, but played without pause.

VII

APOSTLES OF CHARM

A NUMBER OF ORCHESTRAL COMPOSERS, belonging to various periods, seem to defy accurate classification, except for their common ability to write charming music. In some cases they are kept alive in the repertoire by only one or two compositions, but these individual works have often won more popularity than the elaborate creations of greater masters. The consistent appeal of such music to an ever-growing public must be considered an honest tribute to its permanent value.

ANTON DVORAK

B. Mühlhausen, Bohemia, Sept. 8, 1841; d. Prague, May 1, 1904.

This Czech composer might have been included among the modern classicists, since he wrote no fewer than nine symphonies and many other orchestral works. But he is remembered chiefly by one or two outstanding creations (aside from such trifles as the much played *Humoresque*), and in these the element of charm is undeniable.

Dvorak left home at the age of sixteen to avoid becoming a butcher. Having already picked up the violin, he entered the Prague Organ School, where he graduated in 1862. From then on he made a precarious living as a professional violinist, also playing the viola in the National Theatre orchestra at Prague. His first composition to attract attention was a *Hymnus* for mixed chorus and orchestra, introduced March 9, 1872. Three years later he was awarded the Austrian State Prize for a *Symphony in E-flat*, conducted by Smetana at Prague in 1874. Liszt, Brahms, and Bülow encouraged him, and sincerely admired his music. (Brahms picked Dvorak as his own successor.) In time he became organist at St. Adalbert's in Prague, won new honors in England, and from 1892 to 1895 directed the National Conservatory of Music in New York. It was there that Dvorak completed his most famous composition, the symphony *From the New World*, op. 95, in E minor.

There has been much argument concerning this symphony, chiefly as to the extent of Dvorak's borrowings from the folk-music of the American Negro. (He has even been accused of using Indian themes, but the music itself denies any such background.) It is now generally agreed that the symphony is fundamentally Bohemian, but with touches of American material, representing the musical thoughts of a homesick composer who never becomes thoroughly acclimated.

The *New World Symphony* was first played from manuscript at a concert of the New York Philharmonic Society, December 15, 1893, with Anton Seidl conducting and Dvorak present in the audience. The actual work of composition had been completed on May 25th of the same year. The orchestration was largely done at Spillville, Iowa, which contained a strong Bohemian colony.

Both Henry E. Krehbiel, the music critic, and Henry T. Burleigh, the Negro composer and singer, claim to have supplied Dvorak with American themes, but the composer, writing to Oskar Nedbal, conductor of the first Berlin performance in 1900, denied any such indebtedness and said: "I tried to write only in the spirit of those national American melodies."

The opening theme of this deservedly popular symphony, following a slow Introduction, has the definite quality of rag-time (syncopation):

A subsidiary melody shows more of the spirit of a European peasant dance:

The real second subject unmistakably echoes Negro music, with two possible ancestors, the well-known spiritual, *Swing Low, Sweet Chariot*, and a Negro secular song. For purposes of comparison, both these tunes are given below the Dvorak theme:

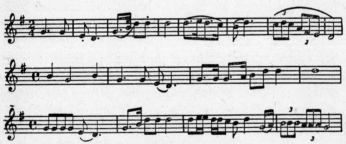

There is considerable development of the opening theme, and all three subjects return in the recapitulation, with the Coda showing a further treatment of the first subject.

The second movement is the familiar Largo (originally called Legenda), best known through such vocal adaptations as *Goin' Home* and *Massa Dear*, but actually Bohemian rather than negroid in its mood. The plaintive slow melody is introduced by the English horn:

A contrast is created by a more agitated theme, leading to reminders of the thematic material of the first movement, in cyclic style.

The Largo returns before the close of the movement, and a Coda repeats the solemn chords which had served as an Introduction.

A brilliant Scherzo follows, built up on snatches of melody, in minor key:

There are two Trios, the first suggesting a country dance, again Bohemian rather than American:

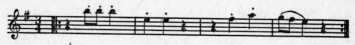

The second Trio has a theme built from major chords. There is a Coda with another reminder of the symphony's opening theme, as well as whispered snatches of the start of the Scherzo, ending in a fortissimo E minor chord.

The Finale begins with an Introduction of chords and octaves, possibly derived from the sequences of the slow movement, then going into a stately theme in the symphony's basic key of E minor:

It has never been pointed out before that this theme might easily have been influenced by the refrain of an American folk-song, *Peter Gray*:

A second theme, of skipping character, contrasts with the opening melody:

Eventually the broad minor theme goes into major key and doubles its time to produce a remarkable and perhaps intentional suggestion of *Yankee Doodle* itself:

There is a recapitulation, and the long, elaborate Coda brings back snatches of all the important themes of the earlier movements, making the symphony truly cyclic in form, with the opening syncopation leading logically to the E major chords of the close.

Dvorak's other symphonies (six published and two unpublished) are seldom heard. The first, op. 60, in D major, dates from 1880. The others are op. 70, in D minor; op. 76 in F; op. 88 in G (1889); one in E-flat, another in D minor, and two unpublished in C minor. Of these only two in addition to the *New World* are played with any regularity, the Second and the Third. The symphony known as Number 2 was actually the fifth in the order of composition. It was commissioned by the London Philharmonic Society and first performed by that orchestra at St. James's Hall under the baton of the composer, April 22, 1885.

The Third Symphony, in F, op. 76, had its first performance at the Crystal Palace, London, April 7, 1888, with August Manns conducting.

Far more popular than these minor symphonies is Dvorak's

Carneval Overture, op. 92, one of a set of three conducted by him at Prague, April 28, 1892, when he was about to depart for New York. These Overtures were originally written and performed as a cycle, Nature, Life and Love, and there is a "Nature" theme that runs through all three:

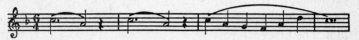

The opening Overture was later given the title *In der Natur*, op. 91, while the last of the trio was called *Otello*, op. 93. Only the *Carneval* is often heard today. It is a lively piece in Sonata form, opening with a brilliant theme which is thoroughly in the spirit of its title:

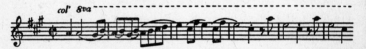

Dvorak's Dramatic Overture, *Husitska*, op. 67, is also occasionally heard. It was written for the festival performance of November 18, 1883, opening the new Bohemian Theatre in Prague. It had been intended as the Introduction to a play by Adolf Subrt, which was never completed. Its subject is the wars of the Hussites, with Johann Ziska as a possible hero. Dvorak used two old melodies as themes, the chorale *St. Wenceslaus* and the Hussite hymn, *All ye who are Warriors of God*, said to have been written by Ziska himself.

A cello Concerto by Dvorak in B minor, op. 104, is still a stand-by with concert performers, and this belongs to the composer's New York period, written between November, 1894 and February, 1895. Victor Herbert's cello Concerto is said to have influenced Dvorak to create this work, and he received some valuable suggestions from Alwin Schroeder, first cellist of the Boston Symphony Orchestra. The dedication, however, was to Hans Wihan, for whom it was actually written. The first performance was by the London Philharmonic, March 19, 1896, with the composer conducting and Leo Stern as soloist, and it was published by Simrock the same year.

Dvorak's violin Concerto in A minor, op. 53, is also played occasionally. It was written in 1879 and revised in May, 1880. Joachim gave it still further revision, and it was dedicated to him. The first performance was in Vienna, December 3, 1883, with Franz Ondricek as soloist.

A set of *Symphonic Variations,* op. 78, written in 1877, was first played in Vienna in 1887. The theme is announced by the strings, and there are twenty-seven Variations, with a fugal Finale.

Dvorak's *Slavonic Dances,* originally written for piano (four hands), have become popular also in their orchestral form. There are two sets of eight each, op. 46 and 72. The best known is probably Number 3 in the first set, in A-flat. These dances made such a success as piano music, after their publication in 1878, that their orchestration by the composer was compulsory. They had their first performance in this form at Prague, May 16, 1879, conducted by Adolf Cech. The second set was published in 1886.

The list of Dvorak's orchestral works is completed with the Symphonic Poems, *The Water Sprite,* op. 107 (1896), *The Golden Spinning-Wheel,* op. 109 (1896), *The Mid-day Witch,* op. 108 (1896), *The Wood Dove,* op. 110 (1896) and *Heroic Song,* op. 111 (1897); the *Slavonic Rhapsodies,* op. 45, a *Romance* for violin and orchestra, op. 11 (1873) and a piano Concerto in G minor, op. 33 (1876).

FRIEDRICH SMETANA

Closely associated with the name of Dvorak is that of Friedrich (Bedrich) Smetana (b. Leitomischl, Bohemia, March 2,

1824; d. Prague, May 12, 1884). He has been called "the father of Bohemian music," and is today best known by his opera, *The Bartered Bride*. Smetana was largely self-taught in music, fighting against parental objections and eventually securing the help of Liszt in opening his own piano school. He conducted the Philharmonic Orchestra of Godeborg in 1856 and that year wrote three symphonic poems, *Richard III*, *Wallenstein's Camp* and *Hakon Jarl*. Later he became active in the opera at Prague, where his *Bartered Bride*, to a libretto by Karl Sabina, was first performed May 30, 1866. Its Overture has become a familiar concert number.

Smetana's most important orchestral work, however, is the cycle of six pieces grouped under the title, *Ma Vlast* (My Country). The first is named *Vyséhrad* (an ancient castle of the Bohemian kings) and the second is the well-known *Ultava* (The Moldau), dated 1874. *Sarka* and *From Bohemia's Meadows and Groves* were written in 1875, *Tabor* (The Camp) in 1878 and *Blanik* in 1879.

The Moldau is a famous river of Bohemia, and this section of the cycle follows a charming program, describing the union of two streams and the gradual development of the resulting river as it flows through the picturesque country, with constant changes in its own character and appearance. The chief theme of *The Moldau* represents the river itself, with something of the quality of a folk-song:

Among Smetana's other works is a *Triumph Symphony* (1853) and a *Festival March*, written for the Shakespeare tercentenary in 1864. The composer suffered from deafness, writing some of his best music while thus handicapped, and his tragic life ended with the loss of his reason.

EDVARD HAGERUP GRIEG

B. Bergen, Norway, June 15, 1843; d. there Sept. 4, 1907.

There is far more cheerfulness in the life of the outstanding Scandinavian composer, and a consistent charm in his music. Grieg studied at the Leipzig Conservatory in 1858, with Richter, Reinecke and others, and later at Copenhagen (1863) with Nils Gade. His first orchestral work was the concert Overture, *In Autumn,* op. 11 (1865). In 1866 he became conductor of the Philharmonic Society of Christiania, and in 1874 he wrote his universally popular music to Ibsen's *Peer Gynt,* originally for two pianos, but now known chiefly through two orchestral Suites. An annuity by the Norwegian Government made it possible for Grieg to devote himself chiefly to creative work and he produced many beautiful songs and piano pieces, three violin sonatas, chamber music, etc. In 1879 he performed his own piano Concerto, in A minor, op. 16, at the Leipzig Gewandhaus. The first public performance had been ten years earlier, in Copenhagen, from manuscript, and the pianist was Edmond Neupert, to whom it was dedicated. The date of composition was 1868, but Grieg made many revisions later. The composer has left a charming story of how Liszt first played it at sight for a small group, and of the master's enthusiastic expressions of approval. The work still ranks among the most popular piano Concertos of all time.

It opens with a drum roll, the piano entering immediately on a crashing chord, followed by a descending sequence and an apparent musical question, which is answered by the orchestra with the first theme, played softly:

This brilliant first movement is followed by an appealing Adagio, whose chief melody is introduced by muted strings:

In the Finale, introduced without a break, the piano plays a short Cadenza and then goes right into the leading subject, which is developed in lively fashion, maintaining interest to the end.

The *Peer Gynt* music has been played by orchestras of all sizes, with a great variety of instrumentation. It is definitely of the salon type, but the charm of its melodic appeal is unfailing. The more popular of the two Suites (op. 55, 1874-5) is the first, which begins with the lovely mood piece known as Morning, built chiefly on this theme:

Then comes the funereal music of Aase's Death. (Aase, pronounced Osa, was Peer Gynt's mother.) Heavy harmonies make up most of this movement:

The third section is Anitra's Dance, Oriental in spirit, and full of a sprightly grace, played by strings and triangle:

The Finale of this Suite is called "In the Hall of the Mountain King," describing the tortures inflicted on Peer Gynt by the evil spirits. Starting softly, in minor key, a single strain of melody works up to a dramatic climax of sound, constantly increasing in both speed and volume:

The second *Peer Gynt* Suite has these titles: Abduction of the Bride; Ingrid's Lament; Arabian Dance; Peer Gynt's Home-coming; Solveig's Song.

One often hears in concert the two *Elegiac Melodies* of Grieg, played by strings alone. They were originally songs, op. 34, with the titles *The Wounded Heart* and *Springtide*, with words by A. O. Vinje (1880). When Grieg turned them into orchestral numbers he changed the names to *Heart Wounds* and *The Last Spring*. The first has this theme:

The Last Spring opens with this plaintive melody:

Grieg is also known orchestrally by a *Romance with Variations*, op. 51, three pieces from *Sigurd Jorsalfar*, op. 56 (Prelude, In the King's Hall; Intermezzo, Borghild's Dream, and Triumphal March), an arrangement of his *Lyric Pieces*, op. 68, and such numbers as the Suite for Strings, *Aus Holberg's Zeit*, op. 40, two *Melodies*, op. 53, *Nordische Weisen*, op. 63, and transcriptions of his songs.

SIR EDWARD ELGAR

B. Broadheath, England, June 2, 1857; d. Worcester, Feb. 23, 1934.

England's chief apostle of musical charm, and a definitely important figure in orchestral literature, is undoubtedly Sir Edward Elgar. His father was an organist who became his first teacher and later took him as an assistant. Young Elgar became conductor of the Worcester Amateur Instrumental Society and eventually succeeded his father as organist at St. George's Church. His Overture, *Froissart*, op. 19, was played at the Worcester Festival in 1890, and his oratorio, *The Dream of Gerontius*, at the Birmingham Festival in 1900.

Elgar's most important orchestral work must be considered the *Enigma Variations*, op. 36, introduced by Hans Richter at the Norwich Festival in 1899. Richter was responsible for some revisions, including the addition of a Coda, and it was in this form that the composer conducted the work at the Worcester Festival, September 13, 1899.

The score consists of a theme and fourteen Variations, each addressed to a personal friend of the composer and presumably describing that person in musical terms. The Enigma is partly in the identity of these people and partly in a "larger theme," which, according to Elgar, never actually appears, but is implied in the music, like a character who remains off-stage throughout a play. The real theme is as follows:

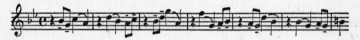

The first Variation has the initials C.A.E., representing Lady Elgar. The theme appears with its rhythm changed, in the second violins, violas, flute and clarinet. The second Variation, marked H.D.S-P., gives the theme to cellos and basses under staccato wood-wind.

Number 3 is initialed R.B.T., showing fragments of the theme in pizzicato violins and oboe, against a counter-theme in the wood-wind. W.M.B. is a spirited, vigorous Variation, with the theme proclaimed by strings, wood-wind and horns. In the fifth Variation, R.P.A., a counter-melody is played first above and then below the theme.

Number 6, Ysobel, has a viola solo, with gentle phrases by the wood-wind and horns. Number 7 is Troyte, a Presto movement. Clarinets embellish the theme in the eighth Variation, W.N. The ninth is called Nimrod, referring to Elgar's friend A. J. Jaeger (literally meaning a huntsman).

Variation 10 is called Dorabella—Intermezzo, full of sparkling joy. The eleventh is initialed G.R.S., probably representing George Roberton Sinclair, an organist and neighbor of Elgar at Hereford. B.G.N. is the twelfth, with cellos predominating. The 13th is marked X.X.X.—Romanza, referring to a sea voyage. The Finale is E.D.U., starting softly and working up to a climax, with a reminiscence of the first Variation before the close.

Elgar's most popular orchestral work is of course the march, *Pomp and Circumstance,* in D major, op. 39, whose Trio appears in the Ode written for the coronation of King Edward VII. The title comes from Shakespeare's *Othello,* Act III, Scene 3: "Pride, pomp and circumstance of glorious war!" At the head of the score the composer placed this verse by Lord de Tabley:

> *Like a proud music that draws men to die,*
> *Madly upon the spears in martial ecstasy,*
> *A measure that sets Heaven in all their veins*
> *And iron in their hands.*

This popular march (there are several others with the same title) is chiefly remembered by the stately melody of the Trio, which is regarded in England almost as a national anthem and often sung to words by Arthur Christopher Benson beginning "Land of Hope and Glory, Mother of the Free!"

This march was dedicated to Alfred Edward Rodewald, founder of the Liverpool Orchestral Society, which first performed it, October 19, 1901.

In addition to the orchestral works mentioned above, Elgar wrote two symphonies, the first in A-flat, op. 55 (1908), the second in E-flat, op. 63, dedicated "to the memory of Edward VII" and first performed at the London Music Festival of 1911; an *Imperial March*, op. 32, written for Queen Victoria's Diamond Jubilee in 1897; a fairly well-known concert Overture, *Cockaigne*, op. 40, introduced in London June 20, 1901; a still more popular violin Concerto in B minor, op. 61, dedicated to and first played by Fritz Kreisler, with the composer conducting, November 10, 1910; a *Coronation March*, op. 65 (1911); a Symphonic Study, *Falstaff*, op. 68 (1913); a Symphonic Prelude, *Polonia*, op. 76 (1915), and a cello Concerto (1919).

FRENCH COMPOSERS OF THE CHARM SCHOOL

In France's considerable contribution to the charming orchestral music of the world an outstanding name is that of Jules Massenet (b. Montaud, May 12, 1842; d. Paris, Aug. 13, 1912). Best known by his operas (*Herodiade, Manon, Thais,* etc.), Massenet wrote a number of effective orchestral pieces, of which several maintain their place in the repertoire.

Most important are the seven Suites of Massenet, the first of which was composed in 1865. The second has the title "Scènes hongroises" (1871); the third, "Scènes dramatiques" (1873); the fourth, "Scènes pittoresques" (1874); the fifth, "Scènes Napolitaines" (1876); the sixth, "Scènes de Feerie" (1879), and the seventh, "Scènes Alsaciennes" (1881). Of these the fourth is the most frequently heard. It consists of a March, Air de Ballet, Angelus and Fête Bohème, the last movement being really a Mazurka, in ballet style. "Scènes pittoresques" was first performed at the Chatelet, Paris, March 22, 1874.

Massenet's three Overtures are also significant, the most

popular having the title *Phèdre*. (The other two are called *Overture de Concert*, 1863, and *Overture Brunaire*, 1899.) The music of *Phèdre*, based upon Racine's drama of 1677, telling of the guilty love of the daughter of Minos and Pasiphae for her stepson, Hippolytus, resulting in his destruction by Poseidon and her own suicide, was composed as an introduction to the play in 1873. It was first performed at one of the Paris Concerts Populaires, February 22, 1874, with Pasdeloup conducting. Twenty-six years later Massenet wrote incidental music for the entire play. Some of the material of the Overture reappears in his opera, *Ariane*. There is a wailing motive at the start and finish, suggesting the tragedy of the ancient story, and the Overture in general follows Racine's version.

An early work by Massenet, the Suite, *Les Erinnyes* (The Furies), was written as incidental music to Leconte de Lisle's tragedy of the same name. It was first played at the Odéon in Paris, January 6, 1873. The music was composed in fifteen days, and created a disagreement between the playwright and the manager of the theatre, Duquesnel, who gave it his complete approval. The dramatist's objections were overcome when Duquesnel threatened to introduce a ballet into the production. The conductor of the premiere was Colonne, with Ysaye as concertmaster. The story of *Les Erinnyes* follows the classic tradition of the killing of Clytemnestra by her son Orestes, after she and her paramour, Aegisthus, had disposed of Agamemnon, and the consequent pursuit of the avenger by the Furies. There are four parts to Massenet's Suite: A Prelude, Scène religieuse, Entr'acte and Finale.

Massenet also wrote a symphonic poem, *Visions* (1890), a *Fantaisie* for cello and orchestra (1897) and a piano Concerto (1903). He is best known, of course, by that popular bit of salon music, the *Meditation* from *Thais*, which has been entrusted to a variety of arrangements.

There is musical solidity as well as charm in the orchestral music of Georges Bizet (b. Paris, Oct. 25, 1838; d. Bougival, June 3, 1875), whose fame rests chiefly on the immensely successful opera, *Carmen*. Bizet's short life did not permit the creation of a great volume of music, but what he did represented a remarkably high standard. The Overture and Entr'actes of Carmen are effective purely as orchestral pieces, and so is the ballet music. But Bizet is best known in the concert hall by the two Suites made from his incidental score to Daudet's play, *L'Arlésienne* (1872). The first begins with an Overture based upon an old Provençal Christmas carol, *The March of the Three Kings,* suggesting the Christmas atmosphere of the play itself.

The second movement is a Minuet, which also has the atmosphere of folk-music. It opens with this charming melody:

Next comes a Romanza, Adagietto, representing a love scene between an old shepherd and the sweetheart of his youth, the wood-wind and strings playing a tender duet. The Finale of this first *L'Arlésienne Suite* is a Carillon, imitating the bells of Christmas Eve, represented by three tones which are played over and over against a dance theme in the strings, with a pastoral section by way of contrast.

The second *L'Arlésienne* Suite contains an Intermezzo, whose chief melody is often sung to the words of the *Agnus Dei*:

A Farandole, one of the liveliest of Spanish dances, supplies the main theme of the most popular movement, preceded by the *March of the Three Kings,* with which the first
Suite opened. Here is the Farandole theme:

Bizet wrote two other Suites, *Roma* and *Jeux d'Enfance*
(Games of Childhood), as well as the Overtures, *La Chasse
d'Ossian* and *Patrie,* op. 19 (1872). The latter was commissioned by Jules Pasdeloup, and introduced by him February
15, 1874.

Emmanuel Chabrier (b. Auvergne, Jan. 18, 1841; d. Paris,
Sept. 13, 1894) is known almost entirely by his orchestral
Rhapsody, *España* (dedicated to Lamoureux, and introduced
at one of his concerts, November 4, 1883). This piece remains
a favorite with concert audiences, and has been much imitated in popular music. Its themes are Spanish dances of the
Jota and Malaguena type, one of which appears also in Wald-
teufel's *España Waltz.* These are typical examples:

Chabrier is occasionally represented on concert programs
by a *Bourrée Fantasque* (1891) and a *Joyeuse Marche* (1890)
dedicated to d'Indy.

There is also Gustave Charpentier (b. Dieuze, Lorraine,
June 25, 1860), composer of the opera *Louise,* whose orches-

tral Suite, *Impressions of Italy,* remains a popular concert
number. It was written at the Villa Medici, while Charpentier
held the Prix de Rome, in 1887, and first played by Colonne,
March 13, 1892, in Paris. The five movements are called
Serenade, At the Fountain, On Mule-back, On the Summits
and Naples.

Edouard Lalo (b. Lille, Jan. 27, 1823; d. Paris, April 22,
1892) is represented on modern orchestral programs by his
Overture to *Le Roi d'Ys* (one of his three operas) and a popular violin Concerto, called *Symphonie Espagnole,* op. 21, written in 1874. Its first performance was at the Chatelet, Paris,
February 7, 1875, with Sarasate as soloist, to whom it was
dedicated. There are five movements, with a Spanish folk-
tune, *The Silversmith,* appearing in the Finale:

Another outstanding theme is the following, which has also
been much imitated in pseudo-Spanish music:

Lalo composed another violin Concerto, op. 20, performed
at Paris in 1874. The Overture to *Le Roi d'Ys* was first played
in 1876, although the premiere of the opera was not until
May 7, 1888. The text was by Edward Blau, and Lalo worked
at the music from 1875 to 1887.

Paul Dukas (b. Paris, Oct. 1, 1865; d. there May 17, 1935)
is famous chiefly for his orchestral Scherzo, *The Sorcerer's
Apprentice,* which became the climax of Walt Disney's *Fan-
tasia.* Its first performance (without benefit of Mickey
Mouse) was by the National Society of Paris, May 18, 1897.
This is outright program music, with a story that goes back

to a dialogue of Lucian, telling of a sorcerer, Pancrates, whose apprentice, Eucrates, tried some of his master's tricks in his absence. He succeeded in making a broom carry water for him, but was then unable to stop it, and when he tried cutting the broom in half, it merely doubled the amount of water in the rising flood. The sorcerer's return stopped the tragedy just in time. Dukas gives the animated broom this theme (slightly suggestive of the familiar "Bum's March"):

Dukas received his direct inspiration for this piece from a ballad by Goethe (*Der Zauberlehrling*), written in 1796. He also wrote a *Symphony in C*, in three parts (1895-6), dedicated to Paul Vidal, who first conducted it at the Paris Opera, January 3, 1897.

The Dukas Overture, *Polyeucte*, written in 1891, was introduced at a Lamoureux concert, January 24, 1892, but not published until 1910. It is based on the tragedy by Corneille (1642), telling of the persecution of Christians in Armenia by the Emperor Decius and the execution of the noble Polyeuctes, who broke the idols in the temple. Dukas wrote two other Overtures, *King Lear* (1883) and *Götz von Berlichingen* (1884), as well as the successful opera, *Ariane et Barbe-Bleu* (1907), and a ballet, *The Peri* (1910), introduced at the Chatelet in April, 1912, with the composer conducting.

An important figure in French music is Ernest Chausson (b. Paris, Jan. 21, 1855; d. Limay, June 10, 1899). His *Symphony in B-flat*, op. 20, is often heard. It was written in 1890 and introduced by the National Society of Paris, April 18, 1891, with a dedication to Henry Lerolle, painter and Chevalier of the Legion of Honor. The symphony is cyclic in form, with the introductory theme reappearing in the Finale.

Chausson's popular *Poème*, for violin and orchestra, op. 25, composed in 1896, was first played by Ysaye at a Colonne concert, April 4, 1897. The same virtuoso assisted in introducing a Chausson Concerto for violin, piano and string quartet, op. 21 (1890) in Brussels, March 4, 1892. The dedication is to Ysaye. Chausson also wrote a symphonic poem, *Viviane*, and other orchestral works.

French orchestral music of the lighter type is to be found in the popular ballets of Leo Delibes (b. St. Germain-du-Val, Feb. 21, 1836; d. Paris, Jan. 16, 1891), *Naila* (1866), *Coppélia* (1870) and *Sylvia* (1876). Gounod's *Funeral March of a Marionette* remains an attractive bit of program music. Benjamin Godard (b. Paris, Aug. 18, 1849; d. Cannes, Jan. 11, 1895) is credited with seven symphonies (one called *Orientale*, op. 84, with its five movements representing different parts of the Orient), as well as Concertos for violin and piano, but owes his fame chiefly to the familiar Berceuse from *Jocelyn*. Gabriel Fauré (b. Pamiers, May 13, 1845; d. Paris, Nov. 9, 1914) wrote excellent orchestral music, including the Suite, *Pelléas et Mélisande*, from the incidental music to Maeterlinck's play, first given in English by Mrs. Patrick Campbell, London, June 21, 1898. The Suite had its first concert performance in Paris (Lamoureux) Feb. 3, 1901.

MISCELLANEOUS ORCHESTRAL COMPOSERS

Karl Goldmark (b. Keszthely, Hungary, May 18, 1830; d. Vienna, Jan. 2, 1915) wrote a respectable number of orchestral works, several of which are fairly well established on concert programs. He was both a violinist and a pianist, making his debut in the latter capacity at Vienna, 1858, playing his own piano Concerto, op. 19. His operas, *The Queen of*

Sheba and *The Cricket on the Hearth,* are occasionally performed, and their Overtures have become concert pieces.

Far more popular, however, is the Overture, *Sakuntala,* op. 13, based on a drama of the same name written in Sanskrit by Kalidasa in the sixth century and considered one of the literary masterpieces of all time. Goldmark's Overture was first played by the Vienna Philharmonic Orchestra, December 26, 1865. The story is that Sakuntala was the daughter of a nymph, and King Dushianta fell in love with her while hunting in the forest. He gave her a ring, with instructions to come to the palace to be his wife. But Sakuntala lost the ring in the river and the King's memory was affected by an evil spell, so that when she turned up she was unrecognized. Eventually the ring was found by a fisherman, the King's memory restored, and Sakuntala reclaimed.

The Overture begins with a slow Introduction, followed by the main theme introduced by two solo cellos and clarinet:

There is a fanfare of brass, later developed, and eventually the main theme returns, with a counter-melody.

Goldmark's First Symphony, in E-flat, has the title *Rustic Wedding,* op. 26. It is actually a Suite in five movements, composed in 1859 and first performed by the Vienna Philharmonic, March 5, 1876, under Hans Richter. It begins with a Wedding March, consisting of twelve Variations and a Finale on a theme announced by the cellos and bass viols:

The second movement is a Rondo, with the title Bridal Song, and the third is a Serenade. The fourth is called "In the Garden" and the Finale is a Dance, of rustic character.

Goldmark's violin Concerto in A minor, op. 28, was first played at Nuremberg October 28, 1878, with Johann Lauterbach as soloist. The first of its three movements has a development section played entirely by the orchestra. The second movement is an Air, with this fairly well known melody:

Another Overture by Goldmark occasionally heard has the title *In Spring Time*, op. 36, and was first performed by the Vienna Philarmonic, December 1, 1889, with the composer conducting. Goldmark's orchestral works include also a *Scherzo* in E minor, op. 19, the *Penthesilea Overture*, op. 31, a *Symphony in E-flat*, op. 35, the Overtures, *Prometheus Bound*, op. 38, and *Sappho*, op. 44, another *Scherzo* in A, op. 45, two more Overtures, *In Italien*, op. 49, and *Aus Jugendtagen* (From Days of Youth), op. 53, and, without opus numbers, a second violin Concerto and a Symphonic Poem, *Zriny*.

Similar in character and importance is the orchestral music of Joachim Raff (b. Lachen, May 27, 1822; d. Frankfort-on-Main, June 25, 1882), a violinist and teacher who early won the attention of Mendelssohn and later toured with Liszt, to whom he is credited with having been very helpful in the onerous details of composition. He was, incidentally, one of the teachers of Edward MacDowell. Raff was himself a prolific composer, producing no fewer than eleven symphonies, nine Overtures, four orchestral Suites, four operas (unperformed), many songs, and a variety of Concertos, sonatas, cantatas, oratorios and chamber music. Of all this material, the public today hears mostly two little violin pieces, *Cavatina* and *La Fileuse*.

Two of the Raff symphonies, however, have known considerable popularity in the past and are still occasionally played. Best known is the one called *Im Walde* (In the Forest), third in the list of eleven, and with the already astonishingly high opus number 153. This symphony, in F, was written at Wiesbaden in 1869 and first performed at Weimar, April 17, 1870, with Karl Stör conducting. It was published in January, 1871. The three movements have definite programs, with the titles Daylight, Twilight (Dreams; Dance of the Dryads) and Night (The Wild Hunt). A theme from the first movement appears again at the end of the symphony, suggesting the effect of dawn.

The Fifth Symphony of Raff, in E, op. 177, has the title *Lenore,* and is also programmatic. The four movements were called by the composer Happiness in Love, Parting, Reunion in Death and Introduction and Ballad (after Bürger's *Lenore*). The *Lenore Symphony* was composed at Wiesbaden in 1872, and had a private performance on December 13th of that year, with Raff conducting. Its first public performance was given by Bilse in Berlin, October 29, 1873. One theme from this *Lenore Symphony* may be worth quoting because of the notoriety it received some years ago in a sentimental novel called *The First Violin,* where it was constantly whistled by the hero.

The remaining symphonies of Raff are as follows: 1. *To the Fatherland,* in D, op. 96 (1859-61); 2. C major, op. 140 (1886); 4. G minor, op. 167 (1871); 6. *Life, Aspiration,*

Suffering, Struggle, Death, Fame, D minor, op. 189 (1873); 7. *In the Alps,* B-flat, op. 201 (1875); 8. *Sounds of Spring,* A, op. 205 (1876); 9. *In Summer,* E minor, op. 208 (1878); 10. *Autumn,* F minor, op. 213 (1879); 11. *Winter,* (posthumously published) A minor, op. 214 (1876-7). The last four were intended as a cycle of the seasons. The Raff Overtures include such titles as *Jubilee, Ein feste Burg, Romeo and Juliet, Othello, Macbeth* and *The Tempest.* There are also a Sinfonietta, a Suite for violin with orchestra (*La Fête d'Amour*) and two cello Concertos.

Chiefly known today by his violin Concertos is Max Bruch (b. Cologne, Jan. 6, 1838; d. Berlin, Oct. 2, 1920), a pianist and composer who also won fame by his choral works (chiefly cantatas, one of which, *Arminius,* he conducted in Boston in 1883), besides writing three symphonies and other orchestral music.

The three violin Concertos of Bruch are still in the repertoire of most concert soloists, with the first and second showing a consistent popularity. The first is in G minor, op. 26, sketched in 1857 and completed in 1865-6. Its first performance was at Coblenz, April 24, 1866, with the composer conducting and Otto von Königslöw as soloist. Joachim, to whom this Concerto was dedicated, suggested some revisions, and introduced the new version in Bremen, January 7, 1868, with Karl Reinthaler conducting. It was published in the same year. An outstanding and characteristic theme from Bruch's First Violin Concerto is the following (Adagio):

The Second Concerto, op. 44, in D minor, was instigated by Sarasate, composed at Bonn in 1877 and played from manuscript on November 3rd of the same year at the Crystal

Palace, London, with August Manns conducting and the solo part played by Sarasate, to whom Bruch dedicated the work. It was published in 1878. Here is the opening theme:

The Third Violin Concerto of Bruch, also in D minor, op. 58, was dedicated to Joachim, who introduced it at Düsseldorf, May 31, 1891, when the composer conducted a festival program made up entirely of his own works.

A *Scottish Fantasie* by Bruch, op. 46, is also occasionally played by violinists in orchestral concerts. It was written in 1879-80 and dedicated to Sarasate, who gave it its first performance in Hamburg, in September, 1880. It was published the same year. Sir Walter Scott was the inspiration for this work, and each of its four movements contains a Scotch folk-tune: 1. *Auld Rob Morris;* 2. *The Dusty Miller;* 3. *I'm a doun for lack o' Johnnie;* 4. *Scots wha hae wi' Wallace bled.*

Bruch's arrangement of the traditional Hebrew melody, *Kol Nidrei,* for cello and orchestra, op. 47, remains one of the popular concert pieces for that instrument. It was written during the composer's residence at Liverpool, 1878-80, and had its premiere at the Leipzig Gewandhaus, October 20, 1881, with Adolph Fischer as soloist. This ancient melody, heard at the beginning of the evening service on the Day of Atonement, but differing markedly in various synagogues, has undergone many arrangements, of which Bruch's is still considered the best.

Sarasate and Joachim both contributed to the orchestral literature of the violin, the former with his *Zigeunerweisen,* still a popular virtuoso piece, and the latter with three Concertos and a set of Variations, besides adding Cadenzas to the

Beethoven violin Concerto and other masterpieces. Joachim also wrote several orchestral Overtures.

Another violinist-composer still popular with virtuosos is Wieniawski, best known by his *Souvenir de Moscow,* op. 6, chiefly a set of Variations on the Russian air, *The Scarlet Sarafan,* originally one of 223 songs by Alexander Warlamoff. Wieniawski also composed two violin Concertos, and had the distinction of being befriended by Tschaikowsky's patroness, Nadejda von Meck, when he himself was destitute. The tune of *The Scarlet Sarafan* has become a familiar one:

A greater contribution was made by Henri Vieuxtemps (b. Verviers, Belgium, Feb. 20, 1820; d. Mustapha, Algiers, June 6, 1881), who wrote six violin Concertos, two cello Concertos and several orchestral works. His first violin Concerto, in E, op. 10, was composed in 1839, at Narva, Russia, where the young violinist was recovering from an illness. It was first played by the composer in St. Petersburg, March 16, 1840, and published in 1842. A supposedly later Concerto in F-sharp minor, op. 19, was actually written first. There is also the popular *Ballade and Polonaise* of Vieuxtemps, op. 38, which the composer introduced as violin soloist in 1861. The *Ballade* is in G minor and the *Polonaise* in G major, with no pause between the two parts.

The spectacular Paganini wrote four Concertos for the violin, of which two are lost. Only the first, in D (originally E-flat), is heard today, and this is often limited to the first movement, which contains a popular, flowing melody:

This Concerto was written in 1820 and published in Paris in 1851. There are also orchestrations of Paganini's *Moto Perpetuo* (by Frederick Stock), *Konzertstück* (by Fritz Kreisler), *Grand Fantasie* (by Cesar Thomson) and *Introduction, Theme and Variations* (by August Wilhelmj).

The cello has been given popularity by David Popper (with a Concerto) and Leon Boëllmann, whose *Symphonic Variations*, op. 25, were first played at a Lamoureux concert in Paris, November 27, 1892, by Joseph Salmon, to whom they are dedicated. This composer also wrote a *Symphony in F* (1893) and other orchestral works, but is remembered only by these Variations, which are closely knit about an attractive theme:

The great pianist, Paderewski, is represented in the orchestral repertoire by a *Symphony in B minor,* op. 24, written in 1907 and first performed by the Boston Symphony Orchestra, February 12, 1909. It is a tribute to Poland, and its third movement has a definite program, actually in the form of a symphonic poem, representing the Polish Revolution of 1863-4. Paderewski also wrote a *Polish Fantasie* for piano and orchestra, op. 19, composed in 1893 and first played on October 4th of the same year at the Norwich Festival, England, under the baton of Alberto Randegger, with the composer as soloist. The dedication is to the Princess de Brancovan. Paderewski's famous *Minuet* is often heard orchestrally as salon music.

An earlier pianist, Moritz Moszkowski, gained some reputation as a composer, with a Symphonic Poem, *Joan of Arc,* op. 19 (1879), a *Ballade* for violin and orchestra, op. 16, piano and violin Concertos, and three Suites, of which the one in F, op. 39, is occasionally heard, particularly the last two movements, Intermezzo and Perpetuum Mobile. It was written for the London Philharmonic Society, and performed by that orchestra, June 2, 1886. Moszkowski's popular *Spanish Dances,* originally written for piano, are often heard orchestrally.

In the class of salon music belongs Ponchielli's famous *Dance of the Hours,* from the opera, *La Gioconda,* now also a favorite in motion-picture theatres. Of similar melodic appeal is Nicolai's Overture to *The Merry Wives of Windsor,* first performed in Berlin, March 9, 1849, two months before the death of its composer.

The Roumanian Georges Enesco often appears on orchestral programs with his *Roumanian Rhapsody* in A, op. 11, no. 1. (There are two more, in D and G minor.) This attractive music is built on authentic Roumanian themes, freely treated. Enesco has also written two symphonies, a Suite, op. 9, and a *Symphony Concertante* for cello and orchestra.

Percy Grainger has kept alive the spirit of English folk-music with his orchestral arrangements of Morris Dances, as well as original creations. His *Shepherd's Hey,* dedicated to Grieg, was first played by Sir Henry Wood at the Queen's Hall, London, Aug. 19, 1912, and contains four English fiddle tunes, including one named "Stow on the Wold." *Country Gardens* is heard orchestrally as well as on the piano, and *Molly on the Shore* is available in a string version. A *Mock Morris* by Grainger was first performed by Balfour Gardiner at the Queen's Hall April 19, 1912, and composed about two years earlier. Of this Grainger says "No folk-music tune-stuffs at all are used herein."

Spain is represented on orchestral programs by Isaac Albeniz and Manuel de Falla. The former wrote mostly for the piano, but his *Catalonia Suite* was created orchestrally and several parts of his *Iberia Suite* have been successfully orchestrated by Fernandez-Arbos. De Falla is best known by his ballet *El Amor Brujo*, produced in 1915, and followed later by *The Three-Cornered Hat*. His *Nights in the Gardens of Spain*, for piano and orchestra, was first played in Madrid in 1916. It contains three movements: At the Generalife, Far-off Dance and In the Gardens of the Sierra of Cordova.

Hugo Wolf's opera, *Der Corregidor*, has the same story as *The Three-Cornered Hat* (also known as *The Mayor and the Miller's Wife*), and the music of its Prelude and Entr'acte is often heard in concert. It was first produced at Mannheim, June 7, 1896, with Hugo Röhr conducting. Wolf's *Italian Serenade*, first written as a string quartet in 1887, became established as an orchestral piece after some editing by Max Reger. There were to have been two more movements, an Intermezzo and a Tarantella, but these were never finished. A Symphonic Poem, *Penthesilea*, based on the Kleist tragedy, has three parts, with the titles: Departure of the Amazons, Penthesilea's Dream of the Feast of Roses, and Combats, Passions, Frenzy, Annihilation.

The Italian-German Ermanno Wolf-Ferrari keeps a foothold on the concert stage with the Overture to his little opera, *The Secret of Suzanne*, while the lively Intermezzo from *The Jewels of the Madonna* maintains its popularity as light music.

Peter Cornelius owes his orchestral survival to one composition, the Overture to *The Barber of Bagdad*, first presented by Liszt at Weimar, December 15, 1858. Cornelius wrote his own libretto, on material from *The Arabian Nights*, and the

orchestration of the Overture had the benefit of revision by
Liszt, Mottl and others.

Engelbert Humperdinck's popular Prelude to the children's
opera, *Hänsel und Gretel,* was also introduced at Weimar, with
Richard Strauss as conductor, December 23, 1893. It begins
with the familiar Prayer, later developing in a livelier style,
with echoes of the witch's music.

The waltzes of the younger Johann Strauss are often heard
in the concert hall as well as on the dance floor. The most popular is still the *Beautiful Blue Danube,* originally written for
male chorus with rather inadequate words. Others include
*Tales from the Vienna Woods, Artist's Life, Wine, Women and
Song,* etc. The Overture to *Die Fledermaus* (The Bat) is
also a popular piece of salon music.

In the same general class are Offenbach's Overture to *Orpheus in Hades,* Franz von Suppé's *Poet and Peasant Overture,* Herold's *Zampa Overture* and the *Raymond* of Thomas.
Auber's Overture to *Massaniello,* the *Mignon Overture* of
Ambroise Thomas, a dainty *Praeludium* by Armas Järnefelt,
and various orchestral works of Svendsen, Sinding, Gade and
other minor composers have a similar appeal.

Of more serious significance are the Englishmen, Granville
Bantock and Sir Frederic Cowen, and the Irish Sir Charles
Villiers Stanford. Bantock is chiefly a choral composer, but
has written symphonies, Overtures, Suites and ballets. Cowen
has to his credit six symphonies, four orchestral Suites, two
Overtures, a Sinfonietta and a piano Concerto. Villiers Stanford is best known by his *Irish Symphony,* op. 28, whose Fi-

nale contains two Irish folk-tunes, *Remember the Glories of Brian the Brave,* and *Let Erin Remember the Days of Old.* He wrote six other symphonies, several Overtures, an *Irish Rhapsody* and a piano Concerto.

Important contemporary works are treated in the next chapter, with a final section devoted to American composers of orchestral music.

VIII

CONTEMPORARY GIANTS

MUCH IMPORTANT ORCHESTRAL MUSIC has been written in the present century, some of it in recent years, by men who are still producing, and promising still more for the future. Some of this music is extreme in its modernism. Some of it adheres to classic traditions. The greater part is still touched with the spirit of romanticism, in spite of vigorous denials by the ultra-modernists. How much of it is destined to achieve permanence is an open question, which only time can answer.

Reserving all American music for a final section of its own, a number of contemporary European composers, most of them alive at this writing, deserve to be discussed, or at least mentioned, under the title of Contemporary Giants. A few are so well established that their place in orchestral literature is already assured. The order of their consideration is not necessarily that of their importance.

JEAN SIBELIUS

B. Tavastehus, Finland, Dec. 8, 1865.

The place of honor among today's creative musicians is almost unanimously given to Finland's grand old man, Sibelius. He has been voted by American radio listeners the most popular composer of serious music on the air. His seven symphonies are frequently played, and an eighth is awaited with interest. His *Finlandia* has become practically the national anthem of his native land, and the appealing little *Valse Triste* is heard in all kinds of instrumental arrangements.

Although intended for a legal career, Sibelius, who had early in life shown unusual musical gifts, was eventually permitted by his mother and uncle to substitute the study of composition for the law. (His father, a surgeon, had died before Jean had reached the age of three.) At the Helsinki Academy of Music he made good progress, writing independently and originally even while turning out the conventionally correct work demanded by his teacher, Wegelius. Later he received some instruction in Vienna, chiefly from Robert Fuchs and Karl Goldmark.

The career of Sibelius has been helped by repeated grants of governmental annuities, as he soon established his importance in the expression of Finnish nationalism. In time he built a secluded home in the forest near Järvenpää, and there he composed most of his great works. His wife was a member of the artistic Järnefelt family.

The sixtieth and seventieth birthdays of Sibelius were celebrated as national festivals in Finland, and honored all over the world, and at this writing he is well on his way toward his eightieth. In addition to his many orchestral works, he has written much choral and chamber music, songs and pieces for the piano and the violin.

THE SIBELIUS SYMPHONIES

All seven of the symphonies by Sibelius are important, and each has a definite individuality. The First, op. 39, in E minor, was composed in 1899, and given its first performance at Helsinki on April 26th of the same year. It has been called the last great symphony of the nineteenth century, and there are those who find in it the influence of Tschaikowsky.

The opening movement begins in slow time, with an introductory theme by the clarinet over a soft rolling of the kettle-drums.

After twenty-eight measures, the principal theme enters in 6-4 time:

There is a subsidiary theme, announced by the flutes, over tremolo strings and harp:

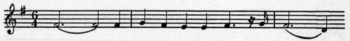

The movement goes through the conventional processes of development and recapitulation, ending with sonorous effects in the brass.

The second movement, also starting slowly, with two introductory measures, presents its main subject through muted violins and cellos, playing in octaves.

A second theme is announced by the horns:

After some stormy development, the section ends tranquilly with a repetition of its opening material.

The third movement is a Scherzo, starting with three measures of pizzicato chords. The chief theme is then introduced by the kettle-drums, alternating with the violins:

The Trio has a new theme, appearing in the brass:

At the end the pizzicato chords are heard, as at the start.

In the Finale an Introduction is derived from the clarinet theme that opened the Symphony. The wood-winds give out the main melody:

There is a second subject by the violins:

Eventually the first theme of the second movement is heard. There is a fugal treatment of the Finale's main theme, reaching an orchestral climax. The clarinet plays the second theme, and after another climax the Symphony ends quietly.

Sibelius' Second Symphony, in D, op. 43, is thus far the most popular of the series. It was begun at Rapallo, Italy, in the spring of 1901, and had its first performance in Helsinki, March 8, 1902, with the composer conducting. Publication was in 1903, with a dedication to Axel Carpelan.

There are conflicting opinions regarding this Symphony. Georg Schneevoight, a friend of the composer, gave it a definite program. The first movement, he said, represented a quiet, pastoral life; the second was patriotic, but timid; the third, full of national feelings, with the Finale expressing comfort and hope for delivery from oppression. Sibelius himself denied any such meaning, and insists that his symphonies are all absolute music, with programs reserved for his tone poems.

After eight measures of Introduction, with a strumming figure in the strings, the leading theme of the first movement is announced by oboes and clarinets:

The second theme is also given to the wood-wind, after bridges of bassoon and string tone:

After development and recapitulation, the strumming strings are heard again at the close.

The second movement is marked Andante, ma rubato. There is a long Introduction by cellos and basses, followed by a lugubrious theme in the bassoons:

The movement develops, poco allegro, and then a long pause leads to a new theme by divided strings:

The third movement, Vivacissimo, has its first theme in the violins:

The second subject is given out by flute and bassoon, three octaves apart:

There is a short Trio, lasting for only thirteen measures, after which the first material is heard in a modified form. The Trio subject returns, going without pause into the Finale, whose main theme is announced by strings and trumpet:

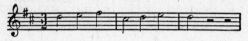

A second subject is suggested by the flute and oboe, and after development and recapitulation, a majestic Coda is formed from the principal theme.

Symphony Number Three is in C major, op. 52, written between 1904 and 1907, and introduced at Helsinki September 25, 1907, with the composer conducting an all-Sibelius program. It is a quiet, restrained work, in classical style. There are only three movements, the second combining the features of an Andante and a Scherzo.

The symphony opens with a folk-like theme by the cellos and basses:

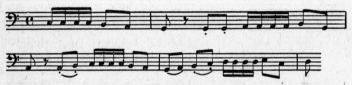

The second subject has touches of syncopation:

In the second movement, there is an alternation of 6-4 and 3-2 time, with two flutes giving out a delicate theme:

The third movement, Moderato, shows the typical Sibelius technique of building a closely knit structure from thematic snatches, apparently unrelated, but gradually brought together in an impressive unity. The oboe is heard at the outset:

The flutes and clarinets introduce another theme:

The final subject is first given to the violas and cellos:

Sibelius finished his Fourth Symphony, in A minor, op. 63, in 1911, and it was introduced at Helsinki on April 3rd of the same year. The composer called it "a protest against the compositions of today" and announced that there was "nothing, absolutely nothing of the circus about it."

The slow first movement is remarkable for its compression, with four notes at the start supplying the thematic germ of the entire movement, in fact of the symphony as a whole:

A solo cello announces the second theme:

The movement ends with a repetition of the opening material.

In the second movement the oboe gives out the chief subject:

A second theme is given to the violins:

There is still a third subject, by the oboe and clarinets:

The third movement is a free fantasy on a fragmentary theme in the cellos:

The Finale is again typical of the Sibelius workmanship, with tiny, episodic themes gradually pieced together, including this one in the first violins:

Sibelius' Fifth Symphony, in E-flat, op. 82, belongs to the year 1915 in its original form, and was introduced on the composer's fiftieth birthday, December 8th of that year, at Helsinki, with Robert Kajanus conducting. It was revised in 1916 and conducted by the composer in its new form on December 14th, at Helsinki. There were still further revisions up to 1919, and on November 24th of that year the Symphony was heard at Helsinki in its final version.

The first two movements are generally considered and played as one, closely linked together by a four-note motto, played by the horn in the first two measures, and creating the opening theme:

The Scherzo section begins with a blithe theme in the wood-wind, and ends in "an uproar of brass and drums."

Then comes a slow movement which may be considered as either the third or the second, with a set pattern of rhythm serving as the basis of variations which are really continuously changing melodies. The simple, innocent theme which may be considered most important is played by pizzicato violins:

In the Finale, Allegro molto, after a rustling of strings, the violas indicate the first theme:

Then the horns introduce what has been called a "bell theme," which is built up to a tremendous climax in its final announcement by the brass:

The Sixth Symphony of Sibelius is thus far his least known, and perhaps least significant. It was described by its composer as "pure, cold water," compared with the champagne and cocktails served, in his estimation, by other creative musicians of today. The orchestral color is quiet and the interest chiefly formal. Its key is D minor, op. 104, and it was completed in January, 1923, with a first performance at Helsinki on February 19th of the same year, the composer conducting.

The first movement contains a characteristic theme, played by the flutes in thirds:

In the second movement the first violins, divided, give out the chief theme, accompanied by chords in the wood-wind:

The Scherzo's opening theme is chiefly rhythmic, with the violins establishing a pattern consisting of an eighth note followed by a sixteenth. The Finale begins with a heroic subject, played by violins, wood-wind and two horns, forte:

There is an agitated development, with a chromatic style contrasting with the earlier emphasis on the diatonic scale. The Coda again stresses the basic idea of the diatonic scale, with particular attention to the interval of the third.

Sibelius completed his Seventh Symphony on March 2nd, 1924, first calling it merely a *Fantasia Sinfonica*, as it is in one movement. The key is C major, op. 105, and the form is compact and "purely classical." The work was published in 1925. It had been intended for one of the English music festivals, but the illness of the composer prevented this introduction. Leopold Stokowski first played it in the United States with the Philadelphia Orchestra, April 3, 1926.

The symphony opens with an ascending scale in the strings, which remains the basic thematic material throughout. But the dominating theme is in the manner of a fanfare, introduced by the solo trombone:

There is much subtlety of design, with small, fragmentary motives again woven together in the typical Sibelius style. Critics have noted "an Olympian serenity and repose," with Lawrence Gilman summing up the symphony as an "enigmatic, puissant and strangely moving work."

THE TONE POEMS OF SIBELIUS

The most popular of all the works of Sibelius is unquestionably his tone poem, *Finlandia*, op. 26, no. 7. This familiar piece may have been written as early as 1894, but first became known as one of a series of musical accompaniments to historical tableaux, given at Helsinki in 1899, ostensibly in aid of newspaper pension funds, but actually as non-censorable expressions of Finnish patriotism. It was first called merely *Finale*, and later known in Russia as *Impromptu*.

While its nationalistic significance is obvious, *Finlandia* is not based on actual folk-tunes. The melodies are original with Sibelius. Its program roughly represents the feelings of an exile on his return home after a long absence.

The music of *Finlandia* begins with an abrupt, agitated, almost angry theme in the brass, followed by an organ-like response of the wood-wind and a prayerful passage in the strings, suggesting the essential earnestness of the Finnish people. A broad, cheerful theme by the strings begins what might be considered a Sonata form. The second and final theme is the melody which has become famous, often fitted to words, and with the development of these musical ideas the tone poem reaches its eloquent conclusion.

Another important orchestral work by Sibelius, *The Swan of Tuonela*, is really the third section of a symphonic poem,

Lemminkainen, op. 22, in four parts, of which only two are generally heard. The first section was called Lemminkainen and the Maidens; the second, His Sojourn in Tuonela, and the final part, Lemminkainen's Home-coming. The program of these pieces is drawn from the Finnish epic, *Kalevala.*

A note on the score of *The Swan of Tuonela* reads thus: "Tuonela, the Kingdom of Death, the Hades of Finnish mythology, is surrounded by a broad river of black water and rapid current, in which the Swan of Tuonela glides in majestic fashion and sings."

Lemminkainen is one of the four outstanding heroes of the *Kalevala,* a jovial, reckless fellow who gets into scrapes from which he is saved by magic, either his own or his mother's. When he woos the daughter of Pohjola, her mother demands that he perform certain tasks, among them the killing of the Swan of Tuonela with a single arrow. Lemminkainen is himself killed by an old, blind cowherd and his body cut in pieces. But his mother rakes the fragments from under a waterfall and, by her magic, pieces them together so that he comes to life again and returns home with her. This is the scene described in the final section of the Symphonic Poem, *Lemminkainen's Home-coming,* op. 22, no. 4, whose music is boisterous and high-spirited.

The Swan of Tuonela has vaguer outlines and fragmentary melodies, following the impressionistic method of suggestion rather than definite musical description. The swan-like melody, which is its chief theme, is first sung by the English horn, accompanied by muted strings and the soft roll of drums. With answering phrases from other instruments, the music works up to a great climax, followed by the softest pianissimo, the strings playing with the bow-sticks instead of the hair, perhaps imitating the faint flapping of wings. A sighing cello phrase brings the work to an end.

Sibelius' first important work was a Symphonic Poem (with

voices) called *Kullervo*, op. 7, dealing with another of the *Kalevala* heroes. It was first performed in Helsinki, April 28, 1892, but is still in manuscript and apparently has never been heard outside of Finland, although it is there considered a huge success.

But the same period (1893) produced the tone poem *En Saga*, op. 9, which was published in 1903, and has now become fairly well known to concertgoers. The title suggests an old tale, but no specific program has ever been announced. The story would seem to be of Scandinavian rather than Finnish origin, with a blending of pathetic and heroic elements. The score is unusual in the absence of kettle-drums. The prevailing tone is somber, reaching a dramatic climax suggestive of battle, and dying away in "elegiac beauty."

In 1893 Sibelius wrote an Overture, *Karelia*, op. 10, and a Suite of the same title, published together in 1906. (The Suite consists of an Intermezzo, a Ballade and a Finale, alla Marcia.) Karelia is one of the principal provinces of Finland, situated in the southeastern part, between the Gulf and Lake Ladoga. Sibelius went there on his honeymoon and later visited Karelia again with his brother-in-law, Eero Järnefelt. It is a wild country, sparsely populated, and its rough beauty stimulated much of the sturdiness in Sibelius' music. The Overture, *Karelia*, begins with a martial subject in the lower strings. The oboe is then heard in a theme derived from this material, and the strings play a second theme. The Overture closes with a sonorous Coda.

Sibelius also wrote some early incidental music to Adolf Paul's *King Christian II* (Ballad, Nocturne, Elegie, Musette, etc.). Minor orchestral works include *The Bard*, *Odlan*, *The Tempest* (Berceuse, Oak Tree, Humoresque, etc.), *Spring Song*, op. 16, *Canzonetta*, *In Memoriam*, *Night-ride and Sunrise*, *Rakastova*, op. 14 (for strings) and a *Romance* in C, op. 42 (also for strings).

The popular *Valse Triste* is from the music (op. 44) to a drama, *Kuolema,* by Sibelius' brother-in-law, Arvid Järnefelt, who utilized it as the accompaniment to a death scene. The chief theme scarcely needs quotation:

Of far greater importance is the symphonic fantasy, *Pohjola's Daughter,* op. 49, for whose materials Sibelius again consulted the *Kalevala* (literally, Abode of Heroes). The composer conducted the premiere of this composition in St. Petersburg (Leningrad), at one of Alexander Siloti's concerts. It has a definite program, describing the spinning maiden sitting on a rainbow, wooed by the hero Lemminkainen, whom she taunts until he leaves her in a rage.

Another important tone poem, *The Oceanides,* op. 73, was written in 1914 for the Litchfield Festival at Norfolk, Connecticut, commissioned by Carl Stoeckel, and first played there, with the composer conducting, June 4, 1914. It has been described as "a grim picture of a churning northern ocean," and made a very favorable impression on the American public and critics.

The Symphony Society of New York commissioned still another tone poem, *Tapiola,* op. 112, written in 1925 and first performed under the baton of Walter Damrosch, December 26, 1926. *Tapiola* is program music of the suggestive rather than descriptive or narrative type. Tapio is the forest god of Finnish mythology, and this tone poem creates the atmosphere of his natural surroundings, contenting itself with a general impressionism in preference to a detailed musical treatment. It represents perhaps the latest stage in Sibelius' development of the tone poem, and its performances are increasingly frequent.

Worth mentioning also is the incidental music to Maeterlinck's *Pelleas and Melisande,* op. 46 (1905), "dreamy and delicate," and that which Sibelius wrote in 1906 for Procope's *Belshazzar's Feast,* op. 51 (Oriental Procession, Solitude, Night Music, Khadra's Dance). There is a *Spring Song,* op. 16 (1891); a Suite, *Scènes Historiques,* op. 25, 1899 (Overture, Scene, Festivo); incidental music to *Swanwhite* (Strindberg), op. 54, 1918, including *Maiden with the Roses,* etc.; another Suite of *Scènes Historiques,* op. 66, 1912 (The Chase, Love Song, At the Drawbridge); incidental music to Knudsen's pantomime, *Scaramouche,* op. 71, 1913; two *Serenades* for violin and orchestra, op. 69, 1913; also music to Hoffmannsthal's *Everyman,* op. 83, 1915; three pieces for orchestra, op. 96, 1920; an *Impromptu,* op. 87; incidental music to Adolf Paul's *Language of the Birds* (1911); besides some unpublished works and much vocal music with orchestral accompaniment, altogether far more than is generally realized.

Of real significance is the Sibelius violin Concerto in D minor, op. 47, composed in 1903 and revised in 1905, when it was also published, with a dedication to Franz von Vecsey. It was first performed by Karl Halir, a member of the Joachim Quartet, in Berlin, October 19, 1905, with Richard Strauss conducting. Maud Powell introduced it to America in 1906, and it has recently become popular through frequent performances by Jascha Heifetz.

This Concerto is not essentially a display piece, but depends upon pure musical values throughout, seldom giving way to the conventions of the form. The first movement is rhapsodic, well paced and timed, with a brilliant Cadenza. The second contains a broad, slow theme for the solo violin. The soloist also announces the chief theme of the Finale, after four measures of repeated D's in the lower strings. This final Allegro is full of humor and vigor, with a skillful use of intricate rhythmic devices. The Concerto as a whole is now recognized as among the masterpieces of its kind.

RICHARD STRAUSS
B. Munich, June 11, 1864.

Even though he has composed nothing of outstanding importance since 1911, Richard Strauss must be treated as a contemporary composer, and at this writing he is still very much alive. The son of Franz Strauss, first horn player in the Munich Court Opera, and Josephine Pschorr, of the famous brewing family, with the advantages of wealth and musical surroundings, Richard was a prodigy at five and a composer at ten. At sixteen he had a symphony conducted by Hermann Levi, a famed Wagnerian interpreter.

Richard Strauss found himself at twenty-one conductor of the Meiningen Orchestra, succeeding his good friend and propagandist, Hans von Bülow. By that time he had come under the influence of Alexander Ritter, husband of Wagner's niece, who introduced him to "the music of the future" and definitely indicated the career he was to follow. A *Burleske* for piano and orchestra and a program symphony, *Aus Italien,* were preludes to the series of tone poems that startled the musical world and are mostly still popular today.

In addition to these important orchestral works, Richard Strauss has written a number of operas, of which the most significant are *Der Rosenkavalier, Salomé* and *Elektra,* some chamber music of merit, ballets and later symphonic works, piano pieces and a number of truly inspired songs. He has been a first class conductor of opera as well as symphonic music and an adequate pianist, particularly in the days when he accompanied his wife, Pauline de Ahna, one of the best Lieder-singers of her day. For many years Richard Strauss has rested on his laurels, but his musical reputation is too securely established to be affected by the apparent decline of his powers during the past thirty years. He is still a giant among contemporary composers.

THE STRAUSS TONE POEMS

Richard Strauss wrote seven Symphonic Poems, six of which have become popular show-pieces in the orchestral repertoire. The earliest was called *Macbeth*, op. 23, and this initial experiment is not often heard today. It was written in Munich, between 1886 and 1887, and introduced at Weimar, October 13, 1890, with Strauss himself conducting. There are two versions, the first having closed with a triumphal march for Macduff, which was later changed so as to keep Macbeth in the limelight.

Macbeth was published in 1891, with a dedication to Alexander Ritter. The music attempts to sum up the character and soul struggles of Shakespeare's protagonist, without any more definite program than is suggested by this quotation from Lady Macbeth, inscribed upon the score: "Hie thee hither, that I may pour my spirits in thine ear, and chastise with the valour of my tongue all that impedes thee from the golden round, which fate and metaphysical aid doth seem to have thee crown'd withal."

Don Juan, op. 20, was the first of the Strauss tone poems to be published (1890) but its composition, at Munich, took place a year later than that of *Macbeth*, 1887-8. The first performance was by the Grand Ducal Court Orchestra at Weimar, November 11, 1889. It was dedicated to a fellow-composer, Ludwig Thuille.

The Don Juan described in the music of Strauss is not the Don Giovanni of Mozart, pursuing amorous adventures for their own sake and finally keeping a fatal rendezvous with the statue of a man he had killed. The character is actually taken from a poem by Niklaus Lenau, whose conception was that of an idealist, looking eternally for the perfect woman and failing to find her. Disgust is the devil that finally fetches

him, and his death is practically a suicide, as he drops his
sword deliberately while fighting a duel.

The Strauss *Don Juan* opens with a magnificent orchestral
outburst expressive of arrogant sensuousness and immediately
establishing the character of the hero.

Three women presumably appear in the musical story,
and it is possible to work out a detailed program in which
almost every phrase of the music plays a part. Yet it is better
to think of the outstanding themes as having only a general
significance. Here is one that appears quite early, expressing
perhaps the general feminine charm that continually appeals
to Don Juan:

Another melody, played mostly by the wood-wind, may
imply the disappointment following each seduction, resulting
in gradual boredom:

Finally, there is a big, pompous theme, intoned by the horns,
in which one may hear the selfishly idealistic hero himself:

A high, dissonant note in the trumpet seems to indicate the
fatal sword thrust, with an orchestral crash and a long silence

to confirm the death of Don Juan, strings and wood-winds playing mournfully at the close.

Next in order among the tone poems of Strauss is *Tod und Verklärung* (Death and Transfiguration), op. 24, composed in Munich in 1888-9, and played from manuscript under the composer's direction at Eisenach, June 21, 1890. The composition was published in April, 1891, with a dedication to Friedrich Rösch.

The program for *Death and Transfiguration* is supplied by a poem by Alexander Ritter, appearing on the fly-leaf of the score. It may be summed up in the following translation: "In a poor little room, dimly lighted and ominously silent, except for the ticking of a clock, there lies on his bed, fallen asleep after an exhausting, desperate struggle with death, a sick man, with a smile on his face, as if he were dreaming of childhood's golden time. Before long the battle begins anew between the desire for life and the power of death, but without victory on either side, and again there is silence. Sleepless, as in a fever delirium, the sufferer sees passing before his inner eye the rosy dawn of innocent childhood, the more daring sport of youth and the ardent striving of manhood that turns obstacles into stepping-stones to higher things, the storm and stress continuing until the hour of death that now strikes. From Heaven descend toward him, resounding grandly, what he had longingly sought here below: world redemption and world transfiguration."

The music of *Death and Transfiguration* may be divided into four sections, which are closely connected and continuous. The opening is in slow time, with a Death motif, in syncopation, pianissimo, played by the second violins and violas. The wood-wind, accompanied by horns and harps, suggest the smile on the dying man's face as he thinks of his youth. The oboe announces a simple melody which may be considered the motif of childhood.

The second section begins Allegro molto agitato, with Death attacking the sick man. Dissonant chords in the orchestra indicate the desperate struggle. There are two distinct "fever" themes, with the chief Death motif heard again, and a final suggestion of the Transfiguration theme which is yet to come.

In the third section the sick man returns to his dreams and visions of the past. The childhood motif returns, followed by other melodic suggestions of hope, youth and manhood and a broader version of the Transfiguration theme. The struggle begins again, with the Death motif predominating, and a final series of ascending fifths, with decisive strokes of the tam-tam and harp, announces the soul's departure.

Transfiguration rules the final section, with a reminiscence of the childhood motif by the strings, the big theme of apotheosis eventually appearing for the first time in its complete form and bringing the whole tone poem to a climax:

The fourth of Richard Strauss' tone poems is perhaps the greatest, and certainly the most popular today: *Till Eulenspiegel's Merry Pranks,* op. 28. It is called by the composer a Rondo, "nach alter Schelmenweise," which could be translated either as "in the old roguish style" or "after an old rogues' tale." In either case the meaning is equally clear.

The name of Eulenspiegel means literally Owlglass or Mirror of Owls. There is an old German proverb (still significant): "Man sees his own faults as little as a monkey or an owl recognizes his ugliness in looking into a mirror." The original Till was a wandering mechanic of Brunswick, appearing in a Volksbuch by Dr. Thomas Murner (1475-1530) and perhaps actually living as much as a century earlier. He was a practical joker of the coarse, earthy type, and some of his tricks would now be considered unprintable. The Till of the

folk-book escaped the gallows and died peacefully in bed, but
Strauss has him hanged for his misdeeds, although he softens
the blow with a musical apotheosis that is the high spot of the
Rondo.

Till Eulenspiegel was composed in Munich, 1894-5, and
had its first performance at a Gürzenich concert in Cologne,
November 5, 1895, with Franz Wüllner conducting. It was
published in September, the same year, dedicated to Dr.
Arthur Seidl.

It is neither necessary nor possible to give a detailed meaning to this brilliant piece. Strauss himself said to Dr. Wüllner:
"It is impossible for me to furnish a program to *Eulenspiegel;*
were I to put into words the thoughts which its several inci-
dents suggest to me they would seldom suffice and might give
rise to offense. Let me leave it, therefore, to my hearers to
crack the hard nut which the Rogue has prepared for them.
By way of helping them to a better understanding it seems
sufficient to point out the two Eulenspiegel motives which, in
the most manifold disguises, moods and situations, pervade
the whole up to the catastrophe, when, after he has been condemned to death, Till is strung up to the gibbet. For the rest,
let them guess at the musical joke which a Rogue has offered
them."

The two motives representing the hero are as follows, the
first introduced by the clarinet and the second by the French
horn, both full of a sparkling mischief:

The opening of the Rondo, however, shows the first Eulenspiegel motif in the charmingly tender form which it again

assumes near the close, where it suggests the apotheosis of the
rascally protagonist and seems to ask forgiveness for his
crimes. Its melodic relation to the clarinet passage above is
obvious:

These materials supply most of the thematic content of *Till
Eulenspiegel's Merry Pranks*. With elaborate orchestration
the composer develops his musical picture, perhaps referring
definitely to such tricks as Till's riding into the market-place,
scattering housewives, tradesmen, goods and chattels, or his
disguise as an unctuous priest, or flirtations with the village
maidens. One lively tune, formed of descending scales, described as a street song (*Gassenhauer*), is worth quoting:

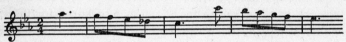

Suddenly the dead march interrupts the merriment. Till has
been brought to trial. His mocking, nonchalant motif still
sounds occasionally through the solemn strains of judgment,
but with less and less confidence. When Till realizes that he is
about to die, a wailing theme is heard (*kläglich*), growing
more and more desperate. Then his own motif carries him aloft
to a sustained high note. His struggles are heard in the music,
growing weaker and finally descending to soft, staccato
chords as his breath gives out. Then comes the epilogue or
apotheosis, completing the tender theme that had been heard
partially at the start, derived from Till's first motif. There is
also a transfiguration of the second Till motif, with a new,
ethereal atmosphere. Finally sadness vanishes. Eulenspiegel
triumphs, even in death. A final reminder of his mocking spirit
leads to closing chords that are musical shouts of laughter.
(Actually Strauss once made pencilled annotations on a score

of this Rondo, substantiating this program, as it is now generally interpreted.)

From the mischief of *Till Eulenspiegel,* Strauss turned to the mysticism of *Also Sprach Zarathustra* (Thus Spake Zarathustra), op. 30, composed in Munich in 1896 and first played at Frankfort-on-Main November 27th of that year, with the composer conducting. This Zarathustra is the creation of Friedrich Nietzsche, not the Zoroaster of Persian legend, but a Superman who preaches the gospel of the Superman. Actually Zarathustra is Nietzsche himself, expounding his views on life and death.

Strauss permitted the publication of the following program for this tone poem: "First movement: Sunrise; man feels the power of God. Andante religioso. But man still longs. He plunges into passion (second movement) and finds no peace. He turns toward science and tries in vain to solve life's problem in a fugue (third movement). Then agreeable dance tunes sound and he becomes an individual, and his soul soars upward while the world sinks far beneath him."

In addition to this explanation, Strauss marked the score of *Thus Spake Zarathustra* with a number of sub-titles, indicating details of meaning in the music. It begins impressively with a solemn motif in the trumpet, leading to a great orchestral climax (including the organ) on a C major chord. The heading "Of the Dwellers in the Back World" refers to those who had looked for a solution in religion, like Zarathustra himself. The horns play a Gregorian Credo.

The next sub-title is "Of the Great Yearning," standing over an ascending passage in B minor for cellos and bassoons, answered by the wood-wind in chromatic thirds. Then comes a passage in C minor, played by the second violins, oboes and horn, whose pathetic strain bears the title "Of Joys and Passions." "Grave Song" (*Grablied*) gives the oboe a tender melody over the Yearning motif in cellos and bassoons. "Of

Science" (*Von der Wissenschaft*) presents a fugal passage, containing all the chromatic steps of the scale, with the responses to the subject coming in always a fifth higher.

Considerably later comes "The Convalescent," in the strings, beginning with cellos and double basses. This is followed by the "'Dance Song" (*Tanzlied*), beginning merrily in the wood-wind. ("The Superman has thrown off the burdens of the common man.") Finally there is a "Night Song" and a "Drunken Song," also called by Nietzsche the "Song of the Night Wanderer," following a fortissimo stroke of the bell, which then dies away after twelve strokes.

The conclusion is mystical, with a forerunner of modern polytonality when Strauss writes simultaneously in two unrelated keys, B major in the high wood-wind and violins, and C major in the basses, pizzicato. "The trombones insist on the unresolved chord of C, E, F-sharp; and in the double basses is repeated C, G, C, the World Riddle." This riddle remains unsolved, by Strauss as well as Nietzsche.

Realism and direct musical imitation appear in the next tone poem of Richard Strauss, *Don Quixote*, which he called "Fantastic Variations on a Theme of Knightly Character," op. 35, with an Introduction and Finale. This composition dates from 1897 in Munich, with a first performance from manuscript at a Gürzenich concert in Cologne, March 8, 1898, Franz Wüllner conducting and Friedrich Grützmacher playing the solo cello part. The score is dedicated to Joseph Dupont.

In spite of its obvious program, this piece could easily pass for absolute music. The Introduction immediately suggests the hero's motif, with "constantly increasing liveliness by other themes of knightly and gallant character." Don Quixote, buried in his reading of chivalric romances, loses his reason and determines to become a knight-errant. According to Cervantes, "through his little sleep and much reading he dried up his brains in such sort as he wholly lost his judgment. His fantasy was filled with those things that he read, of enchantments, quarrels, battles, challenges, wounds, wooings, loves, tempests and other impossible follies."

Fantastic harmonies imply the growing madness of the knight in the Strauss Introduction. The oboe sings of the Ideal Woman, and the trumpets announce that a giant has attacked her and she is being rescued by a knight. The use of mutes on all the instruments, including even the tuba, creates an effect of vagueness and confusion, suggesting the phantasms in Don Quixote's mind, and finally a shrill discord, at the end of a harp glissando, indicates that the knight is actually mad.

The complete theme is introduced by the solo cello, representing the knight himself, and always thereafter associated with that instrument.

Sancho Panza is given an answering theme, first played by bass clarinet and tenor tuba, but later identified regularly with the viola.

This combined thematic material is the basis of ten Variations, each of which supplies the musical description of some adventure of the knight and his squire. In the First Variation, Don Quixote, inspired by the beautiful Dulcinea of Toboso (the Ideal Woman), attacks some windmills, believing they are giants. He is knocked off his horse by the sails, with the mishap musically represented by a run in the wood-wind, a harp glissando and heavy drum-beats.

The Second Variation describes the attack on a flock of sheep, imagined by Don Quixote as the army of the Emperor Alifanfaron. Muted brass gives a realistic imitation of the bleating of the sheep. The knight disables several of the sheep and is stoned by the shepherds.

Variation Three presents Don Quixote and Sancho Panza in a debate on the value of chivalry. The knight speaks nobly of ideals, honor and glory, but the fat squire prefers a life of ease and comfort. Finally the Don loses his temper and bids Sancho hold his tongue.

The Fourth Variation is the episode of the pilgrims (announced by a church theme in the wind instruments). They are carrying a covered image, and Don Quixote interprets the scene as the abduction of a great lady by a band of robbers. He attacks the pilgrims, who knock him senseless and continue on their prayerful way with sacred song. Sancho watches over his unconscious master until he shows signs of life, and then thankfully lies down beside him and goes to sleep, with realistic sounds from the bass tuba and double bassoon.

Number Five among the Variations is the knight's vigil, as he keeps watch over his armor. Dulcinea appears to him in a vision, musically represented by the horn playing the Ideal Woman theme. A Cadenza for harp and violins leads to an orchestral expression of his rapture.

In Variation Six, Sancho Panza points out a common country wench as Dulcinea, and the knight is convinced that an evil spell is responsible for this transformation and vows vengeance. Wood-wind and tambourine suggest the character of the country girl.

The famous Ride through the Air occurs in the Seventh Variation. The two companions sit blindfolded on a wooden horse, imagining that they are flying. Strauss uses an actual wind-machine for realistic effect. A persistent tremolo in the double basses suggests that the pair never really left the ground.

The Eighth Variation is the Journey in the Enchanted Bark. Don Quixote sees an empty boat and is sure that it has been sent to him by some mysterious power for the accomplishment of a glorious deed. His theme becomes a barcarolle as they set forth in the boat. It soon upsets, and they swim back to shore, where they give thanks for their safety, in a religioso passage by the wind instruments.

Don Quixote, once more astride his bony mare, Rosinante, in the Ninth Variation, sees two monks riding along on donkeys. Convinced that they are the magicians who have been working against him, he charges and puts them to flight. An ecclesiastical phrase in the bassoons combines musically with a version of the knight's cello theme.

The Tenth and last Variation depicts the battle between Don Quixote and the Knight of the White Moon, who scores a ridiculously easy victory and at the point of his lance persuades the Don to go home and forget about chivalry. A reminder of the pastoral strain previously used in connection with the sheep episode indicates that the rueful hero will himself settle down as a quiet shepherd.

The Finale is a musical description of the death of Don Quixote. The typical theme of the knight now appears in a new form. The fantastic harmonies of the Introduction have become conventional and commonplace. Don Quixote is now his natural self, "of a mild and affable disposition and of a kind and pleasing conversation." Tremolos in the strings give the first indications of a deadly fever. According to Cervantes, "during the space of three days after he had made his will, he did swoon and fall into trances almost every hour. All the house was in a confusion and uproar; all which notwithstanding the niece ceased not to feed very devoutly, the maidservant to drink profoundly and Sancho to live merrily. For, when a man is in hope to inherit anything, that hope doth deface or at least moderate in the mind of the inheritor the remembrance or feeling of sorrow and grief which of reason he should have by the testator's death." The solo cello utters the knight's last words, recalling his dreams, his fancies and his ambitions, and realizing that they were all empty vanities. In these final passages Strauss reaches sincere emotional heights that he seldom attained elsewhere.

The cycle of Strauss Symphonic Poems is completed by *Ein Heldenleben* (A Hero's Life), op. 40, begun in Munich and finished at Charlottenburg in 1898 and first performed at Frankfort-on-Main, March 3, 1899, with the composer conducting from manuscript and Alfred Hess playing the important violin solos. The composition was dedicated to Willem Mengelberg and his orchestra of the Amsterdam Konzertgebouw, with publication in March, 1899. It is generally agreed that this is an autobiographical piece, with Strauss himself as the hero. The work falls naturally into six sections, each with a definite program.

The composer summed up his intentions by comparing his *Heldenleben* with *Don Quixote*, "whose vain search after heroism leads to insanity," and stating that *A Hero's Life* presented "not a single poetical or historical figure, but rather a more general and free ideal of great and manly heroism—not the heroism to which one can apply an everyday standard of valor, with its material and exterior rewards, but that heroism which describes the inward battle of life, and which aspires through effort and renouncement toward the elevation of the soul."

The music begins with an arrogant, self-confident theme representing the hero himself in his many-sided character, "his pride, emotional nature, iron will, richness of imagination, inflexible and well-directed determination instead of low-spirited and sullen obstinacy." Introduced by strings and horn, this theme is the chief material of the first section, brilliantly developed and reaching a climax in the brass.

The second section deals with "The Hero's Antagonists," a sneering, jealous, backbiting crew, trying to tear down the man whom they envy. Their petty gabble is vividly dramatized by the wood-wind, with emphasis on the dialogue of oboe and flute. This opposition (which may include that of the music critics) is quickly overcome by the Hero, whose theme appears in minor key.

Next comes a section devoted to "The Hero's Helpmate," represented by the solo violin, with a tenderly coquettish theme.

Throughout this section all is peace and sentimental beauty, with a definite love duet, a new theme by the oboe, and a climax of happiness expressed by the violins.

A flourish of trumpets announces the approach of conflict, as the fourth section begins, "The Hero's Battlefield." There is a deliberate, ugly realism in this martial music, with the themes of the Hero and his beloved making themselves audible through the din. Again the Hero is triumphant, but with no real satisfaction in his victory.

"The Hero's Works of Peace" occupy the fifth section, and here it becomes obvious that Strauss is writing about himself, for he quotes literally from several of his well-known compositions. It has been claimed that there are as many as twenty-three such reminiscences, but only a few stand out clearly to the casual listener. One is from the lovely song *Traum durch die Dämmerung* (Dream in the Twilight), and another comes obviously from *Don Juan*. There are recognizable snatches also of *Macbeth*, *Guntram* (an opera), *Till Eulenspiegel, Don Quixote, Zarathustra* and *Death and Transfiguration.*

The final section deals with "The Hero's Renouncement of the World," with a Conclusion which represents "Perfection in contemplative contentment." Resignation takes possession of the Hero's soul. The storms of nature remind him of his own victorious battles. Domestic peace and tranquillity return with the theme of the beloved helpmate. The proud melody of the Hero himself rises again to a sonorous climax. At the close the music becomes almost funereally solemn, perhaps anticipating the death that is inevitable.

OTHER ORCHESTRAL WORKS OF STRAUSS

The notorious *Sinfonia Domestica* of Richard Strauss might easily be included among his tone poems, for it is not really a symphony at all. It is a definite piece of program music, describing a day in the household of the composer, from 7 A.M. to 7 P.M., both hours clearly struck by the clock. There are themes for the father, the mother and the child, with a realistic bit that represents the baby's bath.

The *Domestic Symphony,* op. 53, was written in Berlin in 1903 and published in March of the following year. It was introduced in America March 21, 1904, during the fourth concert of a Strauss Festival at Carnegie Hall, New York, conducted by the composer, with an orchestra organized by Herman Hans Wetzler. It has never found real favor with the public, and is generally considered a mere display of technique, with little or no inspiration.

An *Alpine Symphony,* op. 64, also suffers by comparison with the tone poems, likewise belonging in the class of program rather than absolute music. It was written between 1911 and 1915, with a premiere by the orchestra of the Dresden Royal Opera in Berlin, October 28, 1915, and publication the same year, dedicated to Count Nicolaus Seebach and the Dresden orchestra which introduced it. The instrumentation is as elaborate as any that Strauss ever conceived, but commentators and listeners alike have had difficulty in discovering the necessary spark of inspiration. The program of the *Alpine Symphony* is clearly indicated by such sub-titles as Night, Mountain, Sunrise, Ascent, Entrance into the Forest, Wandering in the Woods, At the Waterfall, Apparition, On Flowery Meadows, On the Alm, Lost in the Thicket and the Underwood, On the Glacier, Dangerous Moments, The Summit and Thunderstorm.

The early *Burleske* of Strauss, for piano and orchestra, representing the composer's first heretical tendencies, was written in 1885-6 when its creator was only twenty-one years old, but already installed as conductor at Meiningen. His friend and predecessor, Hans von Bülow, called it "unplayable," and Strauss himself alluded to it later as "sheer nonsense." It was dedicated to Eugen d'Albert, who played the piano part at its premiere in Eisenach, June 21, 1890, with Strauss himself conducting. The *Burleske* was published in 1894, and has since then become a fairly popular work with the pianistic virtuoso looking for novelty.

An even earlier work is the *Serenade for Wind Instruments*, op. 7, representing Strauss at seventeen, as he wrote it in Munich in 1881. It was dedicated to the composer's teacher, F. W. Meyer, and published in 1883, with its first performance under Franz Wüllner at Dresden, November 27, 1882. It was this piece that first attracted the favorable attention of Hans von Bülow, who conducted it with players from his Meiningen orchestra and became the chief propagandist for the youthful genius who was shortly to become his own successor.

The Symphonic Fantasia, *Aus Italien,* op. 16, was called by Strauss "the connecting link between the old and the new method," and may be considered his first real attempt at the "music of the future." It was dedicated to von Bülow, and had its first performance in Munich, March 2, 1887, with Strauss conducting. There are four movements: On the Campagna, Amid Rome's Ruins, On the Shores of Sorrento and Neapolitan Folk-Life. At one point the melody of Arditi's familiar *Funiculi Funicula* is introduced, evidently under the impression that it is a Neapolitan folk-song.

Excerpts from the Strauss operas are often heard in concert, including the popular waltzes from *Der Rosenkavalier*. The most effective and practical of such selections is the *Dance of the Seven Veils* from *Salomé*. Based on the drama of Oscar Wilde, this opera was a sensation in its day and caused limitless controversy on both sides of the Atlantic. The score dates from 1903-5 and the opera had its premiere at the Dresden Court Opera, December 9, 1905, under the baton of Ernst von Schuch. The *Dance of the Seven Veils* has its touches of Oriental effectiveness and on the whole lives up to its intriguing title. But the music, while technically impressive, has not worn too well and seems to require the stage action and operatic build-up to make it convincing.

IGOR STRAVINSKY

B. Oranienbaum, near St. Petersburg, June 17, 1882.

Somewhat similar to the life of Richard Strauss, at least in its spectacular youth and later decline, is that of the Russian Igor Stravinsky, who still remains one of the most important of contemporary composers in the orchestral field. Starting his creative work somewhat late, as compared with most prodigious musicians, although the son of an opera singer and a musical mother, this modern genius had by 1905 completed the law course at the University of St. Petersburg, then married his second cousin, and for several years wavered in the choice of a career.

Rimsky-Korsakoff, to whom he showed some of his early efforts at composition, at first discouraged him, but eventually gave him some instruction and good advice. For the wedding of Rimsky's daughter Nadia to Maximilian Steinberg, the youthful Stravinsky in 1908 wrote a modest tone poem, *Feu d'artifice* (Fireworks), whose manuscript came back undelivered when his master died a few days later.

But this work and a still earlier *Scherzo fantastique* attracted the attention of Serge Diaghileff, who immediately commissioned Stravinsky to orchestrate a Chopin Nocturne and Waltz for the ballet, *Les Sylphides*. This was so well done that the impresario promptly ordered a complete ballet from the young composer and the result was *L'Oiseau de feu* (The Firebird). Other ballets followed, including such masterpieces as *Petrouschka* and *Le Sacre du printemps* (The Rite of Spring).

After writing *Les Noces villageoises* (The Village Wedding) in 1923, a "secular ballet-oratorio," scored for four pianos, seventeen percussion instruments, solo voices and chorus, Stravinsky abandoned his musical heresies and began to compose in what he called a neo-classic style, imitating Bach and other early masters. As a result the public has definitely lost interest in his work, although his three outstanding ballets are as popular as ever, with or without benefit of staging.

To date the compositions of Stravinsky include also a *Symphony of Psalms,* for chorus and orchestra; *Oedipus Rex,* a dramatic cantata; *Histoire du Soldat, Renard, Apollon Musagète, Perséphone, Pulcinella, Baiser de la Fée, Les Abeilles, Le Rossignol,* symphonies, Concertos, Suites, songs and smaller instrumental pieces.

THE BALLETS OF STRAVINSKY

At least three of the Stravinsky ballets are musically important, with frequent performances on the concert stage. *The
Firebird* was the first to appear, and is still one of the most
popular. It was written between the summer of 1909 and May,
1910, and had its first performance at the Paris Opera, June
25, 1910. Fokine did the choreography, Karsavina danced the
title role, and Gabriel Pierné conducted, with scenery by
Golovin and Bakst.

The story is of the young Prince Ivan, who, wandering in
the night, sees the Firebird plucking golden fruit from a silver
tree. He captures the strange creature, but is satisfied with one
glowing feather, which eventually protects him against the
evil power of the ogre Kastchei, upon whose domain he has
trespassed. Having observed thirteen maidens emerging from
the ogre's castle, and himself obtaining a golden apple, Ivan
defies the magic of Kastchei and enters the dread abode. The
Firebird comes to his rescue and shows him a casket containing an egg which controls the life of Kastchei. The Prince
dashes the egg to the ground, and with its explosion the ogre
dies, the castle vanishes and all the captives are liberated, with
Ivan winning the hand of the most beautiful maiden.

Stravinsky made a concert Suite from the music of this
effective ballet, revising and reorchestrating it in 1919, with a
somewhat simplified instrumentation, and in this form it has
become an exceedingly popular concert number. The Suite is
in five parts, beginning with an Introduction which represents
Kastchei's Enchanted Garden, followed by the Dance of the
Firebird.

Next comes the play of the Princesses with the golden apples
and their dance. The infernal Dance of Kastchei and his Subjects is the real climax of the ballet and a clear forerunner of
the style which was soon to set Stravinsky apart from all other

contemporary composers. A gentle Berceuse serves as a contrast, with muted strings, bassoon and oboe. The Finale consists of music following the death of Kastchei, bringing the Suite to a jubilant conclusion.

Stravinsky finished his second ballet, *Petrouschka,* in Rome, May 26, 1911, and Diaghileff produced it only eighteen days later at the Chatelet in Paris. Nijinsky, Karsavina and Bolm were the principal dancers at the premiere, with Monteux conducting and choreography by Fokine, based on a scenario of Alexandre Benois, who also designed the scenery and costumes. The score was dedicated to Benois when published in 1912.

Petrouschka is ideal ballet material. Its story is the familiar triangle, but the protagonists are puppets, a Ballerina, a Moor and Petrouschka, who is the abused clown with a soul. It has been argued that Petrouschka's woes represent the sufferings of the Russian peasantry, but such symbolism is not necessary for the interest of the story. The scene is a typical Russian Fair, full of bustle and swarming humanity. The showman exhibits his puppets, whom he has endowed with human feelings and passions. In the privacy of their homes we find that Petrouschka is hopelessly in love with the Ballerina, who pities him but inclines to favor the brutal, bullying Moor. When the carnival is at its height, the curtains of the showman's booth suddenly part and Petrouschka rushes out, pursued by the Moor, who kills him with one stroke of his sword. As the crowd gathers around in horror, the showman picks up the battered puppet to show that it is only a doll. But as he walks away, dragging the lifeless form of Petrouschka, the ghost of the tragic clown appears above the booth, shrieking in agony. The showman realizes that his puppet had a soul after all.

The Suite from *Petrouschka,* as generally played in concert, begins with a musical description of the carnival, full of color and dramatic realism. The showman is introduced, and after a Russian dance we meet Petrouschka, the Moor and the Ballerina in her dance. A return to the carnival music brings a dance of the Nurses, the episode of the hand-organ player and the bear and various other dances by characters at the Fair. After the death of Petrouschka, the Suite ends with general dancing. Two folk-tunes occur in the course of the music, both taken from Rimsky-Korsakoff's collection of 100 Russian folk-songs. The first is a Waltz by Joseph Lanner, and the second has the title *Down St. Peter's Road*.

Stravinsky made his deepest impression and most sensational effect with the ballet, *Le Sacre du printemps* (The Rite of Spring). Recently this music has become familiar to a large public by its inclusion in Walt Disney's *Fantasia*, where it is accompanied by animated pictures of geological history, before the dawn of human life on earth. Stravinsky himself used the sub-title *Pictures of Pagan Russia*, and the original name might also be translated Spring Consecration. In its polytonality, dissonance, rhythmic novelty and bold orchestration it is the most extreme and probably the most significant of Stravinsky's works.

The composer had this ballet in mind even before he wrote *Petrouschka*, and discussed the subject with the painter Roerich, who eventually designed the scenery and costumes. He returned to it later, and finished the music in March of 1913. It was introduced at the Champs-Elysées Theatre, Paris, on May 29th of the same year, by Diaghileff's Ballet Russe. Nijinsky was the choreographer and also danced the leading part, with Pierre Monteux conducting. The reception of this apparently enigmatic work by its first audience created one of the scandals of Parisian theatrical history. The laughter, boos, hisses and cat-calls often drowned out the music altogether, and the evening developed into a free fight between rival groups of listeners. But when Monteux first conducted the

Rite as a concert piece at the Casino de Paris, April 5, 1914, it was enthusiastically applauded.

In its concert version *The Rite of Spring* has two parts, The Adoration of the Earth and The Sacrifice. The first part follows this general program: Introduction, Harbingers of Spring, Dance of the Adolescents, Abduction, Spring Rounds, Games of the Rival Cities, The Procession of the Wise Men, The Adoration of the Earth, Dance of the Earth. The second part has the sub-titles: Introduction, Mysterious Circle of the Adolescents, Glorification of the Chosen One, Evocation of the Ancestors, The Sacrificial Dance of the Chosen One.

The music starts with a high-pitched bassoon solo, which "ushers us into the primeval world of Scythia, long before Christianity came to give it history." Insistent rhythms suggest the stamping of feet. Polytonality and polyrhythmic effects are common. The wise men are represented by a persistent figure in the brass. With the opening of the second part the orchestral color becomes more subdued. As the adolescent maidens play their games, a single chord is repeated heavily eleven times. The climax is reached in the Sacrificial Dance of the Chosen One, which creates a physical excitement that is almost unendurable, chiefly by its brutal use of pounding rhythms and "searing discords." The upheavals of *Fantasia,* with its dinosaurs and other monsters, must be considered the mildest possible interpretation of such music.

STRAVINSKY'S MINOR ORCHESTRAL WORKS

Beyond the three great ballets, the representation of Stravinsky in the orchestral repertoire is limited. His early *Fireworks Fantasie,* op. 4, is occasionally heard and still makes an impression with the brilliance of its scoring. Its first performance was at a Siloti concert in St. Petersburg, February 6, 1909, along with the *Scherzo fantastique.* The crackling music actually suggests fireworks, by turns impressionistic and imitative, with realistic touches representing the pin-wheels, explosions of firecrackers, etc.

A piano Concerto, accompanied by wind instruments, completed at Biarritz in April, 1924, was introduced by Koussevitzky in Paris, on May 22nd of the same year, with Stravinsky himself as soloist. The composer called it "a sort of passacaglia or toccata," and refused for a long time to let any other pianist play it, which naturally limited its public performance.

Stravinsky's early opera, *Le Rossignol* (The Nightingale), became eventually a symphonic poem, also practical as a ballet, with the title revised to *Le Chant du rossignol*. It is a clever imitation of Chinese music and worthy of more frequent hearings.

The *Symphony of Psalms* is actually a choral piece, in which the orchestra is largely incidental. It was composed for the fiftieth anniversary of the Boston Symphony Orchestra, but the illness of Koussevitzky forced a postponement, and its first performance was by the Brussels Philharmonic Orchestra in 1930. This is sincerely religious music, mixed with equally sincere sentimentality.

A recent ballet called *The Card Party*, "in three deals," was not taken very seriously. But in 1940 Stravinsky wrote a *Symphony in C major* for the Golden Jubilee of the Chicago Symphony Orchestra, which gave it a world premiere on November 7th of that year. It had been completed August 19th at Beverly Hills, California. The composer conducted the first performance on an all-Stravinsky program. The classic style predominates, with the first movement in Sonata form, the second an Aria, the third a Minuet, Passepied and Fugue, and the Finale a combination of Adagio and Allegro.

Stravinsky's earliest orchestral work was also a symphony, dated 1907, but this is now seldom heard. Two *Little Suites*, however, arranged for small orchestra from piano pieces for four hands, are played occasionally. Their composition dates from the years 1917 to 1925. The first Suite was introduced in Milan, June 17, 1926, and consists of an Andante, Napolitana, Española and Balalaika. The second had its premiere in London, June 8, 1922, with Eugene Goossens conducting. Its four parts include a March, Valse, Polka and Gallop, the last named a parody of Offenbach.

SERGEI RACHMANINOFF

B. Onega, Novgorod, April 1, 1873.

Quite different from the music of Stravinsky is that of another contemporary Russian, Rachmaninoff. He is musically the direct descendant of Tschaikowsky, whom he knew as a boy, and by whom he was definitely influenced. Among his actual teachers were Arensky, Taneieff and his own cousin, Siloti, a pupil of Liszt.

His early friendship with Tschaikowsky made Rachmaninoff a musical conservative and turned him against the nationalistic group. He won the gold medal for composition at the Moscow Conservatory when only nineteen years old, and within a year he had written the famous *Prelude in C-sharp Minor* which was to dog his footsteps the rest of his life. A one-act opera, *Aleko*, was produced in Moscow about the same time.

Rachmaninoff's First Symphony and First Piano Concerto were failures, and it was only by intense mental concentration that he kept himself at the work of composition. His second attempt in each of these forms proved immensely successful.

After a brilliant career as pianist and conductor of opera in Moscow, Rachmaninoff retired to Dresden, where he composed the Symphonic Poem, *The Isle of the Dead,* and other works. Later his tours as a concert pianist brought him to the United States, where he now makes his home, living mostly in New York City.

The works of Rachmaninoff include three symphonies, four piano Concertos, two operas, a *Rhapsody on a Theme of Paganini,* for piano and orchestra, several choral works, a mass and other church music, chamber music, piano pieces and songs. As pianist, conductor and composer he ranks among the greatest of living musicians.

THE RACHMANINOFF SYMPHONIES

Of the three symphonies written by Rachmaninoff, the Second is definitely the most popular. It was written in Dresden in 1908 and performed that season by the Imperial Russian Music Society in Moscow, with the composer conducting. The key is E minor and the dedication is to Taneieff. The symphony is a long one, and generally played with cuts authorized by Rachmaninoff.

After a slow Introduction, the main theme of the symphony appears in the violins:

In the latter part of the first movement this melody is prominent:

The second movement is really a Scherzo, with its chief theme introduced by horns and carried on by the violins:

The third movement, Adagio, is in song form, with three successive melodies, of which the most important is given to the first violins:

The Finale, Allegro Vivace, begins with a lively Introduction, soon followed by a march theme in the wind instruments:

The strings play a second theme, of lyric character. There are reminiscences of earlier thematic material, and a climax is reached with the brass intoning the bass motive of the symphony's Introduction, with the Adagio theme also appearing near the close, as a countermelody to the dance tune of the Finale.

Rachmaninoff's Third Symphony, op. 44, is in A minor, composed in 1935-6, and first performed November 6, 1936, by the Philadelphia Orchestra, with Stokowski conducting. It has only three movements. The first begins with a slow Introduction, proceeding to a faster section (Allegro moderato) in traditional style. The second is marked Adagio ma non troppo and the Finale is an Allegro.

The First Symphony of Rachmaninoff was introduced by Glazounoff at St. Petersburg in 1895, but has since been enveloped in complete obscurity.

RACHMANINOFF'S OTHER WORKS

Of the four piano Concertos by Rachmaninoff, the Second is by far the most popular. After the First had failed completely in a London performance (op. 1, F-sharp minor, 1890-1, revised 1917), the composer despaired of ever writing anything of importance, but was rescued from his morbidity by the psycho-analytical Dr. Dahl, who practically hypnotized him into a state of new confidence and inspiration. The result of this optimistic concentration was the Second Piano Concerto, dedicated to Dr. Dahl himself.

This Second Concerto is in C minor, op. 18, written in 1900 and first performed by the Philharmonic Society of Moscow, October 14, 1901, with the composer at the piano. In 1904 it won the prize of 500 rubles offered by the publisher Belaieff in memory of Glinka. It has become Rachmaninoff's best-loved orchestral work.

The solo piano opens the Concerto with a series of chords, as though groping for the key and theme, which are soon supplied in robust fashion by the strings, decorated by the piano in arpeggio style:

After a short orchestral interlude, the piano announces a second theme in E-flat, the relative major to the opening key of C minor:

These materials are worked out in a fairly strict Sonata form.

At the start of the slow movement, Adagio sostenuto, in E major, the strings offer sustained harmonies, after which the piano introduces an accompaniment figure, over which the flute and clarinet in turn supply a melody which is a foretaste of later thematic material:

A Cadenza for the solo instrument is introduced near the close of the movement, after which some new ideas enter in the Coda.

The Finale opens with staccato strings, in hushed voices (reminiscent of Schubert's *Marche Militaire*) and the piano then announces the first theme. But it is the second theme, first played by the strings and later by the full orchestra and piano, that remains in the memory of the listener, clearly derived from earlier materials yet melodically independent and of climactic sweep:

Rachmaninoff's Third Concerto for piano and orchestra is in D minor, op. 30. It was introduced by the composer during his first American tour, with the New York Symphony Orchestra under Walter Damrosch. This Concerto has not attained the popularity of the second, but is built on similar lines and offers equal musical values.

After a somber opening, the piano and orchestra combine again in a typical strain, with strongly marked rhythm. Later there is a theme of more lyric quality, and after considerable development the piano is given a brilliant Cadenza full of technical difficulties.

The second movement begins with a theme of poignant sadness, in the manner of Tschaikowsky, soon relieved, however, by a brighter melodic line and lively rhythms. The piano is treated as part of the orchestra rather than a virtuoso soloist, and this becomes more and more evident as the movement proceeds directly to the Finale. In the latter one hears thematic materials derived from the first movement, with characteristically shifting rhythms and rich orchestration. A slight slowing of the time leads to a dazzling Coda in which the pace grows faster and faster to the end.

The Fourth Piano Concerto of Rachmaninoff, op. 40, was completed in the summer of 1926 and first performed by the Philadelphia Orchestra, March 18, 1927, with Stokowski conducting and the composer at the piano. It was published in 1928, with a dedication to Nicolas Medtner. There are three movements, the first and last both marked Allegro Vivace, connected by a Largo. There is a brilliant Cadenza in the Finale.

Rachmaninoff's *Rhapsody on a Theme of Paganini,* op. 43, for piano and orchestra, often classed with his four Concertos, is actually a set of twenty-four Variations on a melody from the last of Paganini's twenty-four Caprices. (This subject was also used by Schumann, Liszt and Brahms.) The *Rhapsody* was completed in 1934 on the shores of Lake Lucerne, and introduced on November 7th of that year by the Philadelphia Orchestra in Baltimore, with Stokowski conducting and Rachmaninoff playing the piano part. Recently this composition has been used as musical background for the ballet, *Paganini.*

A tone poem by Rachmaninoff called *The Island* (or *Isle*) *of the Dead,* op. 29, has won a secure place in the orchestral repertoire. It is a piece of impressionistic program music, based on the famous picture of the same name by Arnold Böcklin, the Swiss painter, which Rachmaninoff saw in Paris. The picture itself was inspired by the lonely group of the Ponza Islands, north of the Gulf of Naples, and shows a tomb-like island in the midst of a calm sea, with dark green cypresses overhanging the entrance to a crypt, approached by a boat carrying a coffin, watched over by a white-robed figure. Rachmaninoff's music begins with a somber phrase by the harps, Lento. A persistent figure in the cellos suggests the lapping of the water on the boat. There is a climax of brass, reminiscent of the *Dies Irae*. The second part is calmer in mood, with another suggestion of the opening phrase at the close. *The Island of the Dead* was first performed in Moscow during the summer of 1909, the year of its composition.

SERGE PROKOFIEFF

B. Sontzovka, Russia, April 23, 1891.

A rather enigmatic composer, alternately heretical and conventional, is the Russian Prokofieff, now ranked among the most important of modern creative talents. He was a prodigy, composing his first piece at the age of five, with an opera performed in his home at seven. At ten he began the serious study of composition with Glière, and at thirteen was admitted to the St. Petersburg Conservatory of Music, eventually winning diplomas in piano, composition and conducting.

Prokofieff was a well-established composer by the time he was eighteen years old, writing at first for the piano, but producing a *Sinfonietta in A* for small orchestra, op. 5, in 1909, and following this with an orchestral poem called *Dreams*, two Poems for chorus and orchestra, and another orchestral piece, *Autumn*. Five piano Concertos and two for the violin have given Prokofieff a solid reputation in this field. He is also responsible for five symphonies, a Divertimento, several operas, including the popular *Love of Three Oranges*, some ballets, songs and chamber music, and finally the whimsical *Peter and the Wolf*, which has become widely known through phonograph records.

Prokofieff has spent much time in the United States as a concert pianist and conductor of his own works, but considers Paris his home, with visits to his native Russia whenever possible, at least in pre-war days.

PROKOFIEFF'S SYMPHONIC WORKS

The most popular of Prokofieff's symphonies is a brief work labelled *Classical*, op. 25, composed in 1916-7. It is actually an imitation and occasional modernization of the Mozartian style, and has won success largely through its melodic simplicity and charming instrumentation. The *Classical Symphony* was first performed in Leningrad by the State Orchestra, April 21, 1918, the composer conducting, and was introduced to America by the Russian Symphony Orchestra in December of the same year. The dedication is to Boris Assafieff, who has written on music under the pen name of Igor Gleboff.

There are four movements, although the *Classical Symphony* requires less than a quarter hour for its performance. The predominant key is D major. The first movement, Allegro, contains two themes, both introduced by the first violins, carried out in strict Sonata form.

In the second movement, Larghetto, there is one leading theme, again announced by the first violins, with contrasting episodes in Rondo style. The third movement is a Gavotte, in rather modern terms, with strings and wood-wind immediately announcing the chief subject, and a Trio in which flutes and clarinets take the melody. The Finale, Molto Vivace, goes back definitely to Mozart, with two themes, the first for strings and the second for wood-wind, both treated with witty skill.

Of the four regular symphonies by Prokofieff, only the Third, op. 44, has received much attention from American orchestras. It was written in Paris in 1928, and had its first performance there May 17, 1929, with the Orchestre Symphonique under Monteux. The materials of its four movements are from the Prokofieff opera, *The Flaming Angel*. The

Fourth Symphony, op. 47, was written for the fiftieth anniversary of the Boston Symphony Orchestra.

More important than the Prokofieff symphonies are the Suites made from his ballets. The earliest of these was commissioned by Diaghileff, resulting in an orchestral Suite known as *Scythian* or *Ala and Lolli*, op. 20. This is barbaric music on a barbaric subject. There is dissonance, polytonality, daring orchestration. The four movements follow a definite program, corresponding to the stage action of the ballet.

The first movement is called Invocation to Veles and Ala. Veles represents the sun, highest deity of the Scythians. The music describes the invocation of the sun-worshippers and sacrifices to the beloved Ala, daughter of Veles.

Next comes The Evil-God and Dance of the Pagan Monsters. "The Evil-God summons the seven pagan monsters from their subterranean realms and, surrounded by them, dances a delirious dance."

In the third movement, Night, "the Evil-God comes to Ala in the darkness. Great harm befalls her. The moon rays fall upon Ala, and the moon-maidens descend to bring her consolation."

A climactic Finale describes Lolli's Pursuit of the Evil-God and the Sunrise. Lolli, the Scythian hero, goes forth to fight the Evil-God and save Ala. His life is saved when "the Sun-God rises with the passing of the night and smites the evil deity." The Suite closes with a magnificent musical description of the sunrise.

The *Scythian Suite* was composed in 1914 and first performed at the Imperial Maryinski Theatre, Petrograd, January 29, 1916, with Prokofieff himself conducting.

Prokofieff's ballet, *Le Pas d'Acier* (The Dance of Steel), has also been turned into an orchestral Suite with considerable success. It has a typical Soviet background, emphasizing work on the farms and in the factories of the city. The concert Suite is in six parts: Train of men carrying provision bags; Sailor with bracelet and working woman; Reconstruction of scenery; The Factory; The Hammers and Final Scene.

This ballet was originally produced in Paris, June 7, 1927, and first presented in America by the League of Composers, April 10, 1931, with Stokowski conducting the Philadelphia Orchestra.

After puzzling his hearers with a number of dissonant and difficult compositions, Prokofieff announced that he had written something that everyone could understand in *Peter and the Wolf*, a "symphonic story for children," op. 67. This delightful orchestral piece, with a narrator's voice in the background, proved equally satisfying to adults and may have surprised the composer by its quick rise to popularity. It is today probably his best-known work.

The story is a simple little fairy-tale of a boy who catches a wolf that had swallowed a duck. Peter is assisted by a bird that had escaped from a cat, and hunters from the forest finish the job. All these characters are represented by fairly obvious but charming themes, fully described by the narrator. Prokofieff's little joke has been taken seriously by his listeners, and the result is rather disquieting to lovers of ultra-modernism. *Peter and the Wolf* had its first American performance by the Boston Symphony Orchestra under Koussevitzky, March 25, 1938, with Richard Hale as narrator. Its world premiere was by the Moscow Philharmonic, May 2, 1936, the year of its composition.

A *Divertimento* by Prokofieff, op. 43, is occasionally heard in concert. It was finished in October, 1929, and had its first performance on December 22nd of that year, during a Prokofieff festival, with the composer conducting. There are four movements, with a close relation of thematic materials between the first and the last. The old-fashioned name of Divertimento implies a piece of music in the manner of a Suite, and this composition lives up to the name, although in modern terms.

Quite popular, and increasingly familiar, is the jaunty March from *The Love of Three Oranges*, often heard orchestrally as well as on the piano.

THE PROKOFIEFF CONCERTOS

Prokofieff's First Piano Concerto, in D-flat, op. 10, was written in 1911, and first performed at Moscow in July, 1912, with the composer as soloist. It is in one continuous movement, Allegro brioso, a clear forerunner of the significant works of the same type to come.

The Second Piano Concerto, in G minor, op. 16, dates from 1913, and was introduced at the little town of Pavlosk, near St. Petersburg, in August of that year. The manuscript was lost in the upheavals of the Revolution, but Prokofieff reconstructed it in 1923, with improvements, and the new version had its premiere in Paris, May 8, 1924, under Koussevitzky, with the composer at the piano. There are four movements: Andantino, Scherzo, Intermezzo and Finale.

Prokofieff's Third Piano Concerto is in C major, op. 26, and was composed between 1917 and 1921. Its first performance was in Chicago, December 16, 1921, with the composer as pianist. The first movement goes into an Allegro after a short Introduction. The second is a Theme with Variations. The Finale begins with a staccato theme, interrupted by what Prokofieff calls "the blustering entry of the piano."

The Fourth Piano Concerto of Prokofieff is seldom heard, but the Fifth, in G, op. 55, has won some popularity. Furtwängler first conducted it with the Berlin Philharmonic, October 31, 1932, with the composer as soloist. There are five movements, each having at least four themes, "enough for three Concertos," according to Prokofieff. Melodic and concise, the whole piece runs little over twenty minutes, with the piano employed in "concertante" style, not as a virtuoso instrument.

A violin Concerto by Prokofieff, in D, op. 19, is often played and has already become a standard concert work. It was introduced by Koussevitzky in Paris, October 18, 1923, with Marcel Darrieux as soloist. As in the last piano Concerto, the solo instrument is treated symphonically, as part of the orchestra, rather than in virtuoso style.

Other orchestral works by Prokofieff include a Suite from the ballet, *Chout*, excerpts from the opera, *The Gambler*, a cello Concerto, a Suite from *The Prodigal Son*, and the Incantation, *They are Seven*, for tenor solo, chorus and orchestra.

DMITRI SHOSTAKOVITCH

B. St. Petersburg, now Leningrad, Sept. 25, 1906.

The man who is gradually asserting himself as the most brilliant of contemporary composers is the Soviet representative, Dmitri Shostakovitch. His career has been spectacular from the outset, even though he has spent practically all his time in Leningrad thus far.

Entering the local Conservatory at the age of thirteen, he studied piano with Nikolaieff and composition with Steinberg and Glazounoff. He graduated at nineteen with an amazing technical equipment and the sure touch of a mature composer. His First Symphony, created the same year, became an international sensation. It has been followed by six others, each of individual interest, and all celebrating the political and social ideas of the Soviet Republic.

His opera, *The Nose*, was written in his early twenties, and the later *Lady Macbeth of Mtsensk* (*Katerina Ismailova*) brought him new fame, as well as the condemnation of his

Russian comrades, who felt that he had temporarily deserted his ideals in a search for the lurid and the spectacular. A ballet, *The Limpid Stream,* was similarly criticized on the grounds of a "formalistic" style. Both these works were banned by the Soviet authorities, but Shostakovitch regained political favor through his later symphonies.

In addition to such larger works, Shostakovitch has written much music for the piano, including twenty-four Preludes, a Sonata and a Concerto, chamber music, including a string quartet and a piano quintet, and a number of scores for Russian films. He is unquestionably at the moment the most widely discussed of living composers.

THE SHOSTAKOVITCH SYMPHONIES

Victor Belaieff has described the symphonic style of Shostakovitch as "the negation of thematic development . . . a method which is the converse of Liszt's 'transformation of themes.' " He says: "Shostakovitch not only refrains in general from repeating a theme in its original or in a transformed version—the accepted custom with symphonic composers— but in writing a theme he even avoids the repetition of identical motifs and melodic turns of phrases. One gets the impression that he wants every bar of his composition to be different from the rest. He applies this method also to the distribution of the parts, striving to attain a completely independent design for each of the orchestral parts in the score."

The First Symphony was completed in 1925, "the product," according to Shostakovitch, of his "culminating studies at the Conservatory." It was first heard in Leningrad, May 12, 1926, under the baton of Nicolas Malko. Bruno Walter introduced it to Berlin in November, 1927, and Leopold Stokowski gave it an American premiere with the Philadelphia Orchestra, November 2, 1928.

This First Symphony by Shostakovitch, op. 10, differs from the others in that it is not avowedly "an utterance of political and economic faith." Lawrence Gilman called it "primarily an aesthetic expression rather than a tonal tract." Nicolas Slonimsky finds it largely in the tradition of Rimsky-Korsakoff and Glazounoff, but adds that it "shows some definite departure from traditionalism. Thus, the recapitulation in the first movement reverses the order of the subjects. . . . The harmony of the symphony is far more acrid than any academic training would justify and the linear writing is hardly counterpoint-conscious. There are such strange interludes as a kettle-drum solo. The melody structure is angular, chromatic at times, and then again broad, suggesting a folksong rather than a subject for a symphony. Yet there is enough symphonic academism in this first important work of Shostakovitch to connect it with his academic training."

The four movements of the symphony have the conventional Italian indications of tempo, but with the slow movement coming just before the Finale.

At twenty-one Shostakovitch began his career as, in effect, "Composer-Laureate to the Soviet State," writing his *October Symphony* in 1927 for the tenth anniversary of the Bolshevik Revolution. It was played simultaneously in Moscow, Leningrad, Kiev and Kharkoff as part of the nation-wide celebration and has been repeated annually for a similar purpose.

The *May Day Symphony*, op. 20, written in 1929, has also become an annual rite, "stirring Russians on each succeeding May Day." It is in one movement, with an optional chorus in the last part, singing a Russian text which gives the key to the whole composition, a glorification of work and machinery, addressed to the Proletarians on May Day. The musical materials are loosely organized, but effective.

The Fourth Symphony of Shostakovitch, which followed the unfavorable reception of his *Lady Macbeth* opera, was finished in December, 1936, but withdrawn after a similar criticism of its performance in rehearsal by the Leningrad Philharmonic Orchestra.

With his Fifth Symphony, introduced in Leningrad November 21, 1937, the composer redeemed himself, giving it the sub-title "A Soviet Artist's Reply to Just Criticism." According to Leopold Stokowski, who first played this symphony in America, Shostakovitch here "painted in tone the inner and outer experiences of an artist's life, sometimes expressing the boisterous humor of crowds in the street, as in the fourth part, sometimes painting with ironic splashes of color a gamin-like humor, as in the second part, and sometimes telling by the simplest orchestral means the innermost reveries of his spirit in dark and melancholy coloring, or rising to sublime heights of ecstasy, as in the third part."

This Fifth Symphony is "in the usual sequence of symphonic form." A Moscow critic wrote, after the first performance, that "the composer, while retaining the originality of his art in this new composition, has to a great extent overcome the ostentatiousness, deliberate musical affectation and misuse of the grotesque which had left a pernicious print on many of his former compositions. . . . The fetters of musical formalism, which held the composer captive so long, and prevented him from creating works profound in conception, have been torn off."

The Sixth Symphony of Shostakovitch, op. 53, had its first performance in Moscow, December 3, 1939, and was introduced to America by Stokowski and the Philadelphia Orchestra, November 29, 1940. There are only three movements, the first a Largo, the second really a Scherzo (marked Allegro), and the third, Presto, based on dance rhythms and popular themes from Russian folk-music. Mr. Stokowski's comments include the following: "These three parts are strongly contrasted and are remarkable for the firmness of their melodic outline, rhythm and musical character. . . . Here are harmonic sequences, and several melodies sounding at the same time, making modern counterpoint . . . of great originality and intensity of expression."

A Seventh Symphony by Shostakovitch was presented in Kuibyshev by the Bolshoi Theatre Orchestra, led by S. S. Somosud, March 1, 1942, and had a spectacular American introduction by Toscanini and the NBC Orchestra over the air, July 19, 1942. It was composed during the siege of Leningrad, while Shostakovitch was acting as a firewarden at the Conservatory. A program note quoted the proverb, "When guns speak, Muses keep silent," with the emendation, "Here the Muses speak, together with the guns."

In a broadcast to America, Shostakovitch described his latest symphony as "devoted to the ordinary Soviet people, who have become the heroes of the patriotic war." In an interview the composer mentioned the opening of the first movement "with a calm, lyrical exposition of a theme intended to describe the happy existence of 'ordinary, simple people.' By 'ordinary' I mean not distinguished by any special features or talents—just ordinary, good, quiet people, going about their daily life.

"After this preliminary theme," he continues, "I introduce the main theme, which was inspired by the transformation of these ordinary people into heroes by the outbreak of the war. This builds up into a requiem for those of them who are perishing in the performance of their duty. In the first movement's final passages I introduce something very intimate, like a mother's tears over her lost children. It is tragic, but it finally becomes transparently clear.

"The Scherzo and Adagio movements are of an intermediate character, in which I am moved by the idea that war doesn't necessarily mean destruction of cultural values. The fourth movement can be described by one word—Victory. But my idea of victory isn't something brutal; it's better explained as the victory of light over darkness, of humanity over barbarism, of reason over reaction."

Toscanini called this symphony "inspired," but there was qualified enthusiasm on the part of the American public and critics after its broadcast. The arguments continued after concert performances by Toscanini, Koussevitzky, Stokowski and Rodzinski, and opinions are still in violent disagreement.

A Shostakovitch Concerto for piano, trumpet and strings, op. 35, was first presented by the composer with the Leningrad Philharmonic, October 15, 1933, and introduced to America by Stokowski in one of his Youth Concerts, December 12, 1934, with Eugene List as pianist. There is also a cello Concerto, written in 1934. The two ballets, *The Bolt* and *The Golden Age,* have orchestral significance, as has the substantial volume of film music composed by Shostakovitch.

OTTORINO RESPIGHI

B. Bologna, July 9, 1879; d. Rome, April 18, 1936.

This modern Italian composer belongs among the great men of contemporary orchestral music if only because of his three tone poems, *Fountains of Rome, Pines of Rome* and *Roman Festivals.* He studied with such masters as Martucci, Rimsky-Korsakoff and Max Bruch, taught composition in Bologna and Rome, and toured both Europe and America as a successful conductor of his own works.

Respighi has several operas to his credit, of which *La Campana Sommersa* (The Sunken Bell) was produced at the Metropolitan Opera House in 1928, while a stage triptych, *Maria Egiziaca,* was given its world premiere at Carnegie Hall, New York, in 1932, with the composer conducting the Philharmonic Orchestra.

In addition to the popular Roman cycle, Respighi wrote such orchestral works as *Church Windows, Primavera, Ballade of the Gnomides* and a Suite to *The Birds* of Aristophanes, two ballets, a *Toccata* for piano and orchestra, a *Metamorphose on Modi XII,* some chamber music, pieces for the violin, piano and organ, and transcriptions of Bach and Vivaldi for the modern orchestra.

RESPIGHI'S ROMAN CYCLE

The first of the three Symphonic Poems on various aspects of Roman life, called *The Fountains of Rome,* was written in 1916 and had its first performance under Toscanini in the city it celebrated, February 10, 1918. Four of the famous Roman fountains are described in this music, each representing one section of the score and each, according to the composer, "contemplated at the hour in which its character is most in harmony with the surrounding landscape, or in which its beauty appears most impressive to the observer."

The first part is inspired by the Fountain of Valle Giulia at Dawn. It "depicts a pastoral landscape; droves of cattle pass and disappear in the fresh, damp mists of a Roman dawn."

The second section describes the Triton Fountain at Dawn, introduced by "a sudden loud and insistent blast of horns above the trills of the whole orchestra. . . . It is like a joyous call, summoning troops of Naiads and Tritons, who come running up, pursuing each other and mingling in a frenzied dance between the jets of water."

Next comes the Fountain of the Trevi at Mid-Day, with "a solemn theme, borne on the undulations of the orchestra," which, "passing from the wood to the brass instruments, assumes a triumphal character. Trumpets peal; across the radiant surface of the water there passes Neptune's chariot, drawn by sea-horses and followed by a train of Sirens and Tritons.

The procession then vanishes, while faint trumpet blasts resound in the distance."

The Finale describes the Villa Medici Fountain at Sunset, "announced by a sad theme, which rises above a subdued warbling. It is the nostalgic hour of sunset. The air is full of the sound of tolling bells, birds twittering, leaves rustling. Then all dies peacefully into the silence of the night." (These are the composer's own program notes.)

The second and most popular of the cycle is *The Pines of Rome*, composed in 1924 and first performed at the Augusteum, Rome, in 1925. It was introduced to America by Toscanini, conducting the New York Philharmonic Orchestra at Carnegie Hall, January 14, 1926, with the composer conducting it in Philadelphia the following day. There are again four sections, played without pause. The first describes the Pines of the Villa Borghese. According to the program printed on the score: "Children are at play in the pine grove of the Villa Borghese, dancing the Italian equivalent of 'Ring around a Rosy,' mimicking marching soldiers and battles, twittering and shrieking like swallows at evening."

The scene changes to the Pines Near a Catacomb, beginning with muted and divided strings and soft, muted horns. "We see the shadows of the pines which overhang the entrance to a catacomb. From the depths rises a chant, which re-echoes solemnly, sonorously, like a hymn, and is then mysteriously silenced."

The third section deals with the Pines of the Janiculum, containing a piano Cadenza and a clarinet solo. "There is a thrill in the air. The full moon reveals the profile of the pines of Gianicolo's Hill. A nightingale sings (represented by a gramophone record of a nightingale's song, heard from the orchestra)." (This recording has always been compared unfavorably with musical imitations of the voice of the bird.)

The final part deals with the Pines of the Appian Way, in

march time and "misty dawn." "The tragic country is guarded by solitary pines. Indistinctly, incessantly, the rhythm of innumerable steps. To the poet's fantasy appears a vision of past glories; trumpets blare, and the army of the consul advances brilliantly in the grandeur of a newly risen sun toward the sacred way, mounting in triumph the Capitoline Hill." (This climax has been called the greatest volume of tone ever produced in an orchestra by natural methods.)

The third and last of this trio of effective orchestral works is called *Roman Festivals,* composed in 1928 and given its first performance by Toscanini with the New York Philharmonic Symphony Society at Carnegie Hall, February 21, 1929. Here once more there are four connected parts, designed by Respighi to create "visions and evocations of Roman fêtes," and again the composer permitted a detailed program to be printed in the score.

The first part is called Circus Maximus, and the music describes "the crowded aisles and benches . . ." "the mob, intent upon games, gorged with free food and cheap wine." "The sky is overcast and threatening, but the throng sees only the bright sand of the arena and the purple booth of the Caesar, whom they greet with lusty 'Aves.' A band of Christians is led into the arena, singing a hymn of joy and resignation. The cages of the lions are thrown open, and their howling mingles with the voices of their victims. The song of the martyrs is triumphant—and then obliterated."

Then comes The Jubilee. "Weak and weary, almost despairing, a band of pilgrims plods along the road to Rome. Laboriously they climb to the summit of Monte Mario, and then suddenly bursts upon their vision the incomparable panorama of the Eternal City. 'Rome! Rome!' they shout in frenzied joy, and they join spontaneously in a hymn of praise and thanksgiving, while from the church towers of Rome comes a welcoming reply."

The third section is The October Festival. "The harvest is in; the grapes have given their life-blood for the making of rich wines. The populace takes to the woodlands and the fields, with games and sports and love-making, with hunts and merry music. After nightfall, serenades and swift, cool kisses, and the eternal stratagems of youth."

Finally comes The Epiphany, "religious exaltation transposed into very human revelry. Trumpets are like strident young imperative voices in the crowd. Peasants dance, wildly, heavily, with abandon; the leaping measures of the saltarello are heard, and the harsh, sweet whining of a barrel organ. The uproar is terrific."

Respighi's *Toccata* for piano and orchestra, composed at Capri in August, 1928, was first performed at Carnegie Hall, New York, by the Philharmonic Symphony Society, Mengelberg conducting, on November 28th of the same year, with the composer at the piano. There is also a *Concerto Gregoriano* for violin and orchestra, and a piano Concerto in the Mixolydian mode.

The Metamorphose on Modi XII was written for the fiftieth anniversary of the Boston Symphony Orchestra, to whom it is dedicated, and was given its first performance November 7, 1930, by that organization, with Koussevitzky conducting. It is actually a theme with variations, each variation representing a different mode.

ARNOLD SCHÖNBERG

B. Vienna, Sept. 13, 1874.

Regarded as the arch rebel of modern music, Arnold Schönberg commands respect for his scholarship and admiration for a few examples of his creative genius, regardless of their comprehension by the general public. He studied with the late

Alexander von Zemlinsky, by whom he was strongly influenced and carefully guided, and whose sister, Mathilde, he eventually married. Gustav Mahler also encouraged him and gave him ideals of artistic integrity that made it possible for Schönberg to face the mockery and abuse which have been heaped upon him throughout his career.

Schönberg has been called "the father of atonality," and his system of harmony permits the combination of any tones of the chromatic scale. His compositions show a gradual development from romantic post-Wagnerism to the extremes of cacophony, but his logic is irresistible. As a teacher he has been markedly successful, and his book on harmony, *Harmonielehre,* is considered the final word on the subject. Among his pupils are such men as Alban Berg, Anton Webern and Egon Wellesz.

Exiled from Germany through the rise of Hitler, Schönberg has become an American citizen and now makes his home in Hollywood. His works include several operas, the choral *Gurre-Lieder* and *Pierrot Lunaire,* chamber music, including a quartet in D minor and the sextet, *Verklärte Nacht* (later arranged for string orchestra), several revolutionary pieces for orchestra, some highly original songs and piano music.

SCHÖNBERG'S ORCHESTRAL WORKS

The most popular orchestral music by Schönberg is unquestionably the string arrangement of his sextet, *Verklärte Nacht* (Transfigured Night), a Wagnerian piece in the style of *Tristan und Isolde,* far removed from his later heresies. It was originally composed in 1899 and published in 1905 as opus 4. The orchestral version was published in 1917.

Schönberg's inspiration came from a poem of the same title by Richard Dehmel, in the collection called *Weib und die Welt* (Woman and the World). It tells of a man and woman, walking through a cold, barren landscape, in the moonlight. She confesses her sin: the child that she is to bear is not his. He forgives her, and they find a new understanding in the trans-figured night.

The music creates a succession of moods, closely following the poem, and expressing in turn "the pain of guilt, the agony of confession . . . and the serene loveliness of understanding and forgiveness."

Schönberg's *Five Pieces for Orchestra*, op. 16, written in 1909 and published in 1912, created a sensation when they were first performed by Sir Henry Wood at a London Promenade Concert, September 3, 1912. The composer himself called them "experiments in dissonance," and they represent perhaps his most violent excursions into the realm of cacophony. At a later performance he gave the five parts individual names, as follows: 1. Presentiments; 2. The Past; 3. The Changing Chord; 4. Peripeteia; 5. The Obbligato Recitative.

Schönberg is also represented orchestrally by a *Kammer-symphonie*, a *Theme and Variations* and a *Suite for Chamber Orchestra*. The *Song of the Wood Dove*, for contralto and orchestra, from his *Gurre-Lieder*, is occasionally heard as a concert piece and has won considerable popularity in its recorded form.

ERNEST BLOCH

B. Geneva, Switzerland, July 24, 1880.

Now an American citizen, Ernest Bloch is recognized today as the world's leading creator of music in the Jewish idiom. He studied the violin with Ysaye in Brussels, and composition with Dalcroze in Geneva, Ivan Knorr at Frankfort-on-Main and Ludwig Thuille in Munich, after which he lived in Paris and Geneva, until he came to America in 1916.

Bloch's opera, *Macbeth,* was produced at the Paris Opéra Comique in 1910, and an early symphony, in C-sharp minor (1902), attracted the favorable notice of Romain Rolland. His real success, however, began in the United States. A concert of his works was given by the New York Society of the Friends of Music at Carnegie Hall in 1917, with Artur Bodanzky conducting, and in 1918 Bloch himself conducted a full program of his compositions with the Philadelphia Orchestra. (He had come to this country as conductor for the dancer, Maud Allan.) Later he became director of the Cleveland Institute of Music and the San Francisco Conservatory, and for some years he was subsidized by the family of Jacob and Rosa Stern of San Francisco, so that he could devote himself entirely to composition. The chief fruit of this period was a *Sacred Service,* considered by some his most important work. Bloch also won a prize of $3,000, offered by the magazine, *Musical America,* for his symphony, *America.* Earlier and perhaps more significant orchestral works include his *Three Jewish Poems,* the Hebrew Rhapsody, *Schelomo,* for cello and orchestra, the *Israel Symphony,* several *Psalms* for solo voices and orchestra and a *Concerto Grosso* for strings and piano. Bloch has also composed some significant chamber music, including a prize-winning Suite for viola and piano, *Baal Shem* for violin and piano, a piano quintet, etc.

BLOCH'S ORCHESTRAL MUSIC

The Rhapsody, *Schelomo* (Solomon), for cello and orchestra, has become the best-known work of Ernest Bloch. It was written early in 1916 at Geneva and made a deep impression at the New York concert of 1917. Bloch wrote at the time to Philip Hale: "It is not my purpose, not my desire, to attempt a 'reconstitution' of Jewish music, or to base my works on melodies more or less authentic. I am not an archaeologist.

I hold it of first importance to write good, genuine music, my music. It is the Jewish soul that interests me, the complex, glowing, agitated soul, that I feel vibrating throughout the Bible."

The *Schelomo Rhapsody* has been called a perfect expression of its subject matter. According to one critic (Guido Gatti): "The violoncello, with its ample breadth of phrasing, now melodic and with moments of superb lyricism, now declamatory and with robustly dramatic lights and shades, lends itself to a reincarnation of Solomon in all his glory, surrounded by his thousand wives and concubines, with his multitude of slaves and warriors behind him. His voice resounds in the devotional silence, and the sentences of his wisdom sink into the heart as the seed into a fertile soil."

Another popular work by Bloch is his *Concerto Grosso* for strings and piano. It was begun at Santa Fé, New Mexico, in December, 1924, and finished in Cleveland during April, 1925. Its first public performance was in the Hollywood Bowl, August 15, 1925. The composition follows the form established by Handel, with some modern touches, the piano taking the place of the harpsichord. There is a Prelude, opening with heavily accented chords. The second movement is a melancholy Dirge. This is followed by a Pastorale and Rustic Dances, and the Finale is an elaborate Fugue, closing with reminiscences of the opening movement.

Bloch's "Epic Rhapsody" *America* (1927-8) was dedicated to the memories of Lincoln and Walt Whitman. The latter is represented by a motto on the score: "O America, because you build for mankind, I build for you." The work is programmatic, with sub-titles for each of its three movements, as follows: 1. 1620. The Soil—The Indians—(England)— The Mayflower—Landing of the Pilgrims; 2. 1861-5. Hours of Joy—Hours of Sorrow; 3. 1926. The Present—The Future. Familiar American tunes are embodied in the score, includ-

ing *Old Hundred, Old Folks at Home, Hail Columbia* and
Pop Goes the Weasel, with an anthem at the end, to be sung
by the audience, to which *Yankee Doodle* is added in aug-
mentation. Bloch's much earlier *Israel Symphony,* written
in Geneva, 1912-16, was first conducted by the composer at
Carnegie Hall, New York, May 3, 1917, in the concert of the
Friends of Music, to whose President, Mrs. J. F. D. Lanier,
it was dedicated. The Finale calls for five solo voices, added
to the orchestra.

Bloch's violin Concerto was first performed by Szigeti in
Cleveland, December 15, 1938, Mitropoulos conducting. It
is described by its composer as definitely non-Jewish music.

OTHER CONTEMPORARY COMPOSERS

The list of foreign-born contemporaries writing significant
orchestral music might well be endless. How much of it can
truly be called "great" is largely a matter for the future to de-
cide. There is room here only for a brief account of those compositions which have already established for themselves a
place of some security in the concert repertoire.

Arthur Honegger (b. Havre, March 10, 1892) created
something of a sensation with his "orchestral movement,"
Pacific 231, first performed by Koussevitzky in Paris, May 8,
1924, and later popularized in the United States. It is the
musical representation of a giant locomotive, traveling at high
speed. The composer has made these comments on the work:
"What I wanted to express in the *Pacific* is not the noise of an
engine, but the visual impression and the physical sensation of
it. . . . I have always had a passionate love for locomotives.
To me they are like living creatures. . . . As a subject I have
taken an engine of the 'Pacific' type, known as 231, an engine
for heavy trains of high speed. . . . On a sort of rhythmic

pedal sustained by the violins is built the impressive image of an intelligent monster, a joyous giant." The music is both impressionistic and imitative.

Honegger also wrote a composition called *Rugby*, descriptive of a football game.

Gustav Holst (b. Cheltenham, England, Sept. 21, 1874; d. London, May 25, 1934) is best known by his orchestral Suite, *The Planets*, which requires also a female chorus. There are seven sections to this work, representing in turn Mars, the Bringer of War; Venus, the Bringer of Peace; Mercury, the Winged Messenger; Jupiter, the Bringer of Jollity; Saturn, the Bringer of Old Age; Uranus, the Magician; and Neptune, the Mystic. Holst also wrote a *Cotswolds Symphony*, an *Oriental Suite* and a *Fugal Overture* for orchestra.

Jaromir Weinberger (b. near Prague, Jan. 8, 1896) has contributed a popular Polka and Fugue to orchestral programs, from his opera, *Schwanda, the Bagpiper*. The Polka is a jolly, folk-like tune, intentionally rather clumsy, suggesting the dance of peasants, and the Fugue is rather surprisingly derived from its theme, contrasting musical sophistication with deliberate and charming simplicity.

Recently Weinberger composed a *Lincoln Symphony*, which had its premiere in Cincinnati, under the direction of Eugene Goossens, October 17, 1941. He has given the four movements these descriptive titles: The Hand on the Plow; Scherzo Héroique; O Captain, my Captain! and Deep River (based on the Negro spiritual of the same name). While living in New York City, Weinberger has also composed Variations and a Fugue on *Under the Spreading Chestnut Tree, The Legend of Sleepy Hollow,* a Prelude and Fugue on *Dixie,* and other works.

Paul Hindemith (b. Hanau, Nov. 16, 1895) has been a prolific composer, as well as a virtuoso of the viola, now spending most of his time in America. He is definitely a modernist, but tries sincerely to reach a larger audience than is usually associated with the term and has written much attractive chamber music as well as orchestral works and operas. He is best known in the concert hall by excerpts from his opera, *Mathis der Maler* (Mathis the Painter), inspired by the altar piece of Matthias Grünewald (1480-1530). A symphony of three movements, taken from this opera, was first played by Furtwängler and the Berlin Philharmonic, March 12, 1934 (Angelic Concert, Entombment, The Temptation of St. Anthony).

For the fiftieth anniversary of the Boston Symphony Orchestra Hindemith wrote a piece which he called simply *Concert Music,* for strings and brass instruments. He has also composed five numbers with the title *Chamber Music,* actually orchestral music for various combinations of instruments, a Concerto, *Der Schwanendreher,* and some Symphonic Dances, besides a Concerto for Orchestra and other works. The Overture to Hindemith's opera, *News of the Day,* which had its premiere in Berlin under Klemperer, June 8, 1929, is often heard.

G. Francesco Malipiero (b. Venice, March 18, 1882) has contributed much to the literature of the orchestra, although his music is seldom heard in America. He has a number of operas to his credit, as well as some interesting chamber music. In the Malipiero orchestral list are a symphony and a violin Concerto, with several pieces of program music, carrying descriptive titles.

Alfredo Casella (b. Turin, July 25, 1883) is another Italian who has made valuable contributions to modern orchestral music. He indulges occasionally in satire, but his serious works are also outstanding. Two symphonies and a violin Concerto are to be found in the solid list of his orchestral compositions.

Mario Castelnuovo-Tedesco (b. Florence, April 3, 1895) also has his satirical moments, and there is an intensely human quality in much of his music. He has written two Concertos for the violin and one for the cello, besides an Overture to *The Taming of the Shrew* and other orchestral works.

Darius Milhaud (b. Aix, Provence, Sept. 4, 1892) combines a lyric gift with technical brilliance and is becoming increasingly popular in America. He has written much music for the theatre, as well as chamber music. Among his orchestral pieces are a *Symphonic Suite, Five Etudes* (with piano), *Serenades, Saudades de Brazil* and a piano Concerto.

Alban Berg (b. Vienna, Feb. 9, 1885; d. there, December, 1935) made his greatest impression with the opera, *Wozzeck*, but also wrote important orchestral and chamber music. His orchestral list includes a violin Concerto.

Bela Bartok (b. Nagyszentmiklós, Hungary, March 25, 1881) is best known for his researches in Hungarian folk-music and his skillful treatment of such materials. His music has pronounced nationalistic tendencies, expressed in a modern style. There are two orchestral Suites among his works.

Zoltan Kodaly (b. Keczkemèt, Hungary, Dec. 16, 1882) is generally associated with Bartok as representing the modern expression of Hungarian nationalism and utilizing native folk idioms. His most popular work is the opera, *Háry János*, from which he has made an orchestral Suite that is often heard in the concert hall.

Erno Dohnanyi (b. Pressburg, Hungary, July 27, 1877) has long been an outstanding musical representative of his country as pianist, conductor and composer. His orchestral works include symphonies and piano Concertos, as well as a popular piece called *Ruralia Hungarica,* treating folk materials, and a set of *Variations on a Nursery Tune,* for piano and orchestra, using the familiar ABC melody of childhood as a theme.

A few more names of contemporary composers may be listed here, with space only for a mention of their more important orchestral works. The names are in alphabetical order.

Franco Alfano: *Suite Romantica; Symphony in E; Symphony in C minor.*

Kurt Atterberg: *Rhapsody for Piano and Orchestra; Concert Overture;* Symphonies 1, 2, 3 (*Ocean*), 4, 5 (*Funèbre*), 6; violin Concerto; cello Concerto.

Georges Auric: *Fox-Trot; Nocturne; Suite.*

Arnold Bax: Five Symphonies; *Festival Overture; Four Pieces; Symphonic Variations* (piano); *Tintagel; Summer Music; Mediterranean; Happy Forest; Overture to a Picaresque Comedy; The Tale the Pine Trees Knew.*

Lord Berners: *Three Pieces; Fantaisie Espagnole; Fugue.*

Arthur Bliss: *Concerto for two Pianos and Orchestra; Two Studies; Battle Variations; Hymn to Apollo; Introduction and Allegro; Color Symphony.*

Frank Bridge: *Isabella; Dance Rhapsody; Lament for Strings; Sea Suite; Sir Roger de Coverley.*

Carlos Chavez: *Sinfonia de Antigona; Sinfonia India; Ballets.*

Josef Holbrooke: *The Raven; The Viking; Byron; Skeleton in Armor; Queen Mab; The Bells; Dramatic Choral Symphony; Three Blind Mice; Auld Lang Syne;* violin Concerto; Suites.

Paul Juon: *Symphony in A; Chamber Symphony; Serenade;* two violin Concertos; *Triple Concerto.*

Ernest Krenek: Three Symphonies; Concerto Grosso; violin Concerto.

Constant Lambert: *Prize-Fight; The Bird Actors; Rio Grande; Music for Orchestra; Elegiac Blues;* Symphony.

Nikolai Miaskowsky: Over 20 Symphonies; *The Silence; Alastor; A Tale; Sinfonietta.*

Alexander Mossoloff: *Twilight;* piano Concerto (chamber orchestra); *Iron Foundry.*

Nicholas Nabokoff: *Lyric Symphony;* Piano Concerto; *Le Fiancé.*

Selim Palmgren: *Floden; Pastorale; The Seasons; Finnish Lullaby; The River* (piano); *Metamorphoses* (piano); *April.*

Riccardo Pick-Mangiagalli: *Allegro di Concerto; Notturno e Rondo Fantastico; Sortilegi; Two Preludes; Four Poems; Small Suite; Prelude and Fugue.*

Ildebrando Pizzetti: *Overture for a Tragic Comedy; Poem* (violin); *Rondo Veneziano; Concerto dell' Estate;* cello Concerto; *Canti della Stagione Alta* (piano).

Henri Rabaud: Symphonies in D minor and E minor; *Divertissement on Russian Songs; Eclogue; La Procession Nocturne.*

Roger-Ducasse: *French Suite; Variations on a Solemn Theme; Petite Suite; Nocturne de Printemps; French March; Sarabande; Au Jardin de Marguerite.*

Albert Roussel: Four Symphonies; *For a Spring Festival;* Suites; Concerto; piano Concerto; *Evocations* (chorus).

Victor de Sabata: *Notte di Platon; Juventus; Gethsemane.*

Franz Schreker: *Ekkehard; Romantic Suite; The Birthday of the Infanta; The Wind; Dance Suite; Small Suite for Chamber Orchestra.*

Cyril Scott: Two *Passacaglias; Festival Overture;* violin Concerto; piano Concerto; *Noël; The Melodist and the*

Nightingales (cello); *The Muses; Concertino* (harpsichord); *Poem* (piano).

Alexander Tansman: *Dance of the Sorceress; Symphony in A minor; Symphonic Overture; Toccata;* Two piano Concertos; *Impressions; Symphonic Intermezzo; Four Polish Dances; Two Symphonic Moments; Triptych; Piano Concertino.*

Ernest Toch: *Fanal;* Two piano Concertos; cello Concerto; *Fantastische Nachtmusik; From my Fatherland; Bunte Suite; Westminster Fantasy.*

Vincenzo Tommasini: *Chiari di Luna; Il Beato Regno; Paesaggi Toscani; Prelude, Fanfare and Fugue; Carnival of Venice; Napoli;* violin Concerto.

Hector Villa-Lobos: *Legende Indigène; Suite Paulista; Carneval de Brazil; African Dances; The Golden Centaur.*

Henry Waldo-Warner: *Three Elfin Dances; Hampton Wick; The Broad Highway.*

William Walton: *Portsmouth Point; Sinfonia Concertante;* viola Concerto; violin Concerto; First Symphony.

Egon Wellesz: *Prayers of the Maidens to Mary; Pre-Spring;* violin Suite.

Alexander von Zemlinsky: Three Symphonies; *The Mermaid.*

IX

AMERICA'S OWN

It is difficult to write of America's own music as yet. Only a few works have so definitely established their value that they must be considered a permanent part of the orchestral repertoire. On the other hand, there are hundreds of examples of excellent music in all styles, clamoring for a hearing, and in many cases making a definite impression, if and when they are heard. Any attempt at appraisal would be presumptuous, as well as futile. One can only report what has thus far taken place, and hope for a favorable reaction from future audiences.

The fact of course is that the public performance of serious American music has for many years labored under cruel handicaps, based on a national inferiority complex, the ignorance and prejudice of listeners, the intolerance of critics and the chauvinism of foreign-born conductors and performing artists. The American composer, until recently, has not had a fair chance to be heard. Unfortunately, in too many cases, such hearings as he received made little or no impression. America has long led the world in popular music; but serious music, especially in the orchestral field, has been a stepchild.

This whole subject has been cluttered up with artificial factors, such as social popularity, inside influence, personal salesmanship and commercial backgrounds. The producers of orchestral concerts have almost unanimously labeled Ameri-

can music "bad box-office," and the public has apparently done
its best to justify the term. Actually much music has arrived at
public performance that turned out to be not worth hearing.
On the other hand, there are unquestionably works available
whose success would depend chiefly on repeated hearings.
First performances are no longer difficult to achieve. But
second and tenth and fiftieth performances remain mostly in
the land of dreams, so far as American composers are concerned.

This final chapter will deal, first, with the handful of men
whose creative output has sufficiently asserted its value as to
eliminate real argument (except from stubborn non-conform-
ists), after which there will be at least an attempt to cover
what seems significant in our orchestral field for the present
and possibly the future. Once again the frequency of performance must be used as a guide, so far as detailed discussion
is concerned.

It should be remembered also that American music, in a
little more than fifty years, has passed through what corre-
sponded to the classic, romantic, modern and ultra-modern
schools abroad. Recently all four types of music have flour-
ished simultaneously. Of necessity much of this music has
been imitative of foreign models, and it is not yet possible to
say, in more than a few instances: "This is a definitely and
distinctively American composition."

Our own composers fall quite naturally into three groups:
(1) Those who have written honest, substantial music in the
recognized manner inherited from Europe; (2) Those who
have succeeded in expressing the spirit of America, even in a
fairly obvious fashion, perhaps with the help of programs and
subject matter of popular and national appeal; (3) Those
who have achieved individuality, even originality, with or
without national significance, maintaining an artistic integrity,
no matter what the standards by which they are judged.

From all this material, a few works stand out boldly, of unquestioned importance for all time. A number of others are clearly deserving of attention, and should find their place through the simple process of listening on the part of the public. The rest is largely a matter of guess-work, in which the so-called experts are in complete disagreement, and probably always will be.

OUR ORCHESTRAL PIONEERS

JOHN KNOWLES PAINE (b. Portland, Maine, Jan. 9, 1839; d. Cambridge, Mass., April 25, 1906) is generally considered the father of native orchestral music in the United States, exerting a great influence through his own compositions and his years of teaching at Harvard. Many of his pupils became outstanding composers of the present century. Paine's orchestral works included two symphonies, two Symphonic Poems, Overtures, etc. His Overture to Sophocles' *Oedipus Tyrannus* is still played occasionally, and available on records. It won the gold medal at an international concert in memory of Wagner at Berlin in 1904.

ARTHUR FOOTE (b. Salem, Mass., March 5, 1853; d. Boston, April 9, 1937) was one of Paine's most successful pupils. He is best known today by his chamber music, but wrote several important orchestral works, including an Overture, *In the Mountains,* first performed by the Boston Symphony Orchestra under Gericke in 1887, a Symphonic Prologue, *Francesca da Rimini* (Boston, 1893) and Four Character Pieces after *Omar Khayyam* (1912).

GEORGE WHITEFIELD CHADWICK (b. Lowell, Mass., Nov. 13, 1854; d. Boston, April 7, 1931) became the successor of Paine as leader of our New England group of composers, after studying composition in Germany, and served for many years as director of the New England Conservatory of Music. Chadwick's Symphonic Ballad, *Tam o' Shanter* (1917), still appears occasionally on orchestral programs and may be considered his most popular work. He also wrote six Overtures: *Rip Van Winkle* (1879); *Thalia* (1873); *The Miller's Daughter* (1884); *Melpomene* (1891); *Adonais* (1899) and *Euterp*e (1906). His *Symphonic Sketches* (1907) include *A Vagrom Ballad*, which is also characteristic. A *Suite Symphonique* by Chadwick won the 1911 competition of the National Federation of Music Clubs. There are three symphonies by Chadwick.

HORATIO PARKER (b. Auburndale, Mass., Sept. 15, 1863; d. Cedarhurst, N. Y., Dec. 18, 1919) is best known for his choral works, such as the distinguished oratorio, *Hora Novissima*, and for his operas (two of which, *Mona* and *Fairyland*, won prizes). But he also has some important orchestral compositions to his credit, including a *Symphony in C*, several Overtures and a *Northern Ballad* (1899).

FREDERICK S. CONVERSE (b. Newton, Mass., Jan. 1, 1871; d. Boston, June 8, 1940) is also remembered chiefly as the composer of a prize-winning opera, *The Pipe of Desire*, but figures as a significant creator of chamber music and orchestral works. Among the latter are three symphonies, D minor, C minor and E major; the Overtures, *Youth* and *Euphrosyne;* a Romance, *The Festival of Pan;* a Fantasie, *The Mystic Trumpeter;* a Symphonic Poem, *Ormazd* (Boston, 1912) and a violin Concerto. In 1927 Converse wrote *Flivver Ten Million*, followed in 1928 by *California* and (1929) *American Sketches*.

MRS. H. H. A. BEACH (b. Henniker, N. H., Sept. 5, 1867) also belongs to the New England group, and is best known today as a songwriter and composer of chamber music and piano pieces. Her *Gaelic Symphony,* however, gives her a definite place among our creators of orchestral music, and she has also written a piano Concerto.

EDWARD MACDOWELL (b. New York, Dec. 18, 1861; d. there, Jan. 23, 1908) is generally considered America's leading composer of the older school. His music is of the romantic type, and he is at his best in songs and piano works. Orchestrally MacDowell is most famous for his *Indian Suite* (second in a series of three), and his second piano Concerto. But he also wrote a Symphonic Poem, *Hamlet and Ophelia,* op. 22 (1885), and another called *Lancelot and Elaine,* op. 25 (1888). *Lamia,* after Keats, written in 1888-9, was published posthumously. The *Saracens* and *The Lovely Alda,* published together as op. 30 in 1891, may have been intended as movements of a *Roland Symphony.*

The *Indian Suite,* op. 48, makes use of aboriginal themes, with a distinct program for its five parts: Legend, Love Song, In Wartime, Dirge and Village Festival. It was first performed by the Boston Symphony Orchestra under Emil Paur in New York, January 23, 1896. MacDowell's first piano Concerto, in A minor, op. 15, dates from 1884; the second, in D minor, op. 23, from 1890. Both are still frequently heard, but the second is by far the more important.

HENRY K. HADLEY (b. Somerville, Mass., Dec. 20, 1871; d. New York, Sept. 6, 1937) was the most brilliant and prolific of America's orchestral composers in the romantic style. He was also a conductor of note and founder of the National Association for American Composers and Conductors, which has become a significant organization in the promotion of American music. In addition to several operas and a quantity of chamber music, songs and smaller instrumental pieces, Hadley

composed five symphonies and a number of Overtures and orchestral tone poems.

Hadley's First Symphony, *Youth and Life,* was introduced
in New York in 1897. The Second, called *The Four Seasons,*
won both the Paderewski Prize and that of the New England
Conservatory of Music in 1901. The Third was first played in
Berlin in 1907 and introduced to America a year later by the
Boston Symphony Orchestra. The Fourth, with the title
North, East, South, West (each representing one movement)
was written for the Norfolk Festival of 1911. A Fifth Sym-
phony, *Connecticut Tercentenary,* was also commissioned for
Norfolk by Mr. and Mrs. Carl Stoeckel.

Hadley's concert Overture, *In Bohemia,* first played in
Pittsburgh in 1902, is probably his most popular orchestral
work, although he personally preferred his tone poem, *Salomé,*
introduced in Boston in 1907. The orchestral Rhapsody, *The
Culprit Fay,* won the thousand-dollar prize of the National
Federation of Music Clubs in 1909. Another tone poem,
Lucifer, was commissioned by the Norfolk Festival of 1915.
The Hadley list contains several more works of this type, including *The Streets of Pekin* and *Scherzo Diabolique,* as well
as three Ballet Suites, a cello Concerto and a charming Concertino for piano and orchestra.

EDGAR STILLMAN-KELLEY (b. Sparta, Wisconsin, April 14,
1857) has had a varied and distinguished career as organist,
teacher, critic, conductor and composer. His First Symphony,
Gulliver, is full of humor, and another early work, *Aladdin,*
is a Suite in the Chinese manner. A *New England Symphony*
contains themes based on bird calls, Indian music and Puritan
Psalm tunes. The incidental music to the drama, *Ben Hur*
(1899), makes use of the Greek modes.

Stillman-Kelley's Symphonic Poem, *The Pit and the Pen-
dulum,* was introduced at the Cincinnati Festival in 1925, and

won the composition prize of the National Federation of Music Clubs the same year. A Symphonic Suite, *Alice in Wonderland,* was written for the Norfolk Festival of 1919. Stillman-Kelley has thus stated his views on American music: "The American composer should apply the universal principles of his art to the local and special elements of the subject matter as they appeal to him, and then, consciously or unconsciously, manifest his individuality, which will involve the expression of mental traits and moral tendencies peculiar to his European ancestry, as we find them modified by the new American environment."

RUBIN GOLDMARK (b. New York, Aug. 15, 1872; d. there March 6, 1936), a nephew of the Hungarian Karl Goldmark, was himself a distinguished composer, as well as a noted teacher of composition at the Juilliard Graduate School, and founder and long time President of the New York musicians' club, The Bohemians. Goldmark's *Negro Rhapsody,* 1922, has been a popular piece on American orchestral programs, and his *Hiawatha Overture,* introduced by the Boston Symphony Orchestra in 1900, was highly praised by Huneker and other critics. A tone poem, *Samson,* first played in Boston in 1914, remains in the repertoire, and there is real American spirit in *The Call of the Plains.*

CHARLES TOMLINSON GRIFFES (b. Elmira, N. Y., Sept. 7, 1884; d. New York, April 8, 1920) proved himself in a tragically brief career one of the major creative talents produced in America up to this time. He wrote in the French impressionistic style, yet with an individuality that set him apart from mere imitators. Griffes' most important orchestral work is the tone poem, *The Pleasure Dome of Kubla Khan,* introduced by the Boston Symphony Orchestra shortly before his death in 1920, an atmospheric piece of program music, based on the poem of Coleridge. His *Poem* for flute and orchestra was first played by Georges Barrère with the New York Symphony Orchestra in the same year, Walter Damrosch conducting. One of Griffes' piano pieces, *The White Peacock,* has been orchestrated and thus become his most popular work with an increasingly appreciative public.

ERNEST SCHELLING (b. Belvidere, N. J., July 26, 1876; d. New York, Dec. 8, 1939) won fame through an active career as pianist, conductor and composer, with the distinction of being Paderewski's only pupil. His orchestral works include a *Fantastic Suite,* which he introduced as piano soloist with the Amsterdam Orchestra in 1907; *Impressions from an Artist's Life,* also for piano and orchestra, first played by the Boston Symphony, with the composer as soloist, in 1915; a tone poem, *Morocco,* introduced by the New York Philharmonic in 1927, and the Schelling masterpiece, *A Victory Ball,* describing orchestrally a dance on Armistice Day, and first played by the New York Philharmonic Orchestra in 1923, with Leopold Stokowski conducting. The program of *A Victory Ball* shows the gaiety of the dancers interrupted by the sounds of war, as the spirits of the fallen return, to the roll of drums and the distant sound of Taps. Schelling also wrote a *Symphony in C minor,* a *Symphonic Legend* and a violin Concerto.

HENRY F. GILBERT (b. Somerville, Mass., Sept. 26, 1868; d. Cambridge, May 19, 1928) composed several orchestral pieces that have maintained their activity in performance, with strongly American characteristics. He was MacDowell's first American pupil in composition. Gilbert's *Comedy Overture on Negro Themes* was played by the Boston Symphony Orchestra in 1911. It had been intended as the Overture to an operetta based on the Uncle Remus tales, and it contains

Negro melodies from the Bahamas and the Mississippi steamboats, with a fugue on *The Old Ship of Zion* as a middle section.

A *Negro Rhapsody* was written by Gilbert for the Litchfield County Festival in Norfolk, Conn., in 1913. His *Dance in the Place Congo,* based on five Creole songs of Louisiana, was performed as a ballet at the Metropolitan Opera House, March 23, 1918. Gilbert also wrote a Symphonic Prelude to Synge's *Riders to the Sea,* performed by the MacDowell Memorial Association at Peterborough, N. H., in September, 1914, *Americanesque, Two Episodes, American Dances in Ragtime,* and some smaller works.

MORTIMER WILSON (b. Chariton, Iowa, Aug. 6, 1876; d. New York, Jan. 27, 1932) was a technically proficient composer, with a background of Max Reger's training. He left five symphonies in manuscript, and won recognition and prizes with other orchestral works, including the Suite, *From my Youth,* an *Overture, 1849,* and a Scenic Fantasy called *My Country.*

JAMES P. DUNN (1884-1896), best known as a songwriter, was facile and prolific also in the creation of orchestral music. An *Overture on Negro Themes* was published in 1925, and in 1927 he wrote the tone poem *We,* celebrating Lindbergh's flight, first performed at a New York Stadium Concert on August 27th of that year. Dunn was also responsible for a symphony, a Symphonic Poem, and a Passacaglia and Fugue for orchestra, *The Barber's Sixth Brother,* based on material from *The Arabian Nights.*

GEORGE TEMPLETON STRONG (b. New York, May 26, 1856) spent most of his creative life abroad, after studying at the Leipzig Conservatory. His early works included a symphony,

In the Mountains, and a Symphonic Poem, *Undine,* op. 14. The Philadelphia Orchestra played his *Chorale on a Theme by Hassler* in 1935, and on October 21, 1939, the composer listened in Geneva to a radio performance of his tone poem, *The Night,* played by the NBC Symphony Orchestra under Toscanini. Strong also wrote two other symphonies, two *American Sketches* for violin and orchestra, an orchestral Suite and a Symphonic Poem, *King Arthur.*

BLAIR FAIRCHILD (b. Belmont, Mass., June 23, 1877; d. Paris, April 23, 1933) was also an expatriate for most of his life, having studied with Paine and Spalding at Harvard, and later with Buonamici in Florence and with Widor in Paris. His orchestral works include three Symphonic Tableaux, *East and West;* three Symphonic Poems and a ballet, *Dame Libellule.*

CHARLES SANFORD SKILTON (1868-1941), long a member of the music faculty of the University of Kansas, made a special study of Indian music, and is remembered chiefly for his set of *Indian Dances* (including a lively *War Dance*) which are still heard on orchestral programs.

The field of popular music has produced several composers whose serious works have already proved their permanent significance. Chief among them is GEORGE GERSHWIN (b. Brooklyn, Sept. 26, 1898; d. Hollywood, July 12, 1937) who studied composition with Kilenyi and Rubin Goldmark, among others. His *Rhapsody in Blue* was epoch-making in its proof that jazz idioms could be used effectively in the larger forms, and this work has become a staple of the orchestral repertoire. There are three outstanding themes, of which the slow melody was long used by Paul Whiteman as his signature on the air. It was Whiteman who commissioned and introduced the *Rhapsody* in a famous concert at Aeolian Hall, New York, February 12, 1924, with the composer at the piano.

Gershwin's *Piano Concerto in F* was commissioned by Walter Damrosch for the New York Symphony Orchestra in 1925, and was introduced with the composer again as soloist. It was included by the English conductor, Albert Coates, in his list of "the fifty best musical compositions of all time." The tone poem, *An American in Paris,* likewise commissioned by Dr. Damrosch, has also found a permanent place on orchestral programs. A *Second Rhapsody* by Gershwin was introduced in New York February 5, 1932, by the Boston Symphony Orchestra with Koussevitzky conducting. He also wrote a *Cuban Overture* and *Variations on an Original Theme,* while portions of his opera, *Porgy and Bess,* and orchestral versions of his piano *Preludes* are sometimes heard in the concert hall.

VICTOR HERBERT (b. Dublin, Ireland, Feb. 1, 1859; d. New York, May 26, 1924) also showed the ability to write serious music as well as popular songs and operettas. Himself a cellist, and a conductor of distinction, Herbert wrote two successful cello Concertos, as well as a Suite for that instrument with orchestral accompaniment. The *Dagger Dance* from his opera, *Natoma,* is often played as a concert piece, and there is also a Herbert Suite for strings, as well as the lighter Suite of *Serenades,* introduced by Paul Whiteman on the same program with Gershwin's *Rhapsody in Blue.* Herbert's *American Fantasy* has become the classic potpourri of our patriotic tunes, closing with an elaborate arrangement of *The Star-Spangled Banner,* which Dr. Karl Muck used (under scathing criticism) during the First World War. As the founder of the American Society of Composers, Authors and Publishers, Victor Herbert will be remembered for a telling contribution to America's musical independence, quite aside from his importance as a composer.

CONTEMPORARY AMERICAN CONSERVATIVES

While most of the living American composers are writing in a rather advanced style, there are still a few of the older generation, plus an occasional younger man, who believe in the traditions and conventions of music, trusting to melodic inspiration and a command of form rather than startling distortions, atonality or any other of the individual tricks of modernism.

DANIEL GREGORY MASON (b. Brookline, Mass., Nov. 20, 1873), grandson of Lowell Mason and nephew of William Mason, of a famous musical family, has long been a leader in American music, head of the Music Department of Columbia University, and author of several important books, as well as a distinguished composer. His studies were with Paine, Chadwick and others in America and Vincent d'Indy abroad. His First Symphony, op. 11, in C minor, was composed in 1913-4, and published in 1926, introduced by Stokowski in Philadelphia in February, 1916. A *Prelude and Fugue* for piano and orchestra, op. 20, composed in 1919, was first played by John Powell with the Chicago Symphony Orchestra, in March, 1921. The Festival Overture, *Chanticleer,* op. 27 (1926-8) was introduced by Fritz Reiner in Cincinnati, November, 1928. The score bears a motto from Thoreau: "I do not propose to write an ode to dejection, but to brag as lustily as Chanticleer in the morning, standing on his roost, if only to wake my neighbors up."

Mason's Second Symphony, in A, op. 30 (1928), also had its first performance by Reiner in Cincinnati, November,

1930. A *Suite after English Folk-Songs*, op. 32, written in 1933, was first conducted by Hans Kindler at the Virginia Festival in April, 1934. The Third Symphony of Mason, op. 35, has the title *Lincoln*, and is perhaps his most important work. Composed in 1935-6, it was introduced by Barbirolli and the New York Philharmonic Symphony Orchestra in November, 1937. The first movement is called "The Candidate from Springfield," containing a tune of the 1860's, "The Quaboag Quickstep," along with original material. The second, "Massa Linkum," gives the slaves' point of view, in slow time. The third is a Scherzo, "Old Abe's Yarns," and the Finale, "1865," is a dirge, suggesting the tragedy of Lincoln's death. Mason has also written a *Prelude and Fugue* for string orchestra, op. 37 (1939).

JOHN ALDEN CARPENTER (b. Park Ridge, Illinois, Feb. 28, 1876) is a businessman who also writes excellent music. A student under Paine at Harvard, he later worked with Edward Elgar in England. His most popular orchestral piece is unquestionably the Suite, *Adventures in a Perambulator*, written in 1914, a charming idyl of child life on the Chicago shore of Lake Michigan. The composer's program notes are almost as interesting as the music itself. A Concertino for piano and orchestra (1915) is also full of a conservative charm.

The Birthday of the Infanta was Carpenter's first ballet (1917-8), produced by the Chicago Opera Company in 1919. This was followed by *Krazy Kat* (1921), in a jazzy idiom, and *Skyscrapers* (1923-4), introducing realistic cacophony, presented at the Metropolitan Opera House in 1926. A symphony was written by Carpenter for the Norfolk Festival of 1917, and another, for the fiftieth anniversary of the Chicago Symphony Orchestra, in 1940. This organization also introduced his violin Concerto, with Zlatko Balakovic as soloist, in 1937. His *Danza* was performed by the Boston Symphony Orchestra in 1936. Other orchestral works by Carpenter include *Patterns,* played by the same group in 1932, and *Sea Drift,* based on Walt Whitman, first performed by the New York Philharmonic Symphony Orchestra in November, 1934, under Werner Janssen.

HOWARD HANSON (b. Wahoo, Nebraska, Oct. 28, 1896) may safely be considered a conservative, although his recent music contains plenty of modern touches. As director of the Eastman School of Music of the University of Rochester, he is an outstanding educator and conductor, as well as a helpful propagandist for American music. For these services he was awarded the Henry Hadley Medal in 1938.

Hanson has composed three symphonies, the First called *Nordic,* op. 21, conducted by the composer at the Augusteo in Rome (where he was a Fellow of the American Academy), and since played by many orchestras in the United States. The Second Symphony, *Romantic* (1930), was commissioned by Koussevitzky for the fiftieth anniversary of the Boston Symphony Orchestra. The Third was written primarily for radio, at the request of the Columbia Broadcasting System and introduced on the air September 19, 1937. It consisted originally of three movements, ending in a brief Scherzo. A fourth was added later, with a complete premiere by the NBC Symphony Orchestra. Hanson has also written a *Symphonic Legend,* op. 8, a *Symphonic Rhapsody,* op. 14, five Symphonic Poems: *Before the Dawn* (1920), *Exaltation,* op. 20 (1920), *North and West,* op. 22 (1923), *Lux Aeterna,* op. 24 (1923), and *Pan and the Priest,* op. 26 (1926). A Concerto for organ and orchestra, op. 27, is based on themes from *North and West.* Hanson has also put together a Suite from his opera, *Merry Mount,* which has become a popular concert piece, first conducted by himself and later by Iturbi with the Rochester Philharmonic Orchestra.

DEEMS TAYLOR (b. New York, Dec. 22, 1885) is best known as a radio commentator, but his versatile gifts have been expressed also in books and musical compositions, including three operas, and he was recently elected President of the American Society of Composers, Authors and Publishers. His most popular orchestral work is the Suite, *Through the Looking Glass*, first written for chamber orchestra (1917-9) and later rescored in symphonic style. An earlier Symphonic Poem, *The Siren Song*, won the composition prize of the National Federation of Music Clubs in 1912, and Taylor later wrote a Rhapsody for small orchestra called *Portrait of a Lady* (revised in 1924). The Symphonic Poem *Jurgen* was commissioned by the New York Symphony Society in 1925, and a Suite, *Circus Day*, written for Paul Whiteman the same year, was later rescored for symphony orchestra.

Taylor wrote the ballet, *A Kiss in Xanadu*, for the play, *Beggar on Horseback* and made concert Suites out of his incidental music to *Casanova* and his operas, *Peter Ibbetson* and *Ramuntcho*. Howard Barlow introduced his orchestral Variations, *Marco Takes a Walk*, with the New York Philharmonic Symphony, November 14, 1942.

CHARLES WAKEFIELD CADMAN (b. Johnstown, Pa., Dec. 24, 1881) became a hit writer for the public with two popular songs, *From the Land of the Sky-Blue Water* and *At Dawning*, but has earned the respect of serious music-lovers by his works in the larger forms. Cadman has made a study of American Indian music and frequently used native themes, particularly in the opera, *Shanewis*. His *Thunderbird Suite* (1915) was intended for a play by Norman Bel Geddes (unproduced), but turned out to be an effective concert piece. An *Oriental Rhapsody* (1917) was introduced by the Los Angeles Philharmonic Orchestra in 1920 and later performed in the Hollywood Bowl.

Cadman's *Dark Dancers of the Mardi Gras,* for orchestra with piano obbligato, has been performed many times with the composer as soloist, with a premiere in the Hollywood Bowl under the baton of Raymond Paige. An *American Suite* for strings, based on Indian, Negro and old fiddle tunes, was written in 1937 and first played at the Saratoga Festival of that year. The most important orchestral work of Cadman is probably his symphony, *Pennsylvania,* written in 1939 in the Virgin Islands, already performed by many orchestras, headed by the Los Angeles Philharmonic, March 7, 1940. Most recent of his compositions in this form is the tone poem, *Aurora Borealis,* for piano and orchestra. Early orchestral works include *Three Moods* and the brief composition for strings, *To a Vanishing Race,* introduced in 1914 by the Russian Symphony Orchestra under Modest Altschuler.

JOHN POWELL (b. Richmond, Va., Sept. 6, 1882) is a specialist in American folk-music, with a particular understanding of the materials of the Southern mountaineers and the Negroes. His most important work is a *Negro Rhapsody,* for piano and orchestra, which has been widely played in the United States and was featured by Walter Damrosch in the European tour of the New York Symphony Orchestra, with the composer as soloist. Spirituals and Negro secular music provide the basic themes of this effective composition.

An orchestral Suite by Powell, introduced by the New York Philharmonic in 1940, was called *A Set of Three,* using Virginia tunes, with the movements entitled Snowbird on the Ashbank, Green Willow and Haste to the Wedding. *Natchez on the Hill,* also based on American folk-music, was first played at the Worcester Festival in 1931. Other orchestral works by John Powell include an Overture, *In Old Virginia* (1921), a piano Suite, *At the Fair,* arranged for small orchestra, a *Symphony in A* (1937), and a piano Concerto, still in manuscript. The composer has also spoken of a new symphony, which expresses his newest and most advanced ideas in that form.

EDWARD BURLINGAME HILL (b. Cambridge, Mass., Sept. 9, 1872) studied with Paine, Chadwick and Widor, and for some years headed the Music Department at Harvard. Among his early works was the "fantastic pantomime" for orchestra, *Jack Frost in Midsummer*, introduced by the Chicago Symphony Orchestra in 1907. His two *Stevensoniana Suites* have become quite popular, particularly the second, published by G. Schirmer. Tone poems by Hill have been based on Amy Lowell's *Lilacs* and Poe's *Fall of the House of Usher*. He has written four symphonies, three of which have been repeatedly performed. A *Sinfonietta*, op. 57, in one movement, was introduced by the Boston Symphony Orchestra in Cambridge, March 9, 1933, and another, op. 40A, made from his string quartet, op. 40, had its first performance by the same band in the season of 1935-6. A Concertino for piano and orchestra (with touches of jazz) had a Boston premiere April 25, 1932, with Sanroma as soloist. There is also a Concertino for strings, performed by Koussevitzky in the spring of 1940, and another for piano and orchestra, dated 1938-9, as yet unproduced. An unpublished violin Concerto has been played several times by the Boston Symphony Orchestra with Ruth Posselt as soloist.

DAVID STANLEY SMITH (b. Toledo, Ohio, July 6, 1877), a pupil of Horatio Parker, has headed the Yale School of Music for twenty years, retiring in 1940, but continuing to teach composition. He is a musical architect, with a sound knowledge of form, acquired partly from studies with Thuille and Widor abroad. His First Symphony (F minor, op. 28) was played by the Chicago Symphony Orchestra under Frederick Stock, Dec. 13, 1912, and the second (D major, op. 42) was introduced by the composer at the Norfolk Festival of 1918. A Third Symphony (C minor, op. 60) is dated 1928 and a Fourth (D minor, op. 78), written in 1937, was first performed by the Boston Symphony Orchestra, April 14, 1939, the composer conducting. Other orchestral works by Smith are a *Prince Hal Overture* (his most popular composition), a Symphonic Poem called *Darkness and Dawn, Four Impressions,* op. 40 (1916), a *Fête Galante* for flute and orchestra (1920), a *Cathedral Prelude* for organ and orchestra (1926), an *Epic Poem* (1926), a *Rondo Appassionato* for violin and orchestra, op. 73 (1935), a *Fantasy* for piano and orchestra, 1929, *A Satire,* paired with the Overture *Tomorrow,* op. 66, 1 and 2, (1932-3), a Suite of four pieces called *Flowers,* for chamber orchestra (1924), a *Sinfonietta* for strings (1931), a violin Concerto, op. 69, (1933) and a *Sonatina* for junior string orchestra (1932). The newest Smith works are a *Requiem,* op. 81 (1939), a *Credo,* op. 83 (1941), *Vienna Invicta,* op. 85, and an orchestral *Waltz Rondo* (1941).

HENRY HOLDEN HUSS (b. Newark, N. J., June 21, 1862), teacher, lecturer, composer and pianist, has created much music of the conservative type in his long life. A *Forest Idyl,* for small orchestra, was performed at the Munich Conservatorium in 1884, and a *Rhapsody in C,* for piano and orchestra, in 1885, later played by the composer with the Boston Symphony Orchestra under Gericke. Walter Damrosch conducted a *Festival March* in 1891, written for the fiftieth anniversary of the *New York Tribune.* The Huss *Piano Concerto in B* was introduced by the Boston Orchestra in 1895, with the composer at the piano, Emil Paur conducting, and had many later performances. A violin Concerto in D minor was first played by Maud Powell with the Russian Symphony Orchestra in 1908. *In Memoriam* is an orchestral piece which had its premiere in New York under Plotnikoff in 1937, and in 1938

Frederique Petrides conducted the Huss *Allegretto* for strings at Carnegie Chamber Music Hall. The same auditorium saw the premiere of the orchestral version of a *Legende and Allegretto* from the string quartet originally composed for Ysaye, and in the same year a poem for full orchestra, *Invictus and Peace,* won the first prize of the New York State Federation of Music Clubs. Hans Kindler gave the first performance of another orchestral poem, *La Nuit,* with the National Symphony Orchestra in Washington, and an orchestral version has now been made of two movements of a violin sonata, originally played by Arthur Hartmann and the composer for the Bohemians in New York.

Arthur Farwell (b. St. Paul, Minn., April 23, 1872) has written music in a wide variety of styles, but is still by nature a conservative, making his early studies with such men as MacDowell, Chadwick, Humperdinck and Guilmant and later teaching Roy Harris and others of the modern school. He was the founder of the Wa-wan Press, pioneering in American nationalism and the publication of native works based on folk materials.

Farwell's first orchestral work was the Overture, *Cornell,* op. 9 (1900), based on Indian melodies and student songs and introduced at Ithaca in 1901. *Dawn,* op. 12, dated 1901, for chamber orchestra, is also the result of Indian themes. Similar materials inspired *The Domain of Hurakan,* op. 15 (1903), originally a piano composition, orchestrated in 1909 and first conducted by Arnold Volpe in New York. A *Symbolistic Study,* after Walt Whitman, op. 18, orchestrated in 1922, had its first performance by the Philadelphia Orchestra under Monteux, March 30, 1928. Another *Symbolistic Study,* op. 37 (1912), finally assumed the form of a Concerto for two pianos and strings, and thus shared the prize of the National Federation of Music Clubs in 1939. Most important of Farwell's orchestral works is probably the Suite from Dunsany's *Gods of the Mountain,* op. 52 (1917) symphonically orchestrated in 1927. Recent compositions have included the *Prelude to a Spiritual Drama,* op. 76 (1927), produced in 1936, a *Mountain Song,* op. 90 and a *Rudolph Gott Symphony,* op. 95.

ROSSETTER G. COLE (b. Clyde, Michigan, Feb. 5, 1866) studied with Max Bruch in Europe and spent over thirty years in Chicago as teacher, lecturer, organist and composer. His orchestral works include a *Symphonic Prelude,* op. 28 (1914), first performed by the Chicago Symphony Orchestra under Glenn Dillard Gunn, March 11, 1915; the *Pioneer Overture,* op. 35, composed in 1918 at the MacDowell Colony and introduced by the Chicago Orchestra, March 14, 1919, the composer conducting; a *Heroic Piece* for orchestra and organ, op. 39, also created at the MacDowell Colony and first played in Chicago, February 11, 1924, with a revised version for orchestra alone, May 14, 1939; a *Ballade* for cello and orchestra and two Suites from the opera, *The Maypole Lovers,* the first of which had its concert premiere under Frederick Stock in Chicago, January 9, 1936.

ALBERT STOESSEL (b. St. Louis, Oct. 11, 1894), known first as a concert violinist, now spends most of his time as a conductor and teacher, heading the Orchestra and Opera Departments of the Juilliard Graduate School. Among his orchestral compositions are a *Hispania Suite* (1921), *Minuet Crinoline* (1921), *Cyrano de Bergerac,* a "symphonic portrait" (1922), a *Suite Antique* (1922), *Festival Fanfare* (1933), *Early Americana Suite* (1935), a frequently played *Concerto Grosso* for strings and piano (1936) and a Suite from the opera *Garrick,* which has been performed by leading orchestras in the United States.

DOUGLAS MOORE (b. Cutchogue, Long Island, Aug. 10, 1893) received his musical education from Horatio Parker and David Stanley Smith at Yale, from Ernest Bloch in Cleveland and from d'Indy and Nadia Boulanger abroad. In 1940 he succeeded Daniel Gregory Mason as head of the Music Department at Columbia University. A set of *Four Museum Pieces* for orchestra (Fifteenth Century Armor, A Madonna of Botticini, The Chinese Lion and the Unhappy Flutist, and A Statue by Rodin) was first played by the Cleveland Orchestra in 1923, and the same group a year later introduced Moore's *Pageant of P. T. Barnum,* which has become his most popular work. The music follows the life of the great showman from his Boyhood at Bethel through Joice Heth (Barnum's first exhibit, a 161-year-old Negress), General and Mrs. Tom Thumb, Jenny Lind and a final Circus Parade. A Symphonic Poem, *Moby Dick,* was written in 1928, and a *Symphony of Autumn* had its first performance in Rochester, N. Y., April 2, 1931. An *Overture on an American Tune* (originally called *Babbitt,* after the Sinclair Lewis character) was introduced by David Mannes and the Manhattan Symphony Orchestra on Christmas Day, 1932.

RANDALL THOMPSON (b. New York, April 12, 1899) has made a deep impression as a composer, chiefly through his Second Symphony, in E minor (1930), first played in the season of 1933-4 by the Rochester and New York Philharmonic orchestras. He learned his music at Harvard and later studied with Ernest Bloch, becoming eventually an outstanding teacher himself and for some time heading the Curtis Institute of Music in Philadelphia. Two orchestral tone poems by Thompson are *Pierrot and Cothurnus* (1922) and *The Piper at the Gates of Dawn* (1924). He has also written a *Jazz Poem,* with piano solo (1928). His First Symphony dates from 1929, and he has composed some important choral and chamber music as well.

SAMUEL BARBER (b. West Chester, Pa., March 9, 1910) may be considered the youngest of our contemporary conservatives in music. He is a product of the Curtis Institute, holder of the Prix de Rome in 1935 and of a Pulitzer Prize in 1935 and 1936. His *Symphony in One Movement* was conducted by Artur Rodzinski at the Salzburg Festival of 1937 (after a 1936 premiere in Rome under Molinari), and Toscanini introduced his *Adagio for Strings* with the NBC Orchestra in 1938, later playing it in South America as the only American work in his repertoire. Other orchestral compositions by Samuel Barber are the Overture to Sheridan's *School for Scandal* (1932), first performed by the Philadelphia Orchestra in 1933; *Music for a Scene from Shelley* (1933), introduced by Werner Janssen with the New York Philharmonic Orchestra, March 24, 1935; *Essay for Orchestra* (1937), first played by Toscanini and the NBC Orchestra, November 5, 1938; and a violin Concerto (1940), whose first performance was given by Albert Spalding with the Philadelphia Orchestra under Ormandy, February 7, 1941.

THE NEW SCHOOL

Most of the American composers thus far mentioned are considered hopelessly old-fashioned by the representatives of our newest musical thought and technique. Some of these men are definitely ultra-modern, according to conservative standards. Others are dabbling in a neo-classicism of some sort, while still others merely try to express their musical feelings as honestly as possible, without regard to audience reactions. They have in common a fairly definite hostility to romanticism and post-romanticism, and they strive to express themselves with an economy of means and spareness of instrumentation that often sacrifices obvious emotional values. This new music is scientifically and experimentally interesting, and occasionally it creates effects of genuine significance, even though lacking the conventional appeal of the well-worn classics. Whether it is the music of the future is still to be determined, and whether one likes it or not is entirely a matter of individual taste. It is entirely possible to develop such taste to a point of sincere enjoyment, and it is also far too easy to pretend an appreciation which has no foundation in either knowledge or honesty. The few composers of the new group to be discussed here are necessarily those who have been fortunate or able enough to secure a fair number of public performances by American orchestras.

Roy Harris (b. Lincoln County, Oklahoma, Feb. 12, 1898) is a much disputed but frequently played composer of the new school, unquestionably American in his entire make-up and of real individuality. He studied with Farwell in California and later with Nadia Boulanger in Paris. An early *Andante* for orchestra was selected from a number of manuscripts for performance by the New York Philharmonic Orchestra at the Stadium during the summer of 1926. He won a Guggenheim Fellowship, and in 1931 was subsidized by the Pasadena Music and Arts Association. Later he taught at the Westminster Choir School in Princeton, at Cornell, and in the summer school of Colorado College at Colorado Springs.

The most popular orchestral work of Harris is doubtless the American Overture, *When Johnny Comes Marching Home* (based on the familiar song), commissioned by RCA-Victor for a record, and first performed under the title *From the Gayety and Sadness of the American Scene* by the Los Angeles Symphony Orchestra, December 29, 1932, with Nicolas Slonimsky conducting.

The *Symphony: 1933* was completed by Harris in November of that year, and had its first performance by the Boston Symphony Orchestra under Koussevitzky, January 26, 1934. The composer himself furnished a detailed description of the score, reprinted with the Columbia records, made during the first New York performance, February 2, 1934. According to this, the first movement is "pervaded by a rhythmic motive of 3 plus 2." The second is "a free use of the Rondo principle." The Finale is "a variation development of the theme, stated in the opening."

A Second Symphony was written by Harris in 1934 and first played in 1936, and the same year produced a *Prelude and Fugue* for string orchestra, *Farewell to Pioneers* and a *Time Suite*, commissioned by the Columbia Broadcasting System and first presented over the air, Aug. 8, 1937. This piece is composed from a strict radio angle, with each movement definitely timed for broadcasting.

The Third Symphony (1938), also introduced by Koussevitzky (February 24, 1939), may be considered the most important Harris opus to date. Again the composer supplies a structural outline, dividing the work into five sections, named in order: Tragic, Lyric, Pastoral, Fugue and Dramatic-Tragic. Other orchestral compositions of Roy Harris include a *Chorale* for strings (1933), a violin Concerto, a piano Concerto, a Symphony for High School Orchestra, *Prelude and Fugue for Strings and Trumpets*, a Jazz Symphony (written for Tommy Dorsey), *Western Landscape* (ballet), a *Folk-song Symphony* (with chorus) and *American Creed*, in two movements: Free to Dream and Free to Build, commissioned by the Chicago Orchestra. A Fifth Symphony appeared in 1943.

AARON COPLAND (b. Brooklyn, Nov. 14, 1900) at one time made considerable use of jazz idioms, but has now become an independent composer with a style of his own and great technical facility. He first studied composition with Rubin Gold-mark and later with Nadia Boulanger. He is today President of the American Composers' Alliance, founder of the Yaddo Festivals of American music at Saratoga Springs, and a leading spirit in the League of Composers, as well as a prolific creator of provocative music.

Copland used an early ballet named *Grohg* as the basis for a *Dance Symphony*, which won a share of the RCA-Victor prize of $25,000 in 1929 and was first performed by the Philadelphia Orchestra under Stokowski in April, 1931. His First Symphony was introduced by Walter Damrosch and the New York Symphony Orchestra in 1925 as a symphony for organ and orchestra, with Nadia Boulanger as soloist. Later it was revised and has had frequent performances in its new orchestral form.

Music for the Theatre, still considered one of Copland's best works, was written at the MacDowell Colony in the summer of 1925, and received its first performance in November of that year from the Boston Symphony Orchestra under Koussevitzky. A piano Concerto, of rather jazzy character, was composed in 1926 and played by Copland with the Boston Orchestra the following year. A *Symphonic Ode,* originally intended for the RCA-Victor competition, was completed and performed by the same orchestra in 1932. Another orchestral work, *Statements,* was the result of a commission by the League of Composers in 1935-6, while *Music for Radio* was written for the Columbia Broadcasting System in 1937.

The brilliant *El Salon Mexico* came out of a trip to that country, using typical themes and instrumentation. It was first played over a network of the National Broadcasting Company, with Sir Adrian Boult conducting the NBC Orchestra. An *Outdoor Overture* was written in 1939, presumably for high-school orchestras, and turned out to be one of the most effective pieces yet produced by Copland. Another orchestral work, *The Quiet City,* was one of the selections of the Music Critics' Circle for their New York concert in May, 1942. About the same time his *Portrait of Lincoln* was introduced in concert and on the air by Kostelanetz. Copland's scores for such films as *The City, Of Mice and Men* and *Our Town* have brought him a well-deserved popularity along with the successful ballets, *Billy the Kid* and *Rodeo.* He is aiming constantly at a wider audience and apparently finding it.

ROGER SESSIONS (b. Brooklyn, Dec. 28, 1896) was associated with Copland in one of the earliest efforts in behalf of contemporary American music, the Copland-Sessions Concerts. A student of Horatio Parker and assistant to Ernest Bloch in Cleveland, Sessions spent eight years abroad, winning Guggenheim and Carnegie Fellowships and that of the American Academy in Rome. He now teaches at Princeton, and has also taught at the Dalcroze Institute in New York and at the University of California, besides acting as President of the International Society for Contemporary Music.

The best-known work of Sessions is the orchestral Suite from his incidental music to Andreieff's play, *The Black Maskers,* written in 1928. His First Symphony (1927) and a violin Concerto (1932) were written abroad. Since his return from Europe he has written two more symphonies and three Dirges for orchestra. His work combines impressionism and a modern technique with melodic power and sincerity.

WILLIAM SCHUMAN (b. New York, Aug. 4, 1910) has become an outstanding composer in a comparatively short time, combining the best features of the advanced and the conservative schools and winning consistent success with critics and listeners alike. He is a pupil of Charles Haubiel and Roy Harris and now teaches at Sarah Lawrence College in Bronxville, N. Y., where he also conducts the chorus. Schuman has twice held a Guggenheim Fellowship and won many prizes, including the first Town Hall-League of Composers Award and the award of the New York Music Critics' Circle for orchestral works in 1942, when he was also cited by the National Association for American Composers and Conductors as the best American composer of the season.

Schuman has now written four symphonies, the First, for chamber orchestra, in 1935, and the Second, for full orchestra, in 1937. The Third, completed in January of 1941, was introduced by Koussevitzky and the Boston Symphony Orchestra in the season of 1941-2, with a performance also by Leon Barzin and the National Orchestral Association at Carnegie Hall for the Music Critics' Circle, who gave it first place among the orchestral compositions they had selected. Schuman's Fourth Symphony (1941) was written for the one-hundredth anniversary of the New York Philharmonic Orchestra, scheduled to be played under Artur Rodzinski. An *American Festival Overture* (1939) has been played and recorded by Hans Kindler and the National Symphony Orchestra. It opens with three notes, said by the composer to represent the call used by New York boys in getting together "for an auspicious occasion." Schuman has also written a *Prologue for Chorus and Orchestra* and a secular cantata, *This Is Our Time,* both to words by Genevieve Taggard, and some chamber music, including three string quartets.

CHARLES IVES (b. Danbury, Conn., Oct. 20, 1874) is a modernist who was far ahead of his time. He was experimenting with dissonance and cacophony long before Stravinsky or Schönberg had thought of such things. Today he is respected (though not often played) as one of the most important and original of all American composers. The son of a bandmaster, Ives picked up much of the inherent character of New England music, studying also under Horatio Parker at

Yale. He has made a success of the insurance business, writing music mostly as a sideline, but the significance of his tonal creations is becoming more and more apparent.

Ives has written five symphonies, the First dating from 1896-8, the Second from 1897-1902 (five movements, of which the slow movement was later replaced by another), and the Third, based in part on earlier organ pieces, 1911. His most important work in this form is the symphony called *Holidays*, written mostly in 1913. Each movement represents an American holiday, the first Washington's Birthday, the second Decoration (Memorial) Day, the third the Fourth of July and the Finale Thanksgiving. The composer notes that "these movements may be played as separate pieces." There is humor in this symphony, as well as audacious part-writing, some of the instruments playing at times faster or slower than the rest, as in an amateur band. A Fourth Symphony (actually the Fifth) was composed between 1910 and 1916.

Other orchestral works by Ives include Overtures (based on "the lives and works of literary men"), *Cartoons or Take-offs* (some with a college flavor), a *Set* for theatre or chamber orchestra (1906-11), and three Suites (or Sets), of which the first is called *Three Places in New England* (1903-14): Boston Common, Putnam's Camp and the Housatonic at Stockbridge. (The second Set dates from 1912-15 and the third from 1919-26.) Ives has also written much chamber music, for various combinations of instruments, and a great number of songs.

CARL RUGGLES (b. Marion, Mass., March 11, 1876) is often grouped with Ives as a pioneer in modernism, although his style is quite different, aiming at musical perfection rather than the rugged description and suggestion of picturesque Americana. He has conducted symphony orchestras, maintained a highly individual existence as a composer at Arlington, Vermont, and contributed to the orchestral literature such works as *Portals, Men and Mountains,* and *Sun Treader.*

LAZARE SAMINSKY (b. Odessa, Russia, Oct. 27, 1882) must be considered an American composer, although he has lived here only since 1920, with much of his creative work done in his native Russia. He is a specialist in Jewish music, since 1924 musical director at the Temple Emanu-El in New York. Saminsky is definitely a modernist, a scholar and a technician of the highest order, using whatever styles and methods he considers applicable to the materials of his compositions.

Completing his musical studies at the Petrograd Conservatory, under Rimsky-Korsakoff and other masters, he composed and conducted an Overture (1909-10) and later conducted his *Vigiliae* for orchestra at one of the Koussevitzky concerts in Moscow (February 10, 1913). A Suite, *Orientalia,* followed in May, 1914. Saminsky's First Symphony, *Of the Great Rivers,* op. 10, was conducted by the composer in its first performance at the Imperial Opera House, Petrograd, February 25, 1917 (in the series of Siloti concerts). A Second Symphony, *Of the Summits,* op. 19, was composed in the summer of 1918, and a Third was begun in 1921. After his arrival in America, Saminsky frequently conducted his own works, in addition to their performance by leading orchestras under their regular conductors. The Third Symphony, *Of the Seas,* op. 30, was completed at the MacDowell Colony, and had its premiere in Paris, June, 1925, under the baton of the composer, with the Colonne Orchestra. A *Gagliarda of a Merry Plague,* based on Poe's *Mask of the Red Death,* was also written in 1924 and had its first performance in New York, February 22, 1925.

A Fourth Symphony by Saminsky, op. 35, written in 1926, was first performed in Berlin three years later, and a Fifth

Symphony dates from 1929-30. Other orchestral works by
Saminsky include the Suite, *Ausonia,* op. 39 (1930), *Still
Pageant, Pueblo—A Moon Rhapsody, To a New World* and
Three Shadows, first played by the New York Philharmonic,
February 6, 1936, "a tonal tribute to Edwin Arlington Robin-
son," in three sections called Omen, A Poet and Grass and A
Dirge. Saminsky has also written much ecclesiastical and
chamber music, choruses and songs.

WALTER PISTON (b. Rockland, Maine, Jan. 20, 1894) is
another highly skilled technician, a pupil of Nadia Boulanger,
now teaching music at Harvard. His early *Symphonic Piece*
was introduced by Koussevitzky with the Boston Symphony
Orchestra, March 23, 1928. A Suite for orchestra was composed in 1929 and had its first performance by the Philadelphia Orchestra under Stokowski, April 1, 1932. Next came
a Concerto for orchestra (1933), first played in Boston, March
29, 1934, a Prelude and Fugue (1934) and a Symphony in C
(1937). This symphony, according to the composer, is "without pictorial, narrative, political or philosophical intent." It
begins with a slow Introduction, presenting the motives from
which the work is developed, followed by an Allegro section
in Sonata form, without a Coda. The second movement,
Adagio, is in "a large three-part form," with an opening theme
by the solo English horn. The Finale is in Rondo form, Allegro
con fuoco. The composer conducted its premiere in Boston.

A Concertino for piano and chamber orchestra was commissioned by the Columbia Broadcasting System and introduced on the air, with Howard Barlow conducting and Sanroma as soloist, June 20, 1937. This was followed by Piston's
most popular composition, the ballet, *The Incredible Flutist*
(1938), from which an orchestral Suite has been widely
played. It is definitely program music, with an elaborate story
charmingly presented. Piston has also written a violin Con-

certo, introduced by Ruth Posselt in 1940 with both the Boston Symphony Orchestra and the National Orchestral Association. A *Sinfonietta* for chamber orchestra dates from 1941, with a first performance by Bernard Zighera's ensemble. Piston has composed many smaller chamber works and also published books on harmony.

HENRY COWELL (b. Menlo Park, California, March 11, 1897) has not only been a pioneer among American modernists but a tireless propagandist for our new music. He made an early impression as a pianist by his use of "tone clusters," employing the flat of the hand as well as the elbows and forearms on the keyboard. He has held a Guggenheim Fellowship (1931) and recently devoted much of his time to writing and lecturing on contemporary music.

Cowell's orchestral works include *Synchrony,* for dancers, *Two Appositions, Reel,* a piano Concerto, a Suite for chamber orchestra (in three movements: The Banshee, The Leprechaun and The Fairy Bells), *Six Casual Developments, Ostinato Pianissimo, Exultation* and a *Sinfonietta.* His newest composition, *Tales of Our Countryside,* was among those selected by the New York Music Critics' Circle for a rehearing in 1942 and made an excellent impression.

VIRGIL THOMSON (b. Kansas City, Nov. 25, 1896) has turned out conventional as well as highly unconventional music, meanwhile writing very personal and often provocative reviews in the *New York Herald Tribune.* He was trained at Harvard and the New England Conservatory, later studying with Rosario Scalero and Nadia Boulanger. A long residence in Paris developed his modernistic and impressionistic tendencies, and he was helpful in drawing public attention to such young composers as George Antheil.

Thomson leaped into prominence with his score for the

Gertrude Stein opera, *Four Saints in Three Acts* (1934), which Gilman called "distinguished in its artful banality," but adding that it was "actually very wily and deft and slick, often subtly and wittily allusive." Originality and independence have been characteristic of most of Thomson's music. His orchestral works include a *Symphony on a Hymn Tune*, a Second Symphony, *Two Sentimental Tangos*, musical Portraits of Mayor La Guardia and Dorothy Thompson, and Suites from the ballet, *Filling Station*, and the film score, *The Plow that Broke the Plains*. His music for the documentary film, *The River*, is also effective, and he has written incidental scores for various dramatic productions in New York, as well as the *Living Newspaper* of the WPA.

EDGAR VARESE (b. Paris, Dec. 22, 1885) is undoubtedly the most revolutionary composer now living in America. His studies were with Roussel, d'Indy, Widor, Busoni and Mahler, but he developed ideas of his own that went far beyond even their most heretical beliefs. All the conventions of harmony, melody, rhythm and orchestration have been completely discarded by Varese. His *Hyperprism* created a sensation when introduced by Stokowski with the Philadelphia Orchestra in 1923. Gilman called this music "lonely, incomparable, unique." *Intégrales,* a "tonal expression of stone and steel," was still more extreme in its heresies. Other orchestral works by Varese include his *Three Pieces, Rhapsodie Romane, Bourgogne, Mehr Licht, Gargantua, Amériques* ("new worlds on earth, in the stars and in the minds of men"), *Espace, Arcana* and, for smaller combinations of instruments, *Ionisation, Octandre, Offrandes, Density* and *Equatorial*.

GEORGE ANTHEIL (b. Trenton, N. J., July 8, 1900) was at one time considered an extreme radical in music, but has calmed down with maturity and now writes mostly practical scores for the films. He has twice held Guggenheim Fellowships, and wrote his earlier works abroad. A symphony, *Zingareska,* employing jazz idioms, was played in Berlin in 1922. The notorious *Ballet Mécanique,* for orchestra, player pianos and airplane motors, dates from 1924 and made its composer an international sensation when produced in New York in 1927. A Second Symphony, in F, had been played by Golschmann in Paris in 1926. Antheil wrote incidental music to Sophocles' *Oedipus* for the Berlin State Theatre in 1929, and the same year his ballet, *Fighting the Waves,* was produced in Dublin, at the Abbey Theatre, with words by W. B. Yeats. An opera, *Transatlantic,* created a mild sensation in 1930, and since that time Antheil has written a number of more conventional works, including a *Capriccio* for orchestra (performed by Hanson in Rochester, 1934), *Archipelago* (broadcast in 1935), a ballet, *Dreams,* and an *American Symphony* (1937).

MARC BLITZSTEIN (b. Philadelphia, Pa., March 2, 1905) must be classed with the musical radicals, even though his music to such original dramatic productions as *The Cradle Will Rock* and *No for an Answer* is essentially simple and straightforward, with emphasis chiefly on social significance. His early work, however, was definitely modernistic, after studies with Siloti, Scalero, Boulanger and Schönberg. His composition for radio, *I've Got the Tune,* commissioned by the Columbia Broadcasting System, has been called "an allegory of his development as a composer." Blitzstein also supplied incidental music for the Orson Welles production of *Julius Caesar* and (in collaboration with Virgil Thomson) for the film, *Spanish Earth.* As an orchestral composer he is still something of an unknown quantity, but his significance in the current musical scene cannot be ignored.

DAVID DIAMOND (b. Rochester, N. Y., July 9, 1915) is one of the white-haired boys of the ultra-modern group, thus far a composers' composer, but gradually gaining recognition from the public. He is a product of the Cleveland Institute and Eastman School, numbering Roger Sessions and Nadia Boulanger among his teachers, with a Guggenheim Fellowship and other awards to his credit. His *Psalm for Orchestra* was published by the Juilliard Foundation. His First Symphony (1935) was played by the New York Philharmonic Orchestra in 1942 and selected as one of the outstanding American works of the year by the Music Critics' Circle. Other orchestral compositions by Diamond include a Sinfonietta (1934), a violin Concerto (1936), a Serenade for Strings (1937), an *Elegy in Memory of Ravel* (1938), a *Heroic Piece* (1939), a *Concert Piece* (1940) and a Concerto for Chamber Orchestra (1940). Diamond's orchestral *Variations on an Original Theme* were played at the Eastman Festival in April, 1940.

WALLINGFORD RIEGGER (b. Albany, Georgia, April 29, 1885) belongs among the modern atonalists, even though he is also known as the commercially effective arranger of conventional music for glee clubs, etc. He originally wrote in a straightforward, romantic style, but has become increasingly aggressive in his modernism. His *Study in Sonority,* for ten violins, attracted attention when played by Hanson in Rochester and Stokowski in Philadelphia. This was followed by a *Fantasy and Fugue* for organ and orchestra, a *Prelude and Fugue,* and *Dichotomy* and *Scherzo* for chamber orchestra. Other orchestral works by Riegger are an *American Polonaise,* a *Rhapsody* and *Frenetic Rhythms*. He has also composed a *New Dance* and much ballet music.

DANTE FIORILLO (b. New York, July 4, 1905) is something of an enigma as a composer, combining an enormous output with a minimum of public performance. To a limited circle of admirers he represents a high point in America's creative music, and he has been honored with several Guggenheim Fellowships and a Pulitzer award. Fiorillo's orchestral works include a dozen symphonies, besides Partitas and Concertos of various kinds. With more frequent hearings, he will undoubtedly be given the place he deserves.

THE INBETWEENERS

A number of significant American composers of today are difficult to classify, writing sometimes in the traditional style, but often showing radical tendencies that might group them with the ultra-modernists. It is entirely possible that these "in-between" composers will in some cases prove to have written music of more permanent value than either the conservatives or the extremists.

PAUL CRESTON (b. New York, Oct. 10, 1906), twice holder of a Guggenheim Fellowship, now organist at St. Malachy's Church, New York, has written a variety of compositions, most of which have found a responsive audience. His earliest orchestral work, op. 5, is called *Out of the Cradle Endlessly Rocking* (1934), based on a poem by Walt Whitman. A *Partita* for flute, violin and strings, op. 12 (1937), has been frequently played. The movements are Preamble, Sarabande, Burlesk, Air and Tarantella. A *Threnody* for full orchestra, op. 16 (1938), is autobiographical in content, but, according to the composer, "to be judged, nevertheless, as an abstract musical work." It was introduced by Fritz Reiner with the Pittsburgh Orchestra, December 2, 1938. Two *Choric Dances,* op. 17 (1938), have been scored both for chamber orchestra and with symphonic instrumentation, the first in a slow tempo and the second marked "Majestic-Fast." A symphony, op. 20, was written by Creston in 1940 and successfully presented by the National Youth Orchestra. A Concertino for marimba and orchestra, op. 21 (1940), was commissioned by Frederique Petrides for her Orchestrette Classique, dedicated to her, and produced at Carnegie Chamber Music Hall April 29, 1940, with Ruth Stuber as soloist. A *Prelude and Dance,* op. 25 (1941), had in mind the abilities of high-school orchestras. A *Saxophone Concerto,* op. 26 (1941), was commissioned by the virtuoso, Cecil Leeson, for whom Creston had already written a Suite and a Sonata. A *Pastorale and Tarantella,* op. 28, had a first performance by the National Orchestral Association under Leon Barzin, March 28, 1942. Toscanini played one of his *Choric Dances* in an all-American broadcast, November 1, 1942, and his recognition is steadily growing.

HAROLD MORRIS (b. San Antonio, Texas, 1890) has also been consistently successful as a composer, while teaching piano at the Juilliard School and at Teachers College, Columbia University, and occasionally lecturing and playing in public. An orchestral *Poem* composed by Morris (after Tagore's *Gitanjali*) was introduced by Ysaye with the Cincinnati Symphony Orchestra in 1918 and immediately established the musical importance of its creator. A piano Concerto on Negro themes, first played by the composer with Koussevitzky and the Boston Symphony Orchestra, October 23, 1931, made an even deeper impression, both in Boston and in New York. A note by the composer indicates his use of the spiritual, *Pilgrim's Song,* which "shows the effect of civilization on the slaves of the Southern States and is in great contrast to the rugged, rhythmic character of the African Negro drum-beat, with which the first movement opens." The spiritual is echoed momentarily in the Finale as a link between movements. This piano Concerto was selected for publication by the Juilliard Foundation in 1932. Morris has also written a symphony,

Prospice (based on the Browning poem), introduced by Fabien Sevitzky with the Indianapolis Symphony, and a violin Concerto which won the award of the National Federation of Music Clubs and was broadcast by the NBC Orchestra under Frank Black, with Philip Frank as soloist, in May, 1939. (It was included also in the American programs of Leon Barzin at Carnegie Hall in 1942, with Carol Glenn as the violinist.) The Morris chamber music is as important as his orchestral works. A Suite for strings was introduced by Eddy Brown over Station WQXR and in concert by Wesley Sontag and the Mozart Sinfonietta, and there are two successful piano sonatas, as well as two Trios, the second of which was generally considered the best of the smaller works selected by the Music Critics' Circle in their special concert of May 12, 1942. Another symphonic work by Morris is in preparation, but had not at this writing been heard.

CHARLES HAUBIEL (b. Delta, Ohio, Jan. 31, 1894) has won distinction as a composer in various forms, as well as a teacher and pianist, serving on the faculties of the Juilliard Institute of Musical Art and New York University's Music Department. He is also the organizer and director of the Composers Press, which has published many American compositions on a membership basis. Haubiel's first orchestral piece was called *Mars Ascending* (1925). In 1928 his Symphonic Poem, *Karma*, won the Schubert Centennial Contest of the Columbia Phonograph Company and was recorded a year later, with the composer conducting. It is actually a set of seventeen Symphonic Variations on a Handelian theme, divided into four cycles. The individual Variations all have titles: Ideals, Gaiety, Jesting, Struggles, Achievement, Vision, Pursuit, Disaster, Resignation, Death, Fullfilment, Tranquility, Rest (Nirvana), while the four cycles are called The Soul Ascending, Toward the Abyss, Resurrection and Retrospect. The composition illustrates musically "some philosophic concepts of the Bagavad Gita (the Bible of the Hindus) and may be visualized in pantomime." *Karma* was followed by a *Suite Passacaille* (1931), *Vox Cathedralis* (1934) and the three *Rittrati* (Capriccio, Idyllio and Scherzo) which won second prize in the Swift contest of 1935. *Solari* (1934-6) also contained three sections: Dawn Mists, Meridian and The Plane Beyond, of which the last, a Passacaglia in A minor, shared the prize of the New York Philharmonic in 1938, with the composer conducting that orchestra in its first performance on December 18th of that year. Haubiel's First Symphony (1937) is a set of Variations on the opening theme, otherwise following the traditional Sonata form on a large scale. A set of *Miniatures* (1938) was published for strings in 1939 and later rescored for full orchestra (1940). There is also a *Passacaglia Triptych*, consisting of a Choral Prelude, Air and Variations and a Fugue (1937-9). In addition to purely orchestral works, Haubiel has written in the larger forms for voices with orchestra (*Vision of Saint Joan, Father Abraham,* etc.) and also composed songs and chamber music.

ABRAM CHASINS (b. New York, Aug. 17, 1903) has made his mark as composer, pianist and teacher, serving on the faculty of the Curtis Institute in Philadelphia and the Berkshire Music Center, Stockbridge, Mass., writing articles for magazines, and devoting much time and effort to propaganda for American music. His two piano Concertos are of real importance. The First, in F minor (1928), was introduced by Gabrilowitsch, conducting the Philadelphia Orchestra, Jan. 8, 1929, with the composer at the piano. It is in three movements, ending with a Tarantella. The Second Piano Concerto, in F-sharp minor (1932), also had its premiere in Philadelphia, Stokowski conducting the orchestra, again with the composer as soloist, March 3, 1933. It is in one continuous movement, with Variations on the themes, creating a striking novelty of form. Chasins' tone poem, *Parade,* was conducted for the first time by Toscanini with the New York Philharmonic Orchestra, April 8, 1931, and proved a popular contribution to the repertoire. Even more popular are the *Three Chinese Pieces,* originally written for the piano in 1935, and transcribed for orchestra two years later. The first of the trio is called *Flirtation in a Chinese Garden,* and this made its orchestral debut under Toscanini on the same program with *Parade. A Shanghai Tragedy* is the second piece, introduced by Reiner with the Curtis Orchestra in 1929. The third is called *Rush Hour in Hong Kong,* with a first orchestral performance by the New York Philharmonic under Ernest Schelling, January 10, 1931. These pieces are all frankly program music, descriptive of their titles, with clever instrumentation and sound musicianship expressing novel ideas. In addition to his orchestral works, Chasins has written songs and piano music in the smaller forms.

NICOLAI BEREZOWSKY (b. St. Petersburg, Russia, May 17, 1900) is a concert violinist as well as a composer of note. He has conducted and played in various orchestras, including the New York Philharmonic, is a member of the Coolidge String Quartet, and associated with the Columbia Broadcasting System. Berezowsky has written four symphonies. The First, composed in 1925, had its initial performance by the Boston Symphony Orchestra in 1931, the composer conducting. The Second is dated 1933, with a first performance by Koussevitzky and the Bostonians in 1934. The Third Symphony is dated 1936 and was introduced by Iturbi with the Rochester Philharmonic Orchestra a year later. The Fourth Symphony, op. 27, unperformed at this writing, belongs to the year 1940. Berezowsky also has to his credit a *Hebrew Suite,* composed in 1928 and first performed by Mengelberg with the New

York Philharmonic in 1929; a violin Concerto, played by Carl Flesch in Dresden, 1931, with the composer conducting; a *Concerto Lirico* for cello (1934), first played by Piatigorsky with the Boston Symphony Orchestra; a *Fantasie* for two pianos and orchestra, introduced by Barzin in 1933; a *Sinfonietta* (1931), winner of an NBC prize; *Toccata, Variations and Finale* for string quartet and orchestra (1938), first performed by the Coolidge Quartet with the Boston Symphony, under Koussevitzky; *Introduction and Waltz* for string orchestra, op. 25, broadcast by both NBC and CBS; a viola Concerto, op. 28 (1940), introduced by William Primrose (1941-2); and a clarinet Concerto (1940). Berezowsky has also written much chamber music, for various instrumental combinations.

PAUL NORDOFF (b. Philadelphia, Pa., June 4, 1909) has twice held Guggenheim Fellowships, as well as a Pulitzer Scholarship (1940). He is a pianist, teacher and lecturer, now active at the Philadelphia Conservatory. He has written two piano Concertos (1932 and 1935), a violin Concerto (1939-40) and one for two pianos and orchestra, performed by the composer and Allison Drake with the Federal Symphony Orchestra, New York, in May, 1939. A *Choral Symphony* (Secular Mass) was written in 1933, with *Variations on a Bavarian Dance Theme* in 1935. A *Prelude and Three Fugues* (1935) goes back to an original version for two pianos, presented by the League of Composers in 1933, with one of the Fugues offered orchestrally by Stokowski and the Philadelphians in April of 1937. An orchestral Suite of seven movements (1938) was followed by another for chamber orchestra in 1939 (both including a Tango and a Tarantella), with first performances in St. Louis. Nordoff has also written chamber music and smaller works, many songs, and incidental scores for Katharine Cornell's productions of *Romeo and Juliet* and *Saint Joan,* as well as an untitled opera.

ROBERT MCBRIDE (b. Tucson, Arizona, Feb. 20, 1911) represents a highly individual combination of the popular and the serious in modern music, having had much experience in dance bands, as a virtuoso clarinettist, and also conducting and teaching at Bennington, Vermont, and elsewhere. Much of his playing and creative work is available on records. McBride's orchestral compositions include *Show Piece* (1937), played at the Radio City Music Hall by Erno Rapee; *Prelude to a Tragedy,* introduced by Hans Lange with the New York Philharmonic in 1936, and later conducted in South America by Saminsky; a *Mexican Rhapsody,* written for the Master's degree at the University of Arizona in 1935; *Fugato on a Well-Known Theme* (generally recognized as *The Bum's March*), introduced by Ernest Schelling with the New York Philharmonic in 1939; *Swing Stuff* and *Jingle Jangle,* both played and recorded by the Boston Pops Orchestra under Arthur Fiedler; *Take It Easy Blues,* for string orchestra; and *Strawberry Jam* (*Home Made*), completed in December, 1941, for full orchestra. McBride has also written much for solo instruments and small groups.

BERNARD WAGENAAR (b. Arnhem, Netherlands, July 18, 1894) has been an American citizen since 1927, and now teaches composition at the Juilliard Graduate School, after playing the violin and other instruments in the New York Philharmonic Orchestra under Mengelberg, lecturing and conducting. His orchestral works include a *Divertimento* (1927), first performed by the Detroit Symphony Orchestra under Gabrilowitsch in 1929; a Sinfonietta for small orchestra (1929), introduced by Mengelberg with the New York Philharmonic in 1930 and chosen for the Liège Festival of the International Society for Contemporary Music in September of the same year; three symphonies, of which the First was performed by Mengelberg in October, 1928, the Second by Toscanini, November, 1932, both with the Philharmonic, and the Third at the Juilliard Graduate School, January, 1937, the composer conducting; a Triple Concerto for flute, harp, cello and orchestra (1935), written for the Barrère, Salzedo, Britt Trio, and introduced by them with the Philadelphia Orchestra, March 17, 1938, Ormandy conducting; a *Fantasietta on three British-American Ballads,* for small orchestra, commissioned by the Columbia Broadcasting System, and first broadcast Jan. 26, 1940; and a violin Concerto (1940). Wagenaar has also written much chamber music and songs.

FREDERICK JACOBI (b. San Francisco, Cal., May 4, 1891) was a pupil of Joseffy and Rubin Goldmark, assistant conductor of the Metropolitan Opera, 1913-17, and is now a recognized composer, as well as lecturer and teacher, since 1936 a member of the faculty of the Juilliard Graduate School. A Symphonic Poem, *The Pied Piper,* was written by Jacobi in 1915 and a *California Suite* for orchestra followed in 1917. Another Symphonic Poem, *The Eve of St. Agnes,* dates from 1919, and this was performed by such conductors as Alfred Hertz, in San Francisco, Bodanzky, in New York, and Saminsky, in Paris. A symphony, written in 1922, also had a San Francisco premiere, and a *Suite of Indian Dances* (1927-8) was interpreted by Koussevitzky, Stokowski and other conductors. A cello Concerto is dated 1932, a piano Concerto 1934-5, and a violin Concerto (played by Albert Spalding) 1936-7. *Ave Rota* was written in 1939 for small orchestra and piano, with a *Rhapsody* for harp and string orchestra in 1940. Jacobi's newest orchestral work is an *Ode,* dated 1941.

BERNARD ROGERS (b. New York, Feb. 4, 1893) is a composition pupil of Bloch, Frank Bridge and Nadia Boulanger, a winner of the Pulitzer Prize (1919) and of Guggenheim Fellowships (1927-9). He is now teaching at the Eastman School of Music in Rochester. His substantial list of orchestral works includes three symphonies: the First, *Adonais* (1925), the Second in A-flat (1928), and the Third in C (1936); *Five Fairy Tales* (1934), introduced by Hans Lange with the New York Philharmonic Orchestra in 1936; *Two American Frescoes* (1935), also performed in 1936 by the Philadelphia Orchestra under Stokowski; *Three Japanese Dances* (1933), introduced by Howard Hanson and the Rochester Philharmonic in 1934; *The Supper at Emaus* (1937), also with a Rochester premiere under Hanson (1938); and a *Soliloquy* for flute and strings (1922), which has become popular through a Victor record. Other orchestral works by Rogers are the Suite, *Song of the Nightingale* (1939), after Hans Andersen's story, introduced in 1940 by Goossens and the Cincinnati Orchestra; *The Dance of Salomé* (1939); *The Plains* (*Landscapes* for small orchestra) (1940); *Fantasy* for flute, viola and orchestra (1938); *The Colors of War* (1939); *To the Fallen* (1918); *The Faithful* (1923), an Overture after the Masefield tragedy; and *Fuji in the Sunset Glow* (1925), presented by Walter Damrosch and the New York Symphony Orchestra in 1926. All three of the Rogers symphonies have been performed in Rochester by Dr. Hanson, and the *Adonais* also under Stoessel at Chautauqua, N. Y.

ROBERT MILLS DELANEY (b. Baltimore, Md., 1903) has been a Guggenheim Fellow and Pulitzer prize-winner, studying composition with Nadia Boulanger and Honegger in Paris. He now lives on a ranch in California and has composed much music there. Delaney's orchestral works include several with chorus (of which *John Brown's Song*, with words by

Stephen Vincent Benet, is the most important); a Suite, *The Constant Couple* (1926); a *Pastoral Movement* (1930); two *Symphonic Pieces* (1935 and 1941); a Scherzo called *Work 22* (1938) (played in an all-American program under Izler Solomon at the Metropolitan Opera House); another Suite, *Going to Town* (1940); an Adagio for violin and strings (1935); and a *Short Preface* for clarinet and strings (1940). Delaney has also written chamber music in various forms.

Louis Gruenberg (b. Russia, Aug. 3, 1883) is a baffling combination of the practical and the sentimental, the traditional and the radical, the popular and the serious. Coming to America in his infancy, he developed into a pianist and composer, with training from Busoni and other masters. In recent years he has made his home in Hollywood, where he has written some of his most successful music for the films. (A concert Suite is available from *The Fight for Life*.) Gruenberg made early experiments with the jazz idiom, particularly in chamber music. His *Jazz Suite* was introduced by the Boston Symphony Orchestra in 1930. Still earlier orchestral works were *The Hill of Dreams* and *The Enchanted Isle*. His First Symphony won a share of the Victor prize of 1930 and was first played by the Boston Symphony Orchestra, February 10, 1933. There are also a Second Symphony, two piano Concertos and other orchestral material. The League of Composers in 1934 commissioned Gruenberg's *Serenade to a Beauteous Lady*, first performed by the Chicago Symphony Orchestra, April 4, 1935. It consists of five sections in dance rhythms "expertly orchestrated and full of genuine musical fancy." Gruenberg won his greatest fame with the opera, *The Emperor Jones*, based on the Eugene O'Neill play, with a premiere at the Metropolitan Opera House, January 7, 1933. His treatment of the spiritual, *Standin' in de Need of Prayer*, has been used as a concert number, and is the only portion of the opera that suggests a set aria of the old-fashioned type. Gruenberg has also written songs and chamber music, all showing a definitely modern technique.

WERNER JANSSEN (b. New York, June 1, 1899) has been known as a conductor (named by Sibelius as the best inter- preter of his music) as well as a composer. After leading the New York Philharmonic and Baltimore Symphony Orches- tras, however, he devoted himself chiefly to motion pictures and radio, in which fields he has made both an artistic and a commercial success. His most popular orchestral piece is called *New Year's Eve in New York,* a vivid example of pro- gram music, which has been played by the leading orchestras of America. Janssen has also written a *Louisiana Suite,* con- taining a Dixie Fugue, a *Foster Suite,* and some important chamber music.

HARL McDONALD (b. Boulder, Colorado, July 27, 1899) is a practical composer whose creative work supplements his regular job as manager of the Philadelphia Orchestra. He has written four symphonies. The First, called *Santa Fé Trail,* was introduced by the Philadelphia Orchestra in November, 1934, a frank piece of program music dealing with the history of the Southwest. The Second, a *Rhumba Symphony,* also had its premiere in Philadelphia, October, 1935. Its sub-title, "Reflections on an Era of Turmoil," is carried out graphically in the music, with an actual Rhumba for the Scherzo move- ment, which has been much played as an independent number. The Third Symphony of McDonald is called *Lamentations of Fu Hsuan,* requiring a soprano soloist and chorus. It was in- troduced in Philadelphia in January, 1936. The Fourth, first performed there in April, 1938, is non-programmatic, but ad- mittedly autobiographical in content, with a *Cake-Walk,* in- dividually very popular, as the Scherzo. McDonald has also written two piano Concertos and one for two pianos and orchestra, three Suites, plus one for the harp and orchestra (*From Childhood*), and a number of shorter works, including a *Tragic Cycle, San Juan Capistrano* and an *Overture 1941*. A *Miniature Suite,* attributed to "John C. Smith" (Handel's amanuensis) is really McDonald's own composition, effectively imitating the style of eighteenth-century music. Recently he has won success with the tone poem, *Bataan*.

LEO SOWERBY (b. Grand Rapids, Michigan, May 1, 1895) stands in the happy position of having been (in his own words) "accused by right-wingers of being too dissonant and cacophonous, and by the leftists of being old-fashioned and derivative." He was the first American to receive the Fellowship of the American Academy in Rome, and has recently spent most of his time in Chicago, as organist, teacher and composer. Sowerby's orchestral Suite, *A Set of Four,* was introduced by the Chicago Symphony Orchestra in 1918, and in the same year his Overture, *Comes Autumn Time,* had a first performance by the New York Symphony Orchestra, the latter becoming perhaps his best-known orchestral work. The composer appeared as soloist in his first piano Concerto in 1920, and a symphony followed in 1922. A *Ballad* for two pianos and orchestra was produced during his stay in Rome. Other compositions by Sowerby include a *Medieval Poem* for organ and orchestra and a Concerto for the same combination, a second piano Concerto (1932), introduced by the Boston Symphony Orchestra in 1936, a Second Symphony, a *Passacaglia, Interlude and Fugue,* first heard in Chicago in 1934, the Symphonic Poem, *Prairie,* a *Sinfonietta* for strings and a Suite, *From the Northland*. He wrote a Third Symphony for the 50th anniversary of the Chicago Orchestra, introduced by Dr. Stock, March 6, 1941. Sowerby has also made effective and popular adaptions for orchestra of such tunes as *Money*

Musk and *The Irish Washerwoman,* besides writing chamber music and smaller works for the piano and organ.

WILLIAM GRANT STILL (b. Woodville, Miss., May 11, 1895) is generally considered the most important of America's Negro composers. He studied with Chadwick and Varese, and has held several Guggenheim Fellowships, as well as the Harmon Award, the Rosenwald Fellowship and commissions of various kinds, besides arranging and orchestrating for the popular musicians of Broadway. The International Composers' Guild introduced Still's orchestral *From the Land of Dreams* in New York in February, 1925, and it was considered much too cacophonous for enjoyment. The composer himself called his *From the Journal of a Wanderer* (1926) "a lesson in what not to do," and he also criticized his *Darker America* (1924) as "fragmentary" and "not sufficiently well organized." But when Still began to devote himself to a musical interpretation of the Negro race he met with real and increasing success. Three orchestral works of this character form a trilogy: *Africa,* an *Afro-American Symphony* and a *Symphony in G minor. Africa,* appearing in 1930, was revised five times in the next five years. Its three movements are called Land of Peace, Land of Romance and Land of Superstition. The *Afro-American Symphony* is also dated 1930 and has been perhaps the most played of Still's works, particularly the Scherzo movement. Stokowski introduced the *G minor Symphony* in Philadelphia in December, 1937. *Kaintuck,* for piano and orchestra, was commissioned by the League of Composers and first performed in Los Angeles in 1935. *Lenox Avenue,* written for the Columbia Broadcasting System, had a radio premiere in May, 1937. Recent orchestral works by Still have mostly included singing voices: *Song of the City,* with chorus (written for the New York World's Fair), *Plain Chant for America,* with baritone solo, and the cantata, *And They Lynched Him on a Tree,* requiring a double chorus, contralto and narrator. Other orchestral works by Still include *Log Cabin Ballads, Puritan Epic, Ebon Chronicle, A Deserted Plantation, The Black Man Dances, Beyond Tomorrow, Dismal Swamp* and *Cantcha Line 'em* (on a folk tune). He has also written operas, chamber music and songs.

EMERSON WHITHORNE (b. Cleveland, Ohio, Sept. 6, 1884) is primarily a romantic impressionist, with echoes of the modern French style failing to disturb a fundamental Americanism. His best-known work is the Suite, *New York Days and Nights,* originally written for the piano, but winning its chief popularity in orchestral form. It was chosen as the American representative in the Salzburg Festival of 1923. The four sections are called On the Ferry, Pell Street, A Greenwich Village Tragedy and Times Square. A *Poem* for piano and orchestra was introduced by Gieseking with the Chicago Symphony Orchestra in 1927, with emphasis on syncopation. *Fata Morgana,* first played by the New York Philharmonic in 1928, also offers interesting rhythmic patterns. Whithorne's most romantic work is probably *The Dream Pedlar,* introduced by the Los Angeles Orchestra, January 13, 1931. *Moon Trail,* first performed by the Boston Symphony Orchestra, December 15, 1933, has four musical scenes: Death Valley, The Devil's Kitchen, Palos Verdes and Surf at Malibu. Whithorne has also written three symphonies, two of which were introduced by Goossens in Cincinnati, January 12, 1934 and March 19, 1937, a *Fandango,* played by Sir Thomas Beecham in 1932, and *Sierra Morena,* broadcast by the NBC Symphony Orchestra under Monteux in May, 1939. He is likewise responsible for a ballet, *Sooner and Later,* incidental music to the Eugene O'Neill play, *Marco Millions,* some chamber music, songs and piano pieces.

POPULAR AMERICANS IN
SERIOUS MOODS

There are men in America today who are known primarily
as popular composers but who have proved their ability to contribute quite significantly to the literature of serious music.
Their technique is often astonishing, and if one can eliminate
the preconceived idea that they are limited to Broadway hit
material, one may find much in their works to respect and
admire. George Gershwin had already shown the way, before
his untimely death, and many a cerebral creator of glistening
artificialities might well envy him the sure instinct for emotional expression, the individual melodic gift, and the natural,
unforced musicianship that worked with such telling effect on
his listeners. Probably there is no Gershwin at the moment
among our popular composers. Nevertheless there are several
composers of the Broadway type who have something to say
beyond the obvious appeal of a popular melody, and their importance in the field of orchestral music is becoming more and
more apparent. So far as the response of the public is concerned, there can be no argument as to their significance.

ROBERT RUSSELL BENNETT (b. Kansas City, June 15,
1894) has done amazing work as an arranger and orchestrator
in the field of musical comedy, being responsible for much of
the final effect in the music of Jerome Kern and other composers. The winning of a Guggenheim Fellowship (renewed,
1927-9) and some study with Nadia Boulanger in Paris turned
his mind to more serious musical creation. A symphony by
Bennett won honorable mention in the contest that produced
Bloch's *America*. Other orchestral pieces followed: *Paysage,
Endymion, Sights and Sounds,* and *Abraham Lincoln: A Like-
ness in Symphonic Form*. These last two compositions won
shares of the $25,000 prize offered by Victor in 1929-30. Since

then Bennett has spent much of his time in Hollywood, scoring, composing and conducting music for the films. He has directed a successful program of American music on the air, over the Mutual network. For the New York World's Fair of 1939-40 he created original music to synchronize with the fountain display. A *Charleston Rhapsody* has proved an effective orchestral piece, as has a later *Hollywood Rhapsody*. There is also an *Adagio Eroico,* a *Concerto Grosso,* using a small dance band as concertino, *Six Variations on a Theme of Jerome Kern,* a *March* for two pianos and orchestra, etc. Bennett also wrote an opera, *Maria Malibran,* with a libretto by Robert Simon, presented in 1935 by the Juilliard pupils. For radio he has turned out some humorous "occasional" music, including a *Symphony for the Brooklyn Dodgers* when they were on their way to the pennant in 1941. His orchestral *Etudes* were introduced by Howard Barlow, conducting the New York Philharmonic-Symphony Orchestra, November 5, 1942, emphasizing again his amazing technique.

FERDE GROFÉ (b. New York, March 27, 1892) is another composer who started as an arranger and orchestrator of popular music. He became associated with Paul Whiteman in 1920, and his instrumentation of Gershwin's *Rhapsody in Blue* unquestionably had much to do with its immediate success. In 1931 Whiteman presented Grofé's *Grand Canyon Suite,* and this quickly established the arranger as an original composer in his own right. It has become one of the most popular pieces on the radio, particularly the movement called On the Trail, with its imitation of the halting but sure-footed gait of the donkey, mingled with an occasional "hee-haw." Grofé experimented with modernism in his *Tabloid,* presented at Radio City Music Hall, and with a *Symphony in Steel* (1935). His earlier *Mississippi Suite* (1925) is full of melody and remains one of his most effective works. It was recently included in a high-school music book as one of eight out-standing compositions of permanent value by popular com-posers. Grofé also has to his credit a *Hollywood Suite* (1937), *Knute Rockne, Three Shades of Blue, Metropolis, Ode to Freedom, Wheels, March for Americans, Christmas Eve, Kentucky Derby, Trylon and Perisphere, Café Society Ballet, Hollywood Ballet, Ode to the Star Spangled Banner* and *An American Biography* (based on the life of Henry Ford). In 1937 he gave an entire program of his own compositions at Carnegie Hall.

MORTON GOULD (b. New York, Dec. 10, 1913) began as a serious musician, in fact a prodigy at the piano and in com-position, but found his way into Tin Pan Alley, and is now contributing real excitement to orchestral music, as a com-poser, conductor, arranger and broadcaster. His youth is an asset, and he constantly tries brilliant and daring experiments, to the delight of his listeners. There is novelty and cleverness in all his work, with flashes of inspiration and true creative ability, all tempered by an unerring showmanship. Gould's earliest work of importance is a *Chorale and Fugue in Jazz* (1935), played by Stokowski and the Philadelphia Orchestra in January, 1936. He wrote a symphony in 1936 and a piano Concerto in 1938, in which he has appeared as soloist with leading orchestras. Four *American Symphonettes* are dated 1937-8-9-40, the last being called *Latin-American* and the most frequently played. Fritz Reiner commissioned his *Foster Gallery*, built on the songs of Stephen Foster, with a first per-formance in Pittsburgh, January 12, 1940. A *Homespun Overture* dates from 1939, while 1941 saw the creation of a *Cowboy Rhapsody*, a *Song for Freedom, Lincoln Legend*, a *Concerto for Tap Dancer and Orchestra, Spirituals* and *Jericho* (for band). Gould's most popular individual piece is unquestion-ably the *Pavanne* from the second *American Symphonette*.

Stokowski has performed and recorded the *Guaracho* movement of the *Latin-American Symphonette*. Much of Gould's work has been aimed particularly at school bands and orchestras. He is a thoroughly practical American, who writes music frankly to be played and enjoyed.

MEREDITH WILLSON (b. Mason City, Iowa, May 18, 1902) wrote a popular hit song called *You and I,* and has for some years been well known as an orchestral conductor on the air. He studied music under Wagenaar, Hadley and other masters, also learning the flute from Barrère and playing it for three seasons in Sousa's band. He assisted Hugo Riesenfeld at the Rialto Theatre in New York, where his first orchestral work, *Parade Fantastique,* was produced in 1924. After that Willson played in the New York Philharmonic Orchestra for five years as first flutist, and then drifted into radio, becoming eventually musical director for the entire Western Division of the National Broadcasting Co. His First Symphony, in F minor, known as *San Francisco* was played by the San Francisco Symphony Orchestra in 1936 and later broadcast with great success. A Second Symphony, in E minor, called *The Missions of California,* was completed in April, 1940, and given its premiere by the Los Angeles Philharmonic under Albert Coates. He assisted Charles Chaplin in preparing the music for *The Great Dictator,* and wrote the score of *The Little Foxes* and other motion pictures. Other orchestral works by Meredith Willson include an *O. O. McIntyre Suite* (1936), a *Radio City Suite* (1937), and a tone poem, *Jervis Bay* (1940). He commissioned a series of orchestral compositions by American writers of popular music in the lighter forms made familiar in Europe, putting the results on the air and on records (Decca).

Other popular composers are heard from time to time in more serious works. Jerome Kern was represented on recent programs of the New York Philharmonic and the Cleveland Symphony Orchestras by a *Scenario* made from the melodies of *Showboat*, conducted by Rodzinski, and has also composed an orchestral *Portrait of Mark Twain*, introduced by Kostelanetz. Richard Rodgers has had a ballet performed at the Metropolitan Opera House and in concert. Otto Cesana is known for his *Three Moods*, and Dana Suesse for her *Jazz Concerto, Symphonic Waltzes* and Concerto in E minor for two pianos and orchestra. Vernon Duke, under his real name of Vladimir Dukelsky, has written much orchestral music, including two symphonies and two piano Concertos. Alec Templeton has recently completed a piano Concerto, introduced by him on the air. The dividing line between the popular and the serious is no longer as heavy as it used to be.

AMONG THOSE PRESENT

As with contemporary composers in general, it is necessary to list a number of Americans merely by name and the titles of their important orchestral works. Whether the word "great" can be applied to any of these compositions rests with the future. They are quite likely to develop as much significance as any of the creative American music discussed in greater detail. The order is again alphabetical.

Isidor Achron: Two piano Concertos; *Suite Grotesque* (Gavotte, Minuet, Tango, Polka, Valse).

Joseph Achron: *Hebrew Melody* (violin); *Belshazzar;* three violin Concertos; *Golem Suite; Dance Overture; Dance of the Tsadikim.*

Paul Hastings Allen: Two symphonies; *Serenade; Ex Hocte; O Munasterio.*

Ernst Bacon: Two symphonies; *Country Roads; Prelude and Fugue.*

Edward Ballantine: *Prelude to the Delectable Forest; The Eve of St. Agnes; From the Garden of Hellas; The Awakening of the Woods; Overture to The Piper.*

Samuel L. M. Barlow: *Alba;* piano Concerto; *Babar; Eugenie Waltzes; Biedermeyer Waltzes; Overture to Mon Ami Pierrot; Leda; Sousa ad Parnassum; The Big Tent* (Elephantia; Trapeze; The Bearded Lady; Parade).

Wayne Barlow: *Poem; De Profundis; The Winter's Past; Three Moods for Dancing.*

Hans Barth: Three piano Concertos; Suite; *Pantomime Symphony.*

Marion Bauer: *Symphonic Suite* (string orchestra); *Lament on an African Theme; Indian Pipes; Sun Splendor; Orientale; Faun Song;* Concertino (oboe, clarinet and strings).

John Beach: *Asolani; Phantom Satyr; Orleans Alley; Enter Buffoon.*

John J. Becker: Five Symphonies; two piano Concertos; two Suites; *Soundpieces; A Marriage with Space; Victory March.*

Evelyn Berckman: Ballets, *From the Odyssey* and *County Fair.*

Seth Bingham: *Tame Animal Tunes; Wall Street Fantasy; Passacaglia;* two Suites: *Memories of France* and *The Breton Cadence; Pioneer America.*

Franz C. Bornschein: *Cape Cod Impressions: The Mission Road; Mystic Trumpeter;* violin Concerto; *Three Persian Poems.*

Felix Borowski: Three Symphonies; *Ecce Homo; Semiramis; Youth; The Passionate Springtime; Paintings; Symphonic Elegy; Allegro de Concert* (organ); *Rhapsody* (organ and chamber orchestra); piano Concerto; *Triumphal March; Two Pieces* (strings).

Paul Frederic Bowles: *Yankee Clipper* (ballet); Incidental

music to *Horse Eats Hat; Dr. Faustus; Twelfth Night;* Suite (small orchestra).

Robert Braine: *S. O. S.; The Song of Hiawatha; Concerto in Jazz; The House of Usher; Harlequin and Columbine; City of Dreams; Habañera.*

Gena Branscombe: *Festival Prelude;* Symphonic Suite, *Quebec.*

Henry Brant: Symphonic Overture, *Whoopee;* clarinet Concerto; *The Marx Brothers* (chamber orchestra); *Decision; A Fisherman's Overture: The Great American Goof* (ballet); violin Concerto; *Rhapsody* (viola).

Radie Britain: *Heroic Poem; Southern Symphony; Theme and Variations.*

Mortimer Browning: Concerto for Theremin; *Kemptown Suite* (Cross Roads, Dance, Night Song, County Fair); *Rondo Scherzo* (violin); *Ballet Waltz; Mary Poppins Suite.*

Cecil Burleigh: Three violin Concertos; *Evangeline; Mountain Pictures.*

Carl Busch: *Ozarka;* two symphonies; *The Passing of Arthur; Elegy* (strings).

Theodore Cella: *On a Transatlantic Liner; Through the Pyrenees; Alpine Impressions; Carnival; The Lido.*

Philip Greeley Clapp: *Norge; Symphony in E; Song of Youth; Dramatic Poem* (trombone); *In Summer; Symphony in E minor; Symphony in E-flat; Symphony in D; A Golden Gate Symphony; Symphony in A; Symphony in C; An Academic Diversion* (chamber orchestra); Symphony, *The Pioneers;* piano Concerto; seven Orchestral Preludes; symphony, *Theodore Roosevelt; Fantasy on an Old Plain Chant* (cello); *Prologue to a Tragedy; Overture to a Comedy;* Symphony No. 11.

Mabel Daniels: *Pastoral Ode* (flute and strings); *Deep Forest; Pirates' Island; Fairy Scherzo; In the Greenwood.*

William L. Dawson: *Negro Folk Symphony; Negro Work Song;* Scherzo.

Eric Delamarter: Overture, *The Faun;* Suite, *The Betrothal;* Symphony.

Richard F. Donovan: *Smoke and Steel; Wood Notes; Chamber Symphony; Serenade.*

Arcady Dubensky: *Tartar Song and Dance; From Old Russia; Intermezzo and Compliment; Four Compositions for Orchestra; Gossips* (strings); Suite, *Anno 1600* (strings); *Andante Russe* (strings); Russian Song-Dance (strings); *Fanfare* (brass); *Tom Sawyer Overture; Variations on Foster Themes; Fantasy* (tuba); *Symphony in G minor; Russian Bells; Valse; Andante and Scherzo* (flute); *Prelude and Fugue; Legend; Italian Overture; Concerto Grosso* (strings); *Serenade; Political Suite; Dance Orientale; Recitativo and Fuga Libra; Prelude* (strings); *Meditation* (strings); *Rondo and Gigue* (strings); *Fantasy; Last Fugue.*

Henry Eichheim: *Burma; Java; Bali; Korean Sketch.*

A. Lehman Engel: *Jungle Dance; Introduction and Allegretto; Scientific Creation; Traditions;* Incidental Music to *Within the Gates.*

Carl Eppert: *A Symphony of the City* (Traffic, City Shadows, Speed, City Nights); *The Argonauts; The Pioneer; Little Symphony; Symphony in C minor; Escapade;* Suite, *Vitamins; Concert Waltz Suite.*

Arthur Fickenscher: *Variation Fantasy* (strings): *Dies Irae* (small orchestra); *Willowwood and Wellaway; Day of Judgment; Out of the Gay Nineties.*

Ross Lee Finney: Piano Concerto; violin Concerto; Prelude; *Barbershop Ballad; Slow Piece* (strings); *Serenade* (strings): *Overture for a Drama.*

Isadore Freed: *Jeux de Timbres; Triptyque; Vibrations;*

Pygmalion; Ballad (piano and small orchestra); *Pastorales;* Symphony.

Anis Fuleihan: *Mediterranean Suite* (Shepherds, Peasants, Priests and Priestesses, Musicians, Dancers); *Preface to a Child's Story-Book;* Symphony; Concerto No. 1 (piano and strings); piano Concerto No. 2; *Fiesta; Symphonie Concertante for String Quartet and Orchestra;* Concerto for two pianos; *Epithalamium* (piano and strings); *Invocation to Isis; Divertimento No. 1; Divertimento No. 2* (strings, with oboe, bassoon, trumpet and horn).

Rudolph Ganz: Symphony; *Concert Piece* (piano); *Suite on American Scenes; Animal Pictures.*

Samuel Gardner: Violin Concerto; *Broadway.*

Harvey B. Gaul: *Père Marquette; New England Prelude; Introduction to a Speaker;* Suite, *Fosteriana* (strings); *Three Palestinian Pastels* (strings).

Vittorio Giannini: *Symphony in Memoriam Theodore Roosevelt;* piano Concerto; Suite; *I. B. M. Symphony;* Concerto for two pianos; Opera Ballet; *Prelude, Chorale and Fugue.*

Eugene Goossens: *Kaleidoscope; Tam O'Shanter; The Eternal Rhythm; Rhythmic Dance; Sinfonietta; Three Greek Dances;* Concertino for double string orchestra; *Poem* (viola); *Rhapsody* (cello).

Elliot Griffis: *Symphony in G minor; A Persian Fable; Paul Bunyan, Colossus;* Suite, *Montevallo; Variations for Strings; Fantastic Pursuit* (strings); *Spanish Tango; Julianne: Waltz Memories of Vienna.*

Carl Hugo Grimm: Four Symphonic Poems; two Suites; *Serenade; Erotic Poem; Abraham Lincoln.*

David Guion: *Shingandi* (ballet); Suite; *Little Brown Bulls; Minuet; Alley Tunes;* Transcriptions of *Turkey in the Straw, Arkansas Traveler, Sheep and Goat Walkin' to the Pasture; Mother Goose Suite; The Scissors Grinder; Bar-*

carolle; Southern Nights (Waltz Suite); *The Harmonica Player; Lonesome Whistler; Nocturne in Blue; Two Country Jigs* (in C and D); *Pickaninny Dance.*

Richard Hammond: *Five Chinese Fairy Tales; The Sea of Heaven; West Indian Dances;* Suite, *After Reading The Woman of Andros; Sinfonietta;* two Suites of Dance Music; *Excursion.*

W. Franke Harling: *Jazz Concerto; Venetian Fantasy; Chansons Populaires.*

Bernard Herrmann: *Currier and Ives Suite; The Skating Pond; The City of Brass; Variations on Deep River and Water Boy; Moby Dick* (chorus and soloists); Symphony; *Fiddle Concerto.*

Mary Howe: *Sand; Poem; Dirge; Spring Pastoral; Stars; Whimsy; Coulennes; American Piece; Castellana* (two pianos and orchestra).

Herbert Inch: Symphony; piano Concerto; *To Silvanus; Variations on a Modal Theme;* Suite; Serenade; *Divertimento* (brass).

Philip James: *Station WGZBX; Bret Harte; Song of the Night; Chamber Symphony; Overture on French Noels; Sea-Symphony; Judith;* Suite (chamber orchestra).

Horace Johnson: *Imagery; Streets of Florence; Joyance* (strings); *In the American Manner; Astarte.*

Werner Josten: *Concerto Sacro,* No. 1 and No. 2 (piano and strings); *Jungle; Batouala; Serenade; Symphony for Strings; Symphony in F;* Orchestra Trio.

Homer Keller: *Serenade* (clarinet and strings); Symphony.

Kent Kennan: *Night Soliloquy* (flute and orchestra).

Boris Koutzen: Poem-Nocturne, *Solitude; Symphonic Movement* (violin); *Valley Forge;* Concerto for five solo instruments and strings; *Symphony in C; Concert Piece* (cello).

A. Walter Kramer: *Two Sketches* (Chant Nègre, Valse Triste); *Danse Espagnole* (violin); *Eklog* (violin); *Ro-*

mance in A (violin); *Intermezzo* (strings); *In Elizabethan Days* (strings); *Elegy in C-sharp minor* (strings); *Humoresque on Two American Folk-Tunes: Swanee River* and *Dixie* (strings).

Otto Luening: Two Symphonic Poems; *Divertimento;* two Symphonic Interludes; *Serenade; Dirge;* Symphony; Suite (strings); *Americana; Symphonietta; Prelude to a Hymn-Tune; Concertino* (chamber orchestra).

Quinto Maganini; *Tuolumne; South Wind's Ornithological Suite; Sylvan Symphony; Cuban Rhapsody.*

George Frederick McKay: Three Sinfoniettas; three Lyric Soliloquies; Lyric Poem (strings); Sonatine (clarinet and strings); *Fantasy on a Western Folk-Song; Prairie Portrait; Five Dramatic Moods* (strings); *Harbor Narrative; Epoch; Variants on a Texas Tune; Symphonie Miniature; Introspective Poem* (strings); *Port Royal* (strings); violin Concerto; *To a Liberator* (A Lincoln Tribute); *Symphonic Prelude in American Idiom; Machine-Age Blues.*

Carl McKinley: *Masquerade; Indian Summer Idyl.*

Gian-Carlo Menotti: Overture to *Amelia Goes to the Ball; Pastorale* (piano and strings).

Jerome Moross: Symphony; *Paeans; Biguine; Tall Story.*

Charles Naginski: *Sinfonietta; Children's Suite; The Minotaur* (ballet).

Arthur Nevin: *Lorna Doone Suite; Miniature Suite; Springs of Saratoga; Symphonic Poem; Arizona.*

Arne Oldberg: Two piano Concertos; *The Sea;* two symphonies; Overtures; Orchestral Fantasies; horn Concerto.

Leo Ornstein: Piano Concerto; *Nocturne and Dance of the Fates.*

Courtlandt Palmer: Piano Concerto.

Burrill Phillips: *Selections from McGuffey's Reader; Courthouse Square; Grotesque Dance from a Projected Ballet;*

Symphony Concertante; piano Concerto; Dance; Concert Piece (bassoon and strings).

Solomon Pimsleur: *Symphonic Ballade,* B-flat minor (from *Series of Transformations*); *Meditative Nocturne; The Miracle of Life and the Mystery of Death; Partita* (strings); Symphonic Suite; Symphonic Ode and Peroration; Cycle of Symphonies (*Conflict between Light and Darkness, Lamentation, Man's Inhumanity to Man*); *Dynamic Overture; Symphony to Disillusionment.*

Quincy Porter: *Ukrainian Suite;* Suite in C minor; *Poem and Dance;* First Symphony; *Dance in Three-Time; Two Dances for Radio.*

Gardner Read: *The Lotus-Eaters; The Painted Desert; Sketches of the City; Three Satirical Sarcasms;* Symphony No. 1, A minor; Suite for Strings; *Passacaglia and Fugue; Fantasy* (viola); *Petite Pastorale; Prelude and Toccata;* Symphony No. 2, E-flat minor; *American Circle; Pan e Dafni.*

Alois Reiser: Cello Concerto; *A Summer Evening; From Mt. Rainier; Erewhon; Slavic Rhapsody.*

Leroy Robertson: Concert Overture; *Prelude, Scherzo and Ricercare; Trilogy.*

Edward Royce: *The Fire-Bringers; Far Ocean.*

Beryl Rubinstein: Scherzo; Suite; piano Concerto.

Dane Rudhyar: *The Surge of Fire; To the Real; Ouranos;* Symphony; *Hero Chants; Sinfonietta; Cosmophony.*

Louis Victor Saar: *Rococo Suite; From the Mountain Kingdom of the Great Northwest; Along the Columbia River.*

Carlos Salzedo: *The Enchanted Isle* (harp and orchestra); *Harp Concerto.*

Robert L. Sanders: *Little Symphony in G; Saturday Night* (Barn Dance); violin Concerto; Suite; *Scenes of Poverty and Toil.*

Frederick Preston Search: *Sinfonietta; Exhilaration; Festival Overture;* Symphony No. 1, D major; *The Dream of McKorkle;* Symphonies 3, 4 and 5; *Rhapsody; Romanze* (strings); cello Concerto; *The Bridge Builders.*

Tibor Serly: Two Symphonies; *Six Dance Designs;* viola Concerto; *Prelude and Fugue* (2 harps and strings); *Colonial Pageant; The Pagan City; Alarms and Excursions; Sonata Concertante* (strings); *Transylvanian Suite.*

Bertram Shapleigh: Two Symphonies; Symphonic Prelude; *Poem* (cello); Suites: *Ramayana* and *Gur Amir; Mirage; Aubade; Intermezzo; Nordic Cradle Song.*

Arthur Shepherd: *Dance Episodes on an Exotic Theme; Ouverture Joyeuse; Horizons* (including *The Lone Prairie*); two Symphonies.

Elie Siegmeister: *Prelude* (strings); *Rhapsody; Created Equal; A Walt Whitman Overture; American Holiday.*

Nicolas Slonimsky: *Suite in Black and White; Fragment from Orestes.*

Albert Spalding: Two violin Concertos; Suite.

Timothy Mather Spelman: *Symphony in G minor; Christ and the Blind Man; Dawn in the Woods; Barbaresques; Saints' Days.*

Alexander Steinert: *Southern Night; Leggenda Sinfonica; Concerto Sinfonico* (piano).

Lamar Stringfield: *From the Southern Mountains; Indian Legend; Moods of a Moonshiner; The Legend of John Henry; Negro Parade.*

Edwin J. Stringham: *The Phantom; Three Pastels; Ancient Mariner; Visions; Springtime Overture; Danse Exotique; Italian Symphony; Nocturnes,* 1 and 2; *Fantasy on an American Folk-Tune* (violin).

Gustav Strube: *Symphony in G; Symphonic Prologue;* two violin Concertos; *Sylvan Suite; Americana; Divertimento.*

Burnet C. Tuthill: *Bethlehem* (Pastorale); *Rhapsody: Come Seven;* Symphonic Poem, *Laurentia*.

Donald Tweedy: *L'Allegro; Three Dances;* Ballets; Incidental Music.

David Van Vactor: *Symphony in D; Masque of the Red Death; Chaconne* (strings); Overture, *Cristobal Colon; Passacaglia and Fugue in D minor; Overture to a Comedy; Concerto Grosso;* flute Concerto.

Wesley La Violette: Chorale; First Symphony; violin Concerto; *Prelude and Aria*.

Kurt Weill; *Fantasy, Passacaglia and Hymn; Divertimento; Quodlibet; Flight of Lindbergh*.

Lazar Weiner: *Prelude; Dance; Little Story*.

Adolph Weiss: *American Life; Chamber Symphony; Ballade; Theme and Variations; Five Pieces*.

Mark Wessel: Symphony; *Symphony Concertante* (piano and horn); *Holiday; Song and Dance; Concertino* (flute); *The King of Babylon*.

Hermann H. Wetzler: Overture, *As You Like It; Symphonic Fantasy; Visions; Assisi; Symphonic Dance in Basque Style; Symphonie Concertante* (violin).

Clarence Cameron White: *Bandanna Sketches; From the Cotton Fields; Serenade; Pantomime; Suite on Negro Themes; Prelude to Ouanga; Tambour*.

Paul White: *Five Miniatures; Symphony in E minor; Pagan Festival; To Youth; Feuilles Symphoniques; Boston Sketches; College Caprice*.

APPENDIX

COLUMBIA RECORDS OF
GREAT ORCHESTRAL MUSIC

ALBENIZ:
El Corpus en Sevilla. Madrid Symphony, Arbos. [67709-D]
BACH, J. S.:
Air on the G-string. All-American Orchestra, Stokowski. [X-220]
Brandenburg Concertos, Nos. 1-6. Busch Chamber Players. [M-249, M-250]
Concerto for Two Violins. Szigeti, Flesch. Orchestra, Goehr. [X-90]
Komm, Süsser Tod. All-American Orchestra, Stokowski. [X-220]
Passacaglia and Fugue in C minor. All-American Orchestra, Stokowski. [X-216]
Toccata and Fugue in D minor. All-American Orchestra, Stokowski. [X-219]
Violin Concerto No. 1. Hubermann. Orchestra, Dobrowen. [X-45]
Violin Concerto No. 2. Hubermann. Orchestra, Dobrowen. [M-235]
Violin Concerto in D minor. Szigeti. Orchestra, Stiedry. [M-418]
BALAKIREFF:
Russia. London Philharmonic, Harty. [DB1236, DB1237]
BEETHOVEN:
Coriolanus Overture. Minneapolis Symphony, Mitropoulos. [11175-D]
Egmont Overture. Vienna Philharmonic, Weingartner. [69195-D]
Fidelio Overture. London Philharmonic, Weingartner. [69545-D]
Grosse Fuge. Busch Chamber Players. [X-221]
Leonore Overture No. 2. London Symphony, Weingartner. [X-96]
Leonore Overture No. 3. Minneapolis Symphony, Mitropoulos. [X-173]
Piano Concerto No. 1. Gieseking. Berlin State Opera Orchestra, Rosbaud. [M-308]
Piano Concerto No. 4. Gieseking. Saxon State Orchestra, Böhm. [M-411]

Piano Concerto No. 5. Serkin. Vienna Philharmonic, Walter. [M-500]

Prometheus Overture. Vienna Philharmonic, Weingartner. [68565-D]

Symphony No. 1. Vienna Philharmonic, Weingartner. [M-321]

Symphony No. 2. London Philharmonic, Beecham. [M-302]

Symphony No. 3. Philharmonic-Symphony, Walter. [M-449]

Symphony No. 4. London Philharmonic, Weingartner. [M-197]

Symphony No. 5. Philharmonic-Symphony, Walter. [M-498]

Symphony No. 6. Minneapolis Symphony, Mitropoulos. [M-401]

Symphony No. 7. Vienna Philharmonic, Weingartner. [M-260]

Symphony No. 8. New York Philharmonic-Symphony, Walter. [M-525]

Symphony No. 9. Vienna Philharmonic, Weingartner. [M-227]

Triple Concerto. Odnoposoff, Auber, Morales. Vienna Symphony, Weingartner. [M-327]

Twelve Contra Dances. CBS Orchestra, Barlow. [X-184]

Violin Concerto. Szigeti. Orchestra, Walter. [M-177]

Weihe des Hauses Overture. London Philharmonic, Weingartner. [X-140]

BERG:

Violin Concerto. Krasner. Cleveland Orchestra, Rodzinski. [M-465]

BERLIOZ:

Damnation of Faust: Excerpts. London Philharmonic, Beecham. [X-94]

Roman Carnival Overture. London Philharmonic, Beecham. [68921-D]

Symphonie Fantastique. Cleveland Orchestra, Rodzinski. [M-488]

BIZET:

L'Arlésienne Suite No. 1. London Philharmonic, Beecham. [X-69]

Carmen Suite. London Philharmonic, Beecham. [X-144]

Fair Maid of Perth Suite. London Philharmonic, Beecham. [X-28]

BLOCH:

Violin Concerto. Szigeti. Orchestra, Munch. [M-380]

BORODIN:

Polovtsienne Dances. Leeds Festival Choir. London Philharmonic, Beecham. [X-54]

BRAHMS:

Academic Festival Overture. New York Philharmonic-Symphony, Barbirolli. [X-200]

Haydn Variations. Minneapolis Symphony, Mitropoulos. [X-225]

Minuet from Serenade in D. Chicago Symphony, Stock. [11682-D]

Symphony No. 1. London Symphony, Weingartner. [M-383]

Symphony No. 2. London Philharmonic, Weingartner. [M-493]

Symphony No. 3. London Philharmonic, Weingartner. [M-353]

Symphony No. 4. London Symphony, Weingartner. [M-335]

Tragic Overture. Chicago Symphony, Stock. [X-214]

Violin Concerto. Szigeti. Hallé Orchestra, Harty. [M-117]

BRUCH:

Violin Concerto No. 1. Milstein. New York Philharmonic-Symphony, Barbirolli. [M-517]

CHABRIER:

España Rhapsody. London Philharmonic, Beecham. [71250-D]

CHOPIN:

Piano Concerto No. 1. Kilenyi. Minneapolis Symphony, Mitropoulos. [M-515]

Piano Concerto No. 2. Long. Paris Conservatory Orchestra, Gaubert. [M-143]

CIMAROSA:

Il Matrimonio Segreto Overture. La Scala Orchestra, Molajoli. [7194-M]

CRESTON:

Scherzo. All-American Orchestra, Stokowski. [11713-D]

DEBUSSY:

Iberia. Pittsburgh Symphony, Reiner. [M-491]

L'Après-midi d'un Faune. London Philharmonic, Beecham. [69600-D]

Nocturnes: Nuages, Fêtes, Sirènes. Orchestra, Inghelbrecht. [M-344]

Rhapsody for Clarinet and Orchestra. Goodman. New York Philharmonic-Symphony, Barbirolli. [11517-D]

DELIUS:

Appalachia. London Philharmonic, Beecham. [In M-355]

Brigg Fair. Orchestra, Beecham. [X-30]

Eventyr. London Philharmonic, Beecham. [In M-305]

In a Summer Garden. London Philharmonic, Beecham. [In M-290]

On Hearing the First Cuckoo in Spring. Royal Philharmonic, Beecham. [67475-D]

Over the Hills. London Philharmonic, Beecham. [In M-290]

Paris: A Night Piece. London Philharmonic, Beecham. [In M-305]

Summer Night on a River. London Symphony, Beecham. [17087-D]

The Walk to Paradise Garden. Royal Philharmonic, Beecham. [67474-D]

D'INDY:

Symphony on a French Mountain Air. Long. Colonne Orchestra, Paray. [M-211]

DUKAS:

L'Apprenti Sorcier. Minneapolis Symphony, Mitropoulos. [X-212]

DVOŘÁK:

Carneval Overture. CBS Orchestra, Barlow. [70739-D]

Legende. London Philharmonic, Beecham. [68387-D]

Slavonic Dances Nos. 1 and 3. Minneapolis Symphony, Mitropoulos. [11645-D]

Slavonic Rhapsody. London Philharmonic, Beecham. [X-55]

Symphony No. 5. All-American Orchestra, Stokowski. [M-416]

ELGAR:

Enigma Variations. Hallé Orchestra, Harty. [M-165]

Pomp and Circumstance March. London Philharmonic, Wood. [70364-D]

ENESCO:

Roumanian Rhapsody No. 1. Chicago Symphony, Stock. [X-203]

FAURÉ:

Ballade for piano and orchestra. Long. Orchestra, Gaubert. [X-62]

FRANCK:

Les Eolides. CBS Orchestra, Barlow. [X-145]

Symphonic Variations for Piano and Orchestra. Gieseking. Orchestra, Wood. [X-10]

Symphony in D minor. London Philharmonic, Beecham. [M-479]

GERSHWIN:
  Concerto in F. Levant. Orchestra, Kostelanetz. [M-512]
  Rhapsody in Blue. Templeton. Orchestra, Kostelanetz. [X-196]
GLAZOUNOFF:
  Carnaval Overture. Chicago Symphony, Stock. [11771-D]
  Stenka Razin. Brussels Royal Conservatory Orchestra, Defauw.
    [7202, 7203]
  The Seasons. Orchestra, Glazounoff. [M-284]
GLIÈRE:
  Ilia Mourometz Symphony: Scherzo only. Chicago Symphony,
    Stock. [11697-D]
GLUCK:
  Iphigenie en Aulide Overture. CBS Orchestra, Barlow. [X-138]
GOLDMARK:
  Rustic Wedding Symphony. CBS Orchestra, Barlow. [M-385]
GOULD:
  Guaracho. All-American Orchestra, Stokowski. [11713-D]
GOUNOD:
  Funeral March of a Marionette. London Philharmonic, Wood.
    [7374-M]
GRIEG:
  Peer Gynt Suite. London Philharmonic, Beecham. [X-180]
  Piano Concerto. Gieseking. Orchestra, Rosbaud. [M-313]
  Two Elegiac Melodies. Minneapolis Symphony, Mitropoulos.
    [11698-D]
GRIFFES:
  The White Peacock. CBS Orchestra, Barlow. [17140-D]
HANDEL:
  Alcina Suite. Paris Conservatory Orchestra, Weingartner.
    [X-164]
  Concerto for Viola and Orchestra. Primrose. Orchestra, Goehr.
    [M-295]
  Concerto Grosso No. 5. London Philharmonic, Weingartner.
    [X-142]
  Concerto Grosso No. 6. London Symphony, Weingartner. [X-154]
  Faithful Shepherd. London Philharmonic, Beecham. [M-458]
  Royal Fireworks Music. London Philharmonic, Harty. [X-51]
  The Gods Go A-Begging. London Philharmonic, Beecham.
    [69472-D, 68881-D]
  Water Music. London Philharmonic, Harty. [X-13]

HARRIS:
  Symphony 1933. Boston Symphony, Koussevitzky. [M-191]
HAYDN:
  'Cello Concerto. Feuermann. Orchestra, Sargent. [M-262]
  Concerto for Piano. Roesgen-Champion. Orchestra, Gaillard.
    [X-118]
  Concerto for Trumpet. Eskdale. Orchestra, Goehr. [70106-D]
  Symphony No. 41. Brussels Orchestra, Defauw. [X-14]
  Symphony No. 45. London Symphony, Wood. [M-205]
  Symphony No. 93. London Philharmonic, Beecham. [M-336]
  Symphony No. 94. CBS Orchestra, Barlow. [M-363]
  Symphony No. 98. CBS Orchestra, Barlow. [M-370]
  Symphony No. 99. London Philharmonic, Beecham. [M-264]
  Symphony No. 101. CBS Orchestra, Barlow. [M-459]
  Symphony No. 104. London Philharmonic, Beecham. [M-409]
  "Toy" Symphony. Orchestra, Weingartner. [7242-M]
HOLST:
  St. Paul's Suite. Jacques String Ensemble. [17113, 17114]
  The Planets. London Symphony, Holst. [M-359]
HUMPERDINCK:
  Hansel and Gretel Suite. CBS Orchestra, Barlow. [M-424]
IBERT:
  Escales. Straram Orchestra, Straram. [X-16]
IPPOLITOFF-IVANOFF:
  Procession of the Sardar. Chicago Symphony, Stock. [11738-D]
KERN:
  Mark Twain. Orchestra, Kostelanetz. [X-227]
  Show Boat. Scenario for orchestra. Cleveland Orchestra, Rod-
    zinski. [M-495]
LALO:
  'Cello Concerto. Maréchal. Orchestra, Gaubert. [M-185]
  Symphonie Espagnole. Hubermann. Orchestra, Szell. [M-214]
LISZT:
  A Faust Symphony. Paris Philharmonic, Meyrowitz. [M-272]
  Hungarian Fantasy. Kilenyi. Orchestra, Meyrowitz. [X-120]
  Hungarian Rhapsody No. 2. All-American Orchestra, Stokowski.
    [11646-D]
  Les Préludes. London Symphony, Weingartner. [X-198]
  Orpheus. CBS Orchestra, Barlow. [X-165]
  Piano Concerto No. 1. Sauer. Orchestra, Weingartner. [M-371]

Piano Concerto No. 2. Petri. London Philharmonic, Heward. [M-362]

Spanish Rhapsody. Petri. Minneapolis Symphony, Mitropoulos. [X-163]

Todtentanz. Kilenyi. Orchestra, Meyrowitz. [X-122]

LULLY:

Excerpts from four operas. Orchestra, Cauchie. [M-376]

MACDOWELL:

Suite No. 2. CBS Orchestra, Barlow. [M-373]

MAHLER:

Das Lied von der Erde. Thorborg, Kullman. Orchestra, Walter. [M-300]

Symphony No. 1. Minneapolis Symphony, Mitropoulos. [M-469]

MENDELSSOHN:

Capriccio Brilliant. Graudan. Minneapolis Symphony, Mitropoulos. [X-197]

Fingal's Cave. London Philharmonic, Beecham. [69400-D]

Incidental Music to A Midsummer Night's Dream (Overture, Scherzo, Nocturne, Intermezzo, Wedding March). Cleveland Orchestra, Rodzinski. [M-504]

Piano Concerto No. 1. Dorfmann. Orchestra, Goehr. [X-124]

Ruy Blas. London Philharmonic, Beecham. [70352-D]

Symphony No. 3. Royal Philharmonic, Weingartner. [M-126]

Symphony No. 4. Hallé Orchestra, Harty. [M-167]

Symphony No. 5. CBS Orchestra, Barlow. [M-391]

Violin Concerto. Szigeti. Orchestra, Beecham. [M-190]

MEYTUSS:

Dnieprostroi. Paris Symphony, Ehrlich. [17121-D]

MILHAUD:

Création du Monde. Orchestra, Milhaud. [X-18]

Piano Concerto. Long. Orchestra, Milhaud. [X-67]

MOSSOLOFF:

Steel Foundry. Paris Symphony, Ehrlich. [17121-D]

MOUSSORGSKY:

Khovantchina Prelude. Cleveland Orchestra, Rodzinski. [11657-D]

Night on Bare Mountain. Colonne Orchestra, Paray. [68305-D]

Pictures at an Exhibition. All-American Orchestra, Stokowski. [M-511]

MOZART:

Bassoon Concerto. Camden. Orchestra, Harty. [M-71]

Divertimento in B flat, K. 287. Szigeti. Orchestra, Goberman. [M-322]

Divertimento in D, K. 334. London Philharmonic, Harty. [M-207]

Don Giovanni Overture. London Philharmonic, Beecham. [70365-D]

Eine Kleine Nachtmusik. London Symphony, Weingartner. [X-187]

Magic Flute Overture. Orchestra, Walter. [67660-D]

Marriage of Figaro Overture. London Philharmonic, Beecham. [69058-D]

Piano Concerto in E flat, K. 271. Gieseking. Orchestra, Rosbaud. [M-291]

Piano Concerto in G, K. 453. Dohnanyi. Orchestra, Dohnanyi. [M-111]

Piano Concerto in A, K. 488. Long. Orchestra, Gaubert. [M-261]

Piano Concerto in C minor, K. 491. Casadesus. Orchestra, Bigot. [M-356]

Piano Concerto in B flat, K. 595. Casadesus. New York Philharmonic-Symphony Orchestra, Barbirolli. [M-490]

Symphony No. 25, K. 183. New York Philharmonic-Symphony, Barbirolli. [X-217]

Symphony No. 29, K. 201. London Philharmonic, Beecham. [M-333]

Symphony No. 31, K. 295. London Philharmonic, Beecham. [M-360]

Symphony No. 34, K. 338. Royal Philharmonic, Beecham. [M-123]

Symphony No. 35, K. 385. London Philharmonic, Beecham. [M-399]

Symphony No. 36, K. 425. London Philharmonic, Beecham. [M-387]

Symphony No. 38, K. 504. London Philharmonic, Beecham. [M-509]

Symphony No. 39, K. 543. London Philharmonic, Beecham. [M-456]

Symphony No. 40, K. 550. London Philharmonic, Beecham. [M-316]

Symphony No. 41, K. 551. London Philharmonic, Beecham. [M-194]

NICOLAI:

Merry Wives of Windsor Overture. London Philharmonic, Beecham. [68938-D]

OFFENBACH:

Gaité Parisienne. London Philharmonic, Kurtz. [X-115]

PAGANINI:

Moto Perpetuo. Chicago Symphony, Stock. [11738-D]

PONCHIELLI:

Dance of the Hours. Chicago Symphony, Stock. [11621-D]

PROKOFIEFF:

Classical Symphony. Minneapolis Symphony, Mitropoulos. [X-166]

Peter and the Wolf. Basil Rathbone (Narrator). All-American Orchestra, Stokowski. [M-477]

Violin Concerto No. 1. Szigeti. London Philharmonic, Beecham. [M-244]

RAVEL:

Bolero. All-American Orchestra, Stokowski. [X-174]

Concerto for Piano. Long. Orchestra, Ravel. [M-176]

La Valse. New York Philharmonic-Symphony, Barbirolli. [X-207]

Le Tombeau de Couperin. Minneapolis Symphony, Mitropoulos. [X-222]

Ma Mère l'Oye. CBS Orchestra, Barlow. [X-151]

RESPIGHI:

Pines of Rome. Milan Symphony, Molajoli. [17060-D, 17061-D, 17062-D]

Rossiniana. London Philharmonic, Beecham. [X-56]

The Birds. Brussels Conservatory Orchestra, Defauw. [X-108]

REZNICEK:

Donna Diana Overture. Chicago Symphony, Stock. [11606-D]

RIMSKY-KORSAKOFF:

Capriccio Espagnole. Philharmonic-Symphony, Barbirolli. [X-185]

Flight of the Bumble Bee. All-American Orchestra, Stokowski. [19005-D]

Scheherazade. Cleveland Orchestra, Rodzinski. [M-398]

ROSSINI:
> Barber of Seville Overture. CBS Orchestra, Barlow. [70704-D]
> La Gazza Ladra Overture. London Philharmonic, Beecham. [68301-D]
> Semiramide Overture. London Philharmonic, Beecham. [X-215]
> William Tell Overture. London Philharmonic, Beecham. [X-60]

ROUSSEL:
> Le Festin de l'Araignée. Orchestre des Concerts Straram, Straram. [X-23]

SAINT-SAËNS:
> 'Cello Concerto. Piatigorsky. Chicago Symphony, Stock. [X-182]
> Danse Macabre. Chicago Symphony, Stock. [11251-D]

SCHUBERT:
> 'Cello Concerto (arr. from Arpeggione Sonata). Cassado. Orchestra, Harty. [M-139]
> Fantasie (arr. by Liszt). Kilenyi. Orchestra, Meyrowitz. [M-426]
> Rosamunde Incidental Music. Hallé Orchestra, Harty. [M-343]
> Symphony No. 2. CBS Orchestra, Barlow. [M-420]
> Symphony No. 5. London Philharmonic, Beecham. [M-366]
> Symphony No. 7. Chicago Symphony, Stock. [M-403]
> Symphony No. 8. London Philharmonic, Beecham. [M-330]

SCHUMANN:
> Piano Concerto. Nat (piano). Orchestra, Bigot. [M-196]
> Symphony No. 2. Minneapolis Symphony, Mitropoulos. [M-503]
> Symphony No. 3. Philharmonic-Symphony, Walter. [M-464]
> Symphony No. 4. Chicago Symphony, Stock. [M-475]

SHOSTAKOVITCH:
> Symphony No. 1. Cleveland Orchestra, Rodzinski. [M-472]
> Symphony No. 5. Cleveland Orchestra, Rodzinski. [M-520]

SIBELIUS:
> Festivo. London Philharmonic, Beecham. [68590-D]
> Finlandia. Cleveland Orchestra, Rodzinski. [11178-D]
> Swan of Tuonela. Chicago Orchestra, Stock. [11388-D]
> Symphony No. 1. Orchestra, Kajanus. [M-151]
> Symphony No. 2. Philharmonic-Symphony, Barbirolli. [M-423]
> Symphony No. 5. Cleveland Orchestra, Rodzinski. [M-514]
> Valse Triste. London Philharmonic, Harty. [7322-M]

SMETANA:
> The Bartered Bride Dances. CBS Orchestra, Barlow. [71049-D]

The Bartered Bride Overture. New York Philharmonic-Symphony, Barbirolli. [19003-D]

The Moldau. New York Philharmonic-Symphony, Walter. [X-211]

STRAUSS, JOHANN:
Rediscovered Music of Johann Strauss. CBS Orchestra, Barlow. Two volumes. [M-389, M-445]
Strauss Waltzes. Orchestra, Kostelanetz. [M-481]

STRAUSS, RICHARD:
Also Sprach Zarathustra. Chicago Symphony, Stock. [M-421]
Don Juan. Pittsburgh Symphony, Reiner. [X-190]
Don Quixote. Pittsburgh Symphony, Reiner. [M-506]
Ein Heldenleben. Cleveland Orchestra, Rodzinski. [M-441]
Rosenkavalier Waltzes. Cleveland Orchestra, Rodzinski. [11542-D]
Salome's Dance. Cleveland Orchestra, Rodzinski. [11781-D]
Till Eulenspiegel. Cleveland Orchestra, Rodzinski. [X-210]
Tod und Verklärung. All-American Orchestra, Stokowski. [M-492]

STRAVINSKY:
Baiser de la Fée. London Philharmonic, Dorati. [69840-D]
Capriccio. Stravinsky. Orchestra, Ansermet. [M-152]
Firebird. All-American Orchestra, Stokowski. [M-446]
Le Sacre du Printemps. New York Philharmonic-Symphony, Stravinsky. [M-417]
Les Noces. Orchestra, Stravinsky. [M-204]
Petrouschka. Philharmonic-Symphony, Stravinsky. [X-177]
Symphonie des Psaumes. Straram Orchestra, Stravinsky. [M-162]

TANSMAN:
Triptyque. St. Louis Symphony, Golschmann. [X-47]

TARTINI:
Violin Concerto in D minor. Szigeti. Orchestra. [X-103]

TAYLOR:
Peter Ibbetson Suite. CBS Orchestra, Barlow. [X-204]
Through the Looking Glass. CBS Orchestra, Barlow. [M-350]

TOCH:
Pinocchio: Merry Overture. Chicago Symphony, Stock. [11665-D]

TSCHAIKOWSKY:
Capriccio Italien. New York Philharmonic-Symphony, Beecham. [X-229]

Francesca da Rimini. London Philharmonic, Beecham. [M-447]
Marche Slave. Cleveland Orchestra, Rodzinski. [11567-D]
Nutcracker Suite. Chicago Symphony, Stock. [M-395]
Overture 1812. Cleveland Orchestra, Rodzinski. [X-205]
Piano Concerto No. 1. Petri. London Philharmonic, Goehr.
[M-318]
Romeo and Juliet. Cleveland Orchestra, Rodzinski. [M-478]
Swan Lake. London Philharmonic, Dorati. [M-349]
Symphony No. 4. Minneapolis Symphony, Mitropoulos. [M-468]
Symphony No. 5. London Philharmonic, Beecham. [M-470]
Symphony No. 6. All-American Orchestra, Stokowski. [M-432]
Violin Concerto in D major. Milstein. Chicago Symphony, Stock.
[M-413]
WAGNER:
A Faust Overture. London Philharmonic, Beecham. [X-63]
A Siegfried Idyll. London Philharmonic, Weingartner. [X-139]
Die Götterdämmerung: Siegfried's Rhine Journey, Siegfried's
Funeral March. Paris Conservatory Orchestra, Weingartner.
[X-224]
Die Meistersinger: Excerpts Act III. Pittsburgh Symphony,
Reiner. [X-218]
Die Meistersinger: Overture. Pittsburgh Symphony, Reiner.
[11580-D]
Flying Dutchman Overture. London Philharmonic, Beecham.
[X-107]
Forest Murmurs. Pittsburgh Symphony, Reiner. [11831-D]
Lohengrin Prelude. Pittsburgh Symphony, Reiner. [11772-D]
Lohengrin Prelude Act III. Pittsburgh Symphony, Reiner.
[11644-D]
Parsifal Good Friday Music. Bayreuth Orchestra, S. Wagner.
[67370-D, 67371-D]
Parsifal Prelude. Royal Philharmonic, Walter. [67572, 67573]
Ride of the Valkyries. Pittsburgh Symphony, Reiner. [11644-D]
Tannhäuser Overture. London Philharmonic, Beecham. [X-123]
Tannhäuser Venusberg Music. Pittsburgh Symphony, Reiner.
[X-193]
Tristan Love Music. All-American Orchestra, Stokowski. [M-427]
Tristan: Prelude Act III. Paris Conservatory Orchestra, Wein-
gartner. [69805-D]

WALTON:
Façade. Orchestre Raymonde, Goehr. [69834-D]
WEBER:
Concertino for Clarinet. Kell. Orchestra, Goehr. [69869-D]
Der Freischütz Overture. London Philharmonic, Beecham. [68986-D]
Euryanthe Overture. Chicago Symphony, Stock. [11179-D]
Invitation to the Dance. All-American Orchestra, Stokowski. [11481-D]
Konzertstück for Piano. Casadesus. Orchestra, Bigot. [X-59]
Oberon Overture. London Philharmonic, Beecham. [69410-D]
WEINBERGER:
Schwanda: Polka and Fugue. London Symphony, Harty. [68311-D]
Under the Spreading Chestnut Tree. Cleveland Orchestra, Rodzinski. [X-161]
VAUGHAN WILLIAMS:
Folk Song Suite. CBS Orchestra, Barlow. [X-159]

VICTOR RECORDS OF
GREAT ORCHESTRAL MUSIC

ALFVEN:
Midsummer Vigil. Stockholm Concert Association Orchestra, Grevillius. [M-788]
ARENSKY:
Variations on a Theme by Tschaikowsky. Philadelphia Chamber String Sinfonietta, Sevitzky. [M-896]
AUBER:
Bronze Horse Overture. London Philharmonic, Lambert. [12511]
Masaniello Overture. BBC Symphony, Boult. [11838]
BACH, J. S.:
Brandenburg Concerto No. 1. Ecole Normale Chamber Orchestra, Cortot. [11781, 11782]
Brandenburg Concerto No. 2. Philadelphia Orchestra, Stokowski. [M-59]
Brandenburg Concerto No. 3. Ecole Normale Chamber Orchestra, Cortot. [4225, 4226]

Brandenburg Concerto No. 4. Ecole Normale Chamber Orchestra, Cortot. [7915, 7916]

Brandenburg Concerto No. 5. Ecole Normale Chamber Orchestra, Cortot. [7863, 7864]

Brandenburg Concerto No. 6. Ecole Normale Chamber Orchestra, Cortot. [11264, 11265]

Chaconne (orch. by Stokowski). Philadelphia Orchestra, Stokowski. [Inc. in M-234]

Chorale-Prelude, Wir Glauben All' an einen Gott (orch. by Stokowski). Philadelphia Orchestra, Stokowski. [Inc. in M-59]

Concerto for Four Pianos (Bach-Vivaldi). Pignari, Salles, Leroux, Rolet. Orchestra, Coppola. [M-366]

Concerto for Harpsichord, Flute and Violin. Pessl, Blaisdell, Kroll. String Orchestra, Bamberger. [M-534]

Concerto for Two Violins. Menuhin. Orchestra, Enesco. [7732, 7733]

Concerto No. 2 for Two Pianos. Artur and Karl U. Schnabel. London Symphony, Boult. [M-357]

Ein' Feste Burg. Philadelphia Orchestra, Stokowski. [1692]

Musical Offering, Ricercare. Chamber Orchestra, Fischer. [8660]

Passacaglia (orch. by Stokowski). Philadelphia Orchestra, Stokowski. [Inc. in M-401]

Piano Concerto No. 1. Chamber Orchestra, Fischer. [M-252]

Piano Concerto No. 4. Chamber Orchestra, Fischer. [M-368]

Piano Concerto No. 5. Chamber Orchestra, Fischer. [M-786]

Suites Nos. 1, 2. Busch Chamber Players. [M-332]

Suites Nos. 3, 4. Busch Chamber Players. [M-339]

Violin Concerto No. 1. Menuhin. Orchestra, Enesco. [14370, 14371]

Violin Concerto No. 2. Menuhin. Paris Symphony, Enesco. [M-221]

The Wise Virgins (Ballet Suite, orch. by Walton). Sadler's Wells Orchestra, Walton. [M-817]

BACH, K. P. E.:

Concerto for Orchestra. Boston Symphony, Koussevitzky. [M-559]

Symphony No. 3. NBC String Symphony, Black. [M-390]

BALAKIREFF:

Thamar. Paris Conservatory Orchestra, Coppola. [11349, 11350]

BARBER:
Essay for Orchestra. Philadelphia Orchestra, Ormandy. [18062]
BARLOW:
The Winter's Past. Eastman-Rochester Symphony, Hanson. [Inc. in M-802]
BEETHOVEN:
Consecration of the House Overture. Boston "Pops" Orchestra, Fiedler. [M-618]
Coriolanus Overture. London Symphony, Walter. [12535]
Egmont Overture. New York Philharmonic-Symphony, Mengelberg. [7291]
Fidelio Overture. BBC Symphony, Walter. [11809]
Leonore Overture No. 1. BBC Symphony, Toscanini. [15945]
Leonore Overture No. 3. Vienna Philharmonic, Walter. [M-359]
Piano Concerto No. 1. Schnabel. London Symphony, Sargent. [M-158]
Piano Concerto No. 2. Schnabel. London Philharmonic, Sargent. [M-295]
Piano Concerto No. 3. Schnabel. London Philharmonic, Sargent. [M-194]
Piano Concerto No. 4. Schnabel. London Philharmonic, Sargent. [M-156]
Piano Concerto No. 5. Schnabel. London Symphony, Sargent. [M-155]
Symphony No. 1. BBC Symphony, Toscanini. [M-507]
Symphony No. 2. Boston Symphony, Koussevitzky. [M-625]
Symphony No. 3. NBC Symphony, Toscanini. [M-765]
Symphony No. 4. BBC Symphony, Toscanini. [M-274]
Symphony No. 5. NBC Symphony, Toscanini. [M-640]
Symphony No. 6. BBC Symphony, Toscanini. [M-417]
Symphony No. 7. New York Philharmonic-Symphony, Toscanini. [M-317]
Symphony No. 8. Boston Symphony, Koussevitzky. [M-336]
Symphony No. 9. Philadelphia Orchestra, Stokowski. [M-236]
Violin Concerto. Heifetz. NBC Symphony, Toscanini. [M-705]
BERLIOZ:
Benvenuto Cellini Overture. Paris Symphony, Monteux. [11140, 11141]
Damnation of Faust, Ballet des Sylphes. Victor Concert Orchestra. [20563]

Judges of the Secret Court Overture. BBC Symphony, Boult. [Inc. in M-803]

King Lear Overture. BBC Symphony, Boult. [Inc. in M-803]

Roman Carnival Overture. Boston "Pops" Orchestra, Fiedler. [12135]

Symphonie Fantastique. Paris Conservatory Orchestra, Walter. [M-662]

BIZET:

L'Arlésienne Suite No. 1, Pastorale of Suite No. 2. Philadelphia Orchestra, Stokowski. [M-62]

L'Arlésienne Suite No. 2. Boston "Pops" Orchestra, Fiedler. [M-683]

Jeux d'Enfants, Ballet Suite. London Philharmonic, Dorati. [M-510]

Petite Suite, March and Impromptu. Victor Concert Orchestra. [19730]

Symphony No. 1. London Philharmonic, Goehr. [M-721]

BLISS

Music for Strings. BBC Symphony, Boult. [M-464]

BLOCH:

Concerto Grosso for Piano and String Orchestra. Curtis Chamber Music Ensemble. [M-563]

Schelomo (Cello and orch.). Feuermann. Philadelphia Orchestra, Stokowski. [M-698]

BOCCHERINI:

Cello Concerto in B-flat major. Casals. London Symphony, Ronald. [M-381]

Minuet. Philadelphia Orchestra, Stokowski. [7256]

BORODIN:

In the Steppes of Central Asia. London Symphony, Coates. [11169]

Prince Igor, Dances of the Polovetzki Maidens. Philadelphia Orchestra, Stokowski. [M-499]

Symphony No. 2. London Symphony, Coates. [M-113]

BRAHMS:

Academic Festival Overture. Vienna Philharmonic, Walter. [12190]

Double Concerto. Feuermann, Heifetz. Philadelphia Orchestra, Ormandy. [M-815]

Hungarian Dance No. 1. Philadelphia Orchestra, Stokowski. [1675]

Hungarian Dances Nos. 5 and 6. Boston "Pops" Orchestra, Fiedler. [4321]

Hungarian Dances Nos. 19, 20, 21. BBC Symphony, Boult. [11534]

Liebeslieder Walzer Nos. 1-18. NBC String Symphony, Black. [Inc. in M-455]

Piano Concerto No. 1. Schnabel. London Philharmonic, Szell. [M-677]

Piano Concerto No. 2. Horowitz. NBC Symphony, Toscanini. [M-740]

Serenade No. 2. Alumni Orchestra of National Orch. Assn. [M-774]

Symphony No. 1. NBC Symphony, Toscanini. [M-875]

Symphony No. 2. Philadelphia Orchestra, Ormandy. [M-694]

Symphony No. 3. National Symphony, Kindler. [M-762]

Symphony No. 4. Boston Symphony, Koussevitzky. [M-730]

Tragic Overture. BBC Symphony, Toscanini. [Inc. in M-507]

Variations on a Theme by Haydn. New York Philharmonic-Symphony, Toscanini. [M-355]

Violin Concerto. Heifetz. Boston Symphony, Koussevitzky. [M-581]

BRUCH:

Concerto No. 1. Menuhin. London Symphony, Ronald. [M-124]

Kol Nidrei. Casals. London Symphony, Ronald. [M-680]

BRUCKNER:

Symphony No. 3 (Scherzo). Vienna Symphony. [11726]

Symphony No. 4. Saxonian State Orchestra, Böhm. [M-331]

Symphony No. 5. Saxonian State Orchestra, Böhm. [M-770, M-771]

Symphony No. 7. Minneapolis Symphony, Ormandy. [M-276]

Symphony No. 9. Munich Philharmonic, Hausegger. [M-627]

CHABRIER:

España Rapsodie. Boston "Pops" Orchestra, Fiedler. [4375]

CHADWICK:

Jubilee (No. 1 from Symphonic Sketches Suite). Eastman-Rochester Symphony, Hanson. [Inc. in M-608]

Noël. National Symphony, Kindler. [18274]

CHAUSSON:

Poème. Menuhin. Paris Symphony. [7913, 7914]

Symphony in B-flat major. Paris Conservatory Orchestra, Coppola. [M-261]

CHAVEZ:

Sinfonia India; Sinfonia de Antigona; Chacona. Symphony Orchestra of Mexico, Chavez. [M-503]

CHOPIN:

Concerto No. 1. Rubinstein. London Symphony, Barbirolli. [M-418]

Concerto No. 2. Cortot. Orchestra, Barbirolli. [M-567]

Les Sylphides. London Philharmonic, Sargent. [M-306]

Polonaise Militaire. Boston "Pops" Orchestra, Fiedler. [11947]

COATES:

From Meadow to Mayfair—No. 3—Evening in Town. London Symphony, Coates. [36170]

The Merrymakers. London Symphony, Coates. [36170]

COPLAND:

El Salón México. Boston Symphony, Koussevitzky. [M-546]

Music for the Theatre. Eastman-Rochester Symphony, Hanson. [M-744]

CORELLI:

Concerto Grosso. London Symphony, Walter. [M-600]

DEBUSSY:

Afternoon of a Faun. Philadelphia Orchestra, Stokowski. [17700]

Cloches à travers les feuilles. Paris Conservatory Orchestra, Coppola. [M-363]

Iberia (Images, Set 3, No. 2). New York Philharmonic-Symphony, Barbirolli. [M-460]

La Cathédrale Engloutie, Danse Sacrée et Danse Profane. Philadelphia Orchestra, Stokowski. [M-116]

La Damoiselle Elue. Pasdeloup Orchestra, Coppola. [Inc. in M-363]

La Mer. Boston Symphony, Koussevitzky. [M-643]

L'Ile Joyeuse. Orchestra, Coppola. [12033]

Martyre de St. Sebastien. Paris Conservatory Orchestra, Coppola. [M-767]

Nocturnes. Philadelphia Orchestra, Stokowski. [M-630]

Petite Suite. Orchestra, Coppola. [M-674]

Printemps, Symphonic Suite. Paris Conservatory Orchestra, Coppola. [M-363]

Rhapsody for Clarinet and Orchestra. Hamelin. Orchestra, Coppola. [11433]

Rhapsody for Saxophone and Orchestra. Viard. Orchestra, Coppola. [11426]

DELIBES:

Sylvia Ballet. Minneapolis Symphony, Ormandy. [M-220]

Coppélia Ballet Suite. Boston "Pops" Orchestra, Fiedler. [12527]

DELIUS:

In a Summer Garden. London Symphony, Toye. [9731, 9732]

On Hearing the First Cuckoo in Spring. London Philharmonic, Lambert. [4496]

D'ERLANGER:

The Hundred Kisses. London Philharmonic, Dorati. [M-511]

D'INDY:

Istar—Variations Symphoniques. Paris Conservatory Orchestra, Coppola. [11560]

DOHNÁNYI:

Ruralia Hungarica, 2nd Movement. London Symphony, Dohnányi. [Inc. in M-162]

Suite. Chicago Symphony, Stock. [M-47]

Variations on a Nursery Tune. London Symphony, Collingwood. [M-162]

DUKAS:

Sorcerer's Apprentice. Philadelphia Orchestra, Stokowski. [M-717]

DVOŘÁK:

Carneval Overture. Boston "Pops" Orchestra, Fiedler. [12159]

Concerto in A minor. Menuhin. Paris Conservatory Orchestra, Enesco. [M-387]

Concerto in B minor. Casals. Czech Philharmonic, Szell. [M-458]

Scherzo Capriccioso. Minneapolis Symphony, Ormandy. [8418]

Slavonic Dances, Nos. 1, 2, 3, 6, 8, 9, 10, 12. Czech Philharmonic, Talich. [M-310]

Slavonic Dances, Nos. 4, 5, 7, 11, 13, 14, 15, 16. Czech Philharmonic, Talich. [M-345]

Symphony No. 1. Czech Philharmonic, Talich. [M-874]

Symphony No. 2. Czech Philharmonic, Talich. [M-663]

Symphony No. 4. Czech Philharmonic, Talich. [M-304]

Symphony No. 5. Rochester Philharmonic, Iturbi. [M-899]

ELGAR:

Concerto in B minor. Menuhin. London Symphony, Elgar. [M-174]

Enigma Variations. BBC Symphony, Boult. [M-475]

Introduction and Allegro for Strings. BBC Symphony, Boult. [M-635]

Pomp and Circumstance March No. 1. Boston "Pops" Orchestra, Fiedler. [11885]

Sospiri. BBC Symphony, Boult. [Inc. in M-635]

ENESCO:

Roumanian Rhapsody No. 1. Philadelphia Orchestra, Ormandy. [Inc. in M-830]

Roumanian Rhapsody No. 2. National Symphony, Kindler. [Inc. in M-830]

DE FALLA:

Amor Brujo. Boston "Pops" Orchestra, Fiedler. [12160]

Nights in the Gardens of Spain. Descaves. Paris Conservatory Orchestra, Bigot. [M-725]

Three Cornered Hat Dances. Boston "Pops" Orchestra, Fiedler. [M-505]

FAURÉ:

Elégie. Boston Symphony, Koussevitzky. [14577]

Pavane. National Symphony, Damrosch. [7323]

FRANCK:

Symphony in D minor. San Francisco Symphony, Monteux. [M-840]

Variations Symphoniques. Cortot. London Symphony, Ronald. [8357, 8358]

GERSHWIN:

American in Paris. Victor Symphony, Gershwin. [35963, 35964]

Concerto in F. Sanroma. Boston "Pops" Orchestra, Fiedler. [M-690]

Rhapsody in Blue. Boston "Pops" Orchestra, Fiedler. [M-358]

GLAZOUNOFF:

Concerto in A minor. Heifetz. London Philharmonic, Barbirolli. [M-218]

Danse Orientale. Philadelphia Orchestra, Stokowski. [1335]

GLIÈRE:
Ilia Mourometz—Symphony No. 3. Philadelphia Orchestra, Stokowski. [M-841]
Yablochko. Philadelphia Orchestra, Stokowski. [1675]

GLINKA:
Kamarinskaya. London Symphony, Coates. [11482]
Russlan and Ludmilla Overture. Boston "Pops" Orchestra, Fiedler. [Inc. in M-554]

GLUCK:
Alceste Overture. BBC Symphony, Boult. [12041]
Armide—Musette. Victor Symphony Orchestra. [20563]
Ballet Suite (arr. by Mottl). Boston "Pops" Orchestra, Fiedler. [M-787]
Iphigenia in Aulis: Airs de Ballet. National Symphony, Damrosch. [7321, 7322]

GOLDMARK:
In Springtime Overture. Chicago Symphony, Stock. [6576]
Queen of Sheba: Ballet Music. Chicago Symphony, Stock. [7474]
Rustic Wedding Symphony. Vienna Philharmonic, Heger. [M-103]
Sakuntala Overture. Boston "Pops" Orchestra, Fiedler. [12610]

GOULD:
Foster Gallery. Boston "Pops" Orchestra, Fiedler. [M-727]

GRAINGER:
Londonderry Air. Minneapolis Symphony, Ormandy. [8734]
Molly on the Shore (Irish Reel). Minneapolis Symphony, Ormandy. [8734]

GRIEG:
Elegiac Melodies. London Symphony, Goossens. [12611]
Holberg Suite. London String Orchestra, Goehr. [M-792]
Last Spring. Boston Symphony, Koussevitzky. [Inc. in M-886]
Norwegian Dances. London Symphony, Blech. [11456, 11457]
Peer Gynt Suite No. 1. Orchestra, Barbirolli. [M-404]
Peer Gynt Suite No. 2. Orchestra, Goossens. [9327, 9328]
Piano Concerto. Rubinstein. Philadelphia Orchestra, Ormandy. [M-900]

GRIFFES:
The White Peacock. Eastman-Rochester Symphony, Hanson. [M-608]

GROFÉ:
  Metropolis (A Blue Fantasie). Whiteman's Concert Orchestra.
    [35933, 35934]
HADLEY:
  Concertino for Piano and Orchestra. Howard. Victor Symphony,
    James. [M-634]
HALVORSEN:
  March of the Boyards. Boston "Pops" Orchestra, Fiedler.
    [12175]
HANDEL:
  Alcina Suite. New York Philharmonic-Symphony, Mengelberg.
    [1435, 1436]
  Concerti Grossi Nos. 1 and 5. Collegium Musicum, Diener.
    [M-808]
  Organ Concerto No. 10. Biggs. Fiedler's Sinfonietta. [M-587]
  Organ Concerto No. 11. Biggs. Fiedler's Sinfonietta. [2099, 2100]
  Organ Concerto No. 13. Biggs. Fiedler's Sinfonietta. [M-733]
  Overture in D minor (Trans. by Stokowski). Philadelphia Or-
    chestra, Stokowski. [1798]
  Water Music Suite. Philadelphia Orchestra, Stokowski. [8550,
    8551]
HANSON:
  Merry Mount Suite. Eastman-Rochester Symphony, Hanson.
    [M-781]
  Symphony No. 2. Eastman-Rochester Symphony, Hanson.
    [M-648]
HARRIS:
  Symphony No. 3. Boston Symphony, Koussevitzky. [M-651]
  When Johnny Comes Marching Home. Minneapolis Symphony,
    Ormandy. [8629]
HAYDN:
  Concerto in F major. Roesgen-Champion. Orchestra, Bigot.
    [12042]
  Concerto No. 1. Landowska. Orchestra, Bigot. [M-471]
  18th Century Dance. Philadelphia Orchestra, Stokowski. [7256]
  Symphony No. 67. New Friends of Music Orchestra, Stiedry.
    [M-536]
  Symphony No. 80. New Friends of Music Orchestra, Stiedry.
    [M-536]
  Symphony No. 86. London Symphony, Walter. [M-578]

Symphony No. 88. NBC Symphony, Toscanini. [M-454]

Symphony No. 92. Paris Conservatory Orchestra, Walter. [M-682]

Symphony No. 94. Boston Symphony, Koussevitzky. [M-55]

Symphony No. 96. Vienna Philharmonic, Walter. [M-885]

Symphony No. 97. London Symphony, Weisbach. [M-140]

Symphony No. 100. Vienna Philharmonic, Walter. [M-472]

Symphony No. 101. New York Philharmonic-Symphony, Toscanini. [M-57]

Symphony No. 102. Boston Symphony, Koussevitzky. [M-529]

Symphony No. 104. Chamber Orchestra, Fischer. [M-617]

HINDEMITH:

Der Schwanendreher. Fiedler's Sinfonietta. [M-659]

Matthias the Painter. Philadelphia Orchestra, Ormandy. [M-854]

HOLST:

The Planets. London Symphony, Coates. [11808]

HONEGGER:

Concertino for Piano and Orchestra. Norton. Minneapolis Symphony, Ormandy. [8765]

Pacific 231. Continental Symphony, Coppola. [9276]

HUMPERDINCK:

Hansel and Gretel Dream Pantomime. BBC Symphony, Boult. [11832]

Hansel and Gretel Overture. BBC Symphony, Boult. [11929]

IBERT:

Concertino da Camera for Saxophone and Orchestra. Mule. Orchestra, Gaubert. [M-588]

Divertissement. Boston "Pops" Orchestra, Fiedler. [Inc. in M-324]

IPPOLITOFF-IVANOFF:

Caucasian Sketches. Boston "Pops" Orchestra, Fiedler. [M-797]

KALINNIKOFF:

Symphony No. 1. Indianapolis Symphony, Sevitzky. [M-827]

KELLER:

Serenade. Eastman-Rochester Symphony, Hanson. [Inc. in M-802]

KENNAN:

Night Soliloquy. Eastman-Rochester Symphony, Hanson. [Inc. in M-608]

KERN:
Scenario for Orchestra on themes from Show Boat. Janssen Symphony of Los Angeles, Janssen. [M-906]

KODÁLY:
Dances from Galanta. Boston "Pops" Orchestra, Fiedler. [M-834]
Háry János Suite. Minneapolis Symphony, Ormandy. [M-197]

KREISLER:
Kreisleriana. Minneapolis Symphony, Ormandy. [M-211]

LALO:
Symphonie Espagnole. Menuhin. Paris Symphony. [M-136]

LIADOFF:
Enchanted Lake. Boston Symphony, Koussevitzky. [14078]
Music Box. Boston "Pops" Orchestra, Fiedler. [4390]

LISZT:
Concerto No. 2. De Greef. London Symphony, Ronald. [M-169]
Hungarian Rhapsody No. 1. Boston "Pops" Orchestra, Fiedler. [13751]
Hungarian Rhapsody No. 2. Philadelphia Orchestra, Stokowski. [14422]
Les Préludes (Symphonic Poem No. 3). Philadelphia Orchestra, Ormandy. [M-453]
Mephisto Waltz. Boston Symphony, Koussevitzky. [M-870]
Piano Concerto No. 1. Levitzki. London Symphony, Ronald. [11309, 11310]
Todtentanz. Sanroma. Boston "Pops" Orchestra, Fiedler. [M-392]

LOEFFLER:
Pagan Poem. Eastman-Rochester Symphony, Hanson. [M-876]

MACDOWELL:
Concerto No. 2. Sanroma. Boston "Pops" Orchestra, Fiedler. [M-324]
Dirge (Suite No. 2). Eastman-Rochester Symphony, Hanson. [15657 (Inc. in M-608)]

MAHLER:
Symphony No. 2. Minneapolis Symphony, Ormandy. [M-256]
Symphony No. 5, Adagietto. Vienna Philharmonic, Walter. [12319]
Symphony No. 9. Vienna Philharmonic, Walter. [M-726]

MASSENET:
Le Cid Ballet. San Francisco Symphony, Hertz. [M-56]

McBRIDE:
Mexican Rhapsody. Boston "Pops" Orchestra, Fiedler. [13825]

McDONALD:
Cakewalk (Scherzo from Fourth Symphony). Philadelphia Orchestra, Ormandy. [15377]

Concerto for Two Pianos and Orchestra. Philadelphia Orchestra, Stokowski. [M-557]

Dance of the Workers (Festival of the Workers Suite). Philadelphia Orchestra, Stokowski. [8919]

Rhumba (Rhumba Symphony). Philadelphia Orchestra, Stokowski. [8919]

San Juan Capistrano. Boston Symphony, Koussevitzky. [17229]

Suite from Childhood. Phillips (harp). Philadelphia Orchestra, Ormandy. [M-839]

Symphony No. 1. Philadelphia Orchestra, Ormandy. [M-754]

Two Hebraic Poems. Philadelphia Orchestra, Ormandy. [14903]

MENDELSSOHN:
Calm Sea and Prosperous Voyage Overture. London Symphony, Blech. [11452, 11453]

Fingal's Cave Overture. BBC Symphony, Boult. [11886]

Midsummer Night's Dream Nocturne. BBC Symphony, Boult. [4312]

Midsummer Night's Dream Overture. Boston "Pops" Orchestra, Fiedler. [11919, 11920]

Midsummer Night's Dream Scherzo. New York Philharmonic-Symphony. [7080]

Midsummer Night's Dream Wedding March. Boston "Pops" Orchestra, Fiedler. [11920]

Piano Concerto No. 1. Sanroma. Boston "Pops" Orchestra, Fiedler. [M-780]

Ruy Blas Overture. BBC Symphony, Boult. [11791]

String Octet Scherzo. Boston "Pops" Orchestra, Fiedler. [11947]

Symphony No. 3. Rochester Philharmonic, Iturbi. [M-699]

Symphony No. 4. Boston Symphony, Koussevitzky. [M-294]

Violin Concerto in E minor. Menuhin. Orchestre des Concerts Colonne, Enesco. [M-531]

MENOTTI:
Overture, Amelia Goes to the Ball. Philadelphia Orchestra, Ormandy. [15377]

MIASKOWSKY:

Sinfonietta. NBC String Symphony, Black. [Inc. in M-390]

MOSSOLOFF:

Soviet Iron Foundry. Boston "Pops" Orchestra, Fiedler. [4378]

MOSZKOWSKI:

Bolero and Spanish Dances. Victor Concert Orchestra. [22769]

Perpetual Motion. National Symphony, Damrosch. [7323]

Spanish Dances. Victor Concert Orchestra. [20521]

MOUSSORGSKY:

Boris Godounoff Symphonic Synthesis. Philadelphia Orchestra, Stokowski. [M-391]

Fair at Sorotschinsk, Gopak. London Symphony, Coates. [11443]

Khovantchina Introduction. Boston Symphony, Koussevitzky. [14415]

Khovantchina Persian Dances (arr. Rimsky-Korsakoff). London Symphony, Coates. [11135]

Night on the Bare Mountain. Philadelphia Orchestra, Stokowski. [17900]

Pictures at an Exhibition (Cailliet). Philadelphia Orchestra, Ormandy. [M-442]

Pictures at an Exhibition (Ravel). Boston Symphony, Koussevitzky. [M-102]

MOZART:

Adagio and Fugue, K. 546. Busch Chamber Players. [12324]

Bassoon Concerto, K. 191. Oubradous. Orchestra, Bigot. [M-704]

Clarinet Concerto, K. 622. Kell. London Philharmonic, Sargent. [M-708]

Concerto for Flute and Harp, K. 299. Moyse, Laskine. [M-141]

Cosi Fan Tutti Overture. BBC Symphony, Boult. [11714]

Divertimento No. 10, K. 247. Philadelphia Orchestra, Ormandy. [M-603]

Divertimento No. 15, K. 287. Fiedler's Sinfonietta. [M-434]

Don Giovanni Overture. Glyndebourne Festival Orchestra, Busch. [Inc. in M-423]

Eight German Dances. Minneapolis Symphony, Ormandy. [1722, 1723]

Eine Kleine Nachtmusik, K. 525. Vienna Philharmonic, Walter. [M-364]

Finta Giardiniera Overture, K. 196. Vienna Philharmonic, Walter. [12526]

Flute Concerto No. 1, K. 313. Moyse. Orchestra, Bigot. [M-396]

Flute Concerto No. 2, K. 314. Moyse. Orchestra, Coppola. [M-589]

Horn Concerto No. 3, K. 447. Brain. BBC Symphony, Boult. [M-829]

Idomeneo Ballet Music. Berlin State Opera Orchestra, Blech. [11407]

Il Seraglio Overture. Vienna Philharmonic, Krauss. [11242]

Les Petits Riens Ballet Music. London Symphony, Blech. [11445]

Magic Flute Overture. BBC Symphony, Toscanini. [15190]

Marriage of Figaro Overture. Minneapolis Symphony, Ormandy. [14325]

Overture in B-flat. Société des Concerts Orchestra, Fendler. [12327]

Piano Concerto in E-flat major (two pianos), K. 365. José and Amparo Iturbi. Rochester Philharmonic. [M-732]

Piano Concerto in E-flat major (two pianos), K. 365. Artur and Karl U. Schnabel. London Symphony, Boult. [M-484]

Piano Concerto No. 14, K. 499. Serkin. Busch Chamber Players. [M-657]

Piano Concerto No. 15, K. 450. Ney. Chamber Orchestra, Von Hoogstraten. [M-365]

Piano Concerto No. 17, K. 453. Fischer. Chamber Orchestra. [M-481]

Piano Concerto No. 19, K. 459. Schnabel. London Symphony, Sargent. [M-389]

Piano Concerto No. 20, K. 466. Iturbi. Rochester Philharmonic, Iturbi. [M-794]

Piano Concerto No. 21, K. 467. Schnabel. London Symphony, Sargent. [M-486]

Piano Concerto No. 22, K. 482. Fischer. Chamber Orchestra, Barbirolli. [M-316]

Piano Concerto No. 23, K. 488. Rubinstein. London Symphony, Barbirolli. [M-147]

Piano Concerto No. 24, K. 491. Fischer. London Philharmonic, Collingwood. [M-482]

Piano Concerto No. 26, K. 537. Landowska. Chamber Orchestra, Goehr. [M-483]

Piano Concerto No. 27, K. 595. Schnabel. London Symphony, Barbirolli. [M-240]

Serenade No. 10 for 13 wind instruments, K. 361. Fischer's Chamber Orchestra. [M-743]

Sinfonia Concertante (K. Appendix No. 9) for 4 winds and orchestra. Philadelphia Orchestra, Stokowski. [M-760]

Sinfonia Concertante for violin and viola, K. 364. Spalding, Primrose. New Friends of Music Orchestra, Stiedry. [M-838]

Symphony No. 28, K. 200. Berlin College of Instrumentalists, Stein. [M-502]

Symphony No. 29, K. 201. Boston Symphony, Koussevitzky. [M-795]

Symphony No. 32, K. 319. Chamber Orchestra, Fischer. [M-479]

Symphony No. 34, K. 338. Boston Symphony, Koussevitzky. [M-795]

Symphony No. 35, K. 385. New York Philharmonic-Symphony, Toscanini. [M-65]

Symphony No. 36, K. 425. BBC Symphony, Busch. [M-266]

Symphony No. 38, K. 504. Vienna Philharmonic, Walter. [M-457]

Symphony No. 39, K. 543. BBC Symphony, Walter. [M-258]

Symphony No. 40, K. 550. NBC Symphony, Toscanini. [M-631]

Symphony No. 41, K. 551. Vienna Philharmonic, Walter. [M-584]

Titus Overture. Vienna Philharmonic, Walter. [12526]

Violin Concerto in D major. Menuhin. Paris Symphony, Monteux. [M-246]

Violin Concerto No. 3, K. 216. Menuhin. Paris Symphony, Enesco. [M-485]

Violin Concerto No. 4, K. 218. Kreisler. London Philharmonic, Sargent. [M-623]

Violin Concerto No. 5, K. 219. Heifetz. London Philharmonic, Barbirolli. [M-254]

Violin Concerto No. 7, K. 271a. Menuhin. Symphony Orchestra, Enesco. [M-231]

NICOLAI:

Merry Wives of Windsor Overture. Boston "Pops" Orchestra, Fiedler. [12533]

PADEREWSKI:

Concerto in A minor. Sanroma. Boston "Pops" Orchestra, Fiedler. [M-614]

PAGANINI:
  Concerto No. 1. Menuhin. Paris Symphony. [M-230]
  Moto Perpetuo. NBC Symphony, Toscanini. [M-590]
PAINE, J. K.:
  Prelude to Oedipus Tyrannus. Eastman-Rochester Symphony,
  Hanson. [Inc. in M-608]
PAISIELLO:
  Barber of Seville Overture. Boston "Pops" Orchestra, Fiedler.
  [12519]
PHILLIPS:
  American Dance. Eastman-Rochester Symphony, Hanson. [Inc.
  in M-802]
PIERNÉ:
  March of the Little Lead Soldiers. Boston "Pops" Orchestra,
  Fiedler. [4314]
  Mosquito Dance and Entrance of the Little Fauns. Boston "Pops"
  Orchestra, Fiedler. [4319]
PISTON:
  Incredible Flutist Ballet Suite. Boston "Pops" Orchestra, Fiedler.
  [M-621]
PROKOFIEFF:
  Classical Symphony. Boston Symphony, Koussevitzky. [7196,
  7197]
  Concerto No. 2. Heifetz. Boston Symphony, Koussevitzky.
  [M-450]
  Concerto No. 3. Prokofieff. London Symphony, Coppola. [M-176]
  Lieutenant Kije. Boston Symphony, Koussevitzky. [M-459]
  Love for Three Oranges: Scherzo and March. Boston Symphony,
  Koussevitzky. [14950]
  Pas d'Acier. London Symphony, Coates. [11446, 11447]
  Peter and the Wolf. Boston Symphony, Koussevitzky. [M-566]
PURCELL:
  Suite for Strings. New York Philharmonic-Symphony, Barbirolli.
  [M-533]
  Suite from Dido and Aeneas. Philadelphia Orchestra, Ormandy.
  [M-647]
RACHMANINOFF:
  Piano Concerto No. 1. Rachmaninoff. Philadelphia Orchestra,
  Ormandy. [M-865]

Piano Concerto No. 2. Rachmaninoff. Philadelphia Orchestra, Stokowski. [M-58]

Piano Concerto No. 3. Rachmaninoff. Philadelphia Orchestra, Ormandy. [M-710]

Rhapsody for Piano and Orchestra on a Theme by Paganini. Rachmaninoff. Philadelphia Orchestra, Stokowski. [M-250]

Symphony No. 2. Minneapolis Symphony, Ormandy. [M-239]

Symphony No. 3. Philadelphia Orchestra, Rachmaninoff. [M-712]

RAMEAU-MOTTL:

Three Ballet Pieces for Orchestra. Boston "Pops" Orchestra, Fiedler. [4431]

RAVEL:

Alborada del Gracioso. Minneapolis Symphony, Ormandy. [8552]

Bolero. Boston Symphony, Koussevitzky. [M-352]

Daphnis et Chloe, Suite No. 2. Philadelphia Orchestra, Ormandy. [M-667]

La Valse. Boston Symphony, Koussevitzky. [7413, 7414]

Ma Mère l'Oye Suite. Boston Symphony, Koussevitzky. [7370, 7371]

Pavan for a Dead Princess. Continental Symphony, Coppola. [9306]

Piano Concerto for the Left Hand. Cortot. Paris Conservatory Orchestra, Münch. [M-629]

Rapsodie Espagnole. Philadelphia Orchestra, Stokowski. [8282, 8283]

Tombeau de Couperin. Paris Conservatory Orchestra, Coppola. [12320, 12321]

Valses Nobles et Sentimentales. Paris Conservatory Orchestra, Coppola. [11727, 11728]

REGER:

Variations and Fugue on a Mozart Theme. Saxonian State Orchestra, Böhm. [M-821]

RESPIGHI:

Fountains of Rome. New York Philharmonic-Symphony, Barbirolli. [M-576]

Pines of Rome. Paris Conservatory Orchestra, Coppola. [11917, 11918]

RIMSKY-KORSAKOFF:

Battle of Kershenetz. Boston Symphony, Koussevitzky. [18410]

Capriccio Espagnol. Boston "Pops" Orchestra, Fiedler. [11827, 11828]

Coq d'Or Suite. London Symphony, Goossens. [M-504]

Cortège des Nobles (Funeral March). London Symphony, Coates. [11443]

Grande Paque Russe. Philadelphia Orchestra, Stokowski. [7018]

May Night Overture. London Symphony, Coates. [11424]

Scheherazade. Philadelphia Orchestra, Stokowski. [M-269]

Snow Maiden: Dance of the Tumblers. London Symphony, Coates. [11454]

Symphony No. 2. Paris Conservatory Orchestra, Coppola. [M-210]

ROGERS:

Soliloquy. Eastman-Rochester Symphony, Hanson. [Inc. in M-802]

ROSSINI:

Barber of Seville Overture. New York Philharmonic-Symphony, Toscanini. [7255]

La Gazza Ladra Overture. Boston "Pops" Orchestra, Fiedler. [13751]

La Scala di Seta Overture. BBC Symphony, Toscanini. [Inc. in M-825]

L'Italiana in Algeri Overture. New York Philharmonic-Symphony, Toscanini. [Inc. in M-825]

Semiramide Overture. New York Philharmonic-Symphony, Toscanini. [Inc. in M-825]

William Tell Overture. NBC Symphony, Toscanini. [M-605]

ROSSINI-RESPIGHI:

La Boutique Fantasque Ballet. London Symphony, Goossens. [M-415]

ROUSSEL:

Sinfonietta. NBC String Sinfonietta. [Inc. in M-455]

SAINT-SAËNS:

Carnival of the Animals. Philadelphia Orchestra, Stokowski. [M-785]

Danse Macabre. Philadelphia Orchestra, Stokowski. [14162]

Marche Militaire Française (Suite Algérienne). Continental Symphony. [9296]

Omphale's Spinning Wheel. National Symphony, Kindler. [18358]

Phaëton. Paris Conservatory Orchestra, Coppola. [11431]
Piano Concerto No. 2. De Greef. New Symphony, Ronald.
[M-150]
Piano Concerto No. 4. Cortot. Symphony Orchestra, Münch.
[M-367]
Reverie du Soir. Continental Symphony. [9296]
Suite Algérienne. Continental Symphony, Coppola. [9296]
Symphony No. 3. Symphony Orchestra, Coppola. [M-100]
SATIE-DEBUSSY:
Gymnopédie Nos. 1 and 2. Philadelphia Orchestra, Stokowski.
[1965]
SCHÖNBERG:
Verklärte Nacht. Minneapolis Symphony, Ormandy. [M-207]
SCHUBERT:
Rosamunde Ballet Music. London Symphony, Walter. [12534]
Symphony No. 4. New York Philharmonic-Symphony, Barbirolli.
[M-562]
Symphony No. 5. Berlin State Opera Orchestra, Blech. [M-170]
Symphony No. 8. Boston Symphony, Koussevitzky. [M-319]
Symphony No. 9. London Symphony, Walter. [M-602]
SCHUMAN, WILLIAM:
American Festival Overture. National Symphony, Kindler.
[18511]
SCHUMANN, ROBERT:
Carnaval Ballet Suite. London Philharmonic, Goossens. [M-513]
'Cello Concerto. Piatigorsky. London Philharmonic, Barbirolli.
[M-247]
Manfred Overture. BBC Symphony, Boult. [11713, 11714]
Piano Concerto. Myra Hess. Orchestra, Goehr. [M-473]
Symphony No. 1. Boston Symphony, Koussevitzky. [M-655]
Symphony No. 2. Philadelphia Orchestra, Ormandy. [M-448]
Symphony No. 3. Paris Conservatory Orchestra, Coppola.
[M-237]
Symphony No. 4. London Symphony, Walter. [M-837]
Violin Concerto. Menuhin. New York Philharmonic-Symphony,
Barbirolli. [M-451]
SCRIABIN:
Etudes Nos. 1 and 2. National Symphony, Kindler. [11-8150]
Poem of Ecstasy. Philadelphia Orchestra, Stokowski. [M-125]
Prometheus. Philadelphia Orchestra, Stokowski. [M-125]

SHOSTAKOVITCH:
Age of Gold: Polka. National Symphony, Kindler. [11-8239]
Symphony No. 1. Philadelphia Orchestra, Stokowski. [M-192]
Symphony No. 5. Philadelphia Orchestra, Stokowski. [M-619]
Symphony No. 6. Philadelphia Orchestra, Stokowski. [M-867]
SIBELIUS:
Belshazzar's Feast. London Symphony, Kajanus. [M-715]
En Saga. London Philharmonic, Beecham. [M-658]
Finlandia. Philadelphia Orchestra, Ormandy. [Inc. in M-750]
In Memoriam. London Philharmonic, Beecham. [Inc. in M-658]
Karelia Suite. London Symphony, Goossens. [12830]
Lemminkainen's Homeward Journey. Philadelphia Orchestra, Ormandy. [Inc. in M-750]
Maiden with the Roses (Swan White). Boston Symphony, Koussevitzky. [14355]
Night Ride and Sunset. BBC Symphony, Boult. [M-311]
Pélleas and Mélisande. London Philharmonic, Beecham. [Inc. in M-658]
Pohjola's Daughter. Boston Symphony, Koussevitzky. [M-474]
Rakastava (The Lover). NBC String Symphony, Black. [Inc. in M-455]
Swan of Tuonela. Philadelphia Orchestra, Ormandy. [Inc. in M-750]
Symphony No. 1. Philadelphia Orchestra, Ormandy. [M-881]
Symphony No. 2. Boston Symphony, Koussevitzky. [M-272]
Symphony No. 3. London Symphony, Kajanus. [M-394]
Symphony No. 4. London Philharmonic, Beecham. [Inc. in M-446]
Symphony No. 5. Boston Symphony, Koussevitzky. [Inc. in M-474]
Symphony No. 6. Finnish National Orchestra, Schneevoigt. [M-344]
Symphony No. 7. BBC Symphony, Koussevitzky. [Inc. in M-394]
Tapiola. Boston Symphony, Koussevitzky. [M-848]
Tempest Incidental Music. London Philharmonic, Beecham. [Inc. in M-658]
The Bard. London Philharmonic, Beecham. [Inc. in M-658]
The Oceanides. BBC Symphony, Boult. [Inc. in M-311]
Valse Triste. London Philharmonic, Beecham. [Inc. in M-658]
Violin Concerto. Heifetz. London Philharmonic, Beecham. [M-309]

SMETANA:

From Bohemia's Meadows and Forests. Czech Philharmonic, Kubelik. [Inc. in M-523]

The Bartered Bride, Dance of the Comedians. Minneapolis Symphony, Ormandy. [8694]

The Bartered Bride, Furiant. Minneapolis Symphony, Ormandy. [1761]

The Bartered Bride, Overture. Boston "Pops" Orchestra, Fiedler. [4498]

The Bartered Bride, Polka. Minneapolis Symphony, Ormandy. [8694]

The Moldau. Czech Philharmonic, Kubelik. [Inc. in M-523]

SMITH, J. C.:

Miniature Suite (trans. by H. McDonald). Fiedler's Sinfonietta. [M-609]

SOWERBY:

Comes Autumn Time. Eastman-Rochester Symphony, Hanson. [2058]

SPOHR:

Violin Concerto No. 8. Spalding. Philadelphia Orchestra, Ormandy. [M-544]

STILL, W. G.:

Scherzo from Afro-American Symphony. Eastman-Rochester Symphony, Hanson. [2059]

STRAUSS, JOHANN:

Album of Strauss Waltzes: Wine, Women and Song, Wiener Blut, Artists' Life Waltz, Emperor Waltz, Frühlingsstimmen. Boston "Pops" Orchestra, Fiedler. [M-445]

Egyptian March. Boston "Pops" Orchestra, Fiedler. [10-1019]

Four Novelty Waltzes: Loves of the Poet, Cagliostro, New Vienna Waltz, Lagoon Waltz. Boston "Pops" Orchestra, Fiedler. [M-665]

Indigo March. Boston "Pops" Orchestra, Fiedler. [10-1020]

March from The Gypsy Baron. Boston "Pops" Orchestra, Fiedler. [10-1020]

Music of Johann Strauss: Blue Danube, Fledermaus, Tales from the Vienna Woods, Acceleration Waltz, Gypsy Baron. Minneapolis Symphony, Ormandy. [M-262]

Persian March. Boston "Pops" Orchestra, Fiedler. [10-1019]

STRAUSS, RICHARD:

Alpine Symphony, On the Shores of Sorrento. Chicago Symphony, Stock. [18535]

Also Sprach Zarathustra. Boston Symphony, Koussevitzky. [M-257]

Don Juan. National Symphony, Kindler. [M-914]

Don Quixote. Feuermann. Philadelphia Orchestra, Ormandy. [M-720]

Ein Heldenleben. Philadelphia Orchestra, Ormandy. [M-610]

Le Bourgeois Gentilhomme Suite. Vienna Philharmonic, Krauss. [M-101]

Rosenkavalier Waltzes. Philadelphia Orchestra, Ormandy. [18390]

Symphonia Domestica. Philadelphia Orchestra, Ormandy. [M-520]

Till Eulenspiegels Lustige Streiche. BBC Symphony, Busch. [11724, 11725]

Tod und Verklärung. Philadelphia Orchestra, Stokowski. [M-217]

STRAVINSKY:

Capriccio for Piano and Orchestra. Sanroma. Boston Symphony, Koussevitzky. [M-685]

Firebird. Philadelphia Orchestra, Stokowski. [M-291]

Petrouschka. Philadelphia Orchestra, Stokowski. [M-574]

Sacre du Printemps. Philadelphia Orchestra, Stokowski. [M-74]

SUK:

Fairy Tales—Folk Dance. Chicago Symphony, Stock. [6649]

Serenade for String Orchestra. Czech Philharmonic, Talich. [M-779]

Sokol March. Czech Philharmonic, Kubelik. [4459]

TANSMAN:

Triptyque for String Orchestra. Curtis Chamber Music Ensemble, Bailly. [11944, 11945]

TELEMANN:

Suite for Flute and Strings in A minor. Kincaid. Philadelphia Orchestra, Ormandy. [M-890]

TSCHAIKOWSKY:

Andante Cantabile. Minneapolis Symphony, Ormandy. [1719]

Aurora's Wedding: Ballet. London Philharmonic, Kurtz. [M-326]

Capriccio Italien. Boston "Pops" Orchestra, Fiedler. [M-776]

1812 Overture. Boston "Pops" Orchestra, Fiedler. [M-776]

Eugen Onégin: Waltz. Boston "Pops" Orchestra, Fiedler. [4565]

Francesca da Rimini. New York Philharmonic-Symphony, Barbirolli. [M-598]

Hamlet: Overture, Fantasia. London Symphony, Coates. [M-395]

Marche Slave. Philadelphia Orchestra, Stokowski. [6513]

Nutcracker Suite. Philadelphia Orchestra, Stokowski. [M-265]

Piano Concerto No. 1. Horowitz. NBC Symphony, Toscanini. [M-800]

Romeo and Juliet Overture. Boston Symphony, Koussevitzky. [M-347]

Serenade in C major. BBC Symphony, Boult. [M-556]

Sleeping Beauty: Ballet. Sadler's Wells Orchestra. [M-673]

Swan Lake: Ballet Suite. London Philharmonic, Barbirolli. [11666, 11667]

Symphony No. 2. Cincinnati Symphony, Goossens. [M-790]

Symphony No. 3. National Symphony, Kindler. [M-747]

Symphony No. 4. NBC Symphony, Stokowski. [M-880]

Symphony No. 5. Philadelphia Orchestra, Ormandy. [M-828]

Symphony No. 6. Philadelphia Orchestra, Ormandy. [M-337]

Violin Concerto in D major. Heifetz. New York Philharmonic-Symphony, Barbirolli. [M-356]

VARDELL:

Joe Clark Steps Out. Eastman-Rochester Symphony, Hanson. [2059]

VERDI:

Aida: Ballet Suite. Boston "Pops" Orchestra, Fiedler. [11985]

Aida: Grand March (Act II). Boston "Pops" Orchestra, Fiedler. [11885]

Traviata: Preludes to Acts I and III. NBC Symphony, Toscanini. [18080]

VIEUXTEMPS:

Violin Concerto No. 4. Heifetz. London Philharmonic, Barbirolli. [M-297]

VIVALDI:

Concerto Grosso (Op. 3, No. 11). Boston Symphony, Koussevitzky. [M-886]

Violin Concerto in G minor. Elman. London Symphony, Collingwood. [7585, 7586]

VON SUPPÉ:
Light Cavalry Overture. BBC Symphony, Boult. [11837]
Morning, Noon and Night in Vienna. Boston "Pops" Orchestra,
Fiedler. [12479]

WAGNER:
Das Rheingold: Excerpts. Philadelphia Orchestra, Stokowski.
[M-179]
Die Meistersinger: Entrance of the Meistersingers, Dance of the
Apprentices. Philadelphia Orchestra, Ormandy. [1807]
Die Meistersinger: Overture. Philadelphia Orchestra, Stokowski.
[M-731]
Die Meistersinger: Prelude to Act III. Philadelphia Orchestra,
Stokowski. [1584]
Faust Overture. London Symphony, Coates. [9734]
Götterdämmerung: Siegfried's Rhine Journey and Funeral
March. NBC Symphony, Toscanini. [M-853]
Götterdämmerung Excerpts: Siegfried's Rhine Journey, Sieg-
fried's Death, Brünnhilde's Self-Immolation. Philadelphia Or-
chestra, Stokowski. [M-188]
Parsifal: Prelude and Good Friday Spell. Philadelphia Orchestra,
Stokowski. [M-421]
Rienzi: Overture. Boston "Pops" Orchestra, Fiedler. [M-569]
Siegfried: Synthesis. Philadelphia Orchestra, Stokowski. [M-441]
Tannhäuser: Fest March. Boston "Pops" Orchestra, Fiedler.
[Inc. in M-569]
Tannhäuser: Overture and Venusberg Music, Prelude to Act III.
Philadelphia Orchestra, Stokowski. [M-530]
Tristan and Isolde: Prelude, Liebesnacht, Liebestod. Philadel-
phia Orchestra, Stokowski. [M-508]
Wagnerian Excerpts: Lohengrin, Preludes to Acts I and III;
Götterdämmerung, Dawn and Siegfried's Rhine Journey; Sieg-
fried Idyll. New York Philharmonic-Symphony, Toscanini.
[M-308]
Walküre: Ride of the Valkyries, Wotan's Farewell, The Magic
Fire. Philadelphia Orchestra, Stokowski. [M-248]

WALTON:
Crown Imperial. BBC Symphony, Boult. [12031]
Façade Suite. London Philharmonic, Walton. [12034, 12035]
Violin Concerto. Heifetz. Cincinnati Symphony, Goossens.
[M-868]

WEBER:

> Euryanthe Overture. BBC Symphony, Boult. [12037]
>
> Freischütz Overture. Boston "Pops" Orchestra, Fiedler. [12040]
>
> Invitation to the Waltz. BBC Symphony, Toscanini. [15192]
>
> Oberon Overture. Boston "Pops" Orchestra, Fiedler. [12043]

WEINBERGER:

> Schwanda: Polka and Fugue. Minneapolis Symphony, Ormandy. [7958]
>
> Under the Spreading Chestnut Tree. London Philharmonic, Lambert. [M-654]

WIENIAWSKI:

> Violin Concerto No. 2. Heifetz. London Philharmonic, Barbirolli. [M-275]

VAUGHAN WILLIAMS:

> Fantasia on a Theme by Thomas Tallis. BBC Symphony, Boult. [M-769]
>
> London Symphony. Cincinnati Symphony, Goossens. [M-916]

WOLF-FERRARI:

> Secret of Suzanne: Overture. Boston "Pops" Orchestra, Fiedler. [4412]

INDEX

(Works and Persons Mentioned or Discussed in this Book)